World Economic and Financial Surveys

WORLD ECONOMIC OUTLOOK
September 2003

Public Debt in Emerging Markets

International Monetary Fund

©2003 International Monetary Fund

Production: IMF Graphics Section
Cover and Design: Luisa Menjivar-Macdonald
Figures: Theodore F. Peters, Jr.
Typesetting: Choon Lee

World economic outlook (International Monetary Fund)
World economic outlook: a survey by the staff of the International
Monetary Fund.—1980– —Washington, D.C.: The Fund, 1980–

v.; 28 cm.—(1981–84: Occasional paper/International Monetary
Fund ISSN 0251-6365)
Annual.
Has occasional updates, 1984–
ISSN 0258-7440 = World economic and financial surveys
ISSN 0256-6877 = World economic outlook (Washington)
1. Economic history—1971– —Periodicals. I. International
Monetary Fund. II. Series: Occasional paper (International
Monetary Fund)

HC10.W7979   84-640155

338.5'443'09048—dc19
AACR 2 MARC-S

Library of Congress   8507

Published biannually.
ISBN 1-58906-283-3

Price: US$49.00
(US$46.00 to full-time faculty members and
students at universities and colleges)

Please send orders to:
International Monetary Fund, Publication Services
700 19th Street, N.W., Washington, D.C. 20431, U.S.A.
Tel.: (202) 623-7430   Telefax: (202) 623-7201
E-mail: publications@imf.org
Internet: http://www.imf.org

recycled paper

CONTENTS

Figures

ASSUMPTIONS AND CONVENTIONS

A number of assumptions have been adopted for the projections presented in the *World Economic Outlook*. It has been assumed that real effective exchange rates will remain constant at their average levels during July 1–28, 2003, except for the currencies participating in the European exchange rate mechanism II (ERM II), which are assumed to remain constant in nominal terms relative to the euro; that established policies of national authorities will be maintained (for specific assumptions about fiscal and monetary policies in industrial countries, see Box A1); that the average price of oil will be $28.50 a barrel in 2003 and $25.50 a barrel in 2004, and remain unchanged in real terms over the medium term; that the six-month London interbank offered rate (LIBOR) on U.S. dollar deposits will average 1.3 percent in 2003 and 2.0 percent in 2004; that the three-month interbank deposit rate for the euro will average 2.2 percent in 2003 and 2.4 percent in 2004; and that the three-month certificate of deposit rate in Japan will average 0.1 percent in 2003 and 0.2 percent in 2004. These are, of course, working hypotheses rather than forecasts, and the uncertainties surrounding them add to the margin of error that would in any event be involved in the projections. The estimates and projections are based on statistical information available through late August 2003.

The following conventions have been used throughout the *World Economic Outlook:*

...   to indicate that data are not available or not applicable;

—   to indicate that the figure is zero or negligible;

–   between years or months (for example, 2002–03 or January–June) to indicate the years or months covered, including the beginning and ending years or months;

/   between years or months (for example, 2002/03) to indicate a fiscal or financial year.

"Billion" means a thousand million; "trillion" means a thousand billion.

"Basis points" refer to hundredths of 1 percentage point (for example, 25 basis points are equivalent to ¼ of 1 percent point).

In figures and tables, shaded areas indicate IMF staff projections.

Minor discrepancies between sums of constituent figures and totals shown are due to rounding.

As used in this report, the term "country" does not in all cases refer to a territorial entity that is a state as understood by international law and practice. As used here, the term also covers some territorial entities that are not states but for which statistical data are maintained on a separate and independent basis.

FURTHER INFORMATION AND DATA

This report on the *World Economic Outlook* is available in full on the IMF's Internet site, www.imf.org. Accompanying it on the website is a larger compilation of data from the WEO database than in the report itself, consisting of files containing the series most frequently requested by readers. These files may be downloaded for use in a variety of software packages.

Inquiries about the content of the *World Economic Outlook* and the WEO database should be sent by mail, electronic mail, or telefax (telephone inquiries cannot be accepted) to:

World Economic Studies Division
Research Department
International Monetary Fund
700 19th Street, N.W.
Washington, D.C. 20431, U.S.A.
E-mail: weo@imf.org   Telefax: (202) 623-6343

PREFACE

The analysis and projections contained in the *World Economic Outlook* are integral elements of the IMF's surveillance of economic developments and policies in its member countries, developments in international financial markets, and the global economic system. The survey of prospects and policies is the product of a comprehensive interdepartmental review of world economic developments, which draws primarily on information the IMF staff gathers through its consultations with member countries. These consultations are carried out in particular by the IMF's area departments together with the Policy Development and Review Department, the International Capital Markets Department, the Monetary and Financial Systems Department, and the Fiscal Affairs Department.

The analysis in this report has been coordinated in the Research Department under the general direction of Kenneth Rogoff, Economic Counsellor and Director of Research. The project has been directed by David Robinson, Deputy Director of the Research Department, together with Jonathan D. Ostry, Assistant Director, Research Department.

Primary contributors to this report also include Celine Allard, Tim Callen, James Daniel, Xavier Debrun, Hali Edison, Dalia Hakura, Thomas Helbling, Maitland MacFarlan, Enrique Mendoza, James Morsink, Nicola Spatafora, Marco Terrones, and Cathy Wright. Paul Atang, Nathalie Carcenac, Emily Conover, Carolina Gutiérrez, Toh Kuan, and Bennett Sutton provided research assistance. Nicholas Dopuch, Mandy Hemmati, Yutong Li, Casper Meyer, and Ercument Tulun managed the database and the computer systems. Sylvia Brescia, Celia Burns, and Dawn Heaney were responsible for word processing. Other contributors include Tamim Bayoumi, Nicolas Blancher, Eduardo Borensztein, Barry Bosworth, Chakriya Bowman, Ximena Cheetham, Susan Collins, Ugo Fasano, Ivan Guerra, Aasim Husain, Zubair Iqbal, George Kopits, Paolo Mauro, Christian Mulder, Susanna Mursula, Paul Nicholson, Bright Okogu, Carlos Piñerúa, Alessandro Rebucci, and Ratna Sahay. Marina Primorac of the External Relations Department edited the manuscript and coordinated production of the publication.

The analysis has benefited from comments and suggestions by staff from other IMF departments, as well as by Executive Directors following their discussion of the report on August 25 and 27, 2003. However, both projections and policy considerations are those of the IMF staff and should not be attributed to Executive Directors or to their national authorities.

Although relatively good data are now available on external debt levels for emerging market countries, consistent cross-country data on domestic debt are not so easily obtained. Until 15–20 years ago, this data deficiency was not a big issue, since very few emerging market countries were able to market domestic debt in any significant amounts anyway. The wave of financial liberalizations of the past 15 years has led to a sea change in this situation, however, as Chapter III in this issue of the *World Economic Outlook* illustrates. Emerging market country governments, having widely relaxed financial repression, are now issuing domestic debt at market interest rates in record quantities. Indeed, as the chapter documents, average public debt levels in emerging markets are equal to or exceeding those of many industrialized countries, as a percentage of GDP. Is this a concern? Well, given that the revenue base of the average emerging market country government is much smaller than that of the average industrialized country government, and given that most of the debt crises of the past 10 years have involved domestic debt (albeit sometimes dollar-denominated), the issue certainly merits attention.

The basic finding of Chapter III is that despite current near record-low risk spreads on emerging market debt—the present environment is extraordinarily benign thanks in part to still-low industrialized country interest rates—many countries need to be alert to the possibility that financing problems may arise over the medium term. The chapter looks at sustainability from a number of perspectives, though of course there is no magic cutoff number above which debt becomes unsustainable. Nevertheless, the historical evidence strongly suggests that there will be widespread problems if, over time, emerging market countries do not take measures to rein in expenditures and increase revenues, especially if debt levels continue to rise. Simply put, the current benign financing environment provides a window of opportunity in which countries with particularly acute debt problems need to begin steering debt ratios to safer ground, ideally taking quality measures such as strengthening the tax base and reducing unproductive expenditures. Dealing with long-term pension sustainability, a problem that is of course hardly unique to developing countries, is also critical. (By the way, the *World Economic Outlook* has looked extensively at industrialized country debt issues in the recent past, and we will surely revisit this issue again.)

Despite the increase in public debt, some developing countries are experiencing a rise in external assets. Indeed, many economies, especially in Asia, have been building massive claims on industrial economy governments in the form of foreign exchange reserves. Overall, in the wake of the Asian crisis of the late 1990s, this has to be seen as a welcome development. A comfortable level of reserves gives emerging market economies some measure of padding to deal with shocks and other financial problems that inevitably occur. A question that is increasingly coming to the fore, however, is whether this accumulation of reserves is starting to go too far, especially given the gaping imbalances in global current accounts that we have been warning about in these pages for some time now. So we decided to try to investigate the issue econometrically, to see if one can quantitatively rationalize the recent rise in reserves in terms of any standard explanations. The short answer—given in the second essay of Chapter II, "Are Foreign Exchange Reserves in Asia Too High?"—is that, allowing for some countries' desire to maintain relatively fixed exchange rates, the accumulation until the end of 2001 could be regarded as explainable, or in line with fundamentals. The further run-up in reserves over the past 18 months, however, is much harder to rationalize. Clearly, some element of the reserve increase (which, as the essay shows, is now heavily concentrated in Asia) can be attributed to the same factors that are keeping emerging market debt spreads so narrow. Industrialized country interest rates touched 40- and 50-year lows in 2003, inducing investors to seek higher returns elsewhere. The depreciation of the dollar has also been a factor, as many Asian currencies are linked to the dollar. Going forward, the question is at what point the reserve accumulation should slow or even reverse. From a multilateral perspective, there is a strong case for broadly sharing the burden of adjustment to the inevitable closing of the U.S. current account deficit, and some re-equilibration of real exchange rates has to be part of any solution. However, our analysis suggests that many Asian countries should seriously consider allowing greater exchange rate flexibility even from a domestic perspective, not least because of the high cost of continuing to pile up low-yielding claims on industrialized country governments.

Another reason to adopt a somewhat more flexible exchange rate is to be able to better absorb fluctuations in the exchange rates of the G-3 currencies. The third essay in Chapter II, "How Concerned Should Developing Countries Be About G-3 Volatility?" looks at the impact of G-3 exchange rate volatility on emerging markets and finds that, on the whole, it is less dramatic than one might have expected. However, for countries with relatively fixed exchange rate systems, especially if fixed to a single currency, G-3 exchange rate volatility can be quite problematic. Even a relatively small amount of exchange rate flexibility can be quite helpful.

Finally, with the Bank-Fund annual meetings scheduled to be held in Dubai, it was natural for us to decide to include one essay specifically on the Middle East. The first essay in Chapter II is entitled "How Can Economic Growth in the Middle East and North Africa Region be Accelerated?" The essay, which builds on work on growth and institutions from the last World Economic Outlook, explores different reasons why per capita income growth in the Middle East and North Africa region has been so weak over the past 20 years. The most interesting finding of the chapter perhaps is the differences across the region. In those economies that derive a large share of their income from oil, the large size of the government sector has been the overriding problem, stifling private sector growth and making it hard to diversify production. In countries where oil revenue is significant but not dominant, poor institutions and corruption are the biggest single hindrance to growth. In many of the remaining countries, both issues—overly large governments and poor institutions—are problematic.

We realize that beneath the technical material in analytic Chapters II and III lie many controversial, difficult issues. We do not pretend to have any pat answers, much less of a one-size-fits-all variety. Nevertheless, in the IMF's role in surveillance of the global economy, we cannot afford to shrink away from problems simply because they are difficult. We cannot afford to avoid coming to any tentative conclusions simply because the issues are controversial. We have done our best in these pages to present the issues in the clearest terms using what we believe to be the best available research methods. Nevertheless, we welcome critical comment, and hope that these essays will stimulate others to continue investigating these issues, as they are fundamental and require continued discussion and debate.

Kenneth Rogoff
Economic Counsellor and Director, Research Department

CHAPTER I

ECONOMIC PROSPECTS AND POLICY ISSUES

Following a series of adverse shocks in the first half of 2003, there are now increasing signs of a renewed recovery, and the balance of risks—in April, tilted well to the downside—has improved significantly. But with the pace and robustness of the recovery still unclear, and inflationary pressures low, monetary policies should remain accommodative for the time being; fiscal policies increasingly need to focus on medium-term consolidation, especially given coming demographic pressures. The widening global imbalances, and continuing dependence of global growth on the United States, underscore the need for an acceleration of structural reforms in many countries, along with measures to rein in the U.S. budget deficit over the medium term and, in some cases, a gradual move to greater exchange rate flexibility.

When the last *World Economic Outlook* was published in April 2003, the IMF staff expected—provided the war in Iraq was short and contained—that the global recovery would resume in the second half of the year, with global growth picking up to about 4 percent in 2004 (Table 1.1 and Figure 1.1). In the event, with major hostilities in Iraq indeed ending quickly, forward-looking indicators generally turned up, with equity markets strengthening markedly, accompanied by some pickup in business and consumer confidence, particularly in the United States (Figure 1.2). Concurrent data initially remained weak, with industrial production and trade growth slowing markedly in the second quarter (Figure 1.2), reflecting continued geopolitical uncertainties, the continued aftereffects of the bursting of the equity price bubble, and—particularly in Asia— the impact of Severe Acute Respiratory Syndrome (SARS). Most recently, however, there have been growing signs of a pickup in activity— including investment—particularly in the United States, Japan, and some emerging market countries, notably in Asia. With inflationary pressures very subdued, macroeconomic policies have been eased further across the globe. Interest

rates have been reduced in Europe and the United States, as well as in a number of other industrial and emerging market countries; and fiscal policy has been further relaxed in the United States and a number of Asian countries. That said, the degree of macroeconomic stimulus among the major industrial countries continues to vary widely, with significant stimulus in the pipeline in the United States and the United Kingdom and relatively little in the euro area and Japan (Figure 1.3).

In mature financial markets, the combination of ample liquidity, monetary easing, and the expectation that low policy interest rates will be maintained for longer than earlier thought drove long-run interest rates down to 40-year lows by mid-June. Since that time, long-run interest rates have rebounded, most sharply in the United States (Figure 1.4), apparently reflecting growing expectations of recovery, higher inflationary expectations, and the continuing strong supply of government paper.[1] Even so, the recent rebound has had only a limited effect on equity markets, which have retained their substantial gains since March, and on corporate spreads, which have benefited from actual and anticipated progress in corpo-

---

[1]See the September 2003 *Global Financial Stability Report* for a detailed discussion of financial market developments.

Table 1.1. Overview of the *World Economic Outlook* Projections

(Annual percent change unless otherwise noted)

	2001	2002	Current Projections		Difference from April 2003 Projections[1]	
			2003	2004	2003	2004
World output	**2.4**	**3.0**	**3.2**	**4.1**	—	—
Advanced economies	1.0	1.8	1.8	2.9	−0.1	—
United States	0.3	2.4	2.6	3.9	0.4	0.3
Euro area	1.5	0.9	0.5	1.9	−0.6	−0.4
Germany	0.8	0.2	—	1.5	−0.5	−0.4
France	2.1	1.2	0.5	2.0	−0.7	−0.4
Italy	1.8	0.4	0.4	1.7	−0.7	−0.6
Japan	0.4	0.2	2.0	1.4	1.2	0.4
United Kingdom	2.1	1.9	1.7	2.4	−0.3	−0.1
Canada	1.9	3.3	1.9	3.0	−0.9	−0.2
Other advanced economies	1.6	2.7	1.7	3.0	−0.8	−0.2
Newly industrialized Asian economies	0.8	4.8	2.3	4.2	−1.8	−0.3
Developing countries	4.1	4.6	5.0	5.6	—	−0.2
Africa	3.7	3.1	3.7	4.8	−0.2	−0.4
Sub-Sahara	3.5	3.0	3.1	5.0	−0.7	−0.4
Developing Asia	5.8	6.4	6.4	6.5	0.1	—
China	7.5	8.0	7.5	7.5	—	—
India	4.2	4.7	5.6	5.9	0.5	—
ASEAN-4[2]	2.9	4.3	4.1	4.4	0.2	0.1
Middle East and Turkey[3]	2.0	4.8	5.1	4.6	—	−0.3
Western Hemisphere	0.7	−0.1	1.1	3.6	−0.4	−0.6
Brazil	1.4	1.5	1.5	3.0	−1.3	−0.5
Countries in transition	5.1	4.2	4.9	4.7	0.9	0.6
Central and eastern Europe	3.1	3.0	3.4	4.1	—	−0.2
Commonwealth of Independent States and Mongolia	6.4	4.9	5.8	5.0	1.4	1.0
Russia	5.0	4.3	6.0	5.0	2.0	1.5
Excluding Russia	9.2	5.9	5.4	5.0	0.1	0.1
Memorandum						
World growth based on market exchange rates	1.3	1.9	2.3	3.2	0.1	—
World trade volume (goods and services)	**0.1**	**3.2**	**2.9**	**5.5**	**−1.8**	**−0.7**
Imports						
Advanced economies	−1.0	2.2	2.8	4.8	−1.9	−1.1
Developing countries	1.6	6.0	5.1	7.8	0.4	−0.2
Countries in transition	11.9	6.3	6.6	8.1	0.5	5.0
Exports						
Advanced economies	−0.8	2.2	1.6	5.2	−2.2	−0.6
Developing countries	2.7	6.5	4.3	6.9	0.6	−0.7
Countries in transition	6.0	6.3	5.8	5.6	−0.1	2.9
Commodity prices (U.S. dollars)						
Oil[4]	−14.0	2.8	14.2	−10.5	−10.0	8.8
Nonfuel (average based on world commodity export weights)	−4.0	0.6	5.0	2.4	...	...
Consumer prices						
Advanced economies	2.2	1.5	1.8	1.3	−0.1	−0.4
Developing countries	5.8	5.3	5.9	4.9	0.1	−0.2
Countries in transition	16.2	11.1	9.7	9.1	0.3	1.7
Six-month London interbank offered rate (LIBOR, percent)						
On U.S. dollar deposits	3.7	1.9	1.3	2.0	−0.4	−1.5
On euro deposits	4.2	3.3	2.2	2.4	−0.1	−0.1
On Japanese yen deposits	0.2	0.1	0.1	0.2	—	−0.1

Note: Real effective exchange rates are assumed to remain constant at the levels prevailing during July 1–28, 2003.

[1]Using updated purchasing-power-parity weights, summarized in the Statistical Appendix, Table A.

[2]Includes Indonesia, Malaysia, the Philippines, and Thailand.

[3]Includes Malta.

[4]Simple average of spot prices of U.K. Brent, Dubai, and West Texas Intermediate crude oil. The average price of oil in U.S. dollars a barrel was $24.96 in 2002; the assumed price is $28.50 in 2003, and $25.50 in 2004.

rate restructuring and continued positive risk appetite. In currency markets, the U.S. dollar continued to depreciate through mid-May, reflecting a combination of relatively low interest rates and continued investor concerns about the large U.S. current account deficit, though since then it has strengthened somewhat. Overall, since its peak in early 2002, the U.S. dollar has fallen by some 12 percent in nominal effective terms, matched by a substantial appreciation of the euro, the Canadian dollar, and some other industrial country currencies.

In emerging markets, financing conditions eased significantly through June, aided by low industrial country interest rates and improved sentiment toward a number of key markets, notably Brazil. Financing costs have risen since then, reflecting higher U.S. interest rates, but spreads have continued to decline (Figure 1.5); and while primary issuance has slowed, this appears to have been largely discretionary, with little evidence of an underlying tightening of market access. With capital outflows from many countries slowing, net private capital inflows to emerging markets are projected to rise to over $110 billion in 2003, the highest level since the mid-1990s (Table 1.2). Emerging market currencies have in general been little affected by the fall in the U.S. dollar—indeed, most have depreciated in nominal effective terms since the dollar peak (Figure 1.6). In Asia, which has continued to run large surpluses on both current and capital accounts, this has been accompanied by a very large increase in reserves (see the second essay in Chapter II, "Are Foreign Exchange Reserves in Asia Too High?").

Commodity markets have continued to be heavily influenced by geopolitical developments, the cyclical situation, and supply shocks. After peaking at over $34 a barrel before the war, oil prices fell back sharply in April, but by end-August had returned to $30 a barrel, reflecting a slower-than-expected recovery in Iraq's oil production, persisting tight industrial country inventories, and concerns about the sustainability of current production levels in Nigeria and

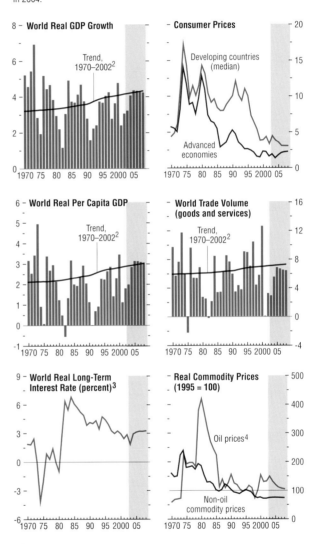

Figure 1.1. Global Indicators[1]
(Annual percent change unless otherwise noted)

Global growth in 2003 is expected to remain subdued, but to return close to trend in 2004.

[1]Shaded areas indicate IMF staff projections. Aggregates are computed on the basis of purchasing-power-parity weights unless otherwise noted.
[2]Average growth rates for individual countries, aggregated using purchasing-power-parity weights; the aggregates shift over time in favor of faster growing countries, giving the line an upward trend.
[3]GDP-weighted average of the 10-year (or nearest maturity) government bond yields less inflation rates for the United States, Japan, Germany, France, Italy, the United Kingdom, and Canada. Excluding Italy prior to 1972.
[4]Simple average of spot prices of U.K. Brent, Dubai, and West Texas Intermediate crude oil.

Figure 1.2. Current and Forward-Looking Indicators

(Percent change from previous quarter at annual rate unless otherwise noted)

Industrial production and trade growth remained weak in the second quarter of 2003, particularly in industrial countries; forward-looking indicators have improved somewhat, most clearly in the United States.

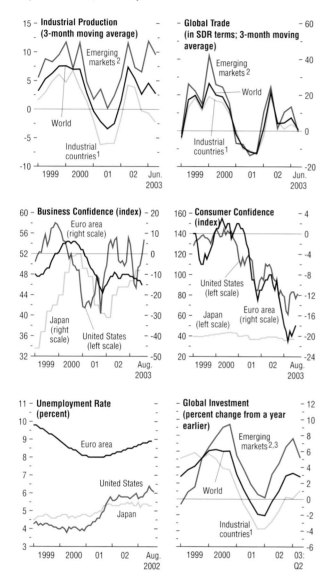

Sources: Business confidence for the United States, the National Association of Purchasing Managers; for the euro area, the European Commission; and for Japan, Bank of Japan. Consumer confidence for the United States, the Conference Board; for the euro area, the European Commission; and for Japan, Cabinet Office (Economic Planning Agency). All others, Haver Analytics.
[1] Australia, Canada, Denmark, euro area, Japan, New Zealand, Norway, Sweden, Switzerland, the United Kingdom, and the United States.
[2] Argentina, Brazil, Chile, China, Colombia, Czech Republic, Hong Kong SAR, Hungary, India, Indonesia, Israel, Korea, Malaysia, Mexico, Pakistan, Peru, the Philippines, Poland, Russia, Singapore, South Africa, Taiwan Province of China, Thailand, Turkey, and Venezuela.
[3] Data for China, India, Pakistan, and Russia are interpolated.

Venezuela. In early September, oil prices fell back, and—while they are expected to remain elevated during the remainder of 2003—they are projected to drop to an average $25.50 a barrel in 2004 in the face of rising supply, including from Iraq; indeed, many oil market analysts see a possibility of a significantly larger price decline. (See Appendix 1.1, "Longer-Term Prospects for Oil Prices.") In contrast, nonfuel commodity prices are projected to rise moderately, aided by rising global activity and the fading of earlier supply shocks (see Appendix 1.2 "Nonenergy Commodity Prices and Semiconductor Markets").

At the current conjuncture, several issues remain important in assessing the speed and nature of the recovery, including:

- *How long will the aftereffects of the bubble— defined broadly as discussed below—persist?* As stressed at the time of the last *World Economic Outlook*, the recent weakness of the world economy has not just been due to the war. The equity boom in the late 1990s was the largest in modern history: the unwinding of its effects is uncharted territory, and it is perhaps not surprising that most observers, including the *World Economic Outlook*, have found it difficult to gauge the aftermath. While the direct impact of equity market losses on household consumption growth should now have peaked, household balance sheets in some countries, notably the United States, remain stretched and housing markets—boosted in part by the aggressive easing of monetary policy in the last three years—are unlikely to provide the same support to the recovery going forward as they did in the past. In addition, the adjustment process in the corporate sector and, to a lesser extent, in the financial sector—eliminating excess capacity, restructuring of balance sheets, and rebuilding defined benefit pension funds—still has some way to go, particularly in Europe; and recent accounting scandals may continue to weigh on corporate confidence.

- *Will the U.S. dollar experience a renewed depreciation, and, if so, will the euro continue to bear the brunt of the offsetting adjustment?* To date, the decline in the U.S. dollar has been relatively orderly and—given the large U.S. current account deficit—generally welcome, and the resulting tightening in financial conditions in the euro area has been largely offset by European Central Bank (ECB) interest rate cuts (see Box 1.1, "Recent Changes in Monetary and Financial Conditions in the Major Currency Areas," p. 14). While the World Economic Outlook projections are, as usual, based on the assumption that real effective exchange rates remain constant, further substantial dollar depreciation cannot be ruled out and would have significant implications for the outlook, especially if the offsetting appreciation continued to be focused on the euro area rather than spread more widely.

Consistent with the signs of renewed recovery discussed above, the IMF staff's baseline forecast continues to project an upturn from the second half of 2003 (Figure 1.7). Global GDP growth is expected at 3.2 percent in 2003, rising to 4.1 percent—close to trend—in 2004, underpinned by reduced geopolitical uncertainties, policy stimulus in the pipeline, a pickup in inventories, the projected decline in oil prices, and a gradual diminution of the aftereffects of the bubble (see Box 1.2, "How Should We Measure Global Growth?" p. 18). Monetary policies are expected to remain accommodative, with a gradual withdrawal of stimulus unlikely to begin until 2004; in Japan, the quantitative easing policy is expected to continue. Looking across individual countries and regions:

- Among the *industrial countries*, recovery will continue to be led by the United States where—despite a weak labor market and considerable excess capacity—current data have shown greatest signs of improvement, forward-looking indicators are strongest, and there is the most policy stimulus in the pipeline (Table 1.3). In the euro area, the forecast has once again been significantly reduced, reflecting continued disappointing private domestic demand and the appreciation of the euro. With the overall policy stance less supportive

Figure 1.3. Fiscal and Monetary Easing in the Major Advanced Countries
(Percent)

Monetary and fiscal policies remain significantly more expansionary in the United States and the United Kingdom than in the euro area and Japan.

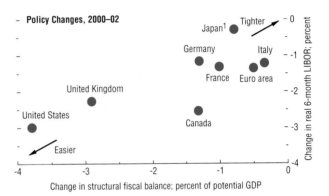

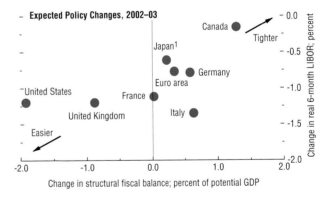

Source: IMF staff estimates.
[1]For Japan, excludes bank support.

Figure 1.4. Developments in Mature Financial Markets

Long-run interest rates have rebounded since mid-June, but remain relatively low by historical standards. Equity markets have continued to rise, accompanied by falling credit spreads.

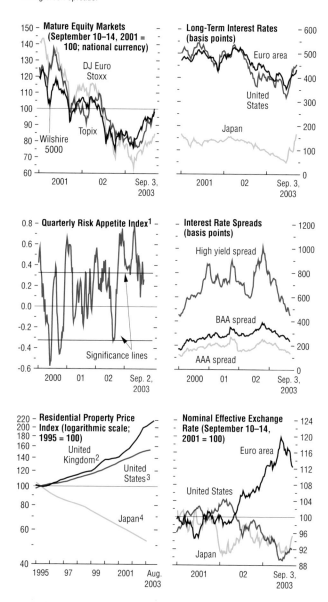

Sources: Bloomberg Financial Markets, LP; State Street Bank; HBOS plc.; Office of Federal Housing Enterprise Oversight; Japan Real Estate Institute; and IMF staff estimates.
[1]IMF/State Street risk appetite indicators.
[2]Halifax housing index as measured by the value of all houses.
[3]House price index as measured by the value of single-family homes.
[4]Urban land price index: average of all categories in six large city areas.

and the region-wide outlook adversely affected by the continuing difficulties in Germany, the projected pickup is expected to be relatively gradual, supported mainly by a gradual pickup in private consumption (underpinned by lower interest rates and the automatic stabilizers) and inventories, and the expected improvement in external demand. In Japan, given the stronger-than-expected second quarter outturn, the stock market pickup, and heightened optimism about the U.S. recovery, the forecast has been revised upward significantly for both 2003 and 2004. However, with the outlook still clouded by deflation and corporate and banking system weaknesses, the pace of recovery is still expected to remain moderate.

- The outlook for *emerging markets* continues to be driven—to differing extents—by developments in industrial countries, external financing conditions, geopolitical factors, and country-specific developments. In emerging markets in Asia, with the effects of SARS now waning, growth is expected to pick up in the second half of 2003 and remain strong in 2004, aided by timely additional policy easing and continued robust growth in China. However, much will depend on a prompt rebound in domestic demand, as well as the pace of the global recovery and a continuation of the nascent recovery in the information technology (IT) sector. Activity in much of Latin America appears to be stabilizing and external confidence in the region—particularly Brazil—has improved markedly. Nonetheless, the recovery remains fragile and, with a number of countries facing significant debt problems and political uncertainties, the region remains vulnerable to a reversal in financial market sentiment. In the Middle East, while the quick end to the conflict in Iraq has boosted confidence, the fragile security situation remains a major source of uncertainty; GDP growth forecasts for the region have been revised upward in 2003 owing to higher oil production, but lower oil prices will adversely affect the outlook in 2004. Reduced geopolitical concerns also benefit Turkey although, to maintain investor confidence, the authorities need to firmly maintain the sustainability of the fiscal position. Growth in the transition countries remains solid, led by Russia and Ukraine; European Union (EU) accession countries continue to benefit from strong direct investment inflows, although weak euro area demand remains an important risk.

- Among the *poorest countries*, GDP growth in sub-Saharan Africa (excluding South Africa) is projected to rise to 3.6 percent in 2003, with the positive effects of improved macroeconomic policies, rising commodity prices, and debt relief under the Heavily Indebted Poor Countries (HIPC) initiative partly offset by continued political instability and adverse weather conditions (the latter—together with the high incidence of HIV/AIDS—contributing to serious food shortages in the Horn of Africa and Southern Africa). GDP growth is expected to pick up markedly in 2004 but, as in the past, this baseline outcome critically depends on a significant improvement in political stability and favorable weather conditions.[2]

Inflationary pressures remain very low. In advanced countries, inflation is projected to be below 2 percent in 2003 for the second year in succession and to fall to 1.3 percent in 2004, the lowest level for 30 years; inflation in developing countries is expected to fall to 5 percent, also a historical low. Against this background, and given the weakness of the global recovery, the possibility of deflation has attracted increased attention.[3] Recently, there has been overt deflation in only a few countries, most importantly Japan; however, inflation in a number of advanced countries is projected at below 1 percent in 2004, uncomfortably close to zero (especially given the general upward bias to measured

[2]In fall *World Economic Outlooks*, sub-Saharan African growth for the year ahead has been overestimated on average by 1.5 percentage points over the past decade, in part because such expectations were not in fact fulfilled.

[3]See Kumar and others (2003) for a detailed discussion.

Figure 1.5. Emerging Market Financial Conditions

Emerging markets spreads have fallen sharply and equity markets have picked up in concert with developments in mature markets.

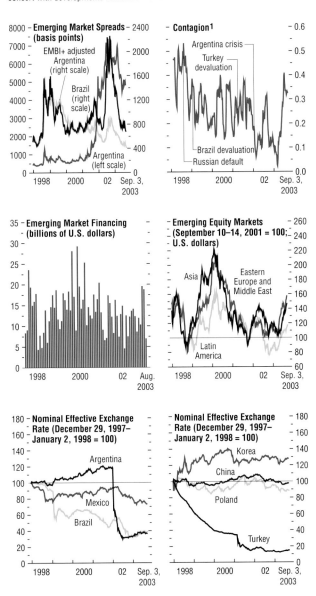

Sources: Bloomberg Financial Markets, LP; Capital Data; and IMF staff estimates.
[1]Average of 60-day rolling cross-correlation of emerging debt market spreads.

Table 1.2. Emerging Market Economies: Net Capital Flows[1]

(Billions of U.S. dollars)

	1995	1996	1997	1998	1999	2000	2001	2002	2003	2004
Total[2]										
Private capital flows, net[3]	192.9	226.5	132.6	77.8	86.7	47.1	42.7	80.3	113.1	93.8
Private direct investment, net	101.5	116.2	143.9	156.0	175.4	165.7	180.9	142.9	143.9	145.2
Private portfolio investment, net	23.9	83.2	63.3	11.0	19.5	−3.8	−51.2	−52.9	−22.9	−16.8
Other private capital flows, net	67.4	27.1	−74.6	−89.2	−108.2	−114.9	−87.1	−9.7	−8.0	−34.6
Official flows, net	49.5	−1.8	42.6	57.6	7.6	−12.8	21.1	7.1	10.1	−16.0
Change in reserves[4]	−117.9	−104.6	−71.1	−49.7	−88.4	−117.2	−122.4	−211.6	−255.1	−148.5
Memorandum										
Current account[5]	−95.2	−89.0	−71.1	−51.1	34.5	126.7	79.1	133.2	128.9	82.3
Africa										
Private capital flows, net[3]	11.3	10.1	4.2	8.1	12.2	0.2	5.2	5.0	8.1	9.5
Private direct investment, net	1.9	3.6	7.8	6.8	9.7	7.9	24.0	11.2	13.3	11.6
Private portfolio investment, net	2.5	2.8	7.0	3.7	8.2	−2.2	−8.8	−0.7	−0.7	0.2
Other private capital flows, net	6.9	3.7	−10.6	−2.4	−5.8	−5.5	−10.0	−5.5	−4.5	−2.3
Official flows, net	5.6	−2.3	3.9	5.6	4.5	5.1	3.5	3.5	4.8	4.4
Change in reserves[4]	−3.1	−6.6	−11.2	2.7	−3.5	−13.1	−12.6	−7.2	−13.9	−11.0
Developing Asia[6]										
Private capital flows, net[3]	99.3	124.6	10.8	−42.1	4.6	−3.3	25.2	57.0	62.4	13.7
Private direct investment, net	55.8	55.0	59.8	60.9	60.6	58.4	50.9	57.8	66.5	59.6
Private portfolio investment, net	22.3	30.0	7.3	−17.2	11.5	4.3	−13.5	−21.1	−10.9	−16.5
Other private capital flows, net	21.2	39.6	−56.3	−85.8	−67.5	−66.0	−12.2	20.2	6.8	−29.4
Official flows, net	3.8	−13.0	17.1	26.1	3.9	1.9	−9.7	−9.9	−7.1	−7.6
Change in reserves[4]	−42.9	−46.9	−15.1	−67.8	−78.9	−49.0	−84.9	−167.1	−159.9	−93.7
Memorandum										
Hong Kong SAR										
Private capital flows, net[3]	−3.5	−7.1	10.8	−8.5	1.1	4.2	−6.6	−24.9	−27.7	−25.6
Middle East and Turkey[7]										
Private capital flows, net[3]	8.1	9.7	17.0	9.6	−1.2	−14.1	−33.6	−15.1	−17.0	−8.0
Private direct investment, net	6.4	5.0	5.3	6.2	4.9	7.9	11.2	6.3	9.3	8.5
Private portfolio investment, net	2.0	1.8	−0.8	−13.0	−1.9	−11.1	−19.5	−16.6	−10.8	−6.1
Other private capital flows, net	−0.3	2.9	12.6	16.4	−4.3	−10.8	−25.4	−4.9	−15.4	−10.3
Official flows, net	4.8	6.5	6.2	4.0	2.4	−5.8	9.6	1.8	2.4	2.2
Change in reserves[4]	−11.8	−22.6	−20.5	9.3	−6.9	−28.7	−8.2	−10.1	−22.5	−11.3
Western Hemisphere										
Private capital flows, net[3]	43.4	76.4	74.4	74.4	53.4	55.3	29.8	7.8	28.3	41.8
Private direct investment, net	24.5	40.3	56.1	61.0	76.3	68.1	69.0	39.6	29.1	36.3
Private portfolio investment, net	3.5	48.0	29.1	25.3	2.5	8.7	−3.8	−7.9	3.7	7.0
Other private capital flows, net	15.4	−11.9	−10.8	−12.0	−25.5	−21.5	−35.3	−23.9	−4.5	−1.4
Official flows, net	19.7	−4.8	9.2	10.2	−2.8	−10.2	23.4	13.6	12.7	−13.0
Change in reserves[4]	−22.9	−28.3	−14.4	7.8	8.6	−2.8	1.1	−1.8	−29.0	−8.9
Countries in transition[8]										
Private capital flows, net[3]	30.7	5.6	26.1	27.8	17.7	9.0	16.0	25.6	31.2	36.7
Private direct investment, net	12.9	12.3	14.9	21.2	23.8	23.4	25.9	27.9	25.8	29.2
Private portfolio investment, net	−6.4	0.5	20.7	12.1	−0.9	−3.4	−5.7	−6.7	−4.2	−1.4
Other private capital flows, net	24.2	−7.2	−9.4	−5.5	−5.2	−11.0	−4.2	4.4	9.6	8.9
Official flows, net	15.6	11.8	6.2	11.7	−0.4	−3.8	−5.6	−1.9	−2.7	−2.1
Change in reserves[4]	−37.2	−0.2	−10.0	−1.7	−7.7	−23.7	−17.8	−25.4	−29.8	−23.5
Memorandum										
Fuel exporters										
Private capital flows, net[3]	5.0	−20.2	9.5	2.6	−27.9	−55.5	−37.2	−52.6	−37.8	−20.2
Nonfuel exporters										
Private capital flows, net[3]	187.9	246.7	123.1	75.1	114.6	102.5	79.8	132.9	150.9	114.0

[1]Net capital flows comprise net direct investment, net portfolio investment, and other long- and short-term net investment flows, including official and private borrowing. Emerging markets include developing countries, countries in transition, Korea, Singapore, Taiwan Province of China, and Israel.
[2]Excludes Hong Kong SAR.
[3]Because of data limitations, other private capital flows, net may include some official flows.
[4]A minus sign indicates an increase.
[5]The sum of the current account balance, net private capital flows, net official flows, and the change in reserves equals, with the opposite sign, the sum of the capital and financial account and errors and omissions. For regional current account balances, see Table 27 of the Statistical Appendix.
[6]Includes Korea, Singapore, and Taiwan Province of China in this table.
[7]Includes Israel and Malta.
[8]Historical data have been revised, reflecting cumulative data revisions for Russia and the resolution of a number of data interpretation issues.

inflation). The risk of a global deflationary spiral appears remote, and inflationary expectations have recently edged up, reflecting increasing expectations of recovery and recent policy measures. However, in an environment of low inflation, the possibility of a temporary period of price declines in the event of an adverse shock remains significant in a number of countries, most importantly Germany, adding to arguments for maintaining a relatively accommodative monetary stance.

While the baseline forecast for global growth is little changed from a few months ago, the balance of risks has improved significantly. Given the quick end to the war, the likelihood of worst-case scenarios has been much reduced since the last *World Economic Outlook*, while policies have been further eased. Indeed, as recent developments in financial markets underscore, it is possible that growth may pick up more quickly than currently expected, particularly in the United States, where productivity growth has been most robust, corporate balance sheet restructuring appears most advanced, and the policy stimulus in the pipeline is particularly large (and, given the expected supplementary budget to finance expenditures in Iraq and Afghanistan, is likely to increase further). While stronger U.S. growth would, of course, benefit the rest of the world, it would come at the cost of exacerbating the already large U.S. current account deficit, underscoring the need to accelerate implementation of measures to reduce the associated medium-term risks, as discussed below. The possibility that oil prices could be lower than expected in 2004 and beyond is also a potential upside risk to global activity.

At the same time, however, downside risks remain, particularly in 2004 and beyond. While geopolitical risks have declined since April they are far from eliminated, as recent tragic events in a number of countries underscore. In addition, beyond the specific risks in Japan, and to a lesser extent Germany, key concerns include the following:

- *The current account imbalances in the global economy and, associated with that, the continued*

Figure 1.6. Selected Countries: Exchange Rate and Interest Rate Developments
(Movement since February 2002; percent)

The fall of the U.S. dollar since its peak in February 2002 has been matched by appreciation in the euro area, Canada, and some smaller industrial countries; in most of the last group, the contractionary impact has been partly or fully offset by monetary easing. Emerging market currencies have generally depreciated.

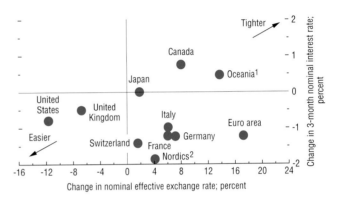

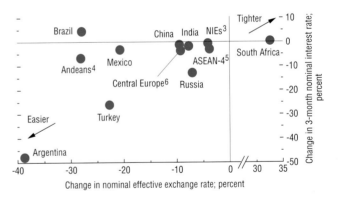

Sources: Bloomberg Financial Markets, LP; and Global Insight.
[1]Australia and New Zealand.
[2]Denmark, Norway, and Sweden.
[3]Hong Kong SAR, Korea, Singapore, and Taiwan Province of China.
[4]Chile, Colombia, Peru, and Venezuela.
[5]Indonesia, Malaysia, the Philippines, and Thailand.
[6]Czech Republic, Hungary, and Poland.

Figure 1.7. Global Outlook
(Real GDP; percent change from four quarters earlier)

After weakening from late 2002, the global recovery is expected to resume in the second half of 2003, led by the United States.

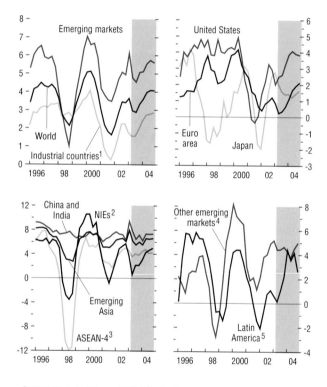

Sources: Haver Analytics; and IMF staff estimates.
[1]Australia, Canada, Denmark, euro area, Japan, New Zealand, Norway, Sweden, Switzerland, the United Kingdom, and the United States.
[2]Hong Kong SAR, Korea, Singapore, and Taiwan Province of China.
[3]Indonesia, Malaysia, the Philippines, and Thailand.
[4]Czech Republic, Hungary, Israel, Pakistan, Poland, Russia, South Africa, and Turkey.
[5]Argentina, Brazil, Chile, Colombia, Mexico, Peru, and Venezuela.

dependence of the world on the outlook for the United States remain a serious concern (Table 1.4). Despite the depreciation of the U.S. dollar, the U.S. current account deficit is projected at 5 percent of GDP in 2003, falling only to 4 percent of GDP by 2008, suggesting that further adjustment will be needed to achieve medium-term sustainability. While the extent, nature, and timing of further dollar adjustment is impossible to predict, history suggests that even an orderly adjustment is likely to be associated with a slowdown in U.S. growth—and, if growth in the rest of the world remains weak, in global growth as well.[4] In addition, a disorderly adjustment—or overshooting—remains an important risk, particularly if the offsetting appreciation continues to be concentrated on a few currencies. Volatility among the major currencies—often associated with currency misalignment—could also be a cause for concern, particularly for developing countries with fixed exchange rates or significant mismatches between the currency structure of trade and external debt (see the third essay in Chapter II, "Is G-3 Exchange Rate Volatility a Serious Concern for Developing Countries?").

- *The recent pickup in investment may not prove enduring, depending in part on the extent to which aftereffects of the bubble persist.* Apart from the direct costs, a more prolonged period of slower growth would make the global economy more vulnerable to new adverse shocks, especially given the still heavy dependence on developments in the United States, the relatively low level of inflation in some countries, and the increasingly limited room for policy maneuver in many countries.

- *In financial markets, as noted in the September* Global Financial Stability Report, *a further sharp rise in bond yields could adversely affect the recovery, particularly if that were not driven by expectations of higher growth.* This would be especially so in countries where house prices have

---

[4]See "How Worrisome Are External Imbalances?" in Chapter II of the September 2002 *World Economic Outlook.*

Table 1.3. Advanced Economies: Real GDP, Consumer Prices, and Unemployment
(Annual percent change and percent of labor force)

	Real GDP				Consumer Prices				Unemployment			
	2001	2002	2003	2004	2001	2002	2003	2004	2001	2002	2003	2004
Advanced economies	**1.0**	**1.8**	**1.8**	**2.9**	**2.2**	**1.5**	**1.8**	**1.3**	**5.9**	**6.4**	**6.7**	**6.6**
United States	0.3	2.4	2.6	3.9	2.8	1.6	2.1	1.3	4.8	5.8	6.0	5.7
Euro area[1]	1.5	0.9	0.5	1.9	2.4	2.3	2.0	1.6	8.0	8.4	9.1	9.2
Germany	0.8	0.2	—	1.5	1.9	1.3	1.0	0.6	7.9	8.6	9.5	9.8
France	2.1	1.2	0.5	2.0	1.8	1.9	1.9	1.7	8.5	8.8	9.5	9.7
Italy	1.8	0.4	0.4	1.7	2.7	2.6	2.8	2.0	9.5	9.0	9.0	9.0
Spain	2.7	2.0	2.2	2.8	2.8	3.6	3.1	2.7	10.5	11.4	11.4	11.0
Netherlands	1.2	0.2	−0.5	1.4	5.1	3.9	2.6	2.0	2.0	2.3	4.2	4.5
Belgium	0.8	0.7	0.8	1.9	2.4	1.6	1.4	1.4	6.7	7.3	8.1	8.3
Austria	0.7	1.0	0.7	1.5	2.3	1.7	1.3	1.2	3.6	4.1	4.4	4.4
Finland	0.7	1.6	1.3	2.6	2.7	2.0	1.8	1.7	9.1	9.1	9.3	9.3
Greece	4.1	4.0	4.0	3.9	3.7	3.9	3.8	3.0	10.4	9.9	9.8	9.7
Portugal	1.6	0.4	−0.8	1.6	4.4	3.7	3.1	2.0	4.1	5.1	6.5	6.7
Ireland	6.2	6.9	1.0	3.8	4.0	4.7	4.0	2.6	3.9	4.4	5.1	5.6
Luxembourg	1.0	0.5	1.5	4.0	2.7	2.1	2.0	1.7	2.6	2.8	3.2	3.3
Japan	0.4	0.2	2.0	1.4	−0.7	−0.9	−0.3	−0.6	5.0	5.4	5.5	5.4
United Kingdom[2]	2.1	1.9	1.7	2.4	2.1	2.2	2.8	2.5	5.1	5.2	5.2	5.2
Canada	1.9	3.3	1.9	3.0	2.5	2.3	2.8	1.7	7.2	7.6	7.9	7.7
Korea	3.1	6.3	2.5	4.7	4.1	2.8	3.3	3.0	3.8	3.1	3.4	3.3
Australia	2.7	3.6	3.0	3.5	4.4	3.0	2.9	2.3	6.7	6.3	6.1	6.0
Taiwan Province of China	−2.2	3.5	2.7	3.8	—	−0.2	0.1	0.8	4.6	5.2	5.3	5.0
Sweden	1.1	1.9	1.4	2.0	3.0	1.6	1.5	2.0	4.0	4.0	4.5	4.2
Switzerland	0.9	0.1	−0.4	1.4	1.0	0.7	0.4	0.5	1.9	2.8	4.2	3.8
Hong Kong SAR	0.5	2.3	1.5	2.8	−1.6	−3.0	−2.6	−1.9	5.1	7.3	7.8	7.5
Denmark	1.4	2.1	1.2	1.8	2.4	2.3	2.5	2.0	4.9	4.9	5.7	5.6
Norway	1.9	1.0	0.6	2.3	3.0	1.3	2.7	1.0	3.6	3.9	4.6	4.7
Israel	−0.9	−1.0	0.7	2.1	1.1	5.7	1.1	0.2	9.4	10.3	10.8	10.6
Singapore	−2.4	2.2	0.5	4.2	1.0	−0.4	0.6	1.2	3.3	4.4	4.9	4.2
New Zealand[3]	2.6	4.4	2.6	2.9	2.7	2.7	2.0	2.0	5.3	5.2	5.4	5.3
Cyprus	4.1	2.2	2.0	3.8	2.0	2.8	3.6	3.5	3.0	3.2	3.4	3.3
Iceland	2.9	−0.5	2.3	3.7	6.6	4.8	2.2	2.1	1.4	2.5	3.0	2.5
Memorandum												
Major advanced economies	0.8	1.6	1.8	2.8	2.0	1.3	1.8	1.1	5.9	6.5	6.8	6.7
European Union	1.7	1.1	0.8	2.0	2.4	2.3	2.2	1.8	7.4	7.7	8.2	8.3
Newly industrialized Asian economies	0.8	4.8	2.3	4.2	1.9	1.0	1.5	1.7	4.1	4.1	4.4	4.2

[1]Based on Eurostat's harmonized index of consumer prices.
[2]Consumer prices are based on the retail price index excluding mortgage interest.
[3]Consumer prices excluding interest rate components.

risen sharply in recent years (notably the United Kingdom, Australia, Ireland, the Netherlands, and to a lesser extent the United States), where such an eventuality would reduce the support that is presently being provided to demand in most of these countries and could increase the risk of a housing bust. In addition, if growth and corporate earnings were to disappoint, the recent rise in equity markets could prove ephemeral, putting renewed pressure on household, corporate, and financial balance sheets.

• *In emerging markets, the recent improvement in financing conditions owes much to temporary cyclical factors and could be reversed if industrial country interest rates were to rise rapidly.* This underscores the need to use the current relatively benign financing conditions to press ahead with measures to address significant medium-term vulnerabilities. In this connection, public sector debt in emerging markets, on average now higher as a percentage of GDP than in industrial countries, is a serious concern, and in many cases is well above the

**Table 1.4. Selected Economies:
Current Account Positions**
(Percent of GDP)

	2001	2002	2003	2004
Advanced economies	**−0.8**	**−0.7**	**−0.9**	**−0.8**
United States	−3.9	−4.6	−5.1	−4.7
Euro area[1]	0.2	0.9	0.8	0.8
Germany	—	2.3	2.4	2.1
France	1.7	1.8	1.2	1.6
Italy	−0.1	−0.6	−1.1	−0.9
Spain	−2.8	−2.4	−2.7	−2.7
Netherlands	2.1	1.3	3.8	3.3
Belgium	4.0	4.7	4.0	4.4
Austria	−2.2	0.7	0.1	−0.2
Finland	7.1	6.9	6.1	5.8
Greece	−6.2	−6.1	−6.6	−6.6
Portugal	−9.6	−7.3	−4.9	−4.2
Ireland	−0.7	−0.7	−1.7	−1.1
Luxembourg	9.3	10.4	10.0	9.8
Japan	2.1	2.8	2.9	2.9
United Kingdom	−1.3	−0.9	−1.0	−0.9
Canada	2.4	2.0	1.6	1.6
Korea	1.9	1.3	1.6	1.8
Australia	−2.4	−4.4	−5.2	−4.8
Taiwan Province of China	6.4	9.1	8.5	8.8
Sweden	3.9	4.5	4.5	3.6
Switzerland	9.1	12.3	10.5	10.5
Hong Kong SAR	7.5	10.8	13.9	14.3
Denmark	2.6	2.7	4.2	4.2
Norway	15.6	13.2	12.5	11.4
Israel	−1.6	−1.2	−0.7	−0.8
Singapore	19.0	21.5	23.7	23.0
New Zealand	−2.6	−3.7	−3.7	−4.1
Cyprus	−4.3	−5.6	−4.9	−4.7
Iceland	−4.0	−0.1	−0.9	−2.1
Memorandum				
Major advanced economies	−1.4	−1.4	−1.6	−1.5
European Union[2]	−0.2	0.5	0.5	0.5
Euro area[2]	−0.3	0.8	0.7	0.7
Newly industrialized Asian economies	5.7	6.8	7.2	7.3

[1]Calculated as the sum of the balances of individual euro area countries.
[2]Corrected for reporting discrepancies in intra-area transactions.

level that would be sustainable if countries do not improve on historical growth and budgetary performance (see Chapter III, "Public Debt Sustainability in Emerging Markets").

Overall, there are increasing signs that the expected pickup in global activity is developing, although it is as yet unclear how broadbased and robust it will be. Against this background, and with inflationary pressures very moderate, macroeconomic policies need to remain supportive. At the same time, policymakers face major medium-term challenges: to reduce the dependence of

global growth on the United States; to foster an orderly reduction in global imbalances; and to strengthen medium-term fiscal positions, especially in view of future pressures from aging populations. In general, monetary policy remains the short-term instrument of choice, and while sustained low policy interest rates run some risk of exacerbating some imbalances—notably in the housing market—these must be balanced against the need to support the recovery and reduce potential deflationary risks. On the fiscal side, with many countries facing substantial medium-term pressures, difficult trade-offs need to be made. In general, the automatic stabilizers should be allowed to operate; beyond that, much depends on country-specific circumstances and constraints, as well as the conjunctural situation. A slower pace of short-term consolidation—or even underlying budgetary deterioration—is clearly of less concern if accompanied by credible plans for future consolidation, by structural reforms to boost future growth, or—perhaps most importantly—by measures to address the future costs of aging populations (the latter having the advantage of having only a limited short-term impact on demand).

Against this background, the main policy priorities would appear to be the following.

• *In industrial countries, monetary policies need to remain accommodative.* In the United States, the federal funds rate is now at the lowest level in 40 years. Even so, given the continued sluggishness of activity, and the potential risks of deflation, the Federal Reserve has appropriately indicated that rates could remain low for a considerable period. Fiscal policy has provided support to demand, but at the cost of a serious deterioration in the long-run outlook; consequently, there is now a pressing need for a credible medium-term framework to restore balance (excluding Social Security) and put Social Security and Medicare on a sound footing (Table 1.5). In the euro area, where inflationary pressures have declined amid weak activity and the appreciation of the euro, the ECB's 50-basis-point reduction in interest rates in June was welcome. Further easing will

Table 1.5. Major Advanced Economies: General Government Fiscal Balances and Debt[1]

(Percent of GDP)

	1987–96	1997	1998	1999	2000	2001	2002	2003	2004	2008
Major advanced economies										
Actual balance	-3.8	-2.1	-1.6	-1.2	-0.3	-1.8	-3.8	-5.1	-4.7	-2.8
Output gap[2]	-0.3	-0.3	-0.2	0.1	1.0	-0.7	-1.4	-2.0	-1.6	—
Structural balance	-3.6	-1.8	-1.4	-1.2	-1.1	-1.7	-3.3	-4.2	-3.8	-2.8
United States										
Actual balance	-4.2	-1.3	-0.1	0.5	1.2	-0.7	-3.8	-6.0	-5.6	-3.0
Output gap[2]	-1.2	-0.5	0.4	1.2	1.8	-1.0	-1.6	-2.1	-1.4	—
Structural balance	-3.8	-1.1	-0.2	—	0.6	-0.5	-3.2	-5.1	-4.9	-3.0
Net debt	54.4	56.4	52.7	48.2	43.3	42.6	44.9	49.1	52.2	54.5
Gross debt	68.4	69.8	65.9	62.7	57.1	57.0	58.8	62.5	65.0	64.8
Euro area										
Actual balance	. . .	-2.6	-2.3	-1.3	0.1	-1.7	-2.3	-3.0	-2.8	-0.7
Output gap[2]	. . .	-1.2	-0.5	0.1	1.2	0.5	-0.7	-2.2	-2.4	-0.1
Structural balance	. . .	-1.6	-1.8	-1.2	-1.5	-2.0	-2.0	-1.7	-1.4	-0.6
Net debt	. . .	62.9	61.4	60.8	58.6	58.4	58.4	59.5	60.0	56.2
Gross debt	. . .	75.4	73.7	72.6	70.2	69.3	69.2	70.4	70.7	65.4
Germany[3]										
Actual balance	-2.4	-2.7	-2.2	-1.5	1.3	-2.8	-3.5	-3.9	-3.9	-1.2
Output gap[2]	0.4	-0.5	-0.4	-0.1	0.9	0.3	-0.9	-2.4	-2.5	—
Structural balance[4]	-2.5	-2.0	-1.7	-1.2	-1.6	-2.9	-2.9	-2.3	-2.3	-1.2
Net debt	31.9	53.4	53.3	54.9	52.8	53.5	55.4	57.8	60.1	59.2
Gross debt	46.4	61.0	60.9	61.2	60.2	59.5	60.8	63.2	65.5	64.6
France										
Actual balance	-3.6	-3.0	-2.7	-1.8	-1.4	-1.4	-3.1	-4.0	-3.5	-0.2
Output gap[2]	-0.8	-3.1	-1.7	-1.0	0.7	0.4	-0.6	-2.1	-2.4	—
Structural balance[4]	-3.0	-1.0	-1.6	-1.1	-1.8	-1.8	-2.8	-2.7	-2.1	-0.2
Net debt	32.6	49.6	49.8	48.8	47.5	48.2	49.2	51.6	53.2	49.3
Gross debt	41.6	59.3	59.5	58.5	57.1	56.8	58.9	61.3	62.9	59.0
Italy										
Actual balance	-10.0	-2.7	-2.8	-1.7	-0.6	-2.6	-2.3	-2.8	-2.6	-1.7
Output gap[2]	0.2	-0.3	-0.1	—	1.0	0.6	-1.0	-2.3	-2.3	—
Structural balance[4]	-9.9	-1.9	-2.8	-1.8	-2.4	-3.1	-2.7	-2.1	-1.7	-1.7
Net debt	101.5	113.8	110.1	108.4	104.5	103.7	101.0	100.9	99.8	93.0
Gross debt	107.3	120.2	116.4	114.6	110.4	109.5	106.7	106.6	105.4	98.3
Japan										
Actual balance	-0.9	-3.8	-5.5	-7.2	-7.4	-6.1	-7.5	-7.4	-6.5	-6.2
Excluding social security	-3.7	-6.0	-7.2	-8.7	-8.5	-6.3	-7.8	-7.6	-6.3	-5.5
Output gap[2]	0.9	1.1	-1.5	-2.5	-1.1	-1.9	-2.8	-2.0	-1.7	-0.1
Structural balance	-1.1	-4.2	-5.0	-6.2	-7.0	-5.4	-6.5	-6.7	-5.9	-6.2
Excluding social security	-3.9	-6.2	-6.9	-8.1	-8.2	-5.9	-7.1	-7.1	-6.0	-5.5
Net debt	18.9	35.3	46.2	52.8	58.6	63.7	72.2	80.0	86.9	103.7
Gross debt	77.6	105.5	117.1	130.5	138.7	148.4	158.4	166.8	174.1	183.2
United Kingdom										
Actual balance	-3.6	-2.2	0.2	1.1	4.0	0.9	-1.3	-2.5	-2.7	-2.5
Output gap[2]	-0.2	0.2	0.5	-0.3	0.2	—	-0.4	-1.1	-1.2	0.1
Structural balance[4]	-3.5	-2.1	—	1.0	1.7	0.8	-1.2	-2.1	-1.9	-2.4
Net debt	28.8	45.4	42.4	40.3	34.4	33.0	33.1	33.5	34.8	38.3
Gross debt	43.0	50.4	47.3	44.8	41.9	38.7	38.3	39.0	40.2	43.7
Canada										
Actual balance	-6.1	0.2	0.1	1.6	3.0	1.4	0.8	1.5	1.5	1.6
Output gap[2]	0.2	-0.9	-0.8	0.6	2.0	0.4	0.4	-0.9	-0.8	-0.1
Structural balance	-6.1	0.8	0.5	1.4	2.1	1.2	0.8	2.1	2.0	1.6
Net debt	73.9	85.8	83.1	74.8	64.7	59.1	56.1	51.7	47.8	33.6
Gross debt	105.8	118.6	116.2	110.8	101.8	99.6	96.0	89.5	83.9	63.4

Note: The methodology and specific assumptions for each country are discussed in Box A1 in the Statistical Appendix.

[1]Debt data refer to end of year. Debt data are not always comparable across countries. For example, the Canadian data include the unfunded component of government employee pension liabilities, which amounted to nearly 18 percent of GDP in 2001.

[2]Percent of potential GDP.

[3]Data before 1990 refer to west Germany. For net debt, the first column refers to 1988–94. Beginning in 1995, the debt and debt-service obligations of the Treuhandanstalt (and of various other agencies) were taken over by general government. This debt is equivalent to 8 percent of GDP, and the associated debt service, to ½ to 1 percent of GDP.

[4]Excludes one-off receipts from the sale of mobile telephone licenses (the equivalent of 2.5 percent of GDP in 2000 for Germany, 0.1 percent of GDP in 2001 and 2002 for France, 1.2 percent of GDP in 2000 for Italy, and 2.4 percent of GDP in 2000 for the United Kingdom). Also excludes one-off receipts from sizable asset transactions.

Box 1.1. Recent Changes in Monetary and Financial Conditions in the Major Currency Areas

Exchange rates among the industrialized countries have been substantially realigned since the peak of the U.S. dollar (in nominal and real effective terms) in February 2002. Most significant has been the dollar's depreciation against the euro—a fall of 20 percent from early 2002 to the end of August 2003—but also noteworthy has been the dollar's weakening against the yen, the pound sterling, and the Canadian dollar (down 10 to 12 percent in each case) and against the Australian dollar (down 20 percent). This box assesses the implications of these movements for short-term prospects in the major regions, especially when developments in interest rates, equity values, and property prices are also taken into account.

Trade-weighted currency movements have been less dramatic than bilateral changes (see Figure 1.4). The U.S. dollar has fallen by 11 percent in nominal effective terms since February 2002—partly reflecting the fact that about one-half of U.S. trade is with developing countries, some of whose currencies have remained stable or depreciated against the dollar over recent years. China and Mexico, for example, are the next-largest suppliers of U.S. imports after Canada, with China maintaining a de facto fixed exchange rate against the dollar and the Mexican peso depreciating about 17 percent against the dollar since February 2002. Individual euro area economies have also faced much smaller effective exchange rate appreciations than suggested by the euro/dollar change—reflecting the significance of intra-European trade, together with the increasing volume of trade with central and eastern Europe. For example, Germany and France have experienced nominal effective exchange rate appreciations of only 5 to 6 percent since early 2002.

Furthermore, recent currency movements have generally been consistent with medium-term fundamentals. As pointed out repeatedly in the *World Economic Outlook* (and elsewhere)

Note: The main author of this box is Maitland MacFarlan.

over recent years, the decline in the value of the U.S. dollar is likely to reflect market concerns about the sustainability of current account imbalances across the major regions—especially the large U.S. deficit. Global current account imbalances eventually will need to be resolved through some reconfiguration of exchange rates and relative demand growth rates. The exchange rate adjustments over the past 18 months are in the direction needed to reduce such imbalances, although the dollar still appears substantially overvalued from a longer-term perspective—implying the likelihood of further downward adjustment. For example, current projections suggest that the U.S. current account deficit may decline by only about 1 percentage point—from 5 to 4 percent of GDP—over the next five years, with the effects of the weaker dollar partly offset by the more rapid recovery expected in the United States than in the euro area and Japan.

In most regions, monetary policy changes have reinforced, or helped to offset, the impact of recent exchange rate developments on overall monetary conditions (a weighted average of the exchange rate, short-term interest rates, and long-term rates). In the United States and the United Kingdom, monetary conditions have eased significantly since early 2002 as a result of both lower interest rates and weaker currencies (see the figure). In the euro area, monetary conditions have been broadly stable over this period, with interest rate reductions offsetting the impact of the euro's appreciation. In Japan, even with massive foreign exchange market intervention, the authorities have only managed to stem the appreciation of the yen, rather than engineer a desirable easing of monetary conditions to combat entrenched deflation. It is also notable that in developing Asia, which by virtue of relatively strong growth rates and external balances would be well placed in comparison with the euro area and Japan to absorb some appreciation, implicit or explicit links to the U.S. dollar have limited the extent to which local currencies have appreciated since the dollar's peak. Overall, then, the cyclically weakest

Monetary Conditions Index[1]
(January 2, 2001 to August 29, 2003 = 100)

Sources: Bloomberg Financial Markets, LP; Global Insight, Inc.; and IMF staff calculations.
[1]Weighted average of nominal short-term and long-term interest rates and the nominal effective exchange rate.

equity and property prices. In general, asset price movements tend to have a stronger influence on consumption and investment in the more capital-market-based financial systems of the United States and United Kingdom, compared with the predominantly bank-based systems of continental Europe and Japan.[1] Over recent years, rising property prices in the United States and, especially, the United Kingdom have offset the downward pressures on household spending from the fall in equity markets (see the first table). While this also appears to be the case in France, property prices in Germany have provided little offset to the large decline in equity market capitalization and, in Japan, falling property prices have reinforced the negative wealth effects from earlier falls in equity markets.

To what degree should recent exchange rate developments influence monetary policy? The *direct* impact of exchange rates on consumer prices appears to have diminished over recent decades, particularly in response to falls in the level and variability of inflation, and may now be very small. While there is substantial variation in estimates of pass-through elasticities—the per-

regions appear to have been the hardest hit by recent currency movements.

This asymmetric impact of changes in monetary conditions across the main regions has in some cases been reinforced by movements in

[1]See the essay on "Is Wealth Increasingly Driving Consumption?" in Chapter II of the April 2002 *World Economic Outlook*. Note that the estimated effects on consumption spending from changes in wealth are spread out over a number of years.

Impact on Household Spending of Asset Price Changes
(Percent change)

	United States	Euro Area	Germany	France	Japan	United Kingdom
Equity markets						
Capitalization[1]	–6	–21	–26	–19	5	–15
Impact on spending	–0.4	–0.2	–0.2	–0.2	—	–1.4
Property markets						
Valuation changes[2]	7	. . .	1	7	–8	30
Impact on spending	0.6	. . .	0	0.3	–0.4	2.4

Sources: National sources; DataStream International; Office of Federal Housing Enterprise Oversight; HBOS plc; Japan Real Estate Institute; and Bundesbank calculations based on Bulwein data.
[1]Percent change from February 2002 to August 2003.
[2]Data for the United States and Japan cover the period Q1:2002 to Q1:2003; for Germany and France, Q4:2001 to Q4:2002; and for the United Kingdom, February 2002 to June 2003.

Box 1.1 *(concluded)*

CPI Impact of Exchange Rate Changes
(February 2002 to end-August 2003)

	Pass-Through Elasticity	Change in Nominal Effective Exchange Rate	CPI Impact
United States	.03	−11	0.3
Euro area	.02	15	−0.3
Japan	.03	4	−0.1
United Kingdom	.08	−7	0.6

Sources: IMF staff estimates; and Gagnon and Ihrig (2002).
Note: Pass-through elasticities for the United States, Japan, and the United Kingdom from Gagnon and Ihrig (2002). The elasticity for the euro area is from IMF (2003a) and may not be strictly comparable—it is prepared on a different methodology and refers to the *core* rather than headline CPI.

cent decrease (increase) in consumer prices in response to a 1 percent appreciation (depreciation) in the exchange rate—some recent studies suggest these may now be only 0.02 to 0.03 in several of the advanced economies (including the United States, the euro area, and Japan).[2] Import prices tend to respond more strongly to exchange rate changes (an estimated one-for-one response in the euro area, for example), but the impact of these changes on consumer prices is moderated by the substantial role of local distribution costs as well as "pricing-to-market" strategies. On this basis, core consumer

[2]See Gagnon and Ihrig (2002) and IMF (2003b).

prices in the euro area would be expected to decline by about 0.3 percent in response to the euro's appreciation since early 2002, the full impact coming through by the end of 2004.[3] Elsewhere, CPI increases (in response to exchange rate depreciations) would also be rather small (see the second table).

The case for monetary policy adjustment to exchange rate changes would be strengthened, however, by the *indirect* impacts of such changes on prices—especially through the demand channel. In the euro area in particular, the potential impact of the stronger euro on exports—the typical growth engine in the initial stages of European recoveries—may further weaken demand, delay recovery prospects, and add to downward pressures on inflation. Hence, recent exchange rate changes may provide scope for further reductions in official euro area interest rates. In the United States and United Kingdom, in contrast, the weakening of exchange rates and overall monetary conditions during the current cycle would tend to add support to the recovery and bring forward the time when a steady withdrawal of monetary stimulus becomes appropriate.

[3]Although less relevant for monetary policy, the impact on *headline* inflation would be higher than this, mainly as a result of the stronger pass-through of oil price changes.

be needed if inflation threatens to undershoot significantly: for instance, if activity fails to pick up quickly or the euro appreciates significantly. In the larger European countries, medium-term fiscal consolidation remains a priority. In these cases, underlying adjustment of ½ percent of GDP a year or, where underpinned by tangible and credible quality consolidation measures and structural reform efforts, cumulative adjustment of 1½ percent of GDP over 2004–06 would appear to provide scope for a reasonable compromise between short- and medium-term policy

trade-offs. Automatic stabilizers should be allowed to operate fully around the consolidation path, even if that results in breaches of the 3 percent of GDP deficit limit. In Japan, despite stronger-than-expected recent data, a much more aggressive monetary policy—accompanied by a clear communication strategy and a commitment to end deflation in a short period—remains essential to turn around deflationary expectations. Given the very high public deficit and debt, modest structural fiscal consolidation appears appropriate. In almost all industrial countries, additional pension and health sector reform is essential to address the future pressures from aging populations.

- *In emerging markets, the policy priorities vary widely across regions.* In Latin America, recent currency appreciation has increased the room for monetary easing in some countries, but—notwithstanding the improvement in financing conditions—it will be critical to ensure that the pace of fiscal consolidation and structural reform is sustained. In Asia, the scope for policy maneuver is greater, and macroeconomic policies have appropriately been eased in a number of countries, in part to offset the impact of SARS. As discussed in Chapter III, in many emerging and developing countries a broad-based effort to improve medium-term public debt sustainability—encompassing tax reforms, improved expenditure control, institutional strengthening, and structural reforms to boost growth—is a central priority.

- *Given the continued need to reduce global dependence on growth in the United States and address global imbalances, the case for structural reform takes on new urgency.* As has been discussed many times in the *World Economic Outlook*, the priorities include labor and product market reforms to boost potential growth in Europe; corporate and financial restructuring in Japan; a greater reliance on domestic demand in emerging markets in Asia, again supported by continued corporate and financial sector reform; and in the United States, measures to boost national savings, particularly through strengthening the medium-term fiscal position. Over the past several years, progress has unfortunately been limited, and in some aspects—notably the U.S. fiscal outlook—the situation has deteriorated. In marked contrast to the situation in the mid-1980s, when the United States last ran a current account deficit of this size, neither Japan nor, to a lesser extent, Europe is well placed to pick up the slack if growth in the United States were to slow. This underscores the need for accelerated efforts to address the issues listed above. In this connection, the recent initiatives in Europe—especially Agenda 2010 in Germany and the recent pension reform in France—are encouraging, although there is much further to go. In many countries, continued efforts to strengthen corporate governance are also required.

- *Policymakers will need to stand ready to manage the effects of a further depreciation in the U.S. dollar, if it were to occur.* To date, the brunt of the adjustment to the depreciation of the dollar has been borne by the euro, the Canadian dollar, and a number of smaller industrial country currencies. As discussed in Box 1.1, this has been broadly in line with medium-term fundamentals, and in most cases there has been scope for offsetting monetary easing. Were the U.S. dollar to depreciate significantly further, most of these countries still have some room for policy action; however, with the degree of undervaluation much less than before, it would be desirable for the necessary currency appreciation to be spread more broadly. The critical need for a more aggressive monetary policy to address deflation in Japan implies, if anything, some downward pressure on the yen. In these circumstances, greater upward exchange rate flexibility in emerging markets in Asia—which is relatively well placed from a cyclical perspective—would significantly facilitate the global adjustment process, given the region's importance in global trade, as well as being desirable for domestic reasons (Chapter II).

In those countries where poverty remains a major concern, GDP growth has remained relatively resilient despite the weakness of the global economy. However, substantial differences across countries remain. In China and, to a lesser extent, India, per capita GDP growth is quite robust; but in sub-Saharan Africa it remains below 1 percent, far from sufficient to meet poverty reduction targets under the Millennium Development Goals. In this connection, it is notable that per capita GDP growth has been significantly stronger in those African countries where political stability has been achieved and where the most progress has been made toward

Box 1.2. How Should We Measure Global Growth?

As estimates of global growth are a key output of global forecasts, such as those reported in the *World Economic Outlook* (WEO), it comes as something of a surprise that the exchange rates used to aggregate growth vary widely across forecasters, with material consequences for the estimated figures. The WEO, together with the Organization for Economic Cooperation and Development (OECD) and a number of private sector organizations, uses purchasing-power-parity (PPP) exchange rates—the exchange rate that equates the cost of a "typical" basket of goods across countries. By contrast, the World Bank and other groups in the private sector use market rates—the rate at which transactions occur in exchange markets. Still others use hybrids between these two main alternatives.

Clearly, the appropriate weighting scheme can depend on the issue being considered. Market weights are appropriate when the outcome is closely linked to the current exchange rate—for example, current accounts. In addition, the well-known identity that the global current account should sum to zero holds only when using market rates. Similar considerations apply to many nominal concepts, as well as some real variables, such as effective demand for a given country, since the profitability of exporters depends on current exchange rates. Reflecting these considerations, the WEO aggregates many variables using market rates, as well as reporting an alternative measure of global growth on this basis in Table 1 of the Statistical Appendix. The main disadvantage of using market rates is their instability over time. For example, the market rate of the euro has appreciated by over one-fourth in real terms against the U.S. dollar since early 2002. Using market rates to add up world GDP would imply that euro area workers have massively increased their productivity compared with their U.S. counterparts over a period when the United States appears to be experiencing a more robust recovery.

Partly as a consequence, PPP exchange rates are generally regarded as providing a better measure of the change in global economic well-being. The greater stability of real exchange rates implied by using PPP means that the resulting estimate of (say) global growth is less affected by short-term changes in the relative importance of countries and regions. In addition, PPP exchange rates are generally thought to provide a more balanced estimate of the relative importance of rich and poor countries. Market rates imply that the vast majority of world output comes from advanced countries, a result generally attributed to the fact that market rates only equate prices of traded goods, and that nontraded goods are relatively more expensive in rich countries. For example, a haircut is much more expensive in New York than in Bombay although the outcome is similar. PPP exchange rates adjust for this bias, so that the weight of advanced countries in global output falls from four-fifths to just over one-half (see Box A1 of the May 2001 *World Economic Outlook*).

PPP weights imply significantly higher global growth than those based on market exchange rates. As developing countries generally grow faster than their industrial counterparts, using PPP exchange rates leads to a higher underlying rate of global growth (see the figure). The differential has become particularly large in recent years, averaging almost 1 percent a year since 1990, largely reflecting rapid growth in China and stagnation in Japan, the major countries whose weights are most affected by the switch from market to PPP exchange rates. Japan's weight in world output halves from 15 to $7\frac{1}{2}$ percent when PPP weights replace market ones, while China's increases from $3\frac{1}{2}$ to $11\frac{1}{2}$ percent.[1] When China and Japan are excluded, the gap between the two weighting schemes falls by over half.

Note: The main author of this box is Tamim Bayoumi

[1]The PPP weight for China is subject to some controversy, as discussed in an appendix available via the Internet at http://pwt.econ.upenn.edu, the website of the Penn World Tables.

Global Growth: Purchasing-Power-Parity Versus Market Exchange Rates
(Percent a year)

Global Growth Using Different Weights, 1990–99
(Percent a year)

	Full Sample	Excluding China and Japan
Penn World Tables PPP weights	3.4	3.0
WEO PPP weights	3.6	3.0
Market exchange rates	2.6	2.7

Sources: Penn World Tables; WEO database; and IMF staff calculations.

One complication with using PPP exchange rates is that, while the exchange rate is adjusted for price distortions between traded and non-traded goods, similar adjustments are difficult to make to national data. As a result, the growth rate for (say) China may be based on internal market prices that put too high a weight on rapidly growing traded goods and too little weight on slower growing services. This implies that global growth may be overstated when PPP exchange rates are used, unless these weights are adjusted over time to reflect the changing pattern of domestic prices. Fortunately, there is a data source—the Penn World Tables—that aggregates output across countries by first converting its components into dollars using U.S. relative prices, thus avoiding this bias. Unfortunately, such calculations are cumber-

some. While not practicable for WEO purposes, they can provide a useful benchmark for more flexible schemes.

Assuming PPP rates are appropriate, the bias coming from using unchanging PPP exchange rates is small compared with that from using market values. The table sets out the growth rate of GDP aggregated across all countries available in the Penn World Tables from 1990–99 using data from the Penn World Tables themselves, as well as aggregating using WEO PPP weights and those derived from market exchange rates. While the WEO PPP aggregation creates an upward bias of 0.2 percent a year, this is considerably smaller than the downward bias from using market exchange rates of 0.8 percent a year. Indeed, once China and Japan are excluded from the calculation, the WEO PPP calculation has no discernable bias, while the market rates continue to show lower growth than the benchmark.

Overall, assuming one wishes to calculate global growth using PPP weights, the current WEO approach provides a relatively accurate estimate of global growth. Further refinements, however, might be able to reduce the upward bias that still occurs compared with calculations using PPP weights calculated on a more careful, but less practical, basis.

macroeconomic stability and structural and institutional reform. This underscores the need to press forward with the region-wide implementation of the New Partnership for Africa's Development (NEPAD), which fully embodies these objectives.

But while improved domestic policies in Africa are crucial, they are not enough: addi-

Figure 1.8. How Much Do Developed Country Policies Help Developing Countries?[1]
(Commitment to development index)

Developed country policies appear only modestly supportive of development, particularly in the largest countries.

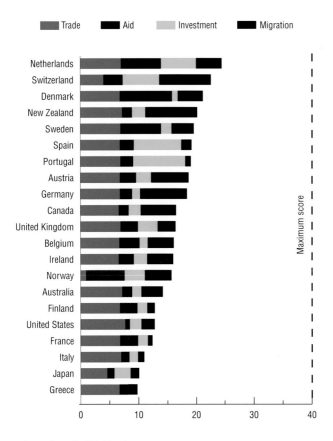

Source: Center for Global Development.
[1]The index measures the impact of advanced country policies on development in the areas of trade, aid, investment, and migration; the maximum score in each category is 10. For details of the calculations, see Birdsall and Roodman (2003).

tional financial assistance from the international community is also essential and—provided appropriate domestic policies are followed—can be effectively absorbed (see Box 1.3, "Managing Increasing Aid Flows to Developing Countries"). Following the Monterrey Summit, progress has been made, including the establishment of the Millennium Challenge Account and additional funding to address the AIDS pandemic by the United States; and the United Kingdom has put forward innovative proposals for an International Financing Facility to finance the achievement of the Millennium Development Goals. While the impact of aid and other key macroeconomic policies in industrialized countries is difficult to measure precisely, recent analysis by the Center for Global Development suggests that in most cases they are far from supportive of development, underscoring the need for further progress to help developing countries meet the Millennium Development Goals (Figure 1.8).

A central and immediate challenge for the global community is to achieve further multilateral trade liberalization under the Doha Round. This would clearly be of enormous benefit to the globe as a whole: as the IMF's Managing Director has stressed, ". . . lowering barriers to trade . . . has been the foundation of the tremendous expansion in global trade and prosperity in the second half of the twentieth century."[5] Moreover, with nearly three-fourths of the world's poor working in the rural sector, competing with industrial country farmers who receive a third of their income in subsidies and other forms of protection, it is clearly also critical for poverty reduction. The developing countries themselves have much to do—and much to gain—from reducing their own trade barriers. But progress in the Doha Round requires leadership from the largest industrial countries, as well

[5]See "Cooperation in Trade and International Financial Integration," speech by Horst Köhler, IMF Managing Director at the WTO General Council Meeting on Coherence, Geneva, May 13, 2003 (available via the Internet: http://www.imf.org/external/np/speeches/2003/051303.htm).

Box 1.3. Managing Increasing Aid Flows to Developing Countries

At the Millennium Summit of the United Nations in September 2000, the global community adopted the Millennium Development Goals encompassing eight socioeconomic objectives related to poverty reduction—including health, gender, education, environment, and global partnership for development—with the number of poor to be halved between 1990 and 2015. Recognizing that achieving these goals would require substantial additional external resources, in the March 2002 Monterrey Consensus the industrial countries were urged to make concrete efforts toward achieving a level of Official Development Assistance (ODA) of 0.7 percent of GNP, a longstanding target so far met by only a handful of industrial countries.

If all industrial countries were to increase their ODA to 0.7 percent of GNP, aid flows to developing countries would increase very substantially (see the figure). Aid flows, which presently average 0.24 percent of industrial countries' GNP, would nearly triple and could reach 70–90 percent of some recipient countries' GDP.[1] Such flows would be unprecedented in size—much higher, for example, than peak capital flows to emerging markets in the mid-1990s (14–15 percent of GDP). Aid has also typically been volatile—in some countries in the 1990s, for example, absolute changes in aid flows exceeded 30 percent of GDP in a single year. With underdeveloped financial markets and relatively closed capital accounts, how should the economies of recipient countries deal with both the large volume and volatility of aid flows?

One concern that has often been raised with respect to aid flows is the so-called Dutch disease. An increase in aid generally increases the demand for both traded and nontraded goods. With the supply of nontraded goods less elastic, higher demand drives up their price relative to that of traded goods and causes the real exchange rate to appreciate. This, in turn, draws resources away from the traded goods sector and

Distributing 0.7 Percent of GDP in Official Development Assistance (ODA) Under Different Scenarios
(ODA in percent of GDP)

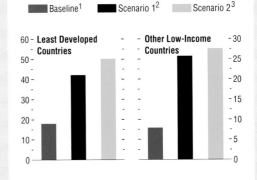

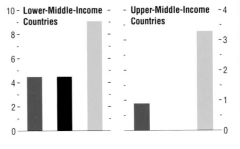

Source: Heller and Gupta (2002).
[1]1996 aid allocation.
[2]Based on Collier and Dollar's (1999) poverty-efficient aid allocation, scaled up for the higher level of allocation implied by the 0.7 percent. China and India are constrained to receive no more than their 1996 share of total aid.
[3]All countries receive the ODA they got in 1996 plus an incremental amount allocated according to Collier and Dollar's (1999) criteria. China and India are constrained to receive no more than their 1996 share of total aid.

causes it to shrink, raising concerns if the traded goods sector is the main source of productivity growth in the economy and aid flows are volatile.[2]

That said, Dutch disease concerns should not be overstated. Recent preliminary results by Prati, Sahay, and Tressel (2003) suggest that a doubling of aid inflows from 10 percent to 20 percent of GDP would lead to a real apprecia-

Note: The main author of this box is Ratna Sahay.
[1]See Heller and Gupta (2002).

[2]See Bulíř and Hamann (2001).

Box 1.3 *(concluded)*

tion of only 6 percent on impact. This effect may vary across countries and could be even smaller if aid translates mostly into higher imports. Moreover, in a number of cases, countries have been able to intervene in the foreign exchange market to limit the exchange rate impact of foreign aid inflows (through buying foreign exchange) and sterilize the monetary impact of the intervention (by selling government paper). Such sterilized intervention can be an effective way of preventing real appreciation in countries with relatively closed capital accounts, but can be expensive because domestic interest rates are generally higher than the interest received on foreign assets.

Managing increasing aid flows requires also choosing their most appropriate form. Grants— as opposed to loans—are the optimal form of aid when aid is intended to raise consumption of the poorest segments of the population, to respond to natural disasters or food shortages, and to provide humanitarian assistance and help the peace process during conflicts. Grants are also appropriate when the magnitude and timing of the returns to public investment are highly uncertain and where the government has limited ability to recoup them through taxation to service debt. If the GDP growth rate of the economy does not increase in response to this type of aid it should not come as a surprise. But grants would help prevent future generations from inheriting debt and reduce the need for debt forgiveness.[3]

Overall, the key issue remains the effectiveness with which aid is used. The main challenges relate to the administrative capacity to manage and use the resources efficiently, the volatility and uncertainty of aid flows, and the potential for fueling corruption. If aid flows are used to finance productivity-increasing investments— for example, in education, health, or infrastructure—Dutch disease concerns are correspondingly reduced. However, raising expenditure on education and health sporadically will

not be sufficient—the spending will need to be well targeted and monitored. In addition, given that it takes time for the quality of human capital to improve, some mechanism will need to be devised to ensure that a higher level of resources can be sustained for at least 10 to 15 years.

If good governance is not in place, the resource transfer is easily captured by the elite with no positive effect on productivity and a worsening of the income distribution in the recipient country. Donors may sometimes face a dilemma if aid helps reduce the absolute number of the poor in a country but at the same time also worsens the income distribution (this is possible when the resource transfer to the elite is much larger than that to the poor). Under these conditions, the overall welfare of the population may increase but corruption may also rise. While in the past, aid appears to have been given to corrupt and noncorrupt governments alike (Alesina and Weder, 2002), greater attention should be paid going forward to the quality of local institutions in future aid decisions. External assistance should be increasingly focused on supporting countries that implement governance reforms and invest in quality human and physical capital, strengthening institutions through technical assistance, and increasing country ownership of programs and projects through the Poverty Reduction Strategy Paper (PRSP) process.

What if policy performance and institutions cannot be strengthened in the short run? Rather than cut off aid, donors should announce multi-year aid commitments with disbursements conditional on good political and economic performance and the dire needs of the poor, thus creating the incentives for recipient countries to reform and making future aid flows more certain. At the same time, countries with good policies and institutions should be allowed to save part of the aid so that the adverse consequences of aid volatility are reduced and disbursements are made commensurate to the absorptive capacity of the country. Dependency on aid can be expected to decline over time as low-income countries succeed in meeting their development goals.

[3]Helbling, Mody, and Sahay (forthcoming).

as a clear commitment by the developing countries to trade integration as a core element of their development strategy. Regrettably, progress to date has generally been disappointing, although recent steps by the European Union toward agricultural reforms are welcome, if still somewhat partial. At the Evian G-7 Summit in May, industrial country leaders renewed their commitment to ensure a successful Doha Round; the WTO Cancun Ministerial meeting in September—which was under way as the *World Economic Outlook* went to press—must be the occasion to match words with action.

North America: Can the United States Remain the Engine of Global Growth?

After a year of recovery, GDP growth in the United States slowed markedly from about mid-2002, owing both to rising geopolitical uncertainties in the run-up to the war in Iraq and to the continued aftereffects of the bursting of the equity price bubble. Amid weak demand and continued substantial excess capacity, inflation has fallen considerably, with core CPI inflation still well below 2 percent. With the substantial depreciation of the U.S. dollar over the past year only just beginning to have an effect, the external current account deficit has continued to break new records; in contrast to previous years, it has been financed primarily by sales of government agency and corporate paper, including to a number of Asian central banks, rather than by equity inflows.

Following the end of the war in Iraq, the recovery has begun to regain momentum. Second quarter GDP data proved stronger than expected, aided by a sharp rise in government expenditures, as well as increasing signs of a pickup in consumption (albeit in part due to very strong automobile sales) and private investment. While labor markets remain sluggish and significant excess capacity persists, forward-looking indicators—notably consumer and business confidence—have strengthened, and monetary and financial conditions have eased further. Fiscal policy has become even more

stimulative with the passage of further tax cuts and higher defense expenditures; equity prices have risen markedly; the dollar has fallen significantly since its peak in early 2002; and long-term interest rates, despite a strong rebound since mid-June, are still low by historical standards. Against this background, the IMF staff continues to project a renewed recovery in the second half of 2003 and 2004, at a somewhat stronger pace than earlier expected, with GDP growth rising above potential from the third quarter onward.

Given the very substantial macroeconomic and other stimuli now in train, a stronger economic upturn is clearly possible. That said, the pace and extent of the pickup in investment may be constrained by relatively high excess capacity along with continued corporate caution in the wake of recent accounting scandals; corporate and household balance sheets, while improving, remain stretched (Figure 1.9); and the substantial support to consumption provided by the housing sector is unlikely to be sustained, while labor market conditions remain relatively soft. More broadly, the record current account deficit—now matched by an equally large general government deficit (Figure 1.10)—is still an important vulnerability. Despite its depreciation over the last year, the dollar still appears overvalued from a medium-term perspective, and the risk that its adjustment may become disorderly—or that it might overshoot—cannot be ruled out.

Against this background, U.S. policymakers have faced a difficult task balancing the need to provide short-term support to the economy while minimizing the risk of exacerbating long-run problems, a task made no easier by the weakness of demand in the rest of the world. Monetary policy has been highly accommodative, and the Federal Reserve has appropriately indicated that this can be maintained for a considerable period; the adoption of a medium-term inflation target could help to anchor inflationary expectations and reduce the risk of an adverse shock leading to unwanted downward pressure on inflation. With low interest rates contributing to a continued boom in house prices, which—after adjustment for inflation—are about 30 percent above

Figure 1.9. United States: Household Balance Sheets
(Percent of disposable income)

Household balance sheets have stopped deteriorating, aided by still buoyant house prices, but remain stretched. The increase in household savings has been financed entirely by lower taxes.

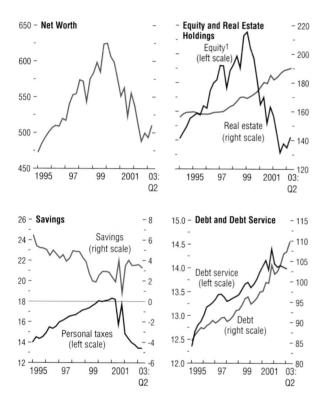

Source: Haver Analytics.
[1]Excluding mutual fund shares, at market value.

their previous peak, concerns have been raised that the current stimulus has been achieved at the risk of a future housing bust, which could have a serious impact on consumption and growth. Such concerns need, however, to be balanced against the certainty of greater current economic weakness in the absence of monetary easing and the risks that it would pose for the United States—and the global economy—at the current conjuncture. And with policy interest rates not expected to be raised until the recovery is on a firm footing, the impact of eventual housing price adjustment would likely be offset by strength elsewhere in the economy. Even so, the elevated level of housing prices is a potential risk, particularly if long-term interest rates were to continue to rise strongly.

On the fiscal side, the general government deficit (covering both the federal government and the states) is projected at over 6 percent of GDP in 2003, compared with a surplus of over 1 percent in 2000—the largest swing in the fiscal position over three years in at least three decades. While this has provided short-term support to the recovery, it has come at the cost of a substantial deterioration in the medium-term fiscal position—in practice, with the U.S. Administration's expenditure and revenue projections appearing relatively optimistic and a further supplementary budget expected to cover expenditures related to Iraq, the outlook may well prove worse. If sustained, higher deficits would offset the longer-term benefits from tax cuts—already reduced by complex and untransparent phasing and sunset arrangements—and make an orderly adjustment of the current account deficit more difficult. In addition, with public debt no longer projected to decline in coming years, no fiscal cushion will be built up in advance of the coming pressures from the retirement of the baby boomers. This would be of less concern if early action to reduce future costs of aging populations were envisaged, but that does not presently appear to be the case (recent proposals in fact increase Medicare spending). Consequently, implementation of a credible medium-term framework to restore broad budgetary balance (excluding Social Security) over the cycle is now even more pressing, along with measures to put the Social Security and Medicare systems on a sound financial footing.

The continued robust growth of labor productivity remains a key strength of the outlook. While this partly reflects the effects of recent labor retrenchment, productivity growth should remain solid in coming years—although not as fast as in the late 1990s—buoyed by continued advances in information technology and the gradual spread of IT-related productivity gains to other sectors of the economy.[6] This, in turn, has been underpinned by the flexibility and investment-friendliness of the U.S. economy, strengths that should continue to be built on in the future, including by continuing to strengthen corporate governance and accounting standards. That said, as noted above, a number of downside risks remain, and based on historical experience even an orderly current account adjustment would likely be accompanied by weaker growth of both GDP and—even more—domestic demand. While such risks are clearly reduced by strong productivity growth, looking forward it seems unlikely that the United States can or should provide the degree of support to the global economy over the medium term that it has in the past.

Following impressive growth in the first three quarters of 2002, GDP growth in Canada has slowed considerably in recent months, reflecting the rapid and sizable appreciation of the Canadian dollar, weaker foreign demand, and a slower pace of inventory accumulation as well as the temporary impact of SARS and mad cow disease. Reflecting these factors, as well as the drop in core inflation to well within the 1–3 percent target range, the Bank of Canada acted in July and September to partially reverse earlier interest rate hikes. Reflecting the projected strengthening in U.S. activity, improving confidence, and

Figure 1.10. United States: Return of the Twin Deficits
(Percent of GDP)

The sharp deterioration in the U.S. fiscal position has led to a reemergence of the twin deficits of the 1980s. With fiscal deficits expected to persist, government debt will now not be reduced in advance of the retirement of the baby boomers.

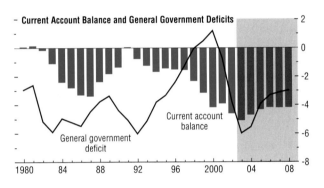

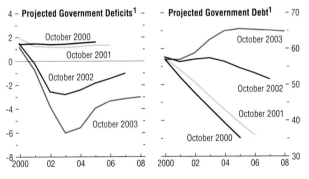

[1]Projections from previous *World Economic Outlooks*.

[6]See "Is the New Economy Dead?" Box 1.2, April 2003 *World Economic Outlook.*

the fading impact of the recent adverse shocks, growth is expected to pick up toward the end of the year. The 2003/04 budget has maintained the commitment to fiscal prudence, and with continued small surpluses projected in the next two years, public debt is expected to be reduced below 40 percent by 2004/05.

Western Europe: Prolonged Weakness with Tentative Signs of a Turnaround

The slowdown in the euro area has been deeper and more prolonged than earlier expected, although recent indicators—notably increases in equity prices and in business confidence—may portend an improvement in economic prospects. Nevertheless, there are still relatively few signs of a broader pickup in real activity: GDP declined in the euro area as a whole in the second quarter of 2003, including in Germany, France, and Italy, implying that Germany and Italy, together with the Netherlands, were in recession; despite some recent strengthening in expectations, indicators of household and business confidence generally remain at depressed levels; unemployment continues to edge up; and industrial production has yet to show a sustained upward trend. The German economy remains weak for the third year in a row, adding to the subpar performance of the euro area as a whole and threatening to hold back the region's recovery prospects. Reflecting these developments, growth projections for the euro area have again been marked down—by about ½ percent in 2003 and 2004—and risks in some countries still appear to be tilted to the downside.

What accounts for these ongoing difficulties in the euro area? Looking at the main components of demand, investment spending has been a key weakness over recent years—driven down by the general over-leveraging of corporate balance sheets during the asset price bubble of the late 1990s and the subsequent slow pace of adjustment. Exacerbating this downturn has been low business confidence and—in Germany—the continued unwinding of the post-reunification

construction boom. Corporate difficulties and the broader legacy of the global equity market bubble have also hit euro area financial institutions. For example, increased loan-loss provisions since 2000 have lowered the capital cushions of euro area banks. The German financial sector had a particularly difficult year in 2002 and, although there have been encouraging signs recently that this deterioration has been arrested—helped by more positive developments in financial markets—further delay in the recovery would nevertheless put additional strains on an already stretched system.

While still uneven across the area, consumption has picked up slowly over the past year, and should receive more support from rising real incomes as inflation declines. Household balance sheets appear to be in generally good shape, with lower debt levels and higher savings rates than in the United States. But offsetting these fundamental strengths has been the poor state of household confidence, influenced by rising unemployment. External trading conditions have also been unfavorable to growth. While exports have been held down mainly by weak demand among the major economies, the substantial appreciation of the euro over the past two years may tend to reduce prospects for an export-led recovery that is as strong as in past regional upturns (Figure 1.11). This appreciation is in the direction implied by medium-term fundamentals, however, and its impact on monetary conditions in the euro area has been largely offset through lower interest rates (see Box 1.1).

Overall, although the worst may now be over, the short-term regional outlook still appears quite weak: recovery prospects are mainly dependent on a pickup in external demand, the low level of interest rates, and a winding down of corporate balance sheet adjustments. Both domestic and external weaknesses appear particularly acute in Germany and, while the recent uptick in the key IFO index of business confidence is encouraging, the economy is not expected to grow in 2003, with a modest upturn in 2004. Growth in France may reach ½ percent this year and about 2 percent in 2004, and the outlook for Italy is slightly lower than this. But, with confidence still weak and an unhelpful external environment, recoveries in these countries may remain hesitant and patchy for some time. Among the smaller euro area countries, domestic activity is particularly depressed in the Netherlands and Portugal; weak growth—1 percent or less in 2003 for the third year in a row—may persist in Austria and Belgium; and growth in Ireland has fallen sharply this year. Growth should remain somewhat more resilient, however, in Spain and especially Greece, aided by relatively buoyant domestic demand (including the impact of Olympic Games–related investment in Greece and stronger investment in Spain). Core inflation in the euro area has declined below 2 percent and is expected to fall further in 2004. There is even a possibility of a period of mildly declining prices in Germany, while above-average inflation rates of some of the smaller economies are expected to diminish—including sizable falls in Ireland, the Netherlands, and Portugal.

Against the background of declining inflation and weak activity, the ECB's decision to lower interest rates by ½ percent in June was fully appropriate. Additional easing will be needed if there is a serious risk of a significant undershooting of inflation—which could occur, for example, if growth does not recover quickly or if the euro were to appreciate significantly. The central bank's clarification that its price stability objective is consistent with inflation below but close to 2 percent indicates its desire to avoid deflation while also accommodating inflation differentials across individual countries. More generally, although monetary policy needs to focus on area-wide conditions, a more activist approach may in certain cases be warranted—especially when downside shocks to individual countries have potentially area-wide spillovers.

Beyond the support provided by the automatic stabilizers, there has been limited scope for fiscal policy to counteract current economic weaknesses, especially in the largest economies. Fiscal deficits in Germany and France are projected to be well above 3 percent of GDP this year and next, and will be close to this level in

Figure 1.11. Euro Area: A Relatively Weak Cyclical Upturn

Euro area exports have picked up less strongly during the latest cycle compared with previous upturns, and investment—hampered by slow corporate balance sheet adjustment—has been particularly weak.

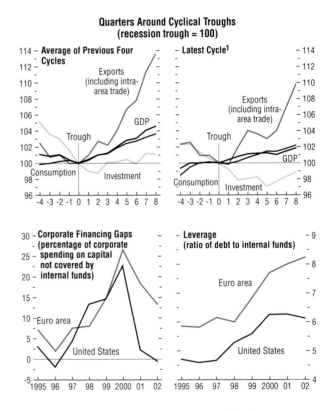

Sources: European Central Bank; U.S. Federal Reserve; and IMF staff estimates.
[1]Latest cyclical trough is taken as 2001:Q4.

Italy, notwithstanding substantial one-off measures. In Germany, tax relief has been advanced to 2004 to support the weak economy, and durable cuts in subsidy and entitlement programs are planned. Looking forward, all euro area economies face significant fiscal pressures from aging populations—especially from about 2010 onward. Public spending on old-age pensions could rise by about 4–5 percent of GDP in several euro area countries over the next 50 years, with increased government spending on health and long-term care amounting to a further 3–4 percent of GDP in some cases. Without offsetting policy measures, these increases would put unbearable strains on public finances and debt burdens. In such circumstances, there is a compelling case for strengthening medium-term fiscal balances. In this regard, countries with weak positions, including the larger economies, should aim to achieve underlying consolidation of ½ percent of GDP a year, or—if backed by tangible and credible quality consolidation measures and structural reform efforts—cumulative adjustment of 1½ percent of GDP over 2004–06; in each case, the automatic stabilizers should be allowed to operate fully around the consolidation path. Such goals should allow countries to achieve a reasonable compromise between short- and medium-term policy trade-offs.

Structural reforms remain key to improving the euro area's economic performance, including meeting the challenges that population aging will imply for longer-term fiscal positions, labor supply, and economic growth. As discussed in the April 2003 *World Economic Outlook*, reforms to improve the competitiveness of European labor and product markets could yield significant dividends in terms of regional output. Several countries have recently introduced or at least proposed substantive reforms, including further liberalization of labor and product markets in Germany, and pension reforms in France, Italy, and Austria. Full implementation of such measures, while important and encouraging, would represent only the beginning of the necessary reform agenda. For example, the recent pension reforms in France—adopted despite substantial public protest—will nevertheless resolve only about two-fifths of the budgetary impact of aging on public pension systems. And the improvements in European labor market performance since the mid-1990s will need to be sustained and deepened if targets adopted at the Lisbon Summit in 2000 are to be reached. The employment rate of older workers, for example, is still under 40 percent (and only 32 percent in France and 28 percent in Italy)—well short of the 50 percent target. Raising effective retirement ages and facilitating employment opportunities for older workers are key elements in a strategy to support labor supply and potential growth in the years ahead.

Turning to countries outside the euro area, growth in the United Kingdom weakened in the first half of 2003, reflecting a slowing of investment and—to a lesser extent—private consumption, as well as a deterioration of external demand. Recent indicators, including business surveys and retail sales, point to an improving outlook. Annual house price inflation has eased in recent months but, at nearly 17 percent in the year to August, remains high. Thus, the risk of an abrupt unwinding cannot yet be ruled out. The labor market has been resilient, with continuing low unemployment and relatively stable earnings growth. In July 2003, the Bank of England cut the policy interest rate by ¼ percent to 3½ percent, responding appropriately to weakening economic prospects, even though inflation remained somewhat above the 2½ percent target owing to temporary factors. Fiscal policy has provided important support for activity during the current slowdown, drawing on the room for maneuver built up over the preceding years. These supportive macroeconomic policies, together with relatively favorable domestic conditions and a gradual improvement in external trade, should support stronger growth in the period ahead.

Elsewhere, 2003 growth projections for Denmark, Norway, and Sweden have been marked down, reflecting weak domestic confidence, rising unemployment, and the poorer international climate. Central banks in all three countries have reduced interest rates since early June and, with inflation declining, further reductions could be considered if weak activity persists. However, policy support already in the pipeline together with an improvement in external conditions is expected to lead to a slow pickup in growth in the second half of 2003 and in 2004. Activity in Switzerland is expected to contract in 2003, although a strengthening in trade and supportive macroeconomic policies should contribute to a modest improvement in 2004. Should recovery again falter, further monetary easing—probably using quantitative measures, as interest rates are close to zero—may be needed to reduce deflation risks, backed by structural policies to improve the dynamism and robustness of growth.

Japan: Bold Measures Needed to Accelerate Restructuring and End Deflation

The initial estimate of second quarter growth in Japan significantly exceeded expectations and this, together with a further upward revision to the first quarter GDP outturn, an improved external environment, and the pickup in stock prices, has led to sizable increases in growth projections for 2003 and 2004. On a more cautious note, however, monthly data have been mixed: exports have been growing strongly and industrial production picked up in July (after falling in the second quarter), but retail sales continue to fall and the apparent strength of business fixed investment in the national accounts data appears at odds with weaker trends in shipments of capital goods and construction materials. Financial conditions are also providing uneven support for recovery: while recent increases in equity prices are encouraging, bond yields have rebounded substantially from their all-time lows reached earlier this year.

Looking forward, although risks have become more balanced, the outlook remains clouded by entrenched deflation and by persistent weaknesses in corporate, financial, and public sector balance sheets. While a stronger global recovery could provide some upside for activity in the remainder of 2003 and 2004, the economy remains vulnerable to a range of domestic and external shocks. Given the limited progress with bank and corporate restructuring, potential falls in equity or bond prices could weaken corporate and financial balance sheets, triggering a rapid cutback in bank lending and dampening investment. Other risks include the impact of a sustained appreciation of the yen on corporate profits, investment, deflation, and net exports; the potential for a pickup in household saving rates if uncertainty about the outlook increases; and the possibility that rising public debt (in the absence of a strategy to restore fiscal sustainability) could trigger sharply higher real interest rates.

To contain these risks, a bold strategy is needed that tackles the underlying weaknesses in the economy. Such a strategy would include rapid and forceful measures to accelerate disposal of nonperforming loans (NPLs) and address the poor quality of capital in the banking sector (building on the Program for Financial Revival announced in October 2002); actions to promote more rapid corporate restructuring, including effective use of the newly established Industrial Revitalization Corporation of Japan (IRCJ); a public commitment by the Bank of Japan to end deflation, backed up by more aggressive quantitative easing and clear communication of this strategy; and a detailed and ambitious plan to restore sustainability to Japan's public finances.

Corporate and financial restructuring remain key to a sustained turnaround in Japan's economic prospects. Both sectors have made some progress in tackling their problems, but severe difficulties persist. The major banks, for example, have continued to lower their NPLs and exposure to equity risk, but the weak economy and stock market have created new problem loans and losses on equities—bringing major banks' losses to nearly 1 percent of GDP in the year to March 2003. Furthermore, the quality of bank capital remains poor, with tax deferred assets (which are only usable if a bank makes

Figure 1.12. Japan: Monetary, Financial, and Fiscal Indicators

Bank lending is still falling, despite rapid base money growth and very low interest rates, while government debt is reaching unsustainable levels.

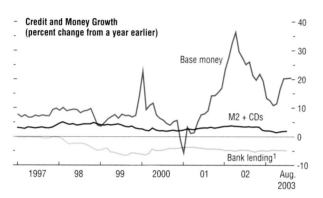

Credit and Money Growth
(percent change from a year earlier)

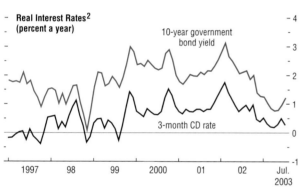

Real Interest Rates[2]
(percent a year)

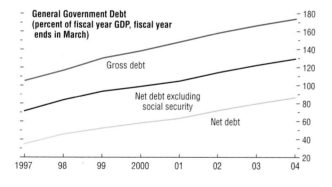

General Government Debt
(percent of fiscal year GDP, fiscal year ends in March)

Sources: Bloomberg Financial Markets; Cabinet Office; Nomura Security; and IMF staff estimates.
[1] End-period.
[2] Deflated by CPI adjusted for changes in indirect taxes and administered prices.

profits, and are not available to meet losses if it fails) accounting for a large share of Tier-1 capital. An external audit that limited the use of such assets in reported capital precipitated the sharp weakening, and subsequent recapitalization with public funds, of Resona Bank in May. This recapitalization, the first under the new Deposit Insurance Law, appears to have gone smoothly, with no enduring financial market fallout, but it needs to be supported by broader reforms to strengthen bank and corporate governance, improve recognition and facilitate disposal of NPLs, and promote bank consolidation. Accelerated disposal of NPLs and targeted use of public funds to recapitalize weak but systemically important banks remain essential to ending the sector's decade-long deterioration. Elsewhere in the financial sector, an improved regulatory framework is needed for life insurance companies, including tighter solvency standards to promote a more accurate assessment of insurers' financial condition.

Financial sector reforms need to be complemented by accelerated corporate restructuring. While aggregate corporate profits have improved over the past year and debt-equity ratios have come down, many companies continue to suffer from high leverage, poor profitability, and excess capacity. Restructuring has been particularly slow among small and medium-sized enterprises and in the construction and retail sectors. Contributing to these delays, banks lack incentives to push ahead with corporate restructuring because of their weak capital bases. Individual banks have also had difficulties in coordinating with other creditors over restructuring plans—an area where the IRCJ could help. To be effective, the IRCJ will need to be insulated from political interference.

While the Bank of Japan's quantitative easing policy has kept short-term interest rates at zero and helped to stabilize the financial system, it has been unable to end deflation, ease deflationary expectations, or promote growth in broad money and bank credit (Figure 1.12). In view of these difficulties, a more aggressive policy approach is clearly needed. This should include setting and communicating a time frame for eliminating deflation; a transparent medium-term inflation target; and sizable purchases of a broader array of assets, which would potentially let monetary policy work through asset prices as well as through the liquidity channel, would help raise the price level, and would allow a strong expansion of base money. Additional purchases of Japanese government bonds (JGBs) would have the added benefit of reducing the private sector's holdings of government debt and hence lowering future interest payments from the public sector to the private sector. Concerns about potential Bank of Japan losses on JGB holdings should not be allowed to detract from the pursuit of price stability, and can in any case be mitigated through loss-sharing arrangements between the central bank and the Ministry of Finance.

The rapid buildup of government debt over the past decade and impending pressures from population aging underscore the need for fiscal consolidation. In view of these concerns, the small reduction in the structural deficit (excluding bank support) envisaged for FY2003 is appropriate. More critical, however, is the need to lay out a clear medium-term strategy to return public finances to a sustainable basis, which may need to go beyond the official targets of keeping expenditure at its current level relative to GDP until FY2006 and eliminating the primary deficit (excluding social security) by the early 2010s. Such a strategy would involve reductions in public spending and revenue-enhancing measures, including broadening of the tax base. Specific measures could include cutting back further on low-value public investment projects, reforming public pension and medical systems, strengthening the corporate and personal income tax bases, and raising the consumption tax.

Latin America: Emerging Stability Provides Opportunity to Accelerate Crisis-Proofing

A tentative recovery appears to be emerging in much of Latin America, although growth is highly differentiated across the region and political uncertainty continues to weigh heavily in some cases. The recovery reflects a number of factors, including a pickup in exports, helped by stronger global growth and substantial real exchange rate depreciations; an improvement in risk appetite, which has underpinned a rally in emerging bond markets and, in a number of cases, pushed secondary market spreads to near all-time lows; and expectations of improved policy fundamentals in some cases.

The recovery nevertheless remains fragile, even under the baseline of gradually improving global growth. A key risk is that the rally in emerging bond markets is not sustained, undercutting growth prospects and macroeconomic stability. A fallback in risk appetite, rising industrial country interest rates, or better prospects for mature-market investments are potential triggers. Sentiment could also be affected by policy slippages in the region or by further sovereign rating downgrades of heavily dollarized economies. Though regional contagion is possible in such circumstances, investment-grade borrowers such as Mexico and Chile would be less vulnerable. Finally, political instability in some countries could undermine a gradually improving economic situation and progress with structural reforms.

The fragility of the recovery underscores the need to implement reforms to make the region more resilient to economic shocks—in short, to "crisis-proof" Latin America's economies. The agenda involves a range of measures, a central one—as suggested in Chapter III—being to bring down public debt to levels more robust to adverse shocks (Figure 1.13), but also including strengthening banking systems and central bank autonomy to pursue low inflation; trade, labor market, regulatory, and judicial reforms; and institutional reforms to improve social equity and governance. It is clear that for some countries, such as Brazil, financial markets are anticipating continued progress on such reforms in the period ahead (see below). The benefits from ambitious reforms are evident—Mexico and Chile's experience in weathering the fallout from

Figure 1.13. Selected Western Hemisphere Countries: Economic Activity, Financial Indicators, and Public Debt

A fragile recovery is under way following the sharpest downturn in two decades. A key policy challenge is to improve the resilience of Latin America's economies to shocks, including by reducing public debt.

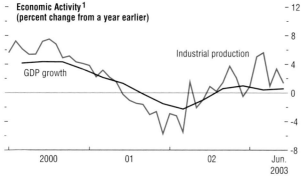

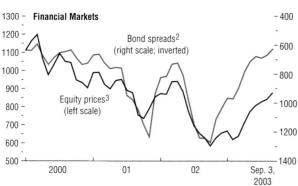

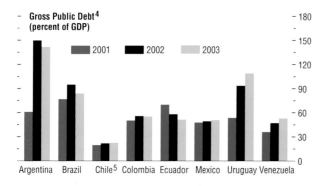

Sources: Bloomberg Financial Markets, LP; Haver Analytics; and IMF staff estimates.
[1]Argentina, Brazil, Chile, Colombia, Mexico, Peru, and Venezuela. Purchasing-power-parity weighted.
[2]EMBI+ in basis points.
[3]MSCI index in U.S. dollars.
[4]Total external and domestic debt. Data for 2003 are IMF staff projections.
[5]General government and public enterprises.

the crisis in Argentina owes much to their efforts to establish more resilient fiscal, monetary, and banking institutions. Equally, however, markets are likely to penalize inaction with higher spreads or lack of access to new funding—thus further delaying the transition to stable growth and magnifying the costs of the downturn.

Turning to individual countries, economic activity (including industrial production and construction) is recovering from a very low base in Argentina; monthly inflation remains low; and the trade balance has posted large surpluses, initially due to import compression, but subsequently reflecting strong growth in exports (Table 1.6). Restrictions on time deposits (the corralón) were successfully removed in April without triggering much impact on bank deposits. Indeed, market indicators have been broadly stable, with the peso appreciating substantially since end-2002, short-term interest rates easing somewhat, and gross international reserves rising. While macroeconomic policies—including a better-than-expected primary fiscal surplus in the first quarter—have been supportive of financial stability, the emerging recovery remains vulnerable to several factors, including unsustainable public finances, lack of progress in dealing with weak banks, a high level of corporate arrears, continuing legal uncertainties, and widespread poverty. The new government needs to press ahead with implementing a credible plan to restore public finances and restructure sovereign debt; strengthen the banking system; advance the restructuring of private corporate debt; and ensure that the poor remain adequately protected during the ensuing transition. In Uruguay, the successful debt exchange has helped to reduce near-term financing needs and improve the debt profile; key challenges remain in the fiscal and banking areas, including the need for firm spending control to meet the government's primary fiscal surplus targets, and faster operational restructuring and asset disposals to reduce remaining fragilities in the banking system.

In Brazil, progress on the policy front has helped strengthen confidence, as seen in the

Table 1.6. Selected Western Hemisphere Countries: Real GDP, Consumer Prices, and Current Account Balance

(Annual percent change unless otherwise noted)

	Real GDP				Consumer Prices[1]				Current Account Balance[2]			
	2001	2002	2003	2004	2001	2002	2003	2004	2001	2002	2003	2004
Western Hemisphere	0.7	−0.1	1.1	3.6	6.4	8.7	10.9	7.0	−2.7	−0.9	−0.8	−1.1
Mercosur[3]	—	−1.1	2.2	3.2	4.9	11.6	14.8	6.7	−3.5	0.4	0.5	−0.2
Argentina	−4.4	−10.9	5.5	4.0	−1.1	25.9	14.3	7.7	−1.7	10.3	5.4	4.5
Brazil	1.4	1.5	1.5	3.0	6.8	8.4	15.0	6.2	−4.6	−1.7	−0.8	−1.5
Chile	3.1	2.1	3.3	4.5	3.6	2.5	3.4	3.0	−1.7	−0.8	−1.0	−1.2
Uruguay	−3.4	−10.8	−1.0	4.5	4.4	14.0	21.6	18.9	−2.8	1.6	1.8	1.3
Andean region	2.0	−0.6	−2.9	4.9	10.6	10.1	13.3	13.7	0.4	1.6	1.3	1.4
Colombia	1.4	1.5	2.0	3.3	7.8	6.3	6.9	5.3	−1.5	−2.2	−2.4	−2.4
Ecuador	5.1	3.4	3.1	5.0	37.7	12.6	8.2	4.4	−2.4	−4.2	−3.8	−2.4
Peru	0.6	5.3	4.0	4.0	2.0	0.2	2.5	2.5	−2.2	−2.1	−2.0	−1.5
Venezuela	2.8	−8.9	−16.7	7.7	12.5	22.4	34.0	40.8	3.1	8.2	9.2	8.2
Mexico, Central America, and Caribbean	0.3	1.1	1.4	3.2	6.6	5.1	5.9	4.5	−3.1	−2.6	−2.5	−2.7
Dominican Republic	3.2	4.1	−3.0	0.5	8.9	5.2	26.1	20.1	−3.4	−4.0	1.0	1.0
Guatemala	2.3	2.2	2.4	3.5	8.9	6.3	5.0	4.0	−5.9	−5.1	−5.5	−4.4
Mexico	−0.2	0.7	1.5	3.5	6.4	5.0	4.6	3.4	−2.9	−2.2	−2.2	−2.7

[1]In accordance with standard practice in the *World Economic Outlook*, movements in consumer prices are indicated as annual averages rather than as December/December changes during the year, as is the practice in some countries.
[2]Percent of GDP.
[3]Includes Argentina, Brazil, Paraguay, and Uruguay, together with Bolivia and Chile (associate members of Mercosur).

real's further appreciation, sharp narrowing of spreads, and the sovereign's early return to the capital markets (with the *real*'s strength facilitating a reduction of the share of exchange rate–linked debt). Nevertheless, growth remains weak—with GDP declining in the second quarter on a seasonally adjusted basis and domestic demand yet to rebound—and the country remains vulnerable to shifting sentiment in the event of policy slippages, given its large external borrowing requirement; the slowing of foreign direct investment inflows; and the fact that spreads are still high in absolute terms. Fiscal discipline remains essential to underpin confidence—especially adherence to the 4¼ percent of GDP primary budget surplus target this year and in the medium term. The recent shift toward monetary policy easing has been appropriate, given the impact of weak activity and the *real*'s appreciation on future inflation. Beyond this, recent progress toward tax and pension reforms needs to be maintained.

In Venezuela, despite the recovery of oil production following the end of the strike in

February, real GDP is expected to decline by 17 percent this year, bringing the cumulative decline to 26 percent over the past two years. Restoration of macroeconomic stability will depend on addressing fiscal and banking vulnerabilities—especially through public sector reform to bring down the non-oil fiscal deficit and implementation of a strategy to deal with the impact on banks' asset quality of the recession in the non-oil sector. Monetary policy tightening is needed to curb pressures on the exchange rate and inflation. A relaxation of foreign exchange controls and structural measures to bolster the non-oil sector remain crucial to securing the reestablishment of investor confidence, economic recovery, job creation, and poverty reduction.

Elsewhere in the Andean region, the outlook depends on making progress in addressing key vulnerabilities. In Colombia, implementation of the authorities' program to ease the public debt burden (including the target of a 2½ percent of GDP fiscal deficit this year) and advance pension and health reforms will be essential to achieving faster growth and low inflation; addressing the nonperforming loan problem in the mortgage banks is another key priority. In Peru, the uncertain political situation underscores the need to maintain an adequate reserve position, keep the flexibility of the exchange regime, preserve the credibility of monetary policy, and follow through on reforms—including tax reform and granting legal protection for bank supervisors— to address the vulnerabilities stemming from the high level of public debt and the high degree of financial dollarization. Containing fiscal and banking vulnerabilities are also key challenges in Ecuador, where political fragmentation is undermining the implementation of reforms, and wage and price trends are inconsistent with the constraints of full dollarization. In Bolivia, while financial conditions have stabilized even as political tensions remain high, there is a need to press ahead with reducing the public sector deficit (while allowing for some increase in poverty-reducing spending), and to implement measures to address bank and corporate sector weaknesses.

Mexico and Chile have both been largely immune from the difficulties affecting many Latin American countries over the past two years, with access to international capital markets on favorable terms having been broadly maintained, downward exchange rate pressures having eased, and Mexico having successfully issued bonds with collective action clauses (CACs) earlier this year. For Mexico, recovery is expected to gather pace in the second half of this year, in line with a pickup in U.S. growth and the pass-through of the recent easing of monetary conditions. A window of opportunity to pursue structural reforms following the July lower house elections should be used (especially to improve labor market flexibility, the bank resolution framework, and private participation in the electricity sector), while further efforts to build consensus on a medium-term fiscal framework are needed to sustain fiscal consolidation. In Chile, earlier cuts in the policy interest rate are helping domestic demand to recover. Monetary policy should continue to focus on

the inflation target, with the exchange rate floating freely except in exceptional circumstances. The fiscal target is broadly adequate and appropriately allows room for the automatic stabilizers to operate. While vulnerabilities remain contained owing to the soundness of the banking system and low public debt, the large external financing needs of the private sector are a potential source of risk going forward, although the majority of corporates' external debt corresponds to companies with foreign parents, which recently have tended to support subsidiaries in difficulty. Moreover, the liquid assets of the private sector cover a significant portion of their short-term external liabilities, with a strong reserve position at the central bank as a healthy backup.

Asia-Pacific Region: Greater Exchange Rate Flexibility Needed for More Balanced Growth

Despite the slowdown since early 2003, the Asia-Pacific countries are again set to be the world's fastest growing region this year and growth is expected to pick up further in 2004 (Table 1.7). A notable feature of recent performance has been the support to output growth provided by net exports, even excluding the crisis period when substantial real depreciations led to very large contributions from external demand (Figure 1.14). While domestic demand is clearly playing a greater role in the region than in the period immediately following the crisis, the global cycle remains a key determinant of cyclical developments in the region, as discussed in the April 2003 *World Economic Outlook*. In the present conjuncture, however, with the U.S. dollar's decline necessitating a rebalancing of global demand, the need to boost the domestic component of growth in Asia is even more pressing. While accelerating structural reforms should be the centerpiece of a strategy to achieve this goal, greater exchange rate flexibility in some countries would also help. The further buildup of foreign exchange reserves in 2002–03 (see the second essay in Chapter II, "Are Foreign

Table 1.7. Selected Asian Economies: Real GDP, Consumer Prices, and Current Account Balance
(Annual percent change unless otherwise noted)

	Real GDP				Consumer Prices[1]				Current Account Balance[2]			
	2001	2002	2003	2004	2001	2002	2003	2004	2001	2002	2003	2004
Emerging Asia[3]	**5.1**	**6.2**	**5.9**	**6.2**	**2.6**	**1.8**	**2.3**	**2.7**	**2.8**	**3.8**	**3.2**	**2.9**
Newly industrialized												
Asian economies	**0.8**	**4.8**	**2.3**	**4.2**	**1.9**	**1.0**	**1.5**	**1.7**	**5.7**	**6.8**	**7.2**	**7.3**
Hong Kong SAR	0.5	2.3	1.5	2.8	−1.6	−3.0	−2.6	−1.9	7.5	10.8	13.9	14.3
Korea	3.1	6.3	2.5	4.7	4.1	2.8	3.3	3.0	1.9	1.3	1.6	1.8
Singapore	−2.4	2.2	0.5	4.2	1.0	−0.4	0.6	1.2	19.0	21.5	23.7	23.0
Taiwan Province of China	−2.2	3.5	2.7	3.8	—	−0.2	0.1	0.8	6.4	9.1	8.5	8.8
ASEAN-4	**2.9**	**4.3**	**4.1**	**4.4**	**6.6**	**5.9**	**3.9**	**3.3**	**5.2**	**5.6**	**4.4**	**3.6**
Indonesia	3.4	3.7	3.5	4.0	11.5	11.9	6.6	5.4	4.9	4.3	2.7	1.9
Malaysia	0.3	4.1	4.2	5.3	1.4	1.8	1.7	2.2	8.3	7.6	8.2	7.1
Philippines	4.5	4.4	4.0	4.0	6.1	3.1	3.0	3.4	1.8	5.4	2.6	1.9
Thailand	1.9	5.3	5.0	5.1	1.5	0.6	1.4	0.1	5.4	6.0	5.3	4.8
South Asia[4]	**4.0**	**4.6**	**5.5**	**5.8**	**3.8**	**4.2**	**4.0**	**4.7**	**−0.2**	**1.2**	**0.8**	**0.3**
Bangladesh	4.8	4.9	5.4	5.8	1.5	3.8	4.5	4.1	−0.8	0.5	0.5	0.3
India	4.2	4.7	5.6	5.9	3.8	4.3	4.0	4.8	−0.2	1.0	0.6	0.3
Pakistan	2.7	4.4	5.4	5.1	3.1	2.9	3.6	4.0	0.4	4.1	3.3	1.0
Formerly centrally												
planned economies[5]	**7.4**	**7.9**	**7.4**	**7.5**	**0.7**	**−0.6**	**0.9**	**1.6**	**1.5**	**2.7**	**1.3**	**1.1**
China	7.5	8.0	7.5	7.5	0.7	−0.8	0.8	1.5	1.5	2.8	1.4	1.3
Vietnam	5.0	5.8	6.0	7.0	−0.4	4.0	4.0	3.5	2.2	−1.1	−3.6	−3.2

[1]In accordance with standard practice in the *World Economic Outlook*, movements in consumer prices are indicated as annual averages rather than as December/December changes during the year, as is the practice in some countries.
[2]Percent of GDP.
[3]Includes developing Asia, newly industrialized Asian economies, and Mongolia.
[4]Includes Bangladesh, India, Maldives, Nepal, Pakistan, and Sri Lanka.
[5]Includes Cambodia, China, Lao People's Dem. Rep., Mongolia, and Vietnam.

Exchange Reserves in Asia Too High?") and the depreciation of effective exchange rates in a number of countries with implicit or explicit links to the U.S. dollar are at least suggestive that incentives for domestically sourced growth may still be blunted in some cases. From a policy standpoint, moreover, further exchange rate flexibility would confer a number of benefits—including reducing risks of future crises, making domestic growth less dependent on the vagaries of the global cycle, lowering holding costs of official reserves, and raising consumption opportunities for local residents in cases where exchange rates may be undervalued—while also helping to resolve global imbalances.

Against this background, the regional slowdown evident since early 2003—which is mostly due to weaker domestic demand—is a concern. Domestic demand slowed markedly, initially reflecting war-related uncertainties and surging

oil prices, and subsequently the impact of SARS. The fall in household credit growth in Korea, due to a tightening of prudential regulations, slower housing price rises, and rising credit card delinquencies, was another factor. Notwithstanding the rapid expansion of intraregional trade, export growth slowed in the early months of the year in several countries—including Korea and the Philippines—reflecting mainly weakness in the electronics sector, although exports are expected to rebound strongly next year given the projected pickup in the United States. While activity surged in China in the first quarter (with GDP growth of 10 percent year-on-year), led by exports and strong investment, growth slowed in the second quarter, mainly reflecting the impact of SARS.

The epidemic's impact has been most visible in tourist arrivals and retail sales, especially in Hong Kong SAR and Singapore (despite the

Figure 1.14. Asia: Composition of Growth, Exchange Rate Volatility, and Reserves

Although domestic demand is playing a larger role than in the immediate aftermath of the crisis, net exports continue to provide a key support for growth in much of the region. Sizable current account surpluses and capital inflows have not resulted in notable real effective exchange rate appreciations, including in the face of the U.S. dollar's weakening since last February, but have been reflected instead in a record buildup of official reserves.

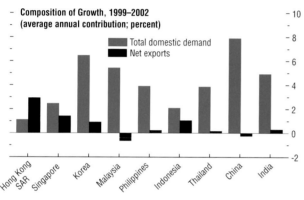

Composition of Growth, 1999–2002
(average annual contribution; percent)

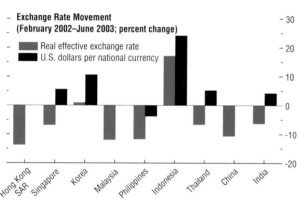

Exchange Rate Movement
(February 2002–June 2003; percent change)

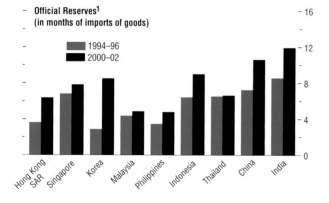

Official Reserves[1]
(in months of imports of goods)

Sources: CEIC Data Company Limited; and IMF staff calculations.
[1]End of period. Average 1995–96 for Indonesia.

larger number of cases in China), but there could be lagged effects on output owing to delayed investment and further effects if the epidemic recurs in the winter. While SARS now appears to have been broadly contained, softness in the IT sector (despite the resolution of war-related uncertainties) remains another key risk, particularly given the recent slowing of electronics exports and weakness of forward-looking indicators, including the book-to-bill ratio. Finally, a reversal of favorable borrowing conditions for emerging markets could create difficulties for countries with very high public debt (e.g., the Philippines), particularly if policies take insufficient account of the risk of a reversal of historically low spreads.

For the most part, the policy response to weaker growth has been appropriate. With inflation contained, monetary policy has been eased in a number of countries, though the continued buildup of official reserves suggests that reforms to increase exchange rate flexibility remained largely on hold. Fiscal stimulus has also been provided in a number of countries to offset the impact of SARS on hard-hit sectors. The scope for easing fiscal policies, however, is much more constrained in countries with chronically high public debt levels, such as India and the Philippines, or significant banking weaknesses. Beyond macroeconomic policies, the key issues remain to resolve nonperforming loan problems (China, Indonesia, the Philippines, Thailand); strengthen insolvency laws to facilitate loan workouts and corporate restructuring (India, Korea, the Philippines, Thailand); implement further corporate governance reforms, including strengthening accounting and auditing practices (Korea); and return banks to private ownership to ensure market-based intermediation practices (Indonesia, Korea).

Turning to individual countries, among the newly industrialized economies, domestic demand remains lackluster in Korea, which may call for further fiscal stimulus, even if the result is a small deficit (excluding the social security balance) this year. Persistent deflation and high unemployment in Hong Kong SAR underscore the need for reforms to bolster competitiveness, while fiscal consolidation over the medium term is needed to underpin confidence in the exchange rate link. Among the ASEAN-4, economic activity in Malaysia and Thailand appears well sustained, partly reflecting supportive macroeconomic policies. In the Philippines, while market pressures have abated, strong efforts are needed to achieve the balanced-budget target even by 2009, and secure a more rapid disposal of banks' NPLs. In Indonesia, growth continues to be fueled by private consumption, with investment remaining sluggish. Sustaining progress on structural reforms (including measures to strengthen the investment climate) remains critical to consolidate the recovery.

In China, the expectation remains that SARS will constitute a temporary shock, with no lasting impact on the medium-term growth outlook, and activity is likely to rebound from the third quarter, helped by continued strong investment and rapid credit expansion, including for consumer lending. The strength of the external position, the desirability of gearing monetary policy more toward domestic stabilization objectives, and the need to facilitate adjustment to structural changes over the medium term underscore the importance of moving gradually to greater exchange rate flexibility. Fiscal consolidation remains a key objective for the medium term, given the sizable contingent liabilities associated with banking weaknesses, pension reform costs, and the need to improve the social safety net and health care. Banking reform, faster asset disposals by asset management companies, and restructuring and privatization of state-owned enterprises remain key structural reform priorities.

In India, while growth is expected to pick up later this year on the back of a recovery in the agricultural sector following last year's drought, the expansion remains well below the 8 percent rate targeted by the authorities, undermining official goals for reducing poverty and regional disparities. A key issue remains the slow pace of fiscal and structural reform. With the general

government deficit set to reach about 10 percent of GDP for a fifth year, and debt plus recorded contingent liabilities nearing 100 percent of GDP, fiscal policy is clearly on an unsustainable path. The absence of consolidation efforts in this year's budget and delays in introducing the value-added tax (VAT) are thus of deep concern. A new fiscal responsibility law was recently approved by India's parliament, providing a framework for the central government to formulate a clear and time-bound plan to achieve a balanced current budget by the target date of 2008. Beyond this, the limited degree of exchange rate flexibility, in the face of continued strong foreign exchange inflows, has contributed to a record buildup of foreign exchange reserves, complicating the implementation of monetary policy. Accelerating structural reforms—including ending regulatory impediments to consolidation in labor-intensive industries; labor market and bankruptcy reforms; and agricultural and trade liberalization—remain essential to stimulate potential growth and reduce poverty. Elsewhere on the subcontinent, while growth has picked up in Pakistan, bold measures are needed to reduce public debt—including by improving tax compliance and reducing subsidies to public enterprises and consumers, while creating room for human development expenditure to address a huge social gap. Although economic recovery is under way in Bangladesh thanks in part to a strengthening of macroeconomic policies, structural reforms—including, on the fiscal side, a sustained revenue effort and a shift in spending toward infrastructure and human capital, reform of the nationalized commercial banks and state-owned enterprises, and trade reform—are critical to raise potential growth and reduce poverty in line with the Millennium Development Goals.

In Australia and New Zealand, the pace of economic growth is expected to slow in 2003, reflecting a number of factors, including the sizable appreciations of the Australian and New Zealand dollars over the past two years, declining commodity prices, and the lingering impact of drought. In Australia, while monetary policy

Table 1.8. European Union Candidates: Real GDP, Consumer Prices, and Current Account Balance
(Annual percent change unless otherwise noted)

	Real GDP				Consumer Prices[1]				Current Account Balance[2]			
	2001	2002	2003	2004	2001	2002	2003	2004	2001	2002	2003	2004
EU candidates	—	**4.3**	**3.9**	**4.3**	**21.1**	**15.8**	**10.1**	**7.3**	**−2.8**	**−3.4**	**−4.1**	**−3.6**
Turkey	−7.5	7.8	5.3	5.0	54.4	45.0	26.0	13.4	2.3	−0.9	−3.2	−1.9
Excluding Turkey	3.1	2.9	3.3	4.1	9.8	5.7	4.1	4.8	−4.5	−4.3	−4.5	−4.4
Baltics	**6.6**	**6.3**	**5.5**	**5.9**	**2.7**	**1.5**	**1.3**	**2.5**	**−6.6**	**−7.6**	**−7.5**	**−6.8**
Estonia	5.0	5.8	5.0	5.1	5.8	3.6	1.7	2.0	−6.1	−12.4	−12.6	−9.2
Latvia	7.9	6.1	5.5	6.0	2.5	1.9	3.0	3.0	−9.6	−7.8	−7.3	−6.8
Lithuania	6.5	6.7	5.8	6.2	1.3	0.3	—	2.5	−4.8	−5.3	−5.7	−5.9
Central Europe	**2.2**	**2.2**	**2.7**	**3.6**	**6.3**	**2.8**	**2.3**	**3.6**	**−4.2**	**−4.2**	**−4.2**	**−4.2**
Czech Republic	3.1	2.0	1.7	2.6	4.8	1.8	0.6	3.5	−5.7	−6.5	−5.7	−5.1
Hungary	3.8	3.3	3.0	3.5	9.2	5.3	4.7	5.5	−3.4	−4.0	−5.7	−5.4
Poland	1.0	1.4	2.9	4.1	5.5	1.9	0.8	2.2	−3.9	−3.5	−3.3	−3.8
Slovak Republic	3.3	4.4	4.0	4.0	7.3	3.3	8.5	8.1	−8.6	−8.2	−6.3	−5.0
Slovenia	2.9	3.2	2.2	3.0	8.4	7.5	5.9	5.0	0.2	1.7	0.9	0.4
Southern and south- eastern Europe	**5.1**	**4.6**	**4.6**	**5.0**	**25.1**	**16.9**	**11.2**	**9.5**	**−5.4**	**−4.0**	**−4.7**	**−4.7**
Bulgaria	4.1	4.8	5.0	5.5	7.5	5.8	2.6	4.2	−6.2	−4.4	−4.6	−4.4
Cyprus	4.1	2.2	2.0	3.8	2.0	2.8	3.6	3.5	−4.3	−5.6	−4.9	−4.7
Malta	−1.2	1.2	2.8	3.8	2.9	2.2	2.0	2.0	−4.5	−3.9	−3.4	−3.4
Romania	5.7	4.9	4.7	5.0	34.5	22.5	15.1	12.0	−5.5	−3.4	−4.8	−4.8

[1]In accordance with standard practice in the *World Economic Outlook*, movements in consumer prices are indicated as annual averages rather than as December/December changes during the year as is the practice in some countries.
[2]Percent of GDP.

has been on hold since the initial withdrawal of stimulus in mid-2002 (not least out of concern that further interest rate cuts could fuel further house price increases), in New Zealand the Reserve Bank cut the overnight cash rate by 25 basis points on three occasions (April, June, and July 2003), citing the impact of slowing economic activity and the sharp appreciation of the currency for the inflation outlook. The short-term outlook for Australia is subject to considerable risks, including a resumption in the appreciation of the Australian dollar, uncertainties about the recovery from the drought, and a rapid cooling off in the housing market following the boom of the past three years. Fiscal policy remains sound in both countries, with public debt continuing to be paid down consistent with principles set out in each country's fiscal responsibility legislation. On the structural side, the priorities include welfare reform to improve work incentives in both Australia and New Zealand and steps to improve labor market flexibility (including liberalizing employment protection) in Australia.

European Union Candidates: Coping with Weakness in the Euro Area

In European Union (EU) accession countries, growth is picking up and the short-term outlook is generally favorable (Table 1.8). Recently, growth in most countries has been supported by both exports and private consumption. GDP is expected to accelerate in 2004, driven by exports, which—along with strengthening corporate profits—are also projected to stimulate investment spending. While exports have thus far been strong, growth prospects in EU accession countries are heavily dependent on the pace of recovery in the euro area, as merchandise exports to the euro area account for 10–35 percent of GDP in most countries (Figure 1.15). Another threat to growth is the appreciation of the euro since February 2002, which has led to some real effective appreciation in those countries whose currencies are closely tied to the euro. Countries with greater shares of exports to the euro area and larger real effective appreciations have seen more highly negative contributions of net exports to growth in 2002–03.

While structural reforms and EU accession will underpin growth over the medium term, there nevertheless are a number of risks around a broadly favorable baseline, even abstracting from the possibility of weaker-than-projected external demand. Fiscal positions are already difficult in many countries and will be exacerbated by population aging and spending pressures from complying with EU environmental standards and absorbing EU development funds (which require domestic fiscal cofinancing). Banking systems appear mostly sound, but private credit has recently grown rapidly and EU entry will likely stiffen bank competition and put pressure on margins. External current account deficits are generally large and, in some countries, are already in unwelcome territory. Finally, there is the risk of sudden capital outflows, as some of the recent inflows appear to have been driven largely by short-term considerations, including convergence trades (that is, the expectation that interest rates will converge to levels prevailing in the euro area as euro adoption nears).

In light of these risks, it is essential to make early and substantial progress on fiscal consolidation, to enhance monitoring of banking systems, and to aggressively pursue growth-enhancing structural reforms. The still-favorable economic environment in the accession countries is conducive to undertaking such reforms. With EU membership slated for mid-2004 in most countries, EU candidates' *goal* of adopting the euro could be an important disciplining force for delivering policies that promote macroeconomic stability, though the *process* of adopting the euro should not be rushed.

Turning to individual countries, growth in Poland is expected to accelerate this year and next, driven by a pickup in investment (as corporate profits rise) and exports (as the recovery in western Europe gains momentum). The large output gap is expected to keep core inflation pressures subdued, possibly allowing a further reduction in interest rates under the inflation targeting framework for monetary policy. However, there are important risks to the out-

Figure 1.15. Selected European Union Accession Countries: Impact of Euro Area and Euro Appreciation

Growth prospects in EU accession countries are heavily dependent on the pace of recovery in the euro area and changes in the value of the euro. Exports to the euro area account for an increasing share of GDP and exchange rates in some countries are closely tied to the euro, with implications for the contribution of net exports to growth.

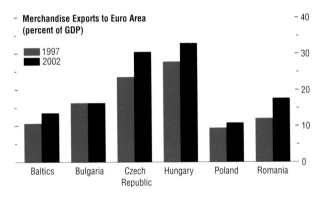

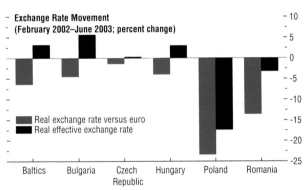

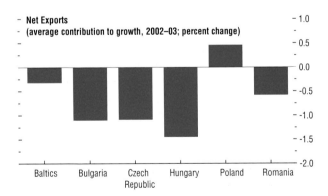

Sources: Haver Analytics; and IMF staff estimates.

look, including the dependence on growth in western Europe, the large fiscal deficit, and the deterioration in credit quality. To improve prospects for durable growth and reduce vulnerabilities, timely implementation of fiscal reform that would significantly reduce the structural budget deficit in the medium term is also essential. Rejuvenating the privatization process is needed to promote enterprise restructuring and reduce fiscal subsidies. Finally, keeping a close watch on bank health is critical.

In Hungary, the devaluation of the forint through July and increases in interest rates underline the dilemma faced by monetary policy, which by itself cannot aim simultaneously to lower inflation and support external competitiveness. As rapid wage growth has fueled inflationary pressures and weakened external competitiveness, wage moderation—especially in the public sector—is essential, including keeping wage increases below the inflation target and encouraging closer cooperation between the social partners. Sizable and early fiscal consolidation is also critical, including restraining spending by securing parliamentary approval for expenditure ceilings in core areas. While the financial system is generally healthy, risks need to be monitored carefully, including rapid credit growth and the adequacy of hedging against foreign exchange risk.

In the Czech Republic, growth is being supported by a widening of the general government deficit, but this fiscal stimulus is unsustainable. The government's recent decision to reduce the deficit to 4 percent of GDP by 2006 is welcome; it will be important to place the largest burden of the adjustment on expenditure restraint, as taxation levels are already high compared with neighboring countries. Given the recent boom in household credit, tighter supervision of banks' internal risk management systems would be desirable. Continued structural reforms, especially strengthening the legal framework and reducing labor market frictions, are essential to a durable improvement in growth. In Slovakia, the large current account and general government deficits underline the importance of per-

manent reductions in fiscal expenditure, supplemented by pension reform. The forthcoming tax reform is expected to improve the transparency and simplicity of the tax code, though the authorities should be ready to address potential fiscal slippages.

In the Baltic countries, the favorable outlook for growth and inflation reflects the solid track record of policies geared toward macroeconomic stability and structural reform. While inflows of foreign direct investment have remained strong, large current account deficits are a concern. As monetary policy is largely constrained by fixed exchange rates, fiscal policy needs to focus on durably reducing nonpriority expenditure to make room for spending needs associated with EU accession, and moving cautiously with respect to tax cuts—either ensuring the revenue-neutrality of reforms (by curtailing tax exemptions and strengthening tax administration) or implementing corresponding expenditure reductions. While banking systems remain healthy, the rapid growth of credit—especially the increase in the ratio of foreign currency loans to foreign currency deposits—underlines the importance of careful credit risk assessments by banks and effective banking supervision.

In Bulgaria and Romania, robust domestic demand is expected to underpin growth, but current account deficits are projected to widen in 2003. In Bulgaria, domestic demand is being fueled by the strong growth of private sector credit, which calls for vigilance from the authorities, including better monitoring of corporate borrowers' foreign currency exposure and hedging. The rapid growth in credit and the widening of the current account deficit point to the need for a continued tight fiscal stance in the remainder of 2003 and 2004. Improvements in tax administration and compliance, as well as implementation of structural reforms in the health, railway, and energy sectors, are essential to achieving a balanced general government budget by 2005. In Romania, domestic demand and inflation are being boosted by rapid wage and credit growth. Further efforts are needed to keep credit expansion under control, to restrain public sector wages, and—more broadly—to harden budget constraints, especially in the energy sector, complemented by the downsizing or liquidation of loss-making state-owned enterprises.

Elsewhere in southeastern Europe, the economic outlook has also continued to improve, though political tensions persist in most countries. Albania, Bosnia and Herzegovina, Croatia, the former Yugoslav Republic of Macedonia, and Serbia and Montenegro have made important strides toward restoring economic growth and reducing inflation, but large current account deficits constitute an important vulnerability. The widening of external deficits in recent months reflected both a dampening of export demand due to the slowdown in western Europe and—in some countries—a surge in imports related to rapid credit growth. To rein in credit growth, monetary conditions have been tightened and prudential supervision of banking systems has been strengthened, but continued careful monitoring is needed. Further progress in fiscal consolidation and structural reform is also essential to stimulate investment and growth and to ensure sustainable external positions.

In Turkey, financial conditions and the short-term economic outlook have improved. Benchmark bond rates have fallen, the currency has appreciated, and the spread on Eurobonds has narrowed. Moreover, with strong output recovery and continued disinflation so far this year, 5 percent output growth and 20 percent inflation in 2003 are within reach. Although the end of the Iraq war has contributed, these results are also partly due to strong actions by the Turkish authorities on reforms related to their candidacy for the European Union and, in the economic sphere, on policies that enabled the completion of the fifth review of the IMF-supported program in early August. Nonetheless, real interest rates remain high, reflecting underlying fragilities and concerns about policy implementation. To address these concerns, the Turkish authorities need to build a strong track record of timely policy implementation and full program ownership. Key in this regard would be the maintenance of

fiscal discipline to safeguard the 6½ percent of GNP primary surplus target.

Commonwealth of Independent States: Structural Reforms Key to Sustaining the Growth Upswing

The Commonwealth of Independent States (CIS) countries have continued to weather the growth slowdown in advanced countries and the ensuing uneven recovery considerably better than expected. Over 1999–2002, GDP growth has averaged about 7½ percent, aided initially by Russia's rebound from the 1998 financial crisis, rising oil prices and energy exports, and—linked to this rise—higher government expenditure and energy sector investment. During 2002, GDP growth was additionally boosted by strong private consumption growth, underpinned by substantial wage and pension increases—particularly but not only in Russia and Ukraine—and strong credit growth as remonetization continued apace, and, in the latter part of the year, by rapid export growth in most countries. In contrast, however, investment activity outside the energy sector has remained subdued, partly reflecting the squeeze on profits coming from wage increases, but more fundamentally the continued inhospitable environment for private investment.

Current indicators suggest that economic activity in early 2003 has remained robust, and GDP growth in the region is projected at 5.8 percent for the year as a whole, 1.4 percentage points higher than expected at the time of the last *World Economic Outlook* (Table 1.9). This is largely due to continued strong growth in the net energy exporters, notably Russia (where growth has been sharply revised upward, reflecting the stronger-than-expected momentum arising from strong real wage growth, favorable liquidity conditions in domestic financial markets, and increased access to international capital markets). With a few exceptions—notably the Kyrgyz Republic, where growth is expected to rebound following a disastrous landslide in 2002—GDP growth elsewhere is expected to

Table 1.9. Commonwealth of Independent States: Real GDP, Consumer Prices, and Current Account Balance

(Annual percent change unless otherwise noted)

	Real GDP				Consumer Prices[1]				Current Account Balance[2]			
	2001	2002	2003	2004	2001	2002	2003	2004	2001	2002	2003	2004
Commonwealth of Independent States	**6.4**	**4.9**	**5.8**	**5.0**	**20.4**	**14.5**	**13.1**	**11.7**	**7.9**	**7.0**	**6.5**	**3.8**
Russia	5.0	4.3	6.0	5.0	20.6	16.0	14.4	12.9	10.8	8.9	8.4	5.2
Excluding Russia	9.2	6.0	5.4	5.0	19.9	11.6	10.4	9.4	−0.7	1.0	—	−1.1
More advanced reformers	**9.9**	**6.6**	**6.6**	**5.9**	**9.9**	**2.9**	**5.6**	**5.1**	**−0.2**	**1.6**	**0.1**	**−1.2**
Armenia	9.6	12.9	7.0	6.0	3.1	1.1	2.2	3.0	−9.5	−7.5	−6.5	−6.3
Azerbaijan	9.9	10.6	9.2	9.1	1.5	2.8	2.7	2.5	−0.9	−12.4	−30.5	−32.6
Georgia	4.7	5.3	4.8	4.5	4.7	5.6	4.4	5.0	−5.6	−6.2	−11.5	−10.9
Kazakhstan	13.5	9.5	9.0	8.0	8.3	5.9	6.4	5.9	−4.0	−1.9	1.3	—
Kyrgyz Republic	5.4	−0.5	5.6	4.0	6.9	2.0	3.3	3.8	−3.3	−3.9	−3.0	−3.7
Moldova	6.1	7.2	6.0	5.0	9.8	5.3	8.1	4.5	−6.1	−6.9	−6.0	−5.4
Tajikistan	10.2	9.1	6.0	4.0	38.6	12.2	14.5	5.0	−7.1	−2.8	−5.0	−4.8
Ukraine	9.2	4.8	5.3	4.8	12.0	0.8	5.5	5.3	3.7	7.7	5.6	4.0
Less advanced reformers[3]	**4.4**	**4.1**	**2.4**	**2.9**	**55.7**	**40.9**	**25.9**	**22.6**	**−2.3**	**−0.5**	**−0.2**	**−1.1**
Belarus	4.7	4.7	4.0	3.2	61.1	42.6	29.0	24.1	−3.6	−2.5	−2.8	−3.4
Uzbekistan	4.1	3.2	0.3	2.5	48.9	38.7	21.9	20.7	−1.0	2.5	4.6	3.1
Memorandum												
Net energy exporters[4]	6.2	4.9	6.2	5.2	19.1	14.8	13.4	12.1	9.4	7.7	7.3	4.3
Net energy importers[5]	7.1	4.8	4.4	4.1	24.9	13.7	12.0	10.7	0.3	3.2	2.1	1.0
CIS-7[6]	6.1	5.7	4.1	4.6	22.5	16.9	11.2	10.2	−2.9	−4.3	−9.4	−10.2

[1]In accordance with standard practice in the *World Economic Outlook*, movements in consumer prices are indicated as annual averages rather than as December/December changes during the year as is the practice in some countries.
[2]Percent of GDP.
[3]Updated data for Turkmenistan not available.
[4]Includes Azerbaijan, Kazakhstan, Russia, and Turkmenistan.
[5]Includes Armenia, Belarus, Georgia, Kyrgyz Republic, Moldova, Tajikistan, Ukraine, and Uzbekistan.
[6]Includes Armenia, Azerbaijan, Georgia, Kyrgyz Republic, Moldova, Tajikistan, and Uzbekistan.

moderate slightly, mainly reflecting a weakening of consumption growth from earlier elevated rates. GDP growth is expected to ease further in 2004, as the oil market–related boost to output in 2003 is reversed and as the deceleration in consumption growth to more sustainable rates continues. Looking forward, while the region should benefit from the expected upturn in global activity, a number of risks remain, notably with respect to the prospects for the oil market (although these are asymmetric across the region, with the poorest countries gaining substantially from lower oil prices); excessive wage increases in a number of countries; and the continued weakness of non-energy-sector investment.

The external current account surplus of the region is expected to weaken over 2003–04, reflecting continued robust demand growth, the recent fall in oil prices, and increased import demand related to foreign direct investment (Azerbaijan, Georgia, and Kazakhstan). Within this, Russia is expected to remain in continued, if declining, surplus. With net capital inflows having strengthened in a number of countries, reserves have risen substantially in some cases, especially in Russia and Kazakhstan. In contrast, net energy importers—with the exception of Ukraine, which has benefited from strong exports and higher transfers—are projected to register rising and in some cases sizable deficits: this is of particular concern in a number of the poor and highly indebted CIS-7 countries (Armenia, Azerbaijan, Georgia, Kyrgyz Republic, Moldova, Tajikistan, and Uzbekistan). While these countries need to maintain appropriately tight fiscal policies, a number also require additional international assistance to ensure progress toward sustainable external debt positions.

Inflation rates across the region have continued to decline, but remain relatively high compared with other developing countries. Within this, however, the situation varies markedly across the region. Among most of the advanced reformers, inflation is well into single digits. In Russia, however, the pace of disinflation has lagged, largely reflecting the continued dilemma between controlling inflation and seeking to limit appreciation of the ruble in the face of large balance of payments inflows and productivity growth, especially in the tradables sector. A more flexible exchange rate policy would allow the inevitable real appreciation to take place while the central bank could appropriately focus on targeting inflation; establishment of the proposed oil stabilization fund (as in Azerbaijan and Kazakhstan) could be helpful in reducing oil price–related real exchange rate volatility. Inflation in the less advanced reformers, while declining, remains very high, particularly in Belarus and Uzbekistan, underscoring the need to strengthen monetary discipline by reining in credit to inefficient public enterprises. In most of the CIS countries, the process of remonetization continues to pose important challenges. With the pace of remonetization difficult to predict, policymakers face unusual difficulty in judging underlying money demand and—because remonetization is inevitably accompanied by rapid credit growth—in managing banking system risks, underscoring the need for further improvements in prudential regulation and supervision.

Looking forward, with the recent boost from higher oil prices and rising real wages unlikely to be sustained, regional growth prospects depend critically on an acceleration of structural reforms. Over the past year, overall progress in most countries has slowed markedly (except in Armenia and Azerbaijan). While the CIS countries lag the EU accession countries in most structural reform areas, the gap appears to be increasing in areas affecting private sector development—enterprise, infrastructure, and financial sector reforms—which is of particular concern given the weakness in non-energy-sector investment (Figure 1.16). While the priorities

Figure 1.16. Real GDP, Investment, and Structural Reforms in the CIS Countries[1]
(Unweighted averages)

The robust growth performance during 1999–2002 helped the CIS countries in overcoming the adverse output dynamics of the early transition years, but lags in structural reform achievements remain a matter of concern.

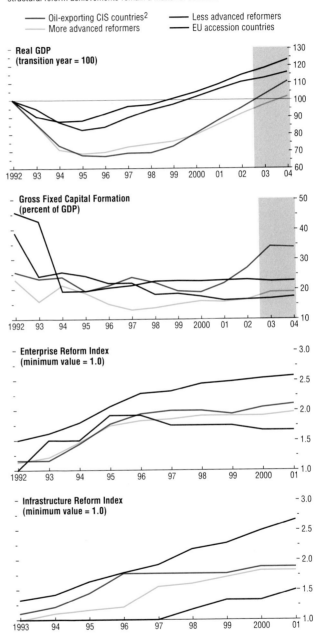

Sources: European Bank for Reconstruction and Development, *Transition Reports;* and IMF staff calculations.

[1]The data is shown in transition time, which for the CIS countries corresponds to the years indicated in the figure. For the other countries' initial year (beginning of transition), see Fischer and Sahay (2000).

[2]Includes Azerbaijan, Kazakhstan, and Russia.

Table 1.10. Selected Middle Eastern Countries: Real GDP, Consumer Prices, and Current Account Balance
(Annual percent change unless otherwise noted)

	Real GDP				Consumer Prices[1]				Current Account Balance[2]			
	2001	2002	2003	2004	2001	2002	2003	2004	2001	2002	2003	2004
Middle East[3]	**4.8**	**3.9**	**5.1**	**4.5**	**8.0**	**8.4**	**10.1**	**10.1**	**6.5**	**4.9**	**7.0**	**3.9**
Oil exporters[4]	**5.0**	**4.5**	**6.0**	**5.0**	**10.1**	**10.4**	**12.6**	**12.2**	**8.9**	**6.5**	**9.0**	**5.2**
Saudi Arabia	1.3	1.0	4.7	2.1	−0.8	−0.6	1.1	1.0	5.1	6.2	10.1	5.4
Iran, Islamic Rep. of	5.9	6.7	6.1	5.7	11.4	15.8	18.0	17.0	5.3	3.0	1.1	−1.2
Kuwait	−1.1	−0.9	4.7	2.2	1.7	1.4	2.0	2.0	26.1	20.9	23.8	18.4
Mashreq[5]	**4.0**	**2.3**	**2.5**	**3.1**	**1.8**	**2.2**	**2.9**	**3.7**	**−1.6**	**−0.5**	**−1.3**	**−1.7**
Egypt	3.5	2.0	2.8	3.0	2.4	2.5	3.2	4.2	—	0.6	1.3	0.9
Jordan	4.2	4.9	3.0	5.5	1.8	1.8	2.5	1.8	−0.1	4.9	4.6	0.2
Memorandum												
Israel	−0.9	−1.0	0.7	2.1	1.1	5.7	1.1	0.2	−1.6	−1.2	−0.7	−0.8

[1]In accordance with standard practice in the *World Economic Outlook*, movements in consumer prices are indicated as annual averages rather than as December/December changes during the year, as is the practice in some countries.
[2]Percent of GDP.
[3]Includes Bahrain, Egypt, Islamic Rep. of Iran, Iraq, Jordan, Kuwait, Lebanon, Libya, Oman, Qatar, Saudi Arabia, Syrian Arab Republic, United Arab Emirates, and Republic of Yemen.
[4]Includes Bahrain, Islamic Rep. of Iran, Iraq, Kuwait, Libya, Oman, Qatar, Saudi Arabia, and United Arab Emirates.
[5]Includes Egypt, Jordan, Lebanon, and Syrian Arab Republic.

vary across countries, in Russia there is a need to reinvigorate reforms to strengthen the banking system, introduce competition in the electricity and transportation sectors, and streamline the civil service and public administration; and in Ukraine, to improve the investment climate, including through tax reform, and to address the financial problems of state-owned enterprises in the energy sector. In the poorer CIS countries, structural reforms need to focus on improving governance and the investment climate. In addition, in the poorer, landlocked CIS-countries (Armenia, Kyrgyz Republic, Tajikistan, and Uzbekistan), lagging infrastructure reforms and intra-CIS trade barriers, some of which are related to transit trade and its (informal) taxation or the distribution of energy from net exporters to net importers, are serious impediments to growth that need to be addressed urgently. Advancing infrastructure development will be challenging, however, given the external financing constraints faced by these countries, and will require improved tax policy and administration and enhanced public expenditure management.

Middle East: Fiscal Reforms Key to Stability and Higher Growth

GDP growth in the Middle East is projected to rise to 5.1 percent in 2003, 1.2 percentage points higher than in 2002 (Table 1.10). The bulk of this increase is due to stronger growth in oil-exporting countries, reflecting primarily higher OPEC oil quotas and oil production before the war (particularly in Saudi Arabia and other countries of the Gulf Cooperation Council[7]), higher average oil prices, and—notably in Iran—the continuing positive impact of recent economic reforms. The early end to major hostilities in Iraq is also a positive factor, although the fragile security situation continues to weigh on activity across the region. In contrast, GDP growth in the Mashreq is expected to pick up more moderately, in part reflecting the relatively close economic links of a number of

[7]Members of the Cooperation Council of the Arab States of the Gulf (GCC) are Bahrain, Kuwait, Oman, Qatar, Saudi Arabia, and the United Arab Emirates.

countries with Iraq (Jordan, Syria) and the adverse effects of the regional security situation on tourism (Egypt, Jordan).

Turning to 2004, GDP growth in the region is expected to fall back somewhat, although once again there are significant differences between oil and non-oil countries. GDP growth in the Mashreq countries is expected to rise modestly further, aided by the upturn in the global economy and reduced geopolitical uncertainties; however, GDP growth in oil producers is expected to decrease owing to falling oil prices and production. But while GDP growth in the region is expected to remain high by historical standards—and the rebuilding of Iraq should be a positive factor (see Box 1.4, "Rebuilding Post-Conflict Iraq")—a number of risks remain. In particular, beyond the fragile security situation, the outlook for the oil market remains subject to considerable uncertainty, and many oil market analysts see downside risks to prices over the medium term (Appendix 1.1), which would clearly have significant implications for oil producers in the region. More generally, public debt burdens across the region are high, particularly in the Mashreq but also in some oil exporters (where such concerns would be exacerbated by further falls in oil prices, especially given relatively high levels of public expenditure (Figure 1.17)). Many countries in the region have taken important steps—for example, apart from those discussed below, Saudi Arabia targets a balanced budget in 2003, which involves expenditure reductions of more than 4 percent of GDP despite higher oil revenue, while in Jordan, a package of revenue measures yielding about 2 percent of GDP—including increased petroleum product prices—was implemented to secure the authorities' lower deficit target for 2003. However, as discussed in Chapter III, these efforts will need to be sustained and, in some cases, strengthened over the medium term.

Looking forward, the key policy issue for Middle Eastern countries is accelerating medium-term growth to reduce generally high unemployment rates and absorb the rapidly

Figure 1.17. Oil Price Cycles and Fiscal Policy in the Middle East

Adjusting government expenditure in response to oil price fluctuation has been key to reducing fiscal deficits in the oil-exporting countries of the Middle East.

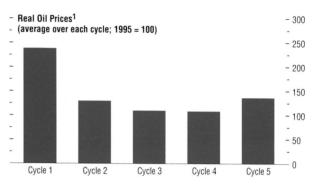

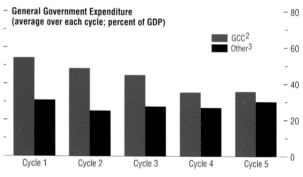

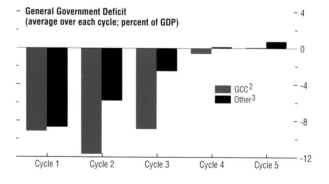

Source: IMF staff calculations.
[1]Drawing on business cycle analysis and methodology used in Chaper III of the April 2002 *World Economic Outlook*, the oil price cycles are identified on the basis of peaks and troughs in real oil prices. Cycle periods: [1]:1981–87, [2]:1988–90, [3]:1991–96, [4]:1997–2000, and [5]:2001–03.
[2]Cooperation Council of the Arab States of the Gulf: Bahrain, Kuwait, Oman, Qatar, Saudi Arabia, and United Arab Emirates.
[3]Islamic Republic of Iran and Libya.

Box 1.4. Rebuilding Post-Conflict Iraq

The role of the IMF in post-conflict situations is primarily to help the countries achieve macroeconomic stability as soon as possible and prepare the ground for long-term sustainable growth. As part of this task, the IMF—in coordination with the World Bank, UN agencies, and other multilateral and bilateral entities—has provided extensive policy advice and technical assistance to improve institutional capacity and policy coordination, as well as its own financial assistance.[1] In terms of policy advice, as a first step the IMF has helped authorities in post-conflict cases develop a macroeconomic framework geared toward quickly restoring macroeconomic stability, with the World Bank playing a supporting role by providing an assessment of sectoral reconstruction and rehabilitation needs. As regards technical assistance, the areas supported by the IMF have included central banking, banking supervision, payments system, public expenditure management, tax policy, compilation of macroeconomic statistics, and external debt monitoring. In the area of policy coordination, the IMF has played a lead role in coordinating policy advice with all institutions involved, while providing support in the preparation and organization of consultative group (CG) and donors' meetings.

In carrying out this work in post-conflict situations, some critical lessons have been learned. Of utmost importance is that institutional and administrative capacity must be restored or enhanced at an early stage; that a macroeconomic framework—underpinned by a simple but realistic policy stance—must be quickly put in place to restore macroeconomic stability and set the ground for a quick resumption of

growth; and that a careful and realistic assessment of external aid flows must be made. The IMF is making use of these lessons on its work in Iraq.

Although Iraq was one of the founding members of the IMF, the IMF has had little official contact with the government of Iraq since the early 1980s. Since that time, Iraq's economy has suffered from the effects of three wars, political repression, intrusive state ownership and control, and international sanctions—all of which has made it difficult to conduct an assessment of the country's economic situation. In addition, there are very few recent economic statistics on Iraq and those that exist cannot be easily interpreted. There is an incomplete recording of transactions, and the use of artificial and highly distorted prices and exchange rates in constructing economic accounts reduces the usefulness of these data.

A UN Security Council Resolution (1483) that lifted all sanctions previously imposed on Iraq (except those relating to arms sales) has facilitated the reintegration of Iraq into the international community. The resolution defines interim institutional arrangements in the country. Among its key provisions, the resolution creates a new structure that governs the treatment of Iraq's assets, revenues, and expenditures until "such time as an internationally recognized, representative government of Iraq is properly constituted." In that context, a Development Fund for Iraq has been established to receive oil export proceeds (net of war reparations) and specified Iraqi assets—including transfers of unused balances from the UN Oil-for-Food Program, which is to be phased out by November 2003. Resources in the Development Fund for Iraq are to be disbursed in a transparent manner at the direction of the Coalition Provisional Authority, in consultation with the Iraqi interim authority. The Development Fund for Iraq—as well as exports of hydrocarbon products—will be audited by independent public accountants to be approved by an International Advisory and Monitoring Board—which is to consist of representatives of the UN

Note: The main author of this box is Carlos Piñerúa.

[1]The IMF's Executive Board has approved post-conflict financial assistance since 1995 to Albania, Bosnia and Herzegovina, Burundi, Republic of Congo, Rwanda, Guinea-Bissau, Sierra Leone, Tajikistan, and the Federal Republic of Yugoslavia. The IMF has also been involved in the economic rebuilding of Afghanistan, Kosovo, and East Timor.

Secretary General, the Managing Director of the IMF, the President of the World Bank, and the Director-General of the Arab Fund for Economic and Social Development.

An IMF staff mission visited Baghdad in June to conduct an initial assessment of the economic and financial situation, and to explore early priorities for advice and technical assistance in the IMF's core areas of responsibility to quickly improve the institutional capacity for policymaking in the country. The IMF has already begun to provide technical assistance in the areas of introduction of a new currency; central bank legislation, commercial bank licensing, and payments system; budget execution and public expenditure management; and the compilation and dissemination of economic statistics. As regards macroeconomic policy, IMF staff is assisting in the development of a macroeconomic framework—including a fiscal budget for 2004 and a monetary and exchange rate policy regime—to ensure that macroeconomic stability is quickly restored and growth resumes as soon as possible. In terms of external assistance, the staff is supporting the work of the Core Group of donors that is organizing a meeting to take place in the second half of October to channel assistance for the rehabilitation and reconstruction of Iraq. Moreover, the staff is helping in the effort to obtain information about the external debt of Iraq as a first step in developing a debt restructuring strategy.

growing labor force. With macroeconomic imbalances outside Lebanon generally moderate—although inflation in Iran remains somewhat high, underscoring the need to slow liquidity growth—the central issues are structural and institutional in nature. As discussed in detail in the second essay in Chapter II ("Why Has Economic Growth in the Middle East and North African Region Lagged Behind?"), the priorities vary across countries, but include reform of the state leading to a reduction in the role of government, strengthening of institutions and governance more generally, further trade liberalization, and diversification away from oil production. Recent progress in structural reforms in the region has been uneven; key achievements include the partial divestment of government equity shares (Iran, Jordan, Oman, and Saudi Arabia); reductions in nontariff barriers (Iran); liberalization of key sectors to foreign direct investment (Iran, Kuwait, Oman, and Qatar); institutional reforms aiming at increasing efficiency in public services delivery (Bahrain, Jordan, and Saudi Arabia); improved tax administration and policies (Egypt, Iran, Jordan, and Lebanon); and financial sector reform (Saudi Arabia and United Arab Emirates). In the GCC countries, the ambitious goal of establishing a monetary union by 2010 will require far-reaching reforms to reduce divergences in key macroeconomic variables, including fiscal positions, and differences in institutions, legal systems, and regulatory practices in the financial sector to prepare the grounds for a common monetary policy framework (see Box 1.5, "Gulf Cooperation Council: Challenges on the Road to a Monetary Union"). In Egypt, the economic outlook has improved following the end of the war in Iraq, and there are signs that tourism—while still depressed—is beginning to pick up. However, confidence and economic growth remain relatively weak, in part owing to continuing foreign exchange shortages in the official market, despite a step-depreciation following the floating of the currency in January and despite resort to administrative measures to boost liquidity. To facilitate market clearing, the pound should be allowed to adjust as needed. On the fiscal side, a multiyear program to ensure long-run sustainability is a priority; in this connection, measures will be required to strengthen the recently adopted budget for 2003/04. In Lebanon, the authorities' strategy of strong fiscal adjustment, large-scale privatization,

Box 1.5. Gulf Cooperation Council: Challenges on the Road to a Monetary Union

Since its inception in the early 1980s, members of the Cooperation Council of the Arab States of the Gulf (GCC)—Bahrain, Kuwait, Oman, Qatar, Saudi Arabia, and the United Arab Emirates—have built on their cultural, political, demographic, and economic ties and commonalities, and have taken significant steps toward economic integration. Barriers to the free movement of national goods, labor, and capital across the GCC countries have been eliminated, and individuals and corporations in the region have been granted national treatment for tax purposes in each country. The customs union was launched on January 1, 2003, and the common external tariff was introduced. The GCC common market is targeted to come into effect in 2007 under a well-defined timetable for intermediate steps.

Effective January 2003, the GCC authorities initiated steps toward the establishment of a monetary union by 2010 and formally pegged their currencies to the U.S. dollar. With appropriate supporting macroeconomic policies, the monetary union will reinforce the beneficial effects of measures already taken to enhance integration and structural reforms presently under way. Although there is limited intraregional trade, the GCC countries face common shocks emanating from oil price volatility, and the planned monetary union should strengthen their ability to address these shocks by promoting policy coordination. It is also likely to reduce transaction costs and increase price transparency, thus resulting in a more stable environment for business and facilitating investment decisions in an expanded market. Moreover, regional growth prospects are likely to benefit from the unification and development of the region's bond and equity markets and improvement in the efficiency of financial services. However, given the similar resource endowment and limited complementarity among the GCC countries, the trade creation

effects could be relatively small. Finally, the cost of monetary union for member countries—in terms of the loss of monetary policy independence and exchange rate flexibility—is likely to be low, because they have not relied on these tools for quite some time under their pegged exchange rate regimes and, given their heavy dependence on oil, external shocks induced comparable effects across GCC countries.

Notwithstanding past progress toward integration, differences in economic performance and policy preferences will necessitate critical decisions for an effective monetary union. Although inflation has traditionally been low in the GCC area, it differs across countries, leading to diverging paths for CPI-based real effective exchange rates. Real growth disparities have also emerged, particularly in non-hydrocarbon sectors. Fiscal positions have not been convergent—reflecting differences in oil dependency and levels of expenditure, with some GCC countries recording fiscal deficits. In the process, government debt has increased considerably in a few of these countries. Moreover, although there are practically no restrictions to capital movements in GCC countries, the financial sectors retain important differences, with capital and securities markets in some member countries still at a rudimentary stage. Differences also exist with respect to institutions, legal systems, and regulatory practices. The authorities are presently working on addressing these differences toward designing the monetary union, while efforts continue to diversify GCC economies, exports, and fiscal revenue away from oil. Initiatives have been taken to select quantitative convergence criteria, coordinate policies in key areas, and design the institutions to support the monetary union.

Three key areas will need to be addressed in the period ahead.
- *Gearing economic policies toward eventual monetary union.* This will require maintaining prudent fiscal policies across member countries to promote fiscal convergence. Under a centralized monetary policy, fiscal discipline including a reduction in public debt will be

Note: The main authors of this box are Zubair Iqbal and Ugo Fasano.

crucial to guard against large differences in members' fiscal stances, which could create tensions, leading to political disagreement and hindering other key macroeconomic convergence requirements. Moreover—given the GCC countries' heavy dependence on volatile oil export receipts and the varying degrees of oil reserves, depletion rates, and government financial wealth—the choice of fiscal convergence criteria and the underlying fiscal rules would be a challenge. In the context of a medium-term fiscal framework, consideration could be given to establishing convergence in terms of non-oil primary balance as a ratio to non-oil GDP along with a well-defined path for the reduction in public debt to an agreed norm. In light of changing trade patterns and economic structures, the current decision to peg the common currency to the U.S. dollar—a policy that has served individual GCC member countries well in the past—could be reconsidered in the future. Alternative options could include pegging to a basket of currencies and possibly a more flexible exchange arrangement. Of course, each option carries its own policy implications and operational requirements. Consideration will also have to be given to the choice of the rates at which to irrevocably fix the bilateral rates.

- *Establishing rules and institutions that will support a monetary union.* Prime among these are laying the basis for establishing key monetary institutions, including a common central bank—charged with making monetary policy decisions; overseeing payments systems; and coordinating efforts toward financial integration—and a single set of monetary policy instruments. These will need to be supported by a common regulatory, legal, and institutional framework. Equally challenging will be the strengthened budgetary procedures and a common fiscal accounting framework that would promote convergence while respecting GCC members' individual characteristics.

- *Strengthening data quality and establishing common data standards to facilitate gauging the convergence process.* A common data framework in all GCC countries will likely prove invaluable in determining union-wide economic policies. A successful monetary union will also require a strong political commitment and the ability to adjust domestic economic policies to deal with the effects of a single currency. In particular, notwithstanding a broadly common resource endowment, different GCC countries may experience differing growth and inflation effects of common exogenous shocks. Experience of other monetary unions has shown that a single monetary policy may not always be optimal for all members of the union. As a result, structural policies that would promote flexibility in labor and product markets will assume greater importance in the planned monetary union.

mobilization of external concessional assistance, and burden sharing with the banking system will, if fully implemented, bring the public debt ratio down significantly from its present level of close to 180 percent of GDP. The initial implementation of the strategy boosted confidence and financial indicators have improved in 2003. Nonetheless, the very high stock remains a large vulnerability.

In Israel, following the deepest recession in its history, GDP growth is expected to turn slightly positive in 2003. Domestic demand remains subdued amid fragile confidence and a difficult security situation, and a modest turnaround in exports—aided by the sharp depreciation in the shekel in 2002, as well as falling real wages—has proved difficult to sustain in the face of a weak global recovery. Given the difficult medium-term fiscal situation, the new government appropriately implemented additional budgetary measures in June to offset weaker-than-expected tax revenues. With inflation projected to fall below 1 percent in 2004, aided by the appreciation of the shekel since late 2002, there appears to be

Figure 1.18. Downturns in Advanced Countries, and Reforms and Growth in Sub-Saharan Africa[1]
(Unweighted averages)

The resilient GDP growth in sub-Saharan Africa during 2000–02 reflected favorable commodity price developments but also improved macroeconomic policies.

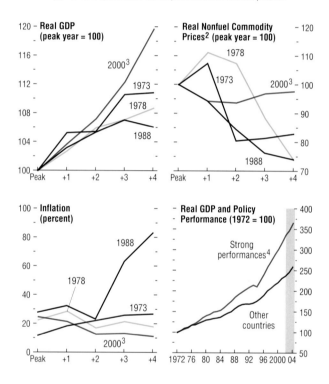

Source: IMF staff calculations.
[1]Peak years identified by local maxima in annual GDP growth of advanced countries at times of major slowdowns in GDP growth.
[2]Nonfuel commodity prices normalized by advanced countries' GDP deflator.
[3]Includes forecasts for 2003–04.
[4]Strong performers are countries with generally strong macroeconomic and structural policies; comprises Benin, Botswana, Burkina Faso, Cameroon, Mali, Mauritius, Mozambique, Rwanda, Senegal, Seychelles, Tanzania, and Uganda.

scope for further monetary easing to support recovery. Economic activity in the West Bank and Gaza remains very depressed, although indications are that the economy stabilized in late 2002. No significant amelioration is likely without a lasting improvement in the security situation accompanied by substantial external support for infrastructure reconstruction.

Africa: Growth Has Been Resilient But Still Far Too Low

Over the past three years, GDP growth in African countries has remained surprisingly resilient in the face of the slowdown in the advanced economies and the ensuing uneven recovery (Figure 1.18). This partly reflected more favorable developments in nonfuel commodity prices, which did not contract as much as in earlier global slowdowns, as well as debt relief under the HIPC initiative. However, external conditions were not the only factor, with the trend toward improved macroeconomic policies in many African countries also playing an important role. In particular, with some exceptions—notably Zimbabwe, Angola, and, to a lesser extent, Nigeria—inflation is now relatively low and government budget deficits are under control. That said, external current account deficits in many countries in sub-Saharan Africa remain relatively high, reflecting in part continued high debt levels but also low savings rates related to low per capita incomes and structural impediments to economic diversification.

In 2003, African GDP growth is projected to edge up slightly, with the expansionary effects of global recovery and increasing nonfuel commodity prices continuing to be offset by adverse local factors—especially weather conditions, political instability, and conflicts—and geopolitical uncertainties (Table 1.11). Within this, GDP growth is expected to pick up in the Maghreb (reflecting favorable weather conditions, expansionary fiscal policy (Algeria), and economic reforms (Morocco and Tunisia)), in west and central Africa (led by Nigeria, where oil production is forecast to rise), and in southern Africa

Table 1.11. Selected African Countries: Real GDP, Consumer Prices, and Current Account Balance
(Annual percent change unless otherwise noted)

	Real GDP				Consumer Prices[1]				Current Account Balance[2]			
	2001	2002	2003	2004	2001	2002	2003	2004	2001	2002	2003	2004
Africa	3.7	3.1	3.7	4.8	12.9	9.3	10.6	7.7	−0.5	−1.3	−0.7	−1.4
Maghreb	4.3	3.3	5.7	4.1	2.6	2.1	2.2	2.8	7.2	4.1	5.8	3.2
Algeria	2.6	4.1	5.9	3.8	4.2	1.4	2.3	3.5	12.9	7.7	12.2	7.5
Morocco	6.3	3.2	5.5	3.4	0.6	2.8	2.0	2.0	4.8	3.0	1.6	1.2
Tunisia	4.9	1.7	5.5	5.8	1.9	2.8	2.5	2.5	−4.3	−3.5	−3.1	−3.2
Sub-Sahara[3]	3.8	3.1	3.6	5.9	21.4	12.7	15.7	11.2	−4.7	−4.7	−4.2	−4.4
Horn of Africa	6.1	3.8	2.6	6.4	1.8	3.6	10.3	6.2	−11.0	−8.2	−7.6	−7.6
Ethiopia	7.7	1.2	−3.8	6.7	−7.1	−7.2	14.6	5.5	−4.2	−6.0	−6.1	−8.3
Sudan	5.3	5.0	5.8	6.5	4.9	8.3	7.0	5.0	−16.9	−11.0	−10.2	−9.4
Great Lakes	2.4	4.2	3.9	5.2	54.4	7.5	8.4	5.2	−5.0	−2.5	−4.7	−6.7
Congo, Dem. Rep. of	−2.1	3.0	5.0	6.0	357.9	27.7	9.1	6.0	−4.7	−2.9	−3.2	−7.0
Kenya	1.2	1.0	1.3	2.6	4.9	2.0	12.4	3.9	−3.5	0.5	−3.1	−6.9
Tanzania	6.1	6.3	5.5	6.3	5.2	4.6	5.3	5.0	−5.0	−2.7	−7.3	−6.5
Uganda	5.5	6.6	5.4	6.0	4.5	−2.0	5.9	5.9	−7.6	−6.4	−5.7	−5.8
Southern Africa	2.8	2.0	2.6	6.4	35.2	38.8	48.8	35.9	−6.5	−3.8	−4.8	−3.9
Angola	3.2	15.3	4.4	11.4	152.6	108.9	95.2	30.1	−15.1	−5.8	−4.3	−3.2
Zimbabwe	−8.8	−12.8	−11.0	5.1	76.7	140.0	420.0	380.0	−3.8	−2.3	−3.2	−9.6
West and Central Africa	4.0	2.8	4.1	5.7	11.6	8.0	8.5	5.8	−2.3	−5.2	−2.9	−3.1
Ghana	4.2	4.5	4.7	5.0	32.9	14.8	26.4	8.6	−5.3	0.6	−1.4	−1.6
Nigeria	2.8	0.5	5.2	2.8	18.0	13.7	12.3	10.6	2.7	−7.0	−1.0	−2.3
CFA Franc Zone	4.9	3.9	3.2	7.9	4.1	3.6	2.8	2.6	−6.1	−4.0	−3.6	−3.0
Cameroon[4]	5.3	6.5	4.0	4.4	2.8	6.3	2.5	2.1	−1.7	−7.2	−5.5	−5.8
Côte d'Ivoire	0.3	−1.8	−3.0	3.0	4.4	3.1	3.5	2.9	−0.7	9.3	7.7	5.3
South Africa	2.8	3.0	2.2	3.0	5.7	9.1	7.7	4.9	−0.3	0.3	−0.7	−0.9
Memorandum												
Oil importers	3.8	2.9	3.2	4.9	11.9	8.4	10.2	7.6	−2.7	−2.0	−2.6	−2.7
Oil exporters	3.2	3.7	5.5	4.2	16.5	12.5	12.0	8.3	5.3	0.5	4.9	2.5

[1]In accordance with standard practice in the *World Economic Outlook*, movements in consumer prices are indicated as annual averages rather than as December/December changes during the year, as is the practice in some countries.
[2]Percent of GDP.
[3]Excludes South Africa.
[4]The percent changes in 2002 are calculated over a period of 18 months, reflecting a change in the fiscal year cycle (from July–June to January–December).

(led by Botswana where mining output is expected to rise). In contrast, GDP growth is projected to slow elsewhere, notably in the Horn of Africa (where Ethiopia continues to face a disastrous famine); the CFA franc zone (where activity in Côte d'Ivoire is expected to decline for the second consecutive year in the face of continued political instability); the Great Lakes region (where tourism has been affected by terror-related risks); and South Africa (partly reflecting the temporary effects of policy tightening). Looking forward, GDP growth—for both the continent as a whole and most major regions—is projected to pick up significantly in 2004. Such an outturn, however, depends criti-

cally on more favorable weather conditions and a substantial reduction in the incidence of conflict and unrest.

But while growth in Africa has been resilient, it clearly remains far too low. To meet the Millennium Development Goals—most importantly, a halving of poverty between 1990 and 2015—growth in sub-Saharan Africa will need to accelerate substantially to about 7 percent a year, well above the rates enjoyed by even the strongest performers during the past decade (about 5 percent). Africa continues to face a wide range of daunting development challenges—including armed conflicts and political instability that undermine macroeconomic stability and the long-term growth potential; weak judicial and legal systems that do not sufficiently protect property rights and hinder private lending; adverse weather conditions and natural disasters that generate high output volatility, to the detriment of long-term growth potential; poor infrastructure and health conditions that hold back productivity growth, thereby aggravating the adverse effects of low savings and investment; and the HIV/AIDS pandemic and tropical diseases that reduce life expectancy and have affected growth prospects in a number of countries. As stressed in the New Partnership for Africa's Development (NEPAD), a multifaceted strategy is needed to address them, including policies aimed at reducing conflict, protecting human rights, and improving political governance; the promotion of competition, trade, and foreign investment, underpinned by measures to strengthen macroeconomic policy frameworks; and a policy focus on developing the pro-poor sectors of health care, education, infrastructure, and agriculture. As discussed above, it is essential that domestic reforms be accompanied by additional external assistance, including higher aid flows, debt relief, and—perhaps most importantly—removal of industrial country restrictions on developing country exports.

In implementing this strategy, two points are worth emphasizing. First, as stressed in the NEPAD—and discussed in detail in the April 2003 *World Economic Outlook*—sustained efforts to strengthen weak institutions, which in many African countries remain a major drag on growth, are critical. In a number of countries, significant progress is being made, for instance through strengthening the regulatory and institutional framework governing private investment (Ghana, Mali, Mauritius, Mozambique, Tanzania, and Uganda); improving governance related to revenues from natural resources (Botswana, Cameroon, and Tanzania); and fiscal capacity building (Burkina Faso, Mali, and Tanzania). However, much remains to be done; with institu-

tions generally deeply rooted in a country's history and culture, domestic ownership is critical to ensure that reforms are tailored to meet specific regional conditions and circumstances.

Second, the experience of the strongest performers in Africa confirms that sound policies do pay off (Figure 1.18). Among the many dimensions of sound policies, three appear particularly important.[8] First, trade openness fosters development and technology transfer, and more open economies have typically outperformed more closed economies;[9] trade openness also fosters competition, which in turn tends to reduce benefits derived from rent seeking and vested interests. Second, appropriately flexible exchange rates and prices are critical for economies that are subject to large commodity price shocks, including most sub-Saharan African economies, which, on average, face larger commodity price volatility in their exports than any other developing country region. Finally, if—as is hoped—the international community follows through with its commitment at Monterrey to sharply increase aid flows, efforts will need to focus on securing the administrative and institutional preconditions for these resources to be used efficiently, and to manage carefully the macroeconomic consequences (Box 1.3). In this connection, given African countries' still large debt burdens and their limited capacity to shoulder additional risk, it would appear highly desirable that such assistance be provided in the form of grants rather than loans.

Turning to the continent's largest economies, GDP growth in South Africa has slowed from late 2002, reflecting earlier monetary tightening in response to inflation rates rising above the target range and the weak recovery in industrial countries. With inflationary pressures now easing, aided by a rebound in the rand and declining food prices, interest rates have appropriately been reduced; domestic demand will also be supported by a mild expansionary impulse from the 2003/04 budget. Consequently, the slow-

---

[8]See also Rogoff (2003).

[9]See Chapter III of the September 2002 *World Economic Outlook* and the references therein.

down is expected to be limited and temporary, with GDP growth picking up to 3 percent in 2004. External vulnerabilities have been significantly reduced with the recent closing of the central bank's net open forward position; however, the economy remains vulnerable to global uncertainties, regional developments, and long-term concerns over HIV/AIDS. The key medium-term policy challenge remains to boost long-run growth so as to reduce very high unemployment rates and poverty; this in turn will require a significant improvement in the investment climate, including through labor market reforms and reduced socioeconomic disparities.

In Nigeria, overall growth in 2003 is projected to pick up sharply on account of oil market developments, while economic activity in the non-oil sectors is expected to remain buoyant. Higher oil prices, together with the peaceful change of government in April's election and a more market-oriented exchange rate policy, have stabilized the international reserves position, which had deteriorated sharply during 2002. However, Nigeria remains highly exposed to oil market developments, and political and civil unrest (as evidenced by the continuing problems in the oil industry). With oil prices projected to fall in coming years, and public debt very high (70 percent of GDP), fiscal consolidation is now urgent and should be accompanied by a more rules-based approach to fiscal policy to avoid oil price–related boom-bust cycles and measures to enhance the transparency and efficiency of public spending. Monetary policy—which was eased substantially in late 2002 and 2003—also needs to be tightened if the authorities' aim of single-digit inflation by end-2003 is to be achieved.

In Algeria, despite an earthquake that rocked the country's center in May, growth in 2003 is projected to strengthen further on account of favorable weather conditions and buoyant construction demand related to demographic conditions but also to reconstruction needs. With

earthquake-related increases in expenditures, the fiscal balance in 2003 will weaken further. Given the outlook for oil prices and the deterioration in budget balances since 2001, the fiscal stance needs to be tightened starting in 2004 to keep the public debt on a sustainable path. A key issue remains the high level of unemployment, the reduction of which will require renewed efforts at stepping up privatization and the restructuring of nonfinancial public enterprises, establishing conditions for an effective real estate market, banking reform, and trade liberalization.

Appendix 1.1. Longer-Term Prospects for Oil Prices

The main authors of this appendix are Aasim Husain, Bright Okogu, and Ximena Cheetham. Paul Nicholson and Chakriya Bowman provided research assistance. The appendix draws on discussions with analysts at Deutsche Bank, Goldman Sachs, J.P. Morgan, Energy Market Consultants, Center for Global Energy Studies, Oxford Institute for Energy Studies, BP, and Shell, as well as officials at the International Energy Agency and the Organization of the Petroleum Exporting Countries.

Oil prices remain a key factor affecting the global economic outlook, as highlighted by recent sharp movements in oil prices and coinciding changes in the pace of economic activity. The decline in the price of oil over the medium term expected by markets and analysts should support global economic prospects, but major shocks in the oil sector could cause oil prices to depart markedly from their projected longer-term path and have serious effects on the overall outlook.

World oil prices have declined markedly in real terms since the late 1970s as the pace of demand growth has moderated and supply has expanded (Figure 1.19).[10] Energy efficiency has

---

[10]Unless otherwise noted, oil prices refer to the simple average petroleum spot price of West Texas Intermediate, U.K. Brent, and Dubai crudes.

Figure 1.19. Oil Prices and Consumption

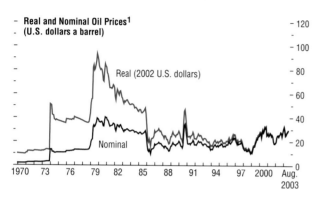

Real and Nominal Oil Prices[1]
(U.S. dollars a barrel)

Real (2002 U.S. dollars)

Nominal

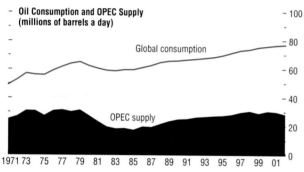

Oil Consumption and OPEC Supply
(millions of barrels a day)

Global consumption

OPEC supply

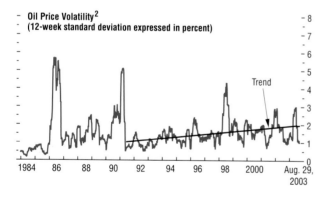

Oil Price Volatility[2]
(12-week standard deviation expressed in percent)

Trend

Sources: International Energy Agency; Bloomberg Financial Markets, LP; and IMF staff estimates.
[1] Average Petroleum Spot Price (APSP).
[2] Based on West Texas Intermediate crude price.

improved steadily, prompted by the oil price shocks of the 1970s, increased taxation, stricter environmental policies, technological advances, and changes in economic structure. As a result, the energy intensity of global output—the amount of energy required to produce a unit of output—has declined at an average rate of about 1 percent a year over the past three decades.[11] The share of oil in world energy consumption has also eased as the use of lower greenhouse gas–emitting fuels (such as natural gas) has increased and, in some countries, policies to promote self-reliance have led to more intensive use of domestically available energy sources, including nuclear power and coal.

World oil consumption growth has averaged about 1.2 percent a year since 1990, less than half the pace of global economic growth. The share of developing countries in world oil consumption has increased, on account of more rapid income growth than in industrial countries and a higher marginal propensity to consume energy products. On the supply side, the increase in oil prices in the 1970s promoted increased investment in exploration and development of production capacity, especially in countries outside the Organization of the Petroleum Exporting Countries (OPEC). Consequently, OPEC's share in world oil production fell from about one-half in the early 1970s to less than one-third in the mid-1980s. Sharply lower oil prices in the mid-1980s lowered oil sector investment, especially in non-OPEC countries, while boosting demand. As a result, non-OPEC production slowed and OPEC, which held significant spare capacity, was able to expand production. Consequently, OPEC's market share recovered to above 40 percent. In recent years, however, OPEC's market share has eased again as oil output in other countries, especially Russia, has increased markedly. Downward pressure on real oil prices over the past three decades has also come from a reduction in oil production costs on account of improved tech-

[11] See IEA (2000), pp. 56–60.

nology, which has expanded recoverable global oil reserves and made these reserves more accessible.

The volatility of crude oil prices has increased over the past decade. Limited spare production capacity—held almost entirely in OPEC countries—and a decline in stocks of crude oil and petroleum products held by private industry, particularly in the United States but also in other OECD countries (Figure 1.20), have contributed to higher oil price volatility as the capacity to respond to temporary shocks with increased output or inventory adjustments has diminished.[12] Changes in OPEC production levels, including temporary disruptions to Iraq's oil production and exports under the oil-for-food program since the late 1990s, have likely contributed to world oil price volatility, as have geopolitical shocks and weather-related shocks to demand. Increased synchronicity of business cycles in the major economies, by widening swings in global oil demand, may also have magnified the amplitude of oil price movements.[13]

Sharp movements in crude oil prices have long been recognized as having a significant effect on the global economy (Figure 1.21). The oil price shocks of the 1970s and the subsequent global economic downturns highlighted the world's dependence on oil. More recent oil price spikes—in 1990 and 2000—were also followed by global economic slowdowns. Indeed, the run-up in oil prices in 2002 and early 2003, as well as the increase in oil price volatility, may have contributed to the slower-than-anticipated pace of the global recovery. Quantitative investigations have found an important relationship between oil prices and economic activity. A recent IMF staff paper considered five channels through which changes in the price of oil could

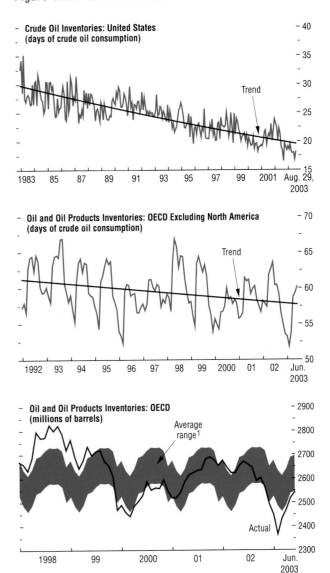

Figure 1.20. Oil Inventories

Crude Oil Inventories: United States
(days of crude oil consumption)

Trend

1983 85 87 89 91 93 95 97 99 2001 Aug. 29, 2003

Oil and Oil Products Inventories: OECD Excluding North America
(days of crude oil consumption)

Trend

1992 93 94 95 96 97 98 99 2000 01 02 Jun. 2003

Oil and Oil Products Inventories: OECD
(millions of barrels)

Average range[1]

Actual

1998 99 2000 01 02 Jun. 2003

Sources: U.S. Department of Energy; American Petroleum Institute; International Energy Agency; and IMF staff estimates.
[1]Average of each calendar month during 1992–2002, plus or minus 75 million barrels.

---

[12]The adoption of efficiency-improving practices such as "just-in-time" stock holdings, technology improvements, and the increased availability of futures and options to hedge oil price risk have allowed some downward trend in commercial stocks without a loss of flexibility.

[13]Chapter II of the October 2001 *World Economic Outlook* documents the increased synchronicity of business cycles.

Figure 1.21. Global Economic Growth and Oil Prices

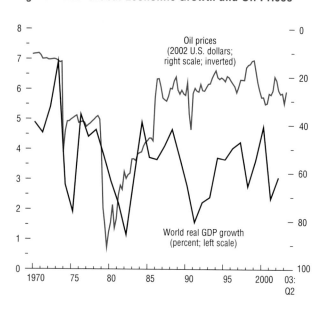

Source: IMF staff estimates.

affect global growth—the transfer of income from oil consumers to producers, changes in the cost of production of goods and services, the impact on overall prices and inflation, the impact on financial markets, and the response of oil supply (through investment) and demand to changes in prices—and found that a sustained $5 a barrel increase in oil prices would lower global economic growth in the following year by 0.3 percent for the world as a whole.[14] Subsequent work has also tried to gauge the effects of confidence and uncertainty in financial markets on economic activity.[15] To the extent that oil price spikes are often associated with sharp declines in confidence and financial asset prices because of common underlying causes, the correlation between oil prices and global growth may well be even higher.

Recent Developments and Near-Term Outlook

The volatility of oil prices has been underscored by their recent sharp rise and subsequent rapid decline. In March 2003, as military action against Iraq became certain, prices fell from over $34 a barrel to $25.5 a barrel in just two weeks. War-related disruptions to oil supply were limited to Iraq, with increases in output by other OPEC members broadly offsetting the loss of Iraqi crude oil exports and a partial loss in Nigerian output in March and April due to civil unrest. The post-strike recovery of Venezuelan production proceeded more quickly than had been anticipated, but questions remain about the extent and sustainability of the recovery. Production in Saudi Arabia also expanded markedly during March to May. A seasonal decline in oil consumption, which followed a surge in demand due to colder-than-expected winter weather in North America, also exerted

[14]IMF (2000). See also Chapter VI of IMF (2003c) for a discussion of the effects of energy price shocks on the U.S. economy.

[15]See Appendix 1.2, "How Will the War in Iraq Affect the Global Economy?" of the April 2003 *World Economic Outlook.*

downward pressure on oil prices. Nevertheless, industry oil inventories, which had in early 2003 fallen to their lowest level in decades, remained low and—together with increased demand by U.S. electricity generation plants and an announcement of a cut in production targets by OPEC[16] as well as setbacks in the recovery of Iraq's oil production—caused oil prices to rise again since May.

The oil price path implied by recent futures contracts suggests that markets expect prices to be sustained near current levels through 2003 before declining to about $25 a barrel by late 2004. The persisting low inventory level, further delays in Iraq's production recovery, and lingering difficulties in Japan's nuclear power sector and the U.S. natural gas sector, which have led to a sizable increase in the use of oil in electricity generation over the past year, could provide support to, and possibly even push up, prices in the near term.[17]

By late next year, however, many analysts believe prices could fall sharply—to levels significantly lower than suggested by current futures prices—once inventories have been replenished and Iraq has returned to near prewar production levels. By late 2004 or early 2005, several large investment projects in deep water facilities in west Africa, Brazil, and the U.S. Gulf of Mexico are also expected to start yielding production, and the completion of the Baku-Tbilisi-Ceyhan pipeline is expected to boost the Caspian region's oil export potential. In such circumstances, barring weather-related or other shocks to oil demand or a resurfacing of political tensions in Nigeria, Venezuela, or elsewhere that could affect supply, there could well be significant downward pressure on oil prices unless OPEC and possibly other major producers lower their production levels.

The divergence between analysts' oil price forecasts for next year and prices implied by current futures contracts may relate to the possibility, albeit remote, of major shocks that could cause oil prices to spike. The futures price—which represents the market's expectation of the probability-weighted average of all potential prices that could prevail at a particular date—does not necessarily correspond to the most likely outcome. For example, if markets were to overwhelmingly expect (with 80 percent probability) prices to decline to $20 a barrel, but at the same time attached some possibility (20 percent) to shocks that would push prices to $40 a barrel in an environment of low oil inventories, the futures price would be about $24 a barrel, markedly higher than the price judged to be most likely.[18] Recent data on options contracts suggest expectations have indeed become somewhat skewed—in late August 2003, markets seemed to be attaching almost a 60 percent probability that spot prices in mid-2004 would be lower than the futures price prevailing at that time (about $26 a barrel), and only a 40 percent chance that spot prices would be higher than the futures price.

Longer-Term Prospects

A high degree of uncertainty surrounds any long-term projection of oil prices. The consensus of forecasts prepared in 1981 envisioned oil prices climbing steadily to over $100 a barrel by the mid-1990s as global oil reserves started to decline and world oil production peaked (Figure 1.22). In the event, such fears have

---

[16]Although the production target was raised in mid-May (effective June 1), the new target represented a cut in actual production from levels in April and May.

[17]Surging U.S. natural gas prices in recent months, and the associated increase in oil consumption, have also contributed to the low U.S. commercial oil inventories position. See Chapter VII of IMF (2003c) for a discussion of energy taxation in the United States.

[18]Calculations using options data by Melick and Thomas (1997) indicate that in mid-January 1991, as military action against Iraq was being launched and markets appeared to perceive some risk of oil supply disruptions, expectations became skewed. Markets seemed to attach about a three-fourths probability to prices declining to below $30 a barrel by April, but also saw about a 15 percent chance that prices would rise above $50 a barrel.

Figure 1.22. Historical Oil Price Forecasts
(2002 U.S. dollars a barrel)

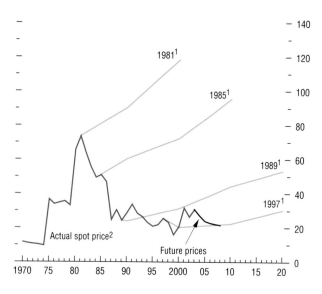

Sources: Bloomberg Financial Markets, LP; Goldman Sachs (2002); and IMF staff estimates.

[1] Average of long-term forecasts prepared by the U.S. Department of Energy and the International Energy Workshop in 1981, 1985, 1989, and 1997, respectively.

[2] West Texas Intermediate petroleum spot price.

proven exaggerated. While shocks have contributed to increased oil price volatility, technological progress, shifts in environmental policies and taxation, and changes in the structure of economies around the world have kept the expected upward trend in oil prices from materializing. Indeed, long-term price forecasts have been revised downward steadily. Even the 1989 consensus forecast, which correctly predicted prices above $30 a barrel in 2000, now appears too high. According to that forecast, oil prices in 2004–05 will average over $35 a barrel, about $12 a barrel above the level implied by current futures contracts maturing in that period.

Current oil futures contracts expiring in 2008 and beyond suggest a further decline in oil prices to about $22 a barrel over the longer term. Notwithstanding the thin trading volumes of futures contracts at distant maturities, the view that oil prices are likely to continue to soften appears to be fairly widespread. Indeed, many market analysts believe that in the absence of serious supply disruptions, longer-term oil prices could well be significantly lower, possibly in the $16–20 range.

Projections for global oil demand growth by various agencies and analysts are in the range of 1–2 percent a year over the long term. Assuming a continued decline in the energy intensity of global output at a pace in line with the trend over the past three decades, and a further moderate decline in the share of oil in primary energy consumption, this range for oil demand growth is broadly consistent with purchasing-power-parity-weighted global real GDP growth of 3–4 percent a year. The bulk of the increase in demand over the longer term will come from developing countries, where the income elasticity of oil demand and the rate of real income growth is expected to be higher than in industrial economies. According to projections prepared by the International Energy Agency (IEA), for example, the share of developing countries in world primary energy demand is expected to rise from 30 percent in 2000 to 34 percent in 2010. Oil consumption in China, in particular, is expected to grow rapidly, and its net oil imports are projected to rise to 9.8 million barrels a day (mbd) by 2030, close to the net imports of the United States in 2000.[19]

While global economic growth will likely remain the principal determinant of oil demand, major technological breakthroughs or changes in energy policies could have striking effects. Steady improvements in energy technology and energy efficiency, including increased use of alternative energy sources such as natural gas, are built into most demand forecasts. However, dramatic technical advances and sharp cost reductions in areas presently under development—such as hydrogen-based energy and fuel cells—could profoundly alter oil consumption patterns. Similarly, marked adjustments in government policies, including changes in energy taxation rates and/or new measures to curb dependence on imported energy products or enhance environmental protection, could also place global oil demand on a significantly different path. Even if the Kyoto Protocol on greenhouse gas emissions does not take effect during the medium term, some countries may well tighten environmental regulations to reduce emissions, possibly through higher energy taxes or a mandated switch to less carbon-intensive fuels.[20]

On the supply side, there is wide consensus among market analysts and energy agencies that global oil reserves are adequate to meet demand over the longer term (Table 1.12). The world reserve replacement rate is presently well above 100 percent, implying that new discoveries and expansion of existing oilfields are more than offsetting current oil consumption. Moreover, technological improvements are expected to further

Table 1.12. Oil Reserves and Production

	Proven Reserves[1] (billions of barrels)	2002 Production (millions of barrels a day)
Conventional oil	**1,048**	**73.1**
Saudi Arabia	262	7.6
Iraq	113	2.0
United Arab Emirates	98	2.0
Kuwait	97	1.9
Iran, Islamic Rep. of	90	3.5
Venezuela	78	2.3
Russia	60	7.7
United States	30	8.1
Libya	30	1.3
Nigeria	24	2.0
China	18	3.4
Qatar	15	0.6
Mexico	13	3.6
Norway	10	3.3
Algeria	9	0.9
Kazakhstan	9	0.9
Brazil	8	1.7
Indonesia	5	1.1
United Kingdom	5	2.5
Others	75	20.2
Undiscovered conventional resources	939	
Canadian oil and Venezuelan heavy bituminous crude oil	580	

Source: BP; International Energy Agency (IEA); and IMF staff estimates.
[1]Oil that has been discovered and is expected to be economically recoverable is called a proven reserve. Oil that is thought to exist and is expected to be economically recoverable is called an undiscovered resource. Data for Saudi Arabia and Kuwait include one-half of Neutral Zone reserves and production.

enhance the accessibility of existing reserves—including deep water oil wells and nonconventional oils such as Canadian oil sands—and bring down production costs further.[21] That said, massive investment, a large portion of which would be in developing countries, will be needed to raise production capacity to meet projected demand.[22]

---

[19]See IEA (2002) pp. 58–69, 89–94, and 237–68.

[20]Okogu (1995) reports that gasoline taxation rates, based on IEA data, in most OECD countries were in the 60–80 percent range in 1993. An important exception was the United States, where the rate of gasoline taxation was about 30 percent.

[21]According to the IEA (2001), total production costs—which include lifting, production, and finding and development costs—for different Canadian oil sands production facilities are in the $5–16 a barrel range. By way of comparison, the IEA (2001) and Goldman Sachs (2002) estimate total production costs at $4–5 a barrel in the Middle East and Russia, and at $10–11 a barrel in Europe and the United States.

[22]Analysts project that cumulative global investment of $1 trillion could be required at various stages of the oil production chain during 2000–30 to meet demand. Of this amount, a substantial portion would need to be invested in developing countries.

Output shares of the major oil-producing regions of the world are expected to change over time, with some of the highest oil-consuming countries increasing their imports of petroleum and petroleum products. Natural decline rates of several mature oilfields in the OECD countries, especially in the North Sea and the United States, have picked up.[23] While higher oil prices and drilling rates in recent years may boost production in the near term, output from these fields is likely to start declining over the longer term. An exception to the projected declining trend among OECD countries may be Canada, where increased investment to exploit oil sands resources could well offset the decline in conventional oil production. According to the IEA's baseline forecast, net oil imports by OECD countries will rise from 23.6 mbd in 2000 to almost 30 mbd in 2010.[24]

Production is likely to rise in several non-OECD countries. Oil production in Russia, which had fallen from over 11 mbd in 1987 (about 18 percent of world output) to 6 mbd in 1996, has recovered to over 8 mbd at present, mainly on account of investment in repairs and maintenance. Such investment could well boost output further, although Russia's oil transport network is beginning to constrain its ability to export oil. Indeed, oil exports are currently at their highest historical levels because domestic consumption, which also fell sharply in the early 1990s, has not rebounded significantly. To further enhance export potential, several major pipeline projects are at various stages of planning and implementation, including a pipeline link to China. These projects, together with prospective investment in large drilling projects, should yield further oil output and export growth over the longer term, although there is considerable variation in views among analysts over the extent and timing of the increase in

Russia's oil production capacity. Outside Russia, other major pipelines and investment projects, such as the Baku-Tbilisi-Ceyhan pipeline, are expected to raise the oil production and export potential of countries in the Caspian region, especially Azerbaijan and Kazakhstan. Recent discoveries of major offshore oil reserves have boosted longer-term production prospects for Brazil and Angola, although successful deployment of advanced deep water technologies will be critical in realizing this output potential. Increases in output are also projected by analysts for other countries in west Africa and for nonconventional oil in Venezuela.

With the bulk of the world's oil reserves and the lowest production costs, OPEC members clearly have the potential to increase production capacity markedly over the long term. The extent of the actual increase, however, will depend on expectations for the "call on OPEC"—the difference between world oil demand and non-OPEC supply—and the availability of investment funds. In view of the high population growth rate and young demographic structure in many OPEC countries, pressures for increased social spending are likely to intensify. This may constrain investment to expand oil production capacity over the longer term, especially since the scope for foreign investment is limited by the prohibition of foreign participation in the upstream oil sector in several countries. There is also considerable uncertainty regarding the call on OPEC over the medium to long term, particularly in view of the wide range of world oil demand forecasts and the uncertainty surrounding the timing and extent of non-OPEC supply expansion. Some analysts believe OPEC will continue to face lower market share over the longer term, while others expect some increase in OPEC output to offset declining production from mature oilfields elsewhere.

[23]OECD countries accounted for about 29 percent of world oil output of 76.6 mbd in 2002. The natural decline rate refers to the rate of decline in production in the absence of new investment in drilling additional wells and enhanced recovery techniques.

[24]See IEA (2002), Tables 3.1 and 3.4. As a share of non-OECD oil output, the IEA projects OECD net oil imports to ease slightly from 44 percent in 2000 to 43 percent in 2010.

Another key uncertainty relates to Iraq. Given its vast oil reserves, an increase in production capacity from 2.5–3 mbd at present to 6 mbd in the long term appears achievable. However, views vary widely over how long this might take and how much investment would be required. Some analysts believe that with a reasonably quick improvement in the security situation, foreign investment could start to flow in and capacity could double in five years. Others note that even with improved security, it will take time to put in place a conducive investment climate, and a marked increase in capacity is unlikely to materialize this decade.

Implications for the Global Economy

The projected decline in oil prices in the near term should help solidify the global economic recovery, and the outlook for further softening of oil prices should support the outlook for the global economy over the longer term. Indeed, there may well be an upside risk to the global outlook if, as many analysts expect, oil prices decline faster than implied by futures prices, on which the global macroeconomic projections are based. At the same time, lower oil prices would weaken growth prospects in oil-exporting countries and, in some cases, affect fiscal sustainability.

Oil prices are likely to remain volatile, however, and future shocks could again affect economic prospects. The uncertainties surrounding the near- and longer-term outlook for world oil demand and supply suggest that oil prices could deviate significantly from the path implied by futures markets. If the trend decline in industry oil inventories continues, the impact of shocks on world oil prices may be magnified, resulting in higher volatility. A further reduction in spare production capacity would have a similar effect. Moreover, since investment projects in the oil sector tend to be lumpy, oil production responds to prices with a lag and in discrete steps. Such a pattern may explain why shocks have persistent effects on oil prices, and possibly also suggests that the eventual (sizable) adjustment of output

may result in a sharp movement of prices in the opposite direction.

Increased cooperation efforts between oil-producing and oil-consuming countries may help reduce oil price volatility, thereby reducing the uncertainties surrounding the longer-term global growth outlook. To this end, the International Energy Forum (IEF) was formed in 1991 to promote dialogue between energy producers and consumers. Participation in the IEF's ministerial meetings has increased to 65 countries over the past decade, and a secretariat of the IEF is soon to be established in Riyadh. Important initiatives being undertaken by the IEF, in cooperation with various international organizations and forums, include the Joint Oil Data Exercise, which aims to assess and improve the quantity, quality, and timeliness of monthly oil data, and efforts to enhance transparent information flow on oil market developments.

Appendix 1.2. Nonenergy Commodity Prices and Semiconductor Markets

The main authors of this appendix are Aasim Husain and Ximena Cheetham. Ivan Guerra and Paul Nicholson provided research assistance.

Nonenergy commodity prices were dampened in the first half of 2003 by weak demand due to war-related uncertainties, SARS-related concerns, and the slower-than-anticipated pace of economic activity. In addition, some unwinding of last year's supply shocks—principally weather-related—led to a reversal of part of the gains in prices during the latter part of 2002. As a result, the nonenergy commodity price index fell by 3.8 percent in Special Drawing Right (SDR) terms in the first half of the year. Owing to the depreciation of the U.S. dollar against other major currencies, however, nonenergy commodity prices rose in dollar terms by 1.6 percent during the first half of 2003.

Looking forward, stronger demand as the global recovery gains momentum is expected to lead to some firming of nonenergy commodity prices toward the end of this year and into next

Figure 1.23. Nonenergy Commodities and Semiconductors

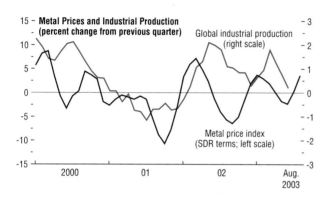

Metal Prices and Industrial Production
(percent change from previous quarter)

Global industrial production
(right scale)

Metal price index
(SDR terms; left scale)

2000   01   02   Aug.
2003

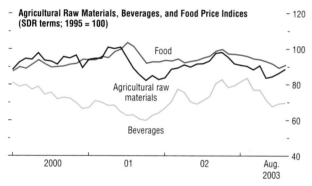

Agricultural Raw Materials, Beverages, and Food Price Indices
(SDR terms; 1995 = 100)

Food

Agricultural raw
materials

Beverages

2000   01   02   Aug.
2003

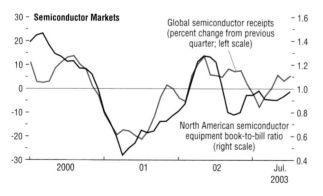

Semiconductor Markets

Global semiconductor receipts
(percent change from previous
quarter; left scale)

North American semiconductor
equipment book-to-bill ratio
(right scale)

2000   01   02   Jul.
2003

Sources: World Semiconductor Trade Statistics; Semiconductor Equipment and Materials International; and IMF staff estimates.

year. In view of the softening of prices so far this year, however, the nonenergy price index is projected to ease by about 2½ percent in SDR terms (but increase by 5 percent in dollar terms) on an annual average basis in 2003, before recovering by 2 percent in 2004. Aside from the possibility of further weather-related or other supply shocks, nonenergy commodity price prospects will clearly be affected by the pace of the global economic recovery, particularly the more cyclically responsive commodity prices such as industrial metals.

Recent developments in industrial metals prices highlight their relationship with global industrial activity (Figure 1.23). Metals prices eased in SDR terms during the second and third quarters of last year as global economic prospects weakened, before picking up moderately toward the end of 2002 and the start of 2003 as overall economic indicators strengthened. However, prices of industrial metals softened once again in the second quarter of this year as the pace of the global recovery proved more tepid than previously expected.

Prices of agricultural raw materials and food and beverage commodities have also eased so far this year, although this appears mainly to be related to the dissipation of the major supply shocks last year. Among food items, cereals prices have fallen markedly from last year's drought-induced peaks and are now near average price levels (in SDR terms) prevailing in 2001. Vegetable oils and meals prices have also edged down this year, but have been supported by a sizable increase in imports by China. Among beverages, cocoa prices have eased markedly on account of stronger-than-expected production and as the anticipated disruptions to export deliveries owing to civil unrest in Côte d'Ivoire did not materialize. While the effects of last year's drought have begun to wear off, coffee prices have drawn support in recent months from crop destruction and increased export retention in some coffee-producing countries. Among agricultural raw materials, wool prices have declined markedly in recent months as wool imports to China slowed sharply amid

SARS concerns. Cotton prices, though well above year-ago levels, have also eased in recent months owing to weaker demand growth in the United States. Rubber prices, by contrast, have risen in the first half of 2003 on increased demand by tire producers, particularly in China.

Global semiconductor sales and other indicators of concurrent activity in the semiconductor sector have started to recover from setbacks in the first part of the year on account of the tepid pace of global economic activity and SARS-related concerns. However, forward-looking indicators such as orders for semiconductor equipment—which is used to produce semiconductors—and surveys of companies' IT-related investment spending plans remain sluggish. While equity prices for the tech sector have outperformed broader stock indices so far in 2003, the outlook for the sector remains tied to overall economic prospects.

References

Alesina, Alberto, and Beatrice Weder, 2002, "Do Corrupt Governments Receive Less Foreign Aid?" *American Economic Review*, Vol. 92 (September), pp. 1126–37.

Birdsall, Nancy, and David Roodman, 2003, *The Commitment to Development Index: A Scorecard of Rich-Country Policies* (Washington: Center for Global Development).

Bulíř, Aleš, and A. Javier Hamann, 2001, "How Volatile and Unpredictable Are Aid Flows, and What Are the Policy Implications?" IMF Working Paper 01/167 (Washington: International Monetary Fund).

Collier, Paul, and David Dollar, 1999, *Aid Allocation and Poverty Reduction*, Development Research Group (Washington: World Bank).

Fischer, Stanley, and Ratna Sahay, 2002, "The Transition Economies After Ten Years," IMF Working Paper 00/30 (Washington: International Monetary Fund).

Gagnon, Joseph, and Jane Ihrig, 2002, "Monetary Policy and Exchange Rate Pass-Through," International Finance Discussion Paper No. 704 (Washington: Board of Governors for the Federal Reserve System).

Goldman Sachs, 2002, *Global Equity Research* (London).

Helbling, Thomas, Ashoka Mody, and Ratna Sahay, forthcoming, "Debt Accumulation in the CIS-7 Countries: Bad Luck, Bad Policies, or Bad Advice?" IMF Working Paper (Washington).

Heller, Peter S., and Sanjeev Gupta, 2002, "Challenges in Expanding Development Assistance," IMF Policy Discussion Paper 02/5 (Washington: International Monetary Fund).

International Energy Agency, 2000, *World Energy Outlook: 2000* (Paris: Organization for Economic Cooperation and Development).

———, 2001, *World Energy Outlook: 2001 Insights* (Paris: Organization for Economic Cooperation and Development).

———, 2002, *World Energy Outlook: 2002* (Paris: Organization for Economic Cooperation and Development).

International Monetary Fund, 2000, *The Impact of Higher Oil Prices on the Global Economy* (Washington). Available via the Internet: http://www.imf.org/external/pubs/ft/oil/2000/oilrep.pdf.

———, 2003a, *Exchange Rate Pass-Through and External Adjustment in the Euro Area: Selected Issues*, IMF Country Report No. 03/292 (Washington).

———, 2003b, *Monetary and Exchange Rate Issues of the Euro Area: Selected Issues*, IMF Country Report No. 03/236 (Washington).

———, 2003c, *United States: Selected Issues*, IMF Country Report No. 03/245 (Washington).

Kumar, Manmohan, and others, 2003, *Deflation: Determinants, Risks, and Policy Options*, IMF Occasional Paper No. 221 (Washington: International Monetary Fund).

Melick, William R., and Charles P. Thomas, 1997, "Recovering an Asset's Implied PDF from Option Prices: An Application to Crude Oil during the Gulf Crisis," *Journal of Financial and Quantitative Analysis*, Vol. 32 (March), pp. 91–115.

Okogu, Bright E., 1995, "Sharing Out the Downstream Barrel: Imbalance May Impact Investment," *Organization of the Petroleum Exporting Countries Bulletin*, Vol. 26 (May).

Prati, Alessandro, Ratna Sahay, and Thierry Tressel, 2003, "Is There a Case for Sterilizing Foreign Aid Inflows?" (unpublished; Washington: International Monetary Fund).

Rogoff, Kenneth, 2003, "Unlocking Growth in Africa," *Finance and Development*, Vol. 40 (June), pp. 56–57.

THREE CURRENT POLICY ISSUES IN DEVELOPING COUNTRIES

This chapter consists of essays on growth in the Middle East and North Africa, reserve accumulation in Asia, and the impact of industrial country exchange rate volatility on developing countries. The first essay examines the causes of the low economic growth in the countries in the Middle East and North Africa (MENA) region over the past two decades. The essay shows that the region's poor growth reflects mainly declining or low growth rates in oil-exporting countries. By contrast, growth in non-oil-exporting countries generally matched that of other developing countries (excluding east Asia), although it was not high enough to create enough new jobs to absorb the rapid expansion of the labor force, resulting in increased unemployment. Using an empirical model, the essay finds that the factors behind the region's weak performance differ across subgroups of countries. Key findings are that, for the members of the Cooperation Council of the Arab States of the Gulf (GCC),[1] high oil revenues that financed excessive government expenditures lowered growth, and that improvements in institutional quality would provide substantial gains for other countries in the MENA region.

The second essay investigates the rapid accumulation of foreign reserves over the past decade in emerging market countries, especially emerging economies in Asia, where the bulk of the increase has occurred. The essay finds that reserves—scaled by imports, short-term external debt, or broad money—in emerging markets have generally risen, quite sharply in many cases. The essay shows that reserves in many emerging market economies have increased more rapidly since 2001 than supported by economic fundamentals, using an empirical model to assess the relative importance of five key factors behind the reserve buildup—economic size, current account vulnerability, capital account vulnerability, exchange rate flexibility, and opportunity cost. After reviewing the main costs and benefits of holding a high level of reserves, the essay concludes that reserves in emerging economies in Asia are now at the point where some slowdown in the rate of accumulation is desirable from both domestic and multilateral perspectives.

The last essay examines the impact of industrial country exchange rate volatility on trade, capital inflows, and the likelihood of exchange rate crises in developing countries. The essay finds that these adverse effects are small for the average country: even the complete elimination of all G-3 (Group of Three industrial countries) exchange rate volatility would boost developing country trade by a modest 1 percent and reduce the probability of exchange rate crises by only 2½ percentage points. Also, these effects arise mainly indirectly, through the impact of G-3 exchange rate volatility on developing country exchange rates, which are more heavily influenced by developing countries' own exchange rate regimes. Simulations indicate that these adverse effects are greatest in those countries that peg to a specific industrial country currency, where external debt is high, and where there is a substantial mismatch between the currency composition of debt and of trade. This suggests that, in many cases, more flexible exchange rate regimes and better hedging may help reduce vulnerabilities. The simulations also find that the beneficial impact on developing countries of any attempt to stabilize G-3 exchange rates could easily be offset by the resulting fluctuations in G-3 interest rates and output.

[1]The members of the GCC are Bahrain, Kuwait, Oman, Qatar, Saudi Arabia, and United Arab Emirates.

How Can Economic Growth in the Middle East and North Africa Region Be Accelerated?

The main author of this essay is Dalia Hakura. Ben Sutton provided research assistance.

Over the past two decades, economic growth in the MENA region has been weaker than in other developing country regions. Indeed, between 1980 and 2001, real per capita GDP in the MENA region did not increase at all, compared with average annual growth of 6.3 percent in east Asia and 1.3 percent in all other developing countries over the same period.[2] The MENA region's poor growth performance during the 1980s and 1990s also contrasts sharply with the 1970s, when annual per capita GDP growth averaged 3 percent, exceeding that of other developing countries (excluding east Asia) by three-fourths of a percentage point.

As discussed below, a closer look at the region's growth performance during 1980–2001 reveals that MENA's poor performance owed much to the dominant share of oil-exporting countries. These—in common with oil exporters in the rest of the world—experienced a significant decline in real per capita GDP in the 1980s and very low growth in the 1990s. In contrast, GDP growth in non-oil-exporting countries was relatively similar to that of other developing countries (excluding those in east Asia). Nonetheless, in the specific circumstances of the MENA countries, such a performance was not good enough; given their relatively high labor force growth, their economies needed to grow considerably faster just to create the necessary job growth. Because this did not happen, unemployment is now high throughout the region[3] and, looking forward, GDP growth will need to be significantly faster to absorb the continuing strong increase in the labor force and bring unemployment down.

Consequently, regional policymakers have for many years focused on how best to improve the region's growth performance (e.g., IMF, 1996; Page, 1998; and Makdisi, Fattah, and Limam, 2000). Unfortunately, while significant progress has been made in eliminating macro-economic imbalances, reducing inflation, and advancing structural reforms in some MENA countries, the trend has not been encouraging—GDP growth in the 1990s remained relatively weak. The persistence of these growth problems suggests that they should be analyzed from a more long-run, structural perspective. Indeed, a number of recent studies, including Abed (2003) and the *Arab Human Development Report* (UNDP, 2002), have pointed to a diverse set of structural causes behind the poor growth performance in the MENA region, including dependence on oil, restrictive trade regimes, weak institutions, political instability, and large public sectors.[4] Extending this literature, this essay uses an empirical model of long-run growth—for the first time including a large number of MENA countries—to analyze MENA's growth performance during the past two decades, focusing on the following questions.

- How different was the MENA region's growth performance during 1980–2001? Have some MENA countries performed better than others?
- Where are the differences between MENA countries and other developing countries when it comes to the main determinants of growth? Are there important differences among MENA countries?
- How much of the growth differential between MENA countries and east Asian countries (the fastest growing group of developing countries) do these differences in growth factors explain? Is the dependence on oil important?
- What policies are needed to strengthen growth in the years ahead?

---

[2]GDP weights in purchasing-power-parity terms are used to construct the regional averages.

[3]Data for seven MENA countries indicates an increase in the unemployment rate from an average of 12.5 percent in 1990 to 15 percent in 2000 (Gardner, 2003).

[4]See also Dasgupta, Keller, and Srinivasan (2002), Keller and Nabli (2002), Sala-i-Martin and Artadi (2002), Makdisi, Fattah, and Limam (2000), Davoodi and Erickson von Allmen (2001), and Alonso-Gamo, Fedelino, and Paris Horvitz (1997).

MENA's Growth Performance in Perspective

The MENA region comprises a group of countries bound together by their geographical location, close historical and cultural ties, and common economic challenges.[5] To account for fundamental differences in economic structure, countries within the region are divided into oil-exporting countries and other MENA countries, which the essay will refer to as non-oil MENA countries (see Appendix 2.1 for country groups and data definitions). The oil-exporting MENA countries are further divided into the members of the GCC—because of their large oil sectors—and other MENA oil exporters.

An initial comparison of the evolution of real GDP per capita over the past two decades suggests that MENA's growth performance has been considerably weaker than that in other developing countries (Figure 2.1). However, this reflects the large share of oil exporters in the MENA region, which—especially the GCC oil exporters—experienced particularly low growth rates. While this performance was broadly similar to that in major oil exporters outside the MENA region—suggesting that common factors, notably related to the oil market, played a key role—the magnitudes of the changes were even larger for MENA, perhaps reflecting sharper changes in oil production in the region.[6] In contrast, non-oil MENA

[5]Specifically, for the purpose of this essay, the region includes Algeria, Bahrain, Egypt, the Islamic Republic of Iran, Jordan, Kuwait, Lebanon, Libya, Morocco, Oman, Qatar, Saudi Arabia, Syrian Arab Republic, Tunisia, the United Arab Emirates, and Yemen.

[6]Since growth in the oil exporters is correlated with crude oil production, the decline in Organization of Petroleum Exporting Countries (OPEC) quotas in the 1980s explains part of the lower growth during that decade, and the recovery of OPEC crude oil production during the 1990s underlies the improved performance of oil exporters during this period. As the oil sector accounts for a larger share of GDP among MENA oil-exporting countries (particularly the GCC countries) than for those outside the region, they are more susceptible to changes in quotas. On the other hand, it should be noted that the relationship between OPEC production quotas and real per capita GDP growth is not necessarily proportional given the considerable scope for output and consumption smoothing in oil-producing countries (through government expenditures).

Figure 2.1. MENA Growth Performance in Comparison[1]
(Average real GDP per capita growth rate; percent)

The MENA region's poor growth performance in the 1980s and 1990s reflects in large part the poor growth in the oil-exporting countries and in part the decelerating growth in the non-oil countries.

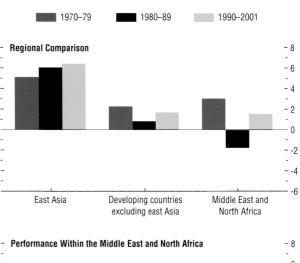

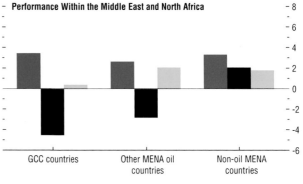

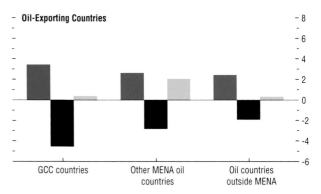

[1]Groups are weighted by GDP at purchasing-power-parity exchange rates.

Figure 2.2. Regional Comparison of Growth Determinants: Macroeconomic and Trade Policy Indicators, 1980–2000

(Simple average)

All MENA subgroups had relatively large governments. In addition, other MENA oil and non-oil MENA countries had relatively overvalued real effective exchange rates and low trade openness.

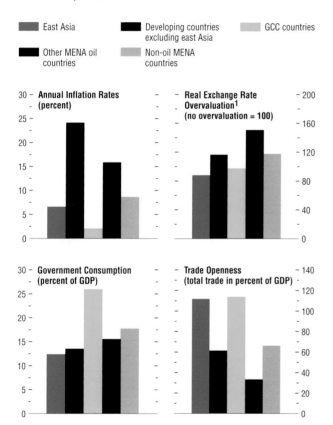

Sources: World Bank, *World Development Indicators;* Dollar (1992)*;* and IMF staff calculations.

[1]Real exchange rate overvaluation shows the average exchange rate misalignment over 1980–2000. It is based on purchasing power parity comparisons, using the Summers-Heston measure, where 100 signifies parity and higher (lower) numbers indicate over-(under-) valuation, following Dollar (1992).

countries, on average, achieved positive rates of growth during all three decades since 1970, which—while well below those achieved in the fast growing countries of east Asia—were comparable to those of other developing countries (excluding east Asia). However, as noted above, this growth performance fell far short of that needed to avoid a sustained rise in unemployment, and the trend was disappointing, as growth rates in the non-oil MENA countries declined from one decade to the next.

What are the causes of MENA's disappointing growth performance? The empirically oriented growth literature has identified a number of fundamental determinants of long-run economic growth that, broadly speaking, fall into six categories. For each of these growth determinants, this section will briefly outline how they are generally thought to affect economic growth and how MENA compares with other developing country regions over 1980–2000.

- *Macroeconomic instability* is often cited as a fundamental reason for poor growth, as (1) high inflation creates uncertainty, which adversely affects productivity and investment, and, as a consequence, economic growth (Fischer, 1993); and (2) overvalued exchange rates reduce the competitiveness of dynamic, outward-oriented sectors. The MENA region's performance with regard to each of these determinants of growth relative to other developing countries varies considerably (see Figure 2.2). The MENA countries generally had average inflation rates of less than 10 percent over the 1980–2000 period, which are below levels typically considered detrimental to growth in developing countries (e.g., Khan and Senhadji, 2000). However, an index of exchange rate misalignment developed by Dollar (1992) suggests that exchange rate overvaluation was particularly relevant in other MENA oil-exporting countries, which score highest in this category. This finding is consistent with the notion that having oil makes countries vulnerable to exchange rate overvaluation (the so-called Dutch disease phenomenon).

In non-oil MENA countries, exchange rate overvaluation was comparable to that of other developing countries.

- *Role of government.* High levels of government consumption can—beyond some threshold—have negative effects on productivity, owing to the adverse effects on savings and the distortions resulting from high levels of taxation (Barro, 1991). The size of government is large in all MENA countries, including in oil-exporting countries, in which oil revenues traditionally financed large government sectors.

- *Trade openness and terms of trade volatility.* Restrictive trade regimes reduce productivity-enhancing effects from competition and international technology transfers (e.g., Coe, Helpman, and Hoffmaister, 1997). In addition, terms of trade volatility creates uncertainty, which is expected to act as a deterrent to growth.[7] The GCC oil exporters stand out as being very open, in terms of both trade openness—an outcome-based measure—and the IMF's trade restrictiveness indicator (Figure 2.3).[8] In contrast, other MENA oil exporters had the most restrictive regime within the region and compared with other developing countries according to both indicators. Non-oil MENA countries were, on average, as restrictive as other developing countries in their trade regime according to the trade openness measure but were more restrictive according to the trade restrictiveness indicator. With regard to terms of trade volatility, the MENA oil exporters experienced larger terms of trade volatility than any other region in the past two decades, reflecting the large fluctuations in oil prices.

- *Quality of institutions.* Recent research has emphasized the strong influence of institutions

Figure 2.3. Trade Restrictiveness Measure, 1997–2002[1]
(Qualitative scale: 1 to 5, simple average)

Other MENA oil countries and non-oil MENA countries had more restrictive trade regimes than all other regions.

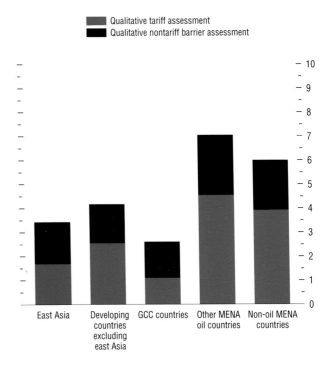

Source: IMF staff calculations.
[1]Each component is scaled 0 to 5, where 5 represents high trade restrictions.

---

[7]Some growth studies have also examined the effect of changes in the terms of trade on growth. An improvement in a country's terms of trade is expected to positively affect real per capita GDP growth if it stimulates an increase in production.

[8]Berg and Krueger (2003) emphasize that outcome-based measures of trade openness can be misleading.

Figure 2.4. Regional Comparison of Growth Determinants: Terms of Trade Volatility, Institutional Quality, Demographics, and Secondary Education, 1980–2000

(Simple average across years and countries unless otherwise noted)

Other MENA oil countries and non-oil MENA countries had relatively low institutional quality while GCC and other MENA oil countries had relatively high terms of trade volatility.

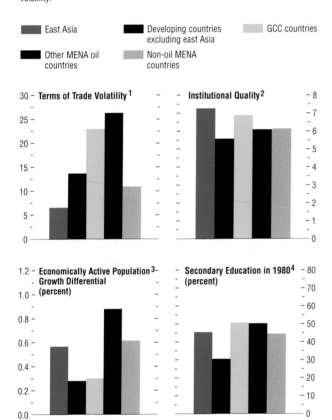

Sources: PRS Group, *International Country Risk Guide;* World Bank, *World Development Indicators;* and IMF staff calculations.

[1]Terms of trade volatility is the standard deviation of the annual percent change in total terms of trade.

[2]Institutional quality is an average of bureaucratic quality, control of corruption, government stability, and rule of law indicators reported in the International Country Risk Guide. Each component is scaled 0 to 12, where 12 represents highest institutional quality.

[3]Economically active population annual growth rate minus total population annual growth rate.

[4]Secondary education is the number of residents enrolled in secondary education programs in percent of the secondary school age population at the beginning of the sample period (1980).

on economic growth, as good institutions encourage productive activities rather than rent seeking, corruption, and other unproductive activities (see Chapter 3 of the April 2003 *World Economic Outlook* and the references therein). In this regard, it has been argued that an abundance of oil wealth negatively affects institutional quality because it encourages rent seeking and corruption (e.g., Sachs and Warner, 1995). Based on a composite index of institutional quality that encompasses the effects of corruption, quality of the bureaucracy, rule of law, and government stability,[9] where higher values indicate better institutions, the GCC countries score higher than the rest of the region and nearly match east Asia's scores (Figure 2.4),[10] while the other MENA oil and non-oil countries score only marginally higher than developing countries excluding east Asia. When it comes to dimensions of institutional quality, the region scores high for stability of government, but in other dimensions, the scores are mixed and vary within MENA country groups (Figure 2.5).

• *Demographics.* The so-called demographic burden—the differential between population and labor force growth—is inversely related to growth (Bloom and Williamson, 1998). The demographic burden was relevant for GCC countries, which, like developing countries excluding east Asia, faced relatively rapid total population growth relative to labor force growth whereas other oil and non-oil MENA countries, like east Asia, experienced relatively rapid growth of the working population relative to the population as a whole (see Figure 2.4).

[9]The data to construct the institutional quality index comes from the *International Country Risk Guide* (see Appendix 2.1 for more details). This is along the lines of research by Knack and Keefer (1995), Barro (1996), Sachs and Warner (1997), and Hall and Jones (1999).

[10]The relative standing of the MENA subgroups vis-à-vis other regions with regard to institutional quality is virtually identical if an alternative indicator of institutional quality developed by Kaufmann, Kraay, and Zoido-Lobatón (1999) is used.

- *Initial conditions.* Growth theory suggests that a country's growth rate is negatively related to its relative initial level of income, as the latter varies inversely with the scope for catching up with the richest countries. In contrast, a larger initial stock of human capital is expected to have a positive influence on growth because it allows a country to engage in research and to adopt new products and ideas developed in advanced economies (Barro, 1991). Per capita income levels vary widely across the MENA region, ranging from one low-income country to three high-income countries, implying that the initial level of income will have a significantly different effect across the countries in the region. The MENA region fares relatively well in terms of the initial stock of human capital measured using the secondary school enrollment ratio when compared with developing countries excluding east Asia, suggesting that it would be difficult to relate the region's poor performance to this factor.[11]

Empirical Analysis of MENA's Growth Performance

After the informal diagnosis of the causes of the MENA region's growth problem, the essay now turns to a formal econometric analysis to identify the relative contribution of each of these factors in explaining the region's poor growth performance. For this purpose, a standard growth model explaining variations in long-

[11]It should be noted, however, that this measure may not adequately capture differences across regions in the quality of education, which affects the productivity of human capital. For instance, Sala-i-Martin and Artadi (2002) argue that the education system in the Arab world does not prepare its citizens for a world of technical change. In addition, the discrepancy between female and male secondary enrollment ratios is relatively high in the MENA region except for the GCC countries, although it should be noted that female secondary enrollment ratios are high in the MENA region compared with other developing country regions. Moreover, UNDP (2002) emphasizes that the MENA region lags substantially behind other regions in female tertiary enrollments.

Figure 2.5. Institutional Quality, 1984–2000
(Scale 1 to 12 with 12 representing highest quality; simple average)

Most subgroups of MENA scored less than other regions for quality of the bureaucracy, rule of law, and control of corruption.

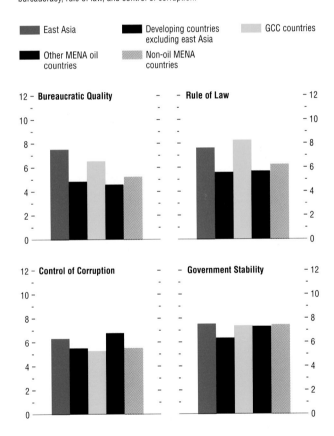

Sources: PRS Group, *International Country Risk Guide;* and IMF staff calculations.

Table 2.1. Growth Regression Results[1]

Explanatory Variables	Including GCC Oil Exporters	Excluding GCC Oil Exporters
Initial income[2]	**−1.21**	**−1.26**
Institutional quality[3]	**0.87**	**0.85**
Trade to GDP	0.003	0.003
Terms of trade volatility (weighted)[4]	−0.0004	***−0.002***
Growth of economically active population minus total population growth	**1.95**	**2.09**
Secondary education, 1980[5]	**0.02**	**0.02**
Government consumption to GDP[6]	***−0.09***	**−0.11**
Inflation rate[7]	−0.001	−0.002
Real exchange rate overvaluation[8]	**−0.01**	**−0.01**
R^2	0.62	0.61
Number of observations	74	71
Number of MENA countries	10	7

Source: IMF staff estimates.

[1]The dependent variable is real per capita GDP growth over 1980–2000. The regressions are estimated using an instrumental variables estimation technique in which the endogenous variables in the regression are the institutional quality and the trade openness variables. Following research by Hall and Jones (1999) and the April 2003 *World Economic Outlook*, the fraction of the population that is English speaking, the fraction of the population speaking one of the major languages of western Europe, and a set of dummy variables that capture a country's legal origin (British, French, or German) are used to instrument for the institutional quality variable. The predicted trade shares computed as for Frankel and Romer (1999) are used to instrument for trade openness. Bold values signify statistical significance at the 5 percent level and bold italics signify significance at the 10 percent level.

[2]Log of initial per capita purchasing-power-parity GDP as reported in the *World Economic Outlook*.

[3]The institutional quality variable is measured as the average of four indices reported in the *International Country Risk Guide*.

[4]Terms of trade volatility is weighted by the share of natural resource exports in GDP in 1980.

[5]Secondary education represents the initial level of secondary education.

[6]This is the ratio of nominal government final consumption to GDP.

[7]Inflation is the average annual inflation rate over 1980–2000.

[8]Real exchange rate overvaluation shows the average exchange rate misalignment over 1980–2000. It is based on purchasing-power-parity comparisons, using the Summers-Heston measure, where 100 signifies parity and higher (lower) numbers indicate over- (under-) valuation, following Dollar (1992).

run growth was estimated for a cross section of 74 countries, including 21 advanced economies (Table 2.1). A key consideration was to include as many MENA countries in the sample as possible, which, given data availability, allowed the model to be estimated for 1980–2000.

The results, which are broadly in line with those in the literature (e.g., Barro, 1991), confirm that higher real per capita growth rates are associated with low initial levels of income, stronger institutions, more open trade regimes, smaller governments, lower terms of trade volatility, higher growth of working-age population relative to total population growth, lower inflation, lower exchange rate overvaluation, and a higher initial level of secondary school enrollment.[12] Perhaps surprisingly, variables capturing a country's abundance of oil were not found to be significant, a point further elaborated on below. All of the explanatory variables are statistically significant except the inflation and trade policy variables;[13] the model, as typically found in growth regression models, explains 62 percent of the cross-country variation in growth rates.

While the model, inevitably, does not provide a full explanation of MENA's growth in the past two decades, it does allow us to identify a number of key factors affecting MENA's growth performance. To illustrate this, following Easterly and Levine (1997), we use the growth model to analyze the causes of the growth differential between the MENA region and the fast-growing developing countries in east Asia. As can be seen in Figure 2.6, the causes of

[12]An instrumental variables estimation technique was used to account for possible endogeneity of some of the explanatory variables. Interactions of the macroeconomic policy variables and the institutions variable (see, for example, Edison and others, 2002) were also included in the regressions to investigate whether there is a nonmonotonic relationship between institutions and growth. However, the interaction terms were not significant and are therefore not reported here. Also, the ratio of private sector credit to GDP, which proxies for the depth of the financial market, was included as an explanatory variable in the regression but was not found to be significant (as in the April 2003 *World Economic Outlook*) and so was not reported.

[13]When the IMF's trade restrictiveness indicator for 1997 is substituted for the trade to GDP ratio, the estimated coefficient is of the correct sign but is also insignificant. The insignificance of the trade and inflation variables is consistent with other recent studies that included a variable of institutional quality. Some have interpreted this as suggesting that institutional quality matters more for growth (e.g., Rodrik, Subramanian, and Trebbi, 2002, and Acemoglu and others, 2002) while others have argued that the significance of the macroeconomic variables depends on the specification of the regression (Sachs, 2003, and Bosworth and Collins, 2003).

weaker growth vary considerably across the MENA subgroups.

- For the GCC countries, the key factors are the relatively high initial income and the relatively large size of the public sector, accounting together for nearly 70 percent of the differential with east Asian countries. The terms of trade volatility, the population growth, and the quality of institutions variables also contribute to explaining the growth differential, albeit to a lesser extent.

- In other MENA oil-exporting countries, higher initial income also plays a key role but after that, lower scores in institutional quality explain the largest fraction of the growth differential. This is followed by exchange rate overvaluation, terms of trade volatility, government consumption, and trade openness variables, respectively.

- For the non-oil MENA countries, consistent with the findings in the April 2003 *World Economic Outlook*, the main variable explaining the growth differential is the institutional quality variable. The government consumption, exchange rate overvaluation, and trade openness variables also matter but to a lesser extent.

Given that a large number of the MENA countries are among the world's main oil exporters, it is important to understand to what extent their dependence on oil has mattered for their long-run growth performance.[14] The main variable that distinguishes the performance of the MENA oil exporters, especially the GCC countries, from east Asian countries as well as oil exporters outside the region is their high initial levels of per

capita income. This finding should not be surprising because soaring oil revenues in the 1970s raised not only income and consumption but also led to a surge in investment spending and rapid capital stock growth, which could be interpreted as reflecting an accelerated catching up (especially in the GCC countries). However, with much of this spending undertaken by governments, it proved relatively inefficient and simply perpetuated the countries' dependence on oil.[15] Therefore, the negative effect on growth of high initial levels of per capita income to some extent also reflects the adverse effects of high oil income on the incentives for economic diversification.[16] Indeed, a growth accounting exercise suggests that capital per worker and total factor productivity declined in the GCC countries during 1980–2000, reflecting the low productivity of initial capital stocks (Box 2.1).

Oil is also likely to have affected growth performance through a number of other channels. In particular, in the GCC countries, high oil revenues have been used to finance very high levels of public employment and wage-related benefits (reflected in the high level of government consumption noted above), hampering labor market flexibility and the development of the non-oil private sector. While other distortions, such as those arising from trade restrictions, are less severe in the GCC, the large size of the government has, in fact, been a veil for other distortions that have impeded diversification of the economies away from oil. Finally, as captured by the terms of trade volatility variable, the fluctuations in the oil prices exposed the private sector

[14]In this context, it should be noted that our framework captures the effects of persistent country characteristics related to oil but not the effects of oil-related country-specific shocks with long-lasting but nevertheless temporary effects on growth (Easterly and others, 1993). Also, as noted above, a variable that measures a country's abundance of oil (the share of fuel exports in total exports) was not found to be significant and was dropped from the final regression. In part, this may be because it is highly correlated with terms of trade volatility, which makes it difficult to isolate its partial effect. Similarly, the effects of changes in the terms of trade were not found to be significant, which may reflect the fact that most of the oil exporters in the sample (for whom movements in the terms of trade would mainly capture movements in the relative price of oil) have oil production quotas in the context of their membership in the OPEC.

[15]See Hausmann and Rigobon (2002) for a complementary discussion.

[16]The coefficient on initial income could also be biased because the GCC countries' initial income was likely to have been negatively correlated with shocks to oil prices and production over the sample period (see Barro and Sala-i-Martin, 1995). However, comparing the coefficients obtained from regressions including and excluding GCC countries from the sample suggests that this bias is at best small and without material implications for the analysis.

Figure 2.6. Decomposition of Growth Differentials Among Subgroups of MENA and East Asian Countries[1]
(Percentage points)

After initial income, government consumption explains the largest fraction of the GCC countries' growth differential, and institutional quality explains the largest fraction of the other MENA oil countries' growth differential. Institutional quality explains the largest fraction of the non-oil MENA countries' growth differential.

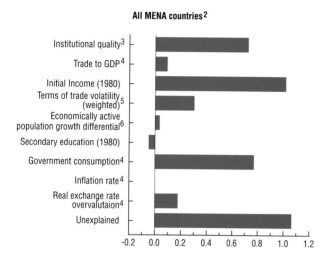

All MENA countries[2]

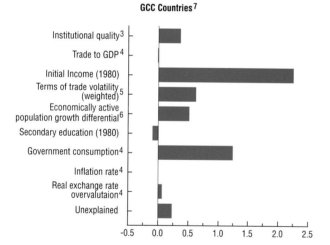

GCC Countries[7]

to boom and bust cycles that are likely to have adversely affected the growth of the non-oil sector. In the other MENA oil exporters, it is also possible that oil revenues may have contributed to weaker institutional quality, for the reasons already noted.

A second factor that has clearly been important for some countries, and is also difficult to capture in formal regressions, is internal and external conflict. Even though countries that were particularly affected by conflicts were excluded from the sample, MENA countries had a higher incidence of conflicts than all other regions (Figure 2.7).[17] To assess the potential impact, the model was reestimated using an institutional quality variable that encompasses the effects of indicators of internal and external conflicts collected by the *International Country Risk Guide*. This increased the explanatory power of the model for some regions,[18] especially for other MENA oil exporters (10 percentage points) and for non-oil MENA countries (4 percentage points),[19] suggesting these factors may indeed be important.

A third characteristic of MENA countries that is clearly different from other regions is the low participation ratios of women in the labor force. Given that female secondary school enrollment ratios are generally high in MENA countries relative to other developing country regions, this prevents a substantial stock of human capital from having a positive impact on the economy (see footnote 11 on the education of women).

---

[17]Lebanon and the Republic of Yemen were excluded from the analysis as they suffered from extended internal conflicts during the period under consideration.

[18]However, there is a high correlation between institutional quality variables (such as those defined in the previous section) and the conflict variables, reflecting the difficulties of running high-quality government operations with conflict. Similarly, weak governance and corruption can even be the instigators of political tensions. This makes it difficult to precisely estimate the effects of the latter from regressions that include the conflict variables as additional explanatory variables.

[19]The results are broadly consistent with the earlier results in the sense that the ranking of the explanatory variables for explaining the growth performance of each MENA subgroup remains unchanged.

Another drawback of low female participation ratios is that they can reduce competition in the labor market. However, female participation ratios rose faster in MENA countries than elsewhere from 1980 to 2000, and in 2000 the gap with other developing countries was generally reduced compared with 1980. While the growth impact is difficult to quantify, this should have boosted growth in MENA countries compared with other regions, everything else being equal. Looking forward, structural reforms aimed at enhancing labor market flexibility that at the same time would facilitate female labor force participation—thereby narrowing the gap with other countries further—could enhance their positive impact on productivity and growth in the MENA region (see also UNDP, 2002, and Klasen, 1999).

Conclusions and Policy Implications

While the MENA region's disappointing growth performance has many causes, the analysis above has identified a number of common factors—the large size of government, the poor quality of institutions (including political instability), misalignment of the real exchange rate, terms of trade volatility, and barriers to trade. The relative importance of the factors varies significantly across the subgroups of MENA countries, however, with the policy implications correspondingly rather different for each MENA subgroup.

- A key source of low growth for the GCC countries appears to have been the large size of public sector consumption, which has been spurred in part by the growth of economic rents in the region. This growth is linked, as described above, to the use of oil revenues to finance subsidies and transfers and high public employment. According to the empirical analysis, the high public sector consumption has accounted for nearly 1¼ percentage points of the growth differential with east Asian countries. This finding underscores the need to reduce the size of government over time, accompanied by structural reforms

Figure 2.6. *(concluded)*

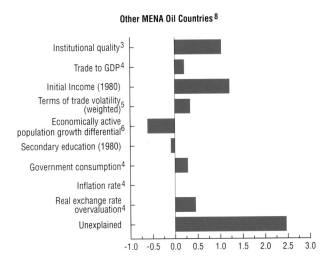

Other MENA Oil Countries[8]

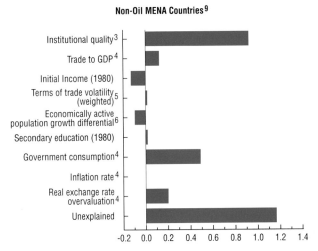

Non-Oil MENA Countries[9]

Sources: Dollar (1992); PRS Group, *International Country Risk Guide;* World Bank, *World Development Indicators*; and IMF staff estimates.

[1] The regression coefficients are applied to the difference between the average values for the explanatory variables for MENA (and its subgroups) and east Asian countries. The calculations use averages for each variable and for all countries in the relevant group for which the data is available and not only the countries included in the regression estimations. The main findings are broadly similar when the calculations are based on average values for the countries included in the regression only.

[2] The growth differential between all MENA countries and the east Asian countries is 4.2 percent.

[3] Simple average 1984–2000.

[4] Simple average 1980–2000.

[5] Standard deviation of the annual percent change in total terms of trade multiplied by the share of natural resource exports in GDP in 1980. This weighting captures the effect of volatility in income flows that is associated with trade in natural resources.

[6] Growth rate of economically active population minus growth rate of total population.

[7] The growth differential between the GCC countries and the east Asian countries is 5.2 percent.

[8] The growth differential between other MENA oil countries and the east Asian countries is 5.4 percent.

[9] The growth differential between non-oil MENA countries and the east Asian countries is 2.7 percent.

Figure 2.7. Indicators of Internal and External Conflict, 1984–2000

(Scale 1 to 12 with 12 representing least conflict; simple average)

Nearly all subgroups of MENA had more internal and external conflicts than other regions.

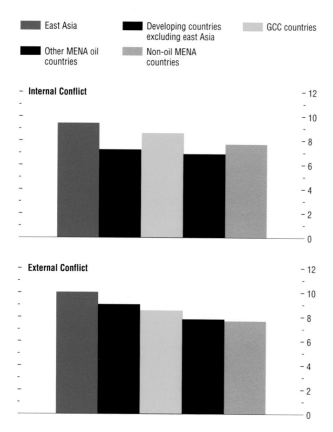

Sources: PRS Group, *International Country Risk Guide;* and IMF staff calculations.

to increase labor flexibility and strengthen the legal and institutional framework for private sector–led growth. Economic diversification and medium-term fiscal rules delinking government spending from oil prices are also important to reduce vulnerability to oil price fluctuations, which—as captured by the terms of trade volatility variable—accounted for more than ½ percentage point of the growth differential with east Asian countries.

- Other MENA oil-exporting countries would gain significantly from improving institutional quality, especially with regard to transparency in government operations, the quality of the bureaucracy, and the strength of the rule of law; indeed, the model suggests that if these could be brought to the level in east Asian countries, annual per capita GDP growth could be increased by 1 percentage point. There would also be a substantial payoff to trade and exchange rate liberalization, which together account for close to 0.7 percentage point of the growth differential with east Asia.

- In the non-oil MENA countries, improving institutional quality is again critical, accounting for 0.9 percentage point of the growth differential with east Asian countries. In addition, despite some progress during the past decade, the size of the public sector remains a drag on growth—if it were reduced to east Asian levels, per capita GDP growth could be boosted by ½ percentage point. More flexible exchange rates and trade liberalization are also priorities (Jbili and Kramarenko, 2003).

In addition to the policy implications outlined above, the evidence in the essay suggests, albeit indirectly, that political tensions and conflicts in the region contributed to the slowdown of growth of other oil exporters and non-oil exporters. Consequently, an improvement in the actual and perceived security situation would be conducive to reviving growth in the MENA region. Moreover, the analysis suggests that further increases in female labor force participation ratios would also support the region's growth prospects.

Box 2.1. Accounting for Growth in the Middle East and North Africa

Over the past two decades, as discussed in the main text, GDP growth in the Middle East and North Africa (MENA) has fallen short of the level required to absorb the rapidly growing labor force. This box looks at the MENA region's growth performance using growth accounting, a methodology that is complementary to the one applied in the main text (e.g., Bosworth and Collins, 2003). This approach breaks down the growth in output per worker into the separate contributions of increases in (physical and human) capital per worker and the residual, typically labeled total factor productivity (TFP), which captures changes in the efficiency with which the factor inputs are used. It is important to note that this residual can also reflect the effects on output of various factors that are not (fully) accounted for by their effects on measured increases in factor inputs, including the effects of war, political turmoil, external shocks, and policy changes.

Using this methodology for the MENA region as a whole, average annual output per worker declined by 0.2 percent annually during the period 1980–2000 (see the table). Within this, physical capital per worker remained almost constant, while the beneficial effects of higher educational attainment (human capital) were offset by a steady and substantial *decline* in TFP. However, there are significant differences between oil-exporting and non-oil MENA countries. For the oil exporters, output per worker fell, on average, by about 1 percent a year during 1980–2000.[1] While human capital improved steadily, this was more than offset by sharp declines in physical capital per worker and TFP. The one exception was Iran, where TFP slightly increased during this period.[2] In contrast, out-

put per worker in the non-oil countries rose by 1.4 percent a year during 1980–2000, which was above the average rate for 45 developing countries outside east Asia (albeit substantially below the rate for east Asian developing countries). Unlike in the oil exporters, over half of this growth was accounted for by increases in physical capital per worker, accompanied again by solid improvements in human capital. Reflecting a pattern common to other developing countries outside east Asia, TFP stagnated (and in a number of countries, including Morocco, Syria, and Jordan, declined).

Three striking aspects of these findings are worth noting.

- First, the contribution to growth from increases in human capital in MENA countries was generally greater than in other developing country regions, including east Asia. In addition, the growth contribution of human capital often exceeds, proportionally, the contributions coming from increases in physical capital and TFP, a pattern not found elsewhere. This finding reflects the sharp rise in the average years of schooling for the population aged 15 and older (the proxy measure for human capital) from just 3.3 years in 1980 to 5.8 years by 2000, which, in turn, reflected the substantial efforts at improving education in the region.[3]

- Second, and less favorably, the growth contribution of physical capital per worker has been small, especially given the relatively high levels of investment. In part, this has reflected the strong growth in the labor force, which, everything else being equal, required more investment (as a percent of GDP) for the capital stock per worker to increase at the same rate as elsewhere. In addition, while the high

Note: The main authors of this box are Barry Bosworth and Susan Collins.

[1]The country coverage differs from that in the main text.

[2]Given the difficulties in measuring the implications of the 1990 invasion on Kuwait's capital stock, the average rate of decline in TFP may be overstated. However, substantial TFP declines are also obtained if the years 1990–91 are omitted from the calculations.

[3]As noted in the table, the contribution from increases in human capital is included in the TFP residual for Saudi Arabia and United Arab Emirates due to data limitations, implying that the "true" TFP declines would be even larger if increases in human capital similar to those in other oil-exporting countries were assumed.

Box 2.1 *(concluded)*

Growth Accounts, 1980–2000[1]

Countries and Regions (number of countries)	Average Annual Rates of Change							
	Output	Output/ worker	Contribution of			Capital/Output		Investment/ Output
			Capital/worker		TFP	1980	2000	
			Physical	Human				
Middle East and North Africa (10)	3.1	−0.2	−0.1	0.6[2]	−0.7	2.1	2.1	22.5
Non-oil countries (5)	4.3	1.4	0.8	0.6	—	2.3	2.5	23.7
Egypt	4.9	2.2	0.9	0.8	0.5	2.3	2.5	27.0
Jordan	3.5	−1.7	0.2	0.6	−2.5	1.9	2.9	27.6
Morocco	3.0	0.5	0.3	0.4	−0.2	2.2	2.4	19.1
Syria	3.8	—	0.5	0.5	−0.9	1.7	2.2	20.3
Tunisia	4.1	1.3	0.5	0.4	0.4	2.8	2.8	26.2
Oil-exporting countries (5)	2.4	−1.1	−0.6	0.6[2]	−1.1	2.0	1.9	19.6
Algeria	2.2	−1.5	−0.3	0.6	−1.8	2.9	3.1	24.7
Iran	3.4	0.7	—	0.6	0.2	2.2	1.9	15.1
Kuwait	0.3	−2.1	0.8	0.6	−3.5	0.9	2.1	18.6
Saudi Arabia	1.4	−3.1	−1.5	. . .	−1.6	1.6	1.1	26.7
United Arab Emirates	2.8	−1.9	−1.4	. . .	−0.5	1.7	1.3	19.7
Other developing countries (45)	3.4	1.0	0.5	0.4	0.1	2.2	2.4	18.0
East Asia (7)[3]	6.4	3.9	2.4	0.5	0.9	1.7	2.8	29.2

Sources: Bosworth and Collins (2003); and World Economic Outlook database.
[1]All regional averages are weighted by GDP at purchasing-power-parity exchange rates.
[2]Excludes Saudi Arabia and United Arab Emirates.
[3]Excludes China.

investment of the 1970s resulted in relatively high ratios of the capital stock to GDP in the early 1980s (see the table), this investment was not always productive, as evidenced by the low growth that ensued. Accordingly, average capital productivity was relatively low during the latter period, diminishing the beneficial effect of high investment ratios on capital stock.

- Third, TFP growth in many countries in the region has been disappointing. While—as noted above—this may partly reflect the variety of shocks that the region has experienced, it also suggests that there is significant scope

to improve the efficiency with which resources are used.

As already noted, the central challenge facing many MENA countries is the relatively high level of unemployment; in contrast, investment and capital-output ratios are now often average to high by developing country standards—particularly in the non-oil-exporting countries. This suggests that, in the past, economic policies and incentives have been focused relatively too much on encouraging investment—not least through the public sector—at the expense of policies that would promote efficiency and create employment.

Are Foreign Exchange Reserves in Asia Too High?

The main author of this essay is Hali Edison. Emily Conover and Yutong Li provided research assistance.

Global foreign exchange reserves have risen sharply over the past decade, with the buildup accelerating over time and the bulk of the increase occurring in emerging market countries

(Figure 2.8). Reserves almost doubled from 4.1 percent of world GDP in 1990 to 7.8 percent of world GDP in 2002, and rapid reserve accumulation has continued in the first half of 2003. The share of global reserves held by emerging market countries rose from 37 percent in 1990 to 61 percent in 2002, with emerging economies in Asia accounting for much of the increase (Figure 2.9). During the recent period of U.S.

dollar weakness, real effective exchange rates in most emerging market economies have depreciated and reserves in emerging economies in Asia have increased at a record pace (see Chapter I).

The rapid accumulation of foreign exchange reserves over the past decade, especially in emerging Asia, raises important questions.

- Why do countries hold reserves? How do economic size, external vulnerability, and exchange rate flexibility affect reserve holdings?
- What are the recent trends in reserves, once they are appropriately scaled?
- What explains a country's reserve holdings in a richer empirical framework? Are reserves in some emerging economies now greater than warranted by fundamentals?
- What are the policy implications? Is it time for emerging economies in Asia to consider slowing the pace of reserve accumulation?

The essay is organized as follows. The first section discusses why countries hold reserves, suggesting that the demand for reserves depends positively on economic size, current account vulnerability, and capital account vulnerability, and negatively on exchange rate flexibility and opportunity cost. Recent trends in reserves scaled by imports, short-term external debt, and broad money are presented next, showing that reserve ratios in emerging market countries have generally increased over the past decade—in some cases quite sharply. The discussion then turns to an empirical model that simultaneously incorporates the various determinants of reserve holdings. The main finding is that reserves in many emerging market economies have increased more quickly since 2001 than warranted by fundamentals. The final section concludes that reserves in emerging economies in Asia are now at the point where some slowdown in the rate of accumulation is desirable from both domestic and multilateral perspectives.

Why Do Countries Hold Reserves?

A country's foreign exchange reserves consist of the financial assets under the control of the

Figure 2.8. Foreign Exchange Reserves
(Billions of U.S. dollars)

The stock of global reserves increased rapidly in the 1990s.

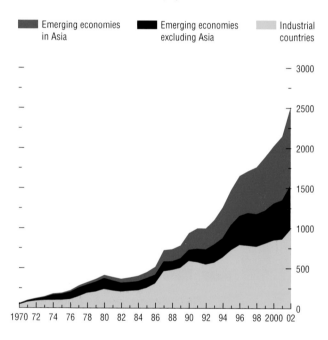

Source: IMF, *International Financial Statistics.*

Figure 2.9. Share of Global Reserves
(Percent of global reserves)

Reserve holding patterns have changed over time, reflecting the surge in reserve accumulation in emerging economies in Asia.

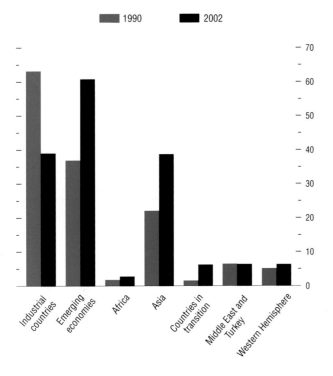

Source: IMF, *International Financial Statistics*.

monetary authority that are readily available for balance of payments financing. While the definition of reserves is straightforward, measuring them is more complicated because of the need to account for future claims on reserves, for example, from derivative contracts (Box 2.2). The ideal solution would be to net out those claims on reserves that might result in immediate drains on reserves and other elements that might overstate gross reserves, yielding a concept of "usable reserves." To help implement this concept, the IMF developed in 1999 a template for reporting reserves, which is now being used by about 50 countries, including 30 emerging market countries. However, data on usable reserves are only available for a very limited period, so this essay focuses on gross foreign reserve assets net of gold.[20]

The main reason why countries hold foreign exchange reserves is to smooth unpredictable and temporary imbalances in international payments. Thus, the basic idea in the theory of the demand for reserves is that a country chooses a level of reserves to balance the macroeconomic adjustment costs incurred if reserves are exhausted (the precautionary motive) with the opportunity cost of holding reserves.[21] Building on this theory, empirical work has identified a relatively stable long-run demand for reserves that is based on a limited set of explanatory variables.[22] There are five key factors that explain reserve holdings.

- *Economic size.* To the extent that international transactions increase with economic size, reserves are expected to rise with population and real GDP per capita.
- *Current account vulnerability.* A more open economy is more vulnerable to external shocks, so greater trade openness would be

[20]Most emerging market countries hold very little gold. Including gold valued at market prices does not affect the conclusions of this essay.

[21]See Heller (1966) and Frenkel and Jovanovic (1981).

[22]See Heller and Khan (1978), Edwards (1983, 1985), Lizondo and Mathieson (1987), Lane and Burke (2001), Flood and Marion (2002), and Aizenman and Marion (2002a, 2002b).

associated with higher reserve holdings. Also, the larger the external shocks (say, export volatility), the higher the level of reserves.

- *Capital account vulnerability.* As with the current account, greater financial openness could be associated with higher crisis vulnerability and thus influence the demand for reserves. In addition, the greater the potential for resident-based capital flight from the domestic currency, the higher the level of reserves.
- *Exchange rate flexibility.* Greater flexibility reduces the demand for reserves, because central banks no longer need a large stockpile of reserves to manage a pegged exchange rate. However, many countries that have adopted more flexible exchange rate regimes (including managed floats) appear reluctant to allow much actual variability.[23] Consequently, it is important to focus on the actual behavior of exchange rates, which suggests that there has in fact been some increase in exchange rate flexibility in recent years, especially in several emerging Asian economies (Figure 2.10).[24]
- *Opportunity cost.* The opportunity cost of holding reserves is the difference between the yield on reserves and the marginal productivity of an alternative investment. The greater the opportunity cost, the lower the level of reserves. With industrial country interest rates hitting 40–50 year lows in many countries (see Chapter I), the cost of holding foreign exchange reserves has likely increased for many emerging economies over the past three years.

[23]See Calvo and Reinhart (2002), who argue that there seems to be a "fear of floating"; see also Reinhart and Rogoff (forthcoming).

[24]The classification of exchange rate regimes is based on Reinhart and Rogoff (2002), which is generally consistent with Baig (2001), Calvo and Reinhart (2002), Hernández and Montiel (2001), and Levy-Yeyati and Sturzenegger (2002). Note that (1) in Asian emerging economies, exchange rate volatility actually declined a little between 1997 and 2002, but not by enough to warrant a reversal of the change in exchange rate clarification; (2) all the results in this paper also hold if the official exchange rate classification is used; and (3) in India, exchange rate flexibility has increased somewhat in recent months.

Figure 2.10. Selected Emerging Economies: Exchange Rate Regimes
(Percent of exchange rate regime with limited flexibility within each group)

Several emerging markets have moved toward more flexible exchange rate arrangements.

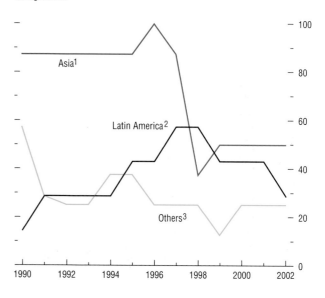

Source: IMF staff estimates based on Reinhart and Rogoff (2004).
[1]China, Hong Kong SAR, India, Indonesia, Korea, Malaysia, the Philippines, and Thailand.
[2]Argentina, Brazil, Chile, Colombia, Mexico, Peru, and Venezuela. Argentina was reclassified in 2002 as a managed floater.
[3]Czech Republic, Hungary, Israel, Pakistan, Poland, Russia, South Africa, and Turkey.

Box 2.2. Measuring Foreign Reserves

The definition of foreign reserves is straightforward, but their measurement is more complicated. Reserves are defined as foreign financial assets controlled by the monetary authorities that are readily available for balance of payments financing.[1] This means that reserves need to be liquid claims in foreign currency on nonresidents under control of the central bank, so that they can be used for operations in the foreign exchange market or repayment of external debt. In practice, there are often claims on reserves that can restrict their availability or result in drains, including derivative positions, the use of reserves as collateral for loans, and the investment of reserves with the government or domestic banks. If such claims need to be met immediately, then some reserve assets cannot be used for balance of payments financing and should not be counted as reserves (see IMF, 2000).

In practice, a useful concept is usable reserves, which nets out any questionable item from reserves. In deriving usable reserves, a primary consideration is the net short position in foreign currency derivatives, which in past crises has severely hindered the availability of reserves. Such positions can quickly become large when the authorities try to defend unsustainable exchange rates through forward sales of foreign currency. For example, in Thailand, forward liabilities contracted by the central bank in support of the domestic currency in 1997 were in excess of $25 billion, a level comparable to gross reserves. Derivatives can impose immediate drains on reserves for two reasons. First, foreign currency derivatives can be subject to margin calls so a movement in the exchange rate can result in an immediate claim on reserves. Second, while few central banks in practice need explicit pledges to take derivative positions, such pledges may be forced upon them in a crisis.

Another important issue in measuring reserves is the valuation of gold. While gold remains an important reserve asset, especially for larger industrial countries, it is no longer the core asset of reserve holdings. For emerging market economies, gold now constitutes only about 3 percent of total reserve holdings, compared with an average of 25 percent in the period 1950–70. If the *level* of reserves is being assessed, then gold should be valued at market prices, to reflect the value it would provide if sold.[2] Even for those emerging market countries with large holdings, gold is likely to be sufficiently liquid at times when the central bank would really need it (for example, during a crisis in the international financial system).[3] If the focus is on the *accumulation* of reserves, then gold could be valued at constant prices, to filter out valuation adjustments.

To help ensure that all the relevant information on the availability of reserves is available in the public domain, the IMF with the support of the G-10 developed in 1999 a template for reporting reserves, which is now being used by over 50 countries.[4] In addition to the gross amount of reserves, the template reports a breakdown of reserves and other foreign currency assets, as well as many potential drains on reserves, such as repayment obligations of the central bank and government. The information on drains is provided to help determine whether such drains pose any limitations on the availability of the reserves, and what claims might reduce reserves in the foreseeable future.[5]

With the introduction of the template, data reporting on reserves has significantly improved.[6] Nevertheless, for statistical analysis, time series on usable reserves are not yet sufficiently long. Thus, for the time being, cross-country empirical studies need to continue to use gross reserves, as is the case for this essay.

---

[2]See IMF (2001), paragraph 135.

[3]Many countries assign a fixed price to gold, which helps to insulate the central bank's accounting profits from fluctuations in the price of gold. It would be undesirable for the central bank's profit remittances to increase just because, say, widespread inflation concerns cause gold to become more valuable.

[4]Countries that subscribe to the IMF's Special Data Dissemination Standards are required to use the template. Other countries are encouraged to do so.

[5]The reserve template allows, in line with standard practice, for several ways of booking certain assets, some of which may lead to an overstatement of reserves. For example, banks may lend securities but keep both the securities and the cash received for the lent securities on their books. This is not a preferred method, but if done the template provides information on the drain to allow for netting (IMF, 2001, paragraph 85).

[6]These data can be accessed via the IMF website at http://www.imf.org/external/np/sta/ir/topic.htm.

Note: The main author of this box is Christian Mulder.
[1]See IMF (1993), paragraph 424.

What Are the Recent Trends in Reserves?

Comparisons of reserve holdings across countries and over time need to be scaled to reflect country characteristics and changes therein over time. Based on the foregoing discussion of the main factors that influence a country's level of reserve holdings, three scaling methods are considered.

- *Months of imports.* This ratio represents the number of months for which a country can support its current level of imports if all other inflows and outflows stop.
- *Short-term external debt based on remaining maturity.* This ratio is an indicator of the likelihood and depth of a financial crisis, as it reflects the country's ability to service external debt falling due in the coming year if external financing conditions deteriorated sharply.
- *Broad money.* Like the ratio to short-term external debt, this ratio is an indicator of reserve adequacy in the event of a financial crisis, as it reflects the potential for resident-based capital flight from the domestic currency.[25]

These three reserve ratios are calculated for the standard set of selected emerging market economies (data limitations preclude calculations for all emerging market countries).[26]

Reserve ratios in emerging market countries have generally increased over the past decade (Figure 2.11). Since the mid-1990s, the ratios of reserves to short-term debt and reserves to imports increased most sharply for emerging economies in Asia, while the ratio of reserves to broad money rose quickly for emerging market countries outside Asia and Latin America. This divergence is not surprising, given that the data for Asia are dominated by China, which is less financially developed and therefore a country in

---

[25]This ratio was used extensively during the gold standard and again by Calvo (1996).

[26]The economies are divided into three regional groups: Asia (China, Hong Kong SAR, India, Indonesia, Korea, Malaysia, the Philippines, Taiwan Province of China, and Thailand), Latin America (Argentina, Brazil, Chile, Colombia, Mexico, Peru, and Venezuela), and others (Czech Republic, Hungary, Israel, Pakistan, Poland, Russia, South Africa, and Turkey).

Figure 2.11. Selected Emerging Economies: Reserve Accumulation

Increases in reserves are apparent for most emerging markets when reserves are scaled by standard ratios.

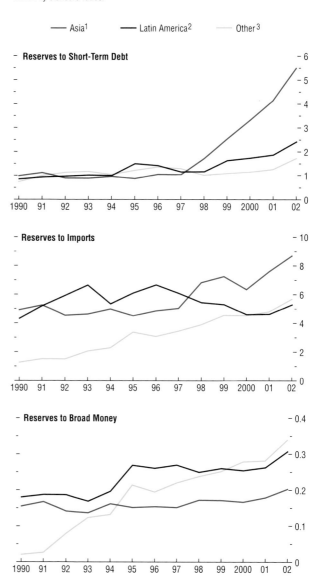

Sources: CEIC Data Company Limited; IMF, *International Financial Statistics;* and IMF staff calculations.
[1]China, Hong Kong SAR, India, Indonesia, Korea, Malaysia, the Philippines, Taiwan Province of China, and Thailand.
[2]Argentina, Brazil, Chile, Colombia, Mexico, Peru, and Venezuela.
[3]Czech Republic, Hungary, Israel, Pakistan, Poland, Russia, South Africa, and Turkey.

Figure 2.12. Selected Emerging Economies in Asia: Reserve Accumulation

In emerging economies in Asia, reserve buildup has been similar across exchange rate regimes.

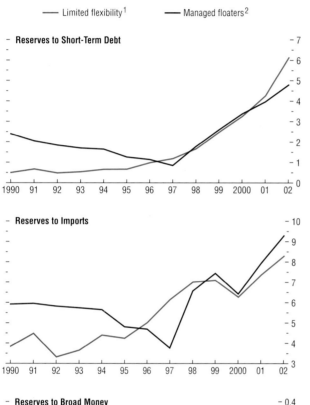

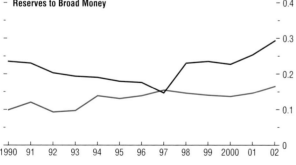

Sources: CEIC Data Company Limited; IMF, *International Financial Statistics;* Reinhart and Rogoff (2004); and IMF staff calculations.
[1]China, Hong Kong SAR, India, and Malaysia.
[2]Indonesia, Korea, the Philippines, Taiwan Province of China, and Thailand.

which high savings are typically channeled into bank deposits. The main exception to the general increase in reserves is Latin America, where the ratio of reserves to imports declined during the second half of the 1990s but that decline has partly reversed in 2002. Within emerging economies in Asia, both economies with limited exchange rate flexibility and those with managed floating exchange rates experienced large increases in reserves (Figure 2.12).

What Explains a Country's Reserve Holdings?

This section develops a richer framework to examine the recent increase in the level of reserves in emerging market economies, moving beyond simple ratios to an empirical model that simultaneously incorporates the various determinants of reserve holdings. Specifically, a multivariate regression model is used to explore the factors discussed above, using data from 1980 through 2002 to capture the most recent surge in reserves.[27] The explanatory variables used in the analysis are the empirical counterparts of the factors discussed above for which data are available (unfortunately, too few historical data on short-term debt are available). The model is estimated using panel data for 122 emerging market countries from 1980 to 1996 and the remaining years are used to compare out-of-sample forecasts with actual reserve buildups.[28]

The simple correlations between reserves and each of the explanatory variables are consistent with the theoretical predictions (Table 2.2). As expected, real reserves are positively and significantly correlated with indicators of economic size (real GDP per capita and population) and

[27]Detailed data on the currency composition of reserves necessary to calculate the impact of valuation changes are not available. However, valuation changes are not believed to have a large input, because most reserves are held in U.S. dollar–denominated assets, and the period under investigation includes times of both U.S. dollar strength and weakness.
[28]This work builds on Aizenman and Marion (2002a, 2002b) by expanding the set of explanatory variables to include measures of financial openness, potential for capital flight, and opportunity cost, and extending the data set through 2002.

Table 2.2. Simple Regressions of Reserves on Explanatory Variables

(Sample: emerging economies, 1980–96)

	Dependent Variable: Real Reserves
Economic size	
Real GDP per capita	1.63**
Population	2.37**
Current account vulnerability	
Ratio of imports to GDP	0.57**
Trade openness	0.16
Export volatility	0.11+
Capital account vulnerability	
Financial openness	0.18
Ratio of broad money to GDP	0.15
Exchange rate flexibility	
Exchange rate volatility	−0.01**
Opportunity cost	
Nominal interest rate differential	−0.01**
Real interest differential	−0.01**

Source: IMF staff estimates.

Notes: All regressions include fixed effects; + denotes significance at 10 percent; * significance at 5 percent; and ** significance at 1 percent.

Table 2.3. Multiple-Variable Regression Results for Reserves

(Sample: emerging economies, 1980–96)

	Dependent Variable: Real Reserves
Real GDP per capita	1.44
	(6.23)**
Population	1.98
	(4.85)**
Imports to GDP	0.44
	(3.58)**
Export volatility	0.09
	(0.92)
Exchange rate volatility	−0.01
	(2.02)*
Number of observations	1,692
R^2	0.91

Source: Estimates based on country fixed effects and a constant.

Notes: Robust *t* statistics in parentheses; * denotes significance at 5 percent; ** denotes significance at 1 percent.

current account vulnerability (the ratio of imports to GDP and export volatility).[29] The correlations between real reserves and indicators of capital account vulnerability (financial openness and the ratio of broad money to GDP, which reflects the potential for capital flight) are correctly signed, but are not significant.[30] Consistent with theory, indicators of both exchange rate flexibility and the opportunity cost of holding reserves are negatively and significantly correlated with real reserves.[31]

The results of the multiple-variable analysis of the demand for reserves are largely in line with those of the simple correlations and with those in

the existing literature (Table 2.3).[32] Explanatory variables with insignificant estimated coefficients have been dropped from the regression, with the exception of export volatility, which has the expected sign and has been found by several other studies to be significant. The empirical model, which includes country fixed effects, accounts for over 90 percent of the variation in reserves and the results are robust.[33] As foreshadowed by the simple correlations, real reserves are positively and significantly related to economic size (both real GDP per capita and population) and current account vulnerability (the ratio of imports to GDP), and negatively and significantly related to exchange rate volatility.[34] Indicators of capital account vulnerability (financial openness

[29]Real reserves are defined as nominal reserves in U.S. dollars deflated by the U.S. consumer price index. Real GDP per capita and population are measured in logs. Export volatility is defined as the standard deviation of real export receipts.

[30]Financial openness is defined as the ratio of capital flows to GDP, which is highly correlated with the stock measure.

[31]Exchange rate volatility is defined as the standard deviation of monthly changes in the exchange rate against the U.S. dollar. The nominal interest differential is the domestic deposit rate minus the interest rate on U.S. treasury bills. The real interest differential deflates nominal interest rates by the respective consumer price inflation rates.

[32]See Flood and Marion (2002) and Aizenman and Marion (2002b).

[33]Four robustness tests were conducted. First, when reserves were redefined to include gold valued at market prices, the coefficient estimates and significance levels were essentially unchanged. Second, when a time trend was added (to take account of the fact that several explanatory variables may be trending and thus lead to spurious results), the main results were unchanged, but as expected the estimates of the coefficients on the trending real GDP per capita and population variables fell. Third, when the model was estimated through 2000, the results—coefficient estimates and forecasts—were consistent with the reported results, suggesting that there is no structural break in the late 1990s as a result of the financial crisis. Fourth, when the model was estimated over different country samples the results were similar.

[34]This analysis implicitly treats exchange rate volatility as an exogenous policy choice.

Figure 2.13. Selected Emerging Economies in Asia: Actual and Predicted Reserves
(Billions of U.S. dollars)

The rapid reserve accumulation in emerging economies in Asia between 1997 and 2001 is consistent with the evolution of fundamentals, but the acceleration in 2002 is not well explained. Reserves are now greater than predicted both in economies with limited exchange rate flexibility and in those with managed floating exchange rates.

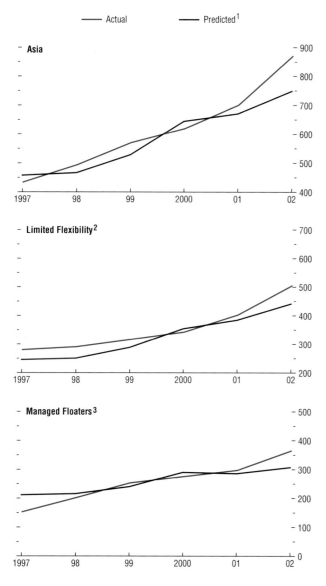

Sources: IMF, *International Financial Statistics;* and IMF staff estimates.
[1]Based on the empirical model described in the main text.
[2]China, Hong Kong SAR, India, and Malaysia.
[3]Indonesia, Korea, the Philippines, Taiwan Province of China, and Thailand.

and the ratio of broad money to GDP) are not significantly correlated with reserves. As in previous empirical studies, the opportunity cost of holding reserves is also not a significant determinant of reserves, reflecting measurement problems and the impact of the correlation between explanatory variables on the precision of the coefficient estimates.

How does the reserve buildup in emerging market economies between 1997 and 2002 compare with the model's forecasts based on evolving fundamentals? For emerging economies in Asia as a whole, reserve accumulation between 1997 and 2001 is broadly in line with the forecast, but the acceleration in 2002 is well in excess of what one would expect based on fundamentals (Figure 2.13).[35] The main drivers of the increase in predicted reserves are rising real GDP per capita and rising population, with the rising propensity to import also making a positive contribution, while falling export volatility subtracted from the predicted buildup. The lower panels of the figure show that, when emerging economies in Asia are divided into economies with limited exchange rate flexibility and those with managed floating exchange rates, most countries in both groups have experienced reserve buildups that exceed the model's forecasts.

By contrast, reserve accumulation in Latin America has been basically flat (Figure 2.14). Actual reserves have fallen slightly, while predicted reserves have risen gently, reflecting the positive impact of population growth that more than offsets negative contributions from falling real GDP per capita and declining import shares (especially in Argentina and Venezuela) as well as from rising exchange rate volatility. The lower panels of the figure show that Mexico is primarily responsible for the excess of actual reserves over predicted reserves in recent years. Also, actual reserves in Mexico have risen considerably over the past five years, while actual reserves in other emerging markets countries in Latin America have trended down.

[35]In some individual countries, excess reserves became apparent somewhat earlier.

Reserves in other emerging market countries have also increased, though significantly less sharply than in emerging economies in Asia (Figure 2.15). Until 2001, this increase was in line with that predicted by fundamentals, reflecting improving living standards, growing populations, and greater import penetration. The lower panels of the figure show that Russia is largely responsible for the excess of actual reserves over predicted reserves in recent years, reflecting mainly the large increase in the value of oil exports. Actual reserves in other emerging market countries in 2002 were broadly in line with predicted reserves.

What Are the Policy Implications?

The previous analysis suggests that foreign exchange reserves in some emerging market economies have recently increased more quickly than warranted by traditional considerations. The rapid accumulation of reserves between 1997 and 2001 was broadly in line with fundamentals, but the surge in reserves in 2002—which has continued into 2003—was above the level predicted by the model. This surge in reserves has been largely driven by increases in the current account and to a lesser extent by capital flows. Emerging market economies in Asia, as well as some others like Russia and Mexico, account for much of the excess of actual reserves over predicted reserves.

Holding excess reserves entails costs and benefits, which can be divided into three main categories: crisis prevention, domestic issues, and multilateral concerns.

Crisis Prevention

First, there is considerable evidence that higher reserves reduce both the likelihood of a crisis and the depth of a crisis, should one occur.[36] Thus, reserves serve as a cushion against

---

[36]There is by now a large empirical literature on Early Warning Systems (EWS), including Berg and Pattillo (1999a), Berg and others (1999), Edison (2000), and Goldstein, Kaminsky, and Reinhart (2000).

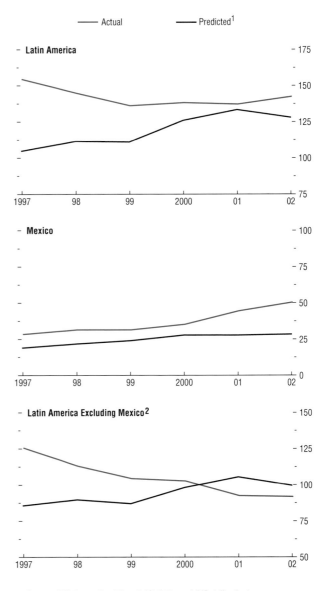

Figure 2.14. Selected Emerging Economies in Latin America: Actual and Predicted Reserves
(Billions of U.S. dollars)

Reserve holdings in Latin America have been relatively flat. Mexico's reserves have risen more quickly than predicted by fundamentals.

Sources: IMF, *International Financial Statistics;* and IMF staff estimates.
[1]Based on the empirical model described in the main text.
[2]Argentina, Brazil, Chile, Colombia, Peru, and Venezuela.

Figure 2.15. Selected Other Emerging Economies: Actual and Predicted Reserves
(Billions of U.S. dollars)

The reserve buildup over the past five years is broadly in line with fundamentals, except for the surge in 2002. Actual reserves in Russia are now well above their predicted levels.

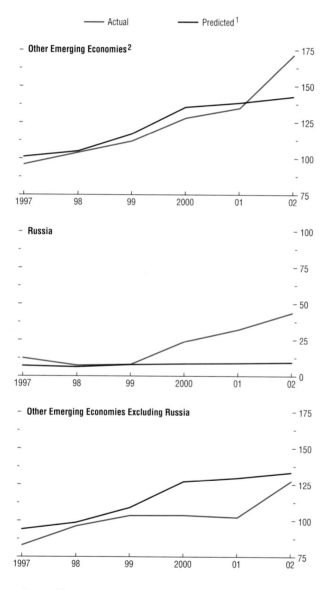

Sources: IMF, *International Financial Statistics;* and IMF staff estimates.
[1]Based on empirical model described in the main text.
[2]Czech Republic, Hungary, Israel, Pakistan, Poland, Russia, South Africa, and Turkey.

Table 2.4. Benefits of Eliminating Consumption Volatility (Upper Bounds)
(Percent of GDP)

	Risk Aversion	
	Low	High
Output volatility		
Low	0.11	0.21
High	0.22	0.45

Note: Calculations based on Obstfeld and Rogoff (1999), p. 330, equation 75. Ljungqvist and Sargent (2000) suggest that values of relative risk aversion between 2 (low) and 4 (high) are reasonable.

an undesired shortage of international currency that would damage the economy. One way of thinking about the value of this cushion is in terms of smoothing consumption. An upper bound on the value of holding reserves is a country's willingness to pay for the elimination of all consumption volatility. Clearly, this willingness to pay increases with risk aversion and output volatility. As shown in Table 2.4, this willingness to pay could range from zero to about ½ percent of GDP, given sensible values of risk aversion and output volatility.[37] Given the experience in emerging market countries over the past decade, it would certainly be understandable if this motive were a factor behind the reserve buildup.[38] To the extent that higher reserves lower crisis vulnerability, they can also help to lower borrowing costs and limit exposure to changing market sentiment.

However, there are limits to the level of reserves needed to prevent financial crises. The empirical literature on the emerging market crises of the 1990s, including work done at the IMF, suggests that a ratio of reserves to short-term debt above 1 marks an important reduction in crisis vulnerability, as long as the current account balance is not out of line and the exchange rate is not misaligned (Box 2.3). The rationale is that, if reserves exceed short-term debt, then a country

[37]This calculation is based on Obstfeld and Rogoff (1999), who show that the cost of exclusion from global capital markets is a function of how much volatility a country faces.
[38]Lee (2003) suggests that the insurance motive helps to explain the high level of reserves held by many Asian economies.

Table 2.5. Illustrative Sterilization Costs
(Percent of GDP)

	Expected Depreciation	
	0 Percent	5 Percent
Interest spread		
5 percent	0.5	0.0
10 percent	1.0	0.5

Note: Table is based on the assumption that reserve accumulation is 10 percent of GDP.

Table 2.6. Selected Emerging Market Countries: Sources of Reserve Accumulation,[1] 2001–02
(Billions of U.S. dollars)

	Increase in Reserves	Current Account	Capital and Financial Account[2]	Errors and Omissions
Asia[3]	252.5	194.0	50.3	8.2
Latin America[4]	1.7	−53.3	63.1	−8.0
Other[5]	39.7	38.9	9.4	−8.6

Source: World Economic Outlook database.
[1]In balance of payments terms.
[2]Excluding change in reserves.
[3]China, Hong Kong SAR, India, Indonesia, Korea, Malaysia, the Philippines, Taiwan Province of China, and Thailand.
[4]Argentina, Brazil, Chile, Colombia, Mexico, Peru, and Venezuela.
[5]Czech Republic, Hungary, Israel, Pakistan, Poland, Russia, South Africa, and Turkey.

can be expected to meet its obligations over the forthcoming year and thus avoid rollover problems that stem from concerns about liquidity. While the ratio of reserves to short-term debt is now between 1 and 2 in Mexico, it is much higher in emerging economies in Asia, so there is a real question about whether a further buildup in reserves in these latter economies would do much to reduce crisis vulnerability.[39]

In addition, to the extent that rapid reserve accumulation reflects exchange rate rigidity, it might actually *increase* vulnerability to a crisis. Exchange rate rigidity can boost capital inflows by reinforcing the perception of a one-way bet, given a positive interest differential. The prolonged buildup in interest-sensitive capital inflows, and associated increase in unhedged foreign currency exposure in the corporate sector, can increase the economy's vulnerability, and possibly even increase the risk of a crisis. In conjunction with exchange rate rigidity, a high level of reserves can create moral hazard in the private sector by discouraging companies and households from taking out adequate insurance against the risk of exchange rate variability.

Domestic Costs

Second, there are important costs to holding and accumulating foreign exchange reserves.

The cost of holding reserves is the difference between the interest paid on the country's public debt and the interest earned on reserves, typically the interest rate on U.S. treasury or similar debt.[40] In most emerging market countries, domestic assets earn a higher return than foreign assets. In addition, the reserve buildup is typically sterilized—that is, the central bank reduces net domestic assets to offset the increase in net foreign assets.[41] The cost of sterilization depends positively on the amount of reserve accumulation and the interest spread (net of the risk premium), and negatively on the expected depreciation of the domestic currency. The cost of sterilizing a reserve accumulation of 10 percent of GDP (which has been fairly typical recently in emerging economies in Asia) can range from zero to 1 percent of GDP, depending on the interest spread and the expected exchange rate depreciation (Table 2.5).[42]

Rapid reserve accumulation may also reflect an undervalued exchange rate. Table 2.6 shows that while Latin America (including Mexico) ran a current account deficit over the past two years,

---

[39]Also, reserves help to prevent crises only if the crises are of the speculative attack variety; if the fundamentals are out of line, then additional reserves do not help and actually may make things worse, because of the associated fiscal costs (Kletzer and Mody, 2000).

[40]An increase in reserves implies an equal increase in public debt; equivalently, if the additional reserves were not added to the central bank's assets, then the same amount of public debt could have been purchased by the central bank.

[41]If the reserve buildup is not sterilized, then it boosts base money growth, fueling inflationary pressures, as in China and Russia.

[42]This range is somewhat higher than the estimates in the literature—¼ to ½ percent of GDP (see Khan and Reinhart, 1995)—because of the large assumed reserve accumulation.

Box 2.3. Reserves and Short-Term Debt

Following the crises in several emerging market countries in the late 1990s, the assessment of reserve adequacy for crisis prevention has increasingly focused on the ratio of reserves to short-term external debt by remaining maturity (see IMF, 2000; and Wijnholds and Kapteyn, 2001). While other factors such as the scope for capital flight by residents and the quality of private debt management also need to be taken into account, short-term debt is the main source of capital outflow and the capital (and not the current) account is a key source of external risk.[1] A large empirical literature has found the ratio of reserves to short-term debt to be closely related to the likelihood and depth of crises.[2]

A benchmark value of 1 for the ratio of reserves to short-term debt is important for crisis prevention. If reserves exceed short-term debt, then—in the absence of a current account deficit and capital flight by nonresidents—a country can be expected to meet its external cash flow needs at least for the forthcoming year, which can help prevent rollover problems that stem from concerns about liquidity. Indeed, capital market access for emerging economies that are fundamentally solvent does not usually dry up for more than three to six months. Thus, a ratio of reserves to short-term debt of 1 provides a cushion to weather interruptions in capital market access and reestablish market confidence.

The practical relevance of the benchmark of 1 for the ratio of reserves to short-term debt is supported by formal empirical work. Bussière and Mulder (1999) estimate the level of reserves that corresponds to averting a crisis during three periods of external financing pressures for emerging market countries. They find that the necessary level broadly corresponds to a ratio of

Selected Emerging Markets: Ratio of Reserves to Short-Term Debt and Crisis Indicator

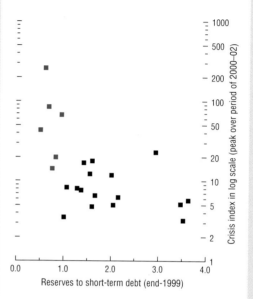

Sources: BIS *Consolidated International Banking Statistics;* IMF *International Financial Statistics;* and IMF staff estimates.

reserves to short-term debt of 1, though an external current account deficit or a significantly overvalued exchange rate imply significantly higher required reserves.[3] This is illustrated in the figure, which shows for selected emerging market countries a scatter plot of the ratio at the end of 1999 and crisis pressures over 2000–02. Crisis pressures are measured as a weighted average of the loss in reserves and the change in the exchange rate, with the weight varying inversely with the variance. Countries with a ratio of reserves to short-term debt less than 1—that is, short-term debt

Note: The main authors of this box are Christian Mulder and Nicolas Blancher.

[1]For developing countries with little or no access to private capital markets, the focus remains on current account–related measures of reserve adequacy, including the level of imports.

[2]See Berg and Pattillo (1999a), Berg and others (1999), Edison (2000), and Goldstein, Kaminsky, and Reinhart (2000).

[3]Note that additional reserves may be second-best to policies such as improved private sector debt risk management, which reduce the need for reserves, and may in fact worsen risk management if reserve buildup is associated with excessive nominal exchange rate stability.

that exceeded reserves—tended to suffer greater crisis pressures during 2000–02.[4]

[4]For reasons of data availability and uniformity, short-term external debt is based on the Joint BIS-IMF-OECD–World Bank Statistics on External Debt (http://www1.oecd.org/dac/debt/). Specifically, it sums lines G (Liabilities to banks from the consolidated BIS statistics), H (debt securities issued abroad), and I (nonbank trade credits, official and officially guaranteed by 25 OECD countries).

In sum, the ratio of reserves to short-term debt is an important indicator of reserve adequacy for crisis prevention for countries with sizable but uncertain private capital market access. While the threshold level of reserves needed to avoid a crisis is difficult to determine precisely, a ratio of reserves to short-term debt of 1 serves as a useful benchmark, absent an external current account deficit or a significantly overvalued exchange rate.

emerging economies in Asia and other emerging market countries ran large current account surpluses. While exchange rate depreciation can help to boost external demand in the aftermath of a crisis, it eventually becomes important to shift to domestic sources of growth. An undervalued exchange rate can have potentially harmful effects on growth and welfare by reducing consumption, lowering domestic investment, and excessively increasing exposure to external shocks. In general, an appropriately valued exchange rate enhances the economy's ability to adjust to rapid productivity growth and greater trade and financial integration with the global economy.

Multilateral Concerns

Finally, from a multilateral perspective, the current account surpluses in many emerging market countries are the largest counterpart to the U.S. current account deficit. In 2002, the current account surplus for emerging economies in Asia was $133 billion, larger than that of Japan ($113 billion) or the euro area ($72 billion). And while faster growth of domestic demand in the euro area and Japan would clearly be welcome, neither area appears particularly well placed to generate this in the short run. Thus, an eventual narrowing of the U.S. current account deficit from its present unsustainable level will likely require emerging economies in Asia to share in the adjustment, to prevent an undue burden of adjustment on other countries.

However, during the recent period of U.S. dollar weakness, the relative price adjustment has in fact fallen on the euro area, along with some small industrial countries. In emerging economies in Asia, the rapid reserve buildup and stability of exchange rates against the U.S. dollar have meant that real effective exchange rates have actually depreciated. As a region with highly open economies, emerging economies in Asia have a strong interest in the smooth rotation of demand from the United States to other parts of the world, to ensure that global growth does not slow unnecessarily and to maintain the orderly adjustment of exchange rates, not least to keep protectionist pressures at bay. This region is clearly an important part of the global economy, accounting for about 20 percent of world trade.

In conclusion, the rapid buildup of foreign exchange reserves in some emerging economies is understandable from a number of perspectives, but may now be approaching the point where some slowdown in the rate of accumulation is desirable. From both the domestic and the multilateral perspective, there would be advantages for growth in emerging economies in Asia to become more reliant on domestic demand, accompanied by a steady reduction in current account surpluses over the medium term. While such a strategy involves many elements, including further progress in structural reforms, one key aspect will be to allow greater exchange rate flexibility. It would be helpful for countries with managed floats to intervene less in the foreign exchange market and for some countries where exchange rate flexibility has been limited—notably China—to gradually move to greater flexibility, as has long been advocated by the IMF.

How Concerned Should Developing Countries Be About G-3 Exchange Rate Volatility?

The main author of this essay is Nikola Spatafora. Bennett Sutton provided research assistance; Alessandro Rebucci and Susanna Mursula implemented the Global Economy Model simulations.

The post–Bretton Woods floating exchange rate period has been characterized by volatile, unpredictable exchange rate movements. Such unpredictability can be costly, both directly and through the potential for associated exchange rate misalignments. Indeed, these issues have come to the fore over recent years as the dollar appreciated rapidly against other major currencies, resulting in widening international imbalances that are an increasing source of policy concern (see, for instance, Chapter II of the September 2002 *World Economic Outlook*). Even after the recent depreciation of the dollar, in particular against the euro, the possibility of a rapid realignment of the major currencies remains a significant risk for the global economy.

This essay examines the potential spillover effects on developing countries of volatility across the three major currency areas, the United States, Japan, and the euro area—a topic that has received limited attention in the existing literature. The impact of such exchange rate movements on advanced economies has already been extensively analyzed and generally found to be small (see, for instance, Appendix 1.2 of the April 2002 *World Economic Outlook*, and Appendix II of the May 2001 *World Economic Outlook*). Linked to this, the potential effects of coordinating industrial country policies to lower their exchange rate volatility are generally believed to be limited

Figure 2.16. Industrial Country Real Exchange Rate (RER) Volatility

(Standard deviation of monthly percentage growth rate of the RER over the preceding two years)

The volatility of industrial country RERs increased substantially after the collapse of the Bretton Woods system.

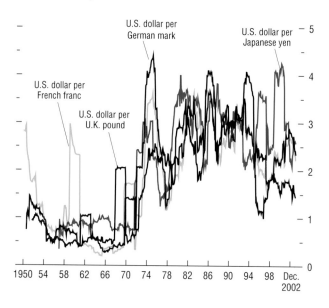

Sources: Global Financial Data; IMF, *International Financial Statistics;* U.S. Board of Governors of the Federal Reserve System, *Banking and Monetary Statistics;* and IMF staff estimates.

and ambiguous.[43] However, developing countries could be particularly vulnerable to exchange rate spillovers because the less developed nature of their financial markets and their limited ability to borrow in their own currencies could hamper adjustment to external disturbances. For instance, it has been argued that the Asian and Argentine crises partly reflected inflexibilities, including formal or informal dollar pegs, which made it difficult to adjust to G-3 exchange rate shocks, and in particular to the misalignments associated with an appreciation of the dollar.

Why Might G-3 Exchange Rate Volatility Be a Concern?

The analysis starts from some broad observations.

- *Industrial country real exchange rate (RER) volatility increased substantially after the breakdown of the Bretton Woods system* (Figure 2.16). In particular, there were significant spikes in volatility after the oil price shocks, around the periods of rapid dollar realignment starting in 1985 and in 1995, and again in the late 1990s. This short-run volatility has been accompanied by significant long-run G-3 exchange rate misalignments, as typified by the sharp dollar overvaluation of the mid-1980s.
- *Even after Bretton Woods, between one-half and two-thirds of all developing countries de facto continued pegging their exchange rate to industrial country currencies* (Figure 2.17). The exchange rate inflexibility induced by such pegs may increase their potential vulnerability to G-3 exchange rate instability.[44]

---

[43]Most studies find that international monetary policy coordination is likely to yield few benefits, relative to having the G-3 central banks follow good domestic monetary policies; in addition, effective international coordination could actually require greater exchange rate volatility. See Rogoff (2003) and Obstfeld and Rogoff (2002).

[44]Pegs remained popular among both large and small countries and across all major regions, including the Western Hemisphere, Africa, and developing Asia (the last less so after the crises of the late 1990s). Most pegs were to the dollar, but African countries often pegged to the French franc.

Figure 2.17. Share of Countries on a Hard or Crawling Peg

(Percent of countries within group with de facto pegged exchange rate regime, simple average unless otherwise noted)

Even after the breakdown of the Bretton Woods system, many developing countries de facto continued pegging their exchange rate to industrial country currencies.

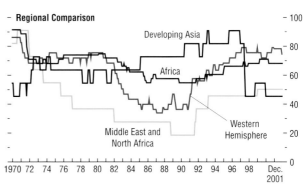

Sources: Reinhart and Rogoff (2002); and IMF staff calculations.
[1]Excludes transition economies.

Figure 2.18. Volatility in Industrial Countries' Real Exchange Rates (RERs) and Developing Countries' Real Effective Exchange Rates (REERs)[1]
(Standard deviation of monthly percentage growth rate of the exchange rate over the preceding year)

There is a significant correlation between volatility in industrial countries' RERs, and in developing countries' REERs.

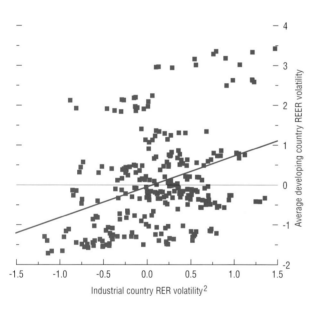

Sources: IMF, *International Financial Statistics;* and IMF staff estimates.
  [1]The volatility of an exchange rate is defined as the standard deviation of its monthly percentage growth rate over the preceding year. Here, all volatilities are plotted as deviations from their country-specific means, to control for fixed country-level characteristics. Further, the volatilities at any given point in time are averaged across all developing countries, to abstract from the significant cross-sectional heterogeneity discussed in the text.
  [2]Defined as a weighted average of the volatilities of the real U.S. dollar / yen and U.S. dollar / deutsche mark exchange rates (see Appendix 2.2 for details).

- *Partly as a result, the volatilities of major industrial countries' real exchange rates and of developing countries' real effective exchange rates (REER) are correlated.* Increases in G-3 RER volatility are on average associated with an increase of over one-half the size in the volatility of developing countries' own REER (Figure 2.18).[45]
- *Greater volatility in developing countries' REER has been associated with greater exchange rate misalignments.* Shocks to real exchange rates are sufficiently persistent for volatility to translate into longer-lived fluctuations. Overall, if REER volatility increases by one standard deviation, then the average misalignment (defined as the average deviation of the exchange rate from trend) increases by about 5 percentage points (Figure 2.19).[46]

The thrust of the limited existing literature is that G-3 exchange rate instability can indeed disrupt developing countries through both trade and finance channels. On the trade side, depending on a developing country's exchange rate regime and on its trade partners, G-3 exchange rate volatility may lead to volatility and uncertainty in the developing country's REER, and/or may require a costly geographical reorientation of trade as relative competitiveness changes vis-à-vis different partners. Both effects increase the riskiness and reduce the attractiveness of trade and investment. This is particularly true in developing economies, which are characterized by a faster pass-through of exchange rates into prices and limited access of firms to financing.[47]

Building on these financial issues, developing countries' financial markets are also less sophisticated. In many cases, the absence of (liquid) futures markets precludes all but costly hedging (say, through the building up of reserves, as discussed in the second essay in this chapter).

  [45]G-3 RER volatility is defined as a weighted average of the volatilities of the real dollar/yen and dollar/deutsche mark exchange rates (see Appendix 2.2 for details).
  [46]These estimates assume the underlying equilibrium path of the exchange rate is relatively stable over time (see Appendix 2.2 for details).
  [47]In addition, the floating rate period was associated with greater volatility in many commodity prices (Cashin and McDermott, 2002, and Cuddington and Liang, 1999).

Further, the fact that developing countries can generally only borrow in foreign currency, and their limited diversification with respect to the currency composition of external debt, suggest that exchange rate swings may have important effects on wealth and debt sustainability (see Chapter III). This limited ability to borrow and lend implies that exchange rate volatility may have larger welfare effects than in advanced economies (Bergin and Tchakarov, 2002).

Indeed, if trade and debt are denominated in different currencies, this may cause tensions for policymakers. In particular, it may be difficult to stabilize both competitiveness and debt service in the face of volatility in G-3 exchange rates (Slavov, 2002). This mismatch between trade and financial links, which has not been analyzed empirically before, is measured here in terms of the correlation between the geographical structure of trade links and the currency composition of external debt (see Appendix 2.2 for details). This correlation is in general far from perfect, and varies widely across countries (Figure 2.20). Clearly, these issues are most important for emerging markets that enjoy significant access to private capital flows, rather than poorer countries whose debt service is mainly on concessional, less volatile terms.

The Argentine crisis provides an illustration of how these effects can help contribute to a costly crisis. During the 1990s, Argentina was pegged to the dollar and borrowed in this currency. Its largest trading partners, however, were Brazil (reflecting the impact of Mercosur) and the European Union. Over much of this period, Brazil's currency was pegged to the dollar, so that a large share of Argentina's trade was tied to the U.S. currency. However, after Brazil's exchange rate crisis in 1999, the Brazilian *real* depreciated sharply and started floating. Argentina then faced both a sharp loss in competitiveness and an increased mismatch between its trade and debt. Given the latter, the former could not be remedied without undermining the sustainability of Argentina's (dollar-denominated) debt burden.

Any assessment of the costs of industrial country exchange rate volatility, however, must also

Figure 2.19. Volatility and Misalignment of Developing Countries' Real Effective Exchange Rates (REERs)

Volatility in developing countries' REERs is also associated with REER misalignments.

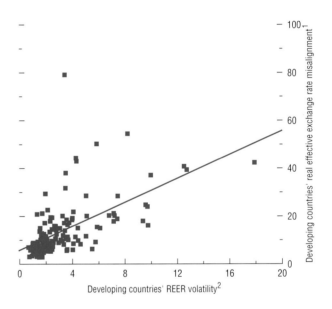

Sources: IMF, *International Financial Statistics;* and IMF staff calculations.
[1] Misalignment is defined as the absolute value of the 12-month moving average of the detrended real effective exchange rate. In this figure, the misalignment for any given country is averaged over all observations.
[2] Standard deviation of monthly percentage growth rate of the REER over the preceding year. In this figure the volatility for any given country is averaged over all periods.

Figure 2.20. Correlation Between the Structure of Trade Links and of Financial Links[1]

The correlation between the geographical structure of trade and the currency composition of external debt varies widely, and is generally lower in crisis countries.

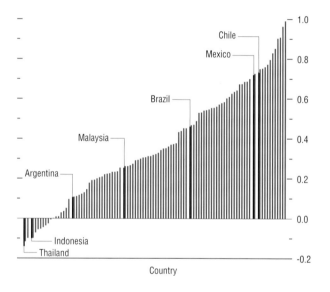

Country

Sources: IMF, *International Financial Statistics;* World Bank, *World Development indicators;* and IMF staff estimates.
[1]Defined as follows: two sets of weights are constructed for each country, at each date. The first is based on the currency composition of debt, using the major currencies: U.S. dollar, Japanese yen, German deutsche mark, British pound, French franc, Swiss franc, and others. The second set of weights gives the geographical composition of trade, broken down in an analogous way, with the exception that all trade with any country that is pegged to, say, the U.S. dollar is for these purposes counted as part of the trade with the United States. Finally, we compute the correlation between these two sets of weights. For this chart, we also take averages for each country over all available observations.

take into account two countervailing considerations. First, G-3 exchange rate volatility is only one among several sources of uncertainty, both domestic and external, affecting developing countries. Even confining ourselves to exchange rate instability, it should be noted that this varies widely among developing countries. Further, the "average" exchange rate volatility in developing countries is larger, and fluctuates more over time, than is true for industrial countries, even though many developing countries peg their exchange rates (Figure 2.21).[48] Second, reducing exchange rate uncertainty across the G-3 could result in more volatility in other variables. In particular, and even though it is difficult to assess the precise tradeoff, it could lead to higher volatility in G-3 interest rates and output (Reinhart and Reinhart, 2001, 2002), which would impose its own costs (see Chapter II of the October 2001 *World Economic Outlook*). Hence, it is even possible that acting to reduce industrial country exchange rate volatility could increase overall developing country instability.[49]

What Do the Data Tell Us?

Quantitatively, how important are all these arguments? The large literature analyzing the effect of volatility in an industrial country's own exchange rate on its trade generally points to small effects (MacDonald, 2000; McKenzie, 1999; Côté, 1994). The impact, however, appears to be larger in developing countries, consistent with their less sophisticated financial structure (Calvo and Reinhart, 2000, summarize the literature).[50]

[48]For instance, in our sample, the mean level of exchange rate volatility across developing countries, its standard deviation across countries, and its standard deviation over time are all much larger than average G-3 exchange rate volatility.

[49]That said, to the extent that G-3 exchange rate volatility reflects the presence of bubbles, sterilized intervention might be used to deflate such bubbles, reducing instability in both exchange rates *and* interest rates. See, for instance, Bergsten (2003).

[50]The evidence also suggests that currency unions stimulate trade significantly (Rose, 2000, 2001, 2002; Parsley and Wei, 2001).

Turning to the specific issue of the effect of G-3 exchange rate instability on developing countries, the limited number of existing studies provide mixed evidence. Esquivel and Larraín (2002) find relatively large effects: a 1 percentage point increase in G-3 exchange rate volatility reduces real exports of developing countries by about 2 percent, and increases the probability of exchange rate crises by 2½ percentage points. Likewise, dollar-euro volatility has been found to negatively affect domestic employment and domestic investment in Argentina and Brazil (Belke and Gros, 2002).

On the other hand, Reinhart and Reinhart (2001, 2002) find that periods of relatively high volatility in G-3 real exchange rates are not associated with significantly diminished capital flows to developing countries, with lower portfolio investment being offset by higher foreign direct investment. In contrast, they find that periods of relatively high volatility in U.S. short-term interest rates do appear associated with sharp changes in capital flows. Also, most studies of the factors that predict exchange rate or debt crises emphasize the role of exchange rate misalignment, rather than volatility (see, for instance, Kaminsky, Lizondo, and Reinhart, 1998).

To illustrate and refine these findings, a broad sample of over 120 developing countries over the period 1980–2001 is now examined. Briefly, cross-country panel regressions are used to analyze whether G-3 exchange rate volatility affects trade, capital flows, and/or the probability of an exchange rate crisis in developing countries (Appendix 2.2 provides more details about the data and methodology). Throughout, standard specifications are adopted, augmented by measures of G-3 RER volatility, as well as measures of a country's own REER volatility, misalignment, and/or trade-finance mismatch (depending on the specific regression). The latter variables also help capture the potential indirect effects of industrial country volatility. Results are reported for the full sample, for countries on an exchange rate peg (to help examine the impact of a country's exchange rate regime), and for a narrow sample of 21 emerging markets that

Figure 2.21. Developing Country Real Effective Exchange Rate (REER) Volatility
(Standard deviation of monthly percentage growth rate of the REER over the preceding year)

There are huge differences across developing countries in REER volatility, reflecting the impact of many factors other than G-3 real exchange rate volatility (RER).

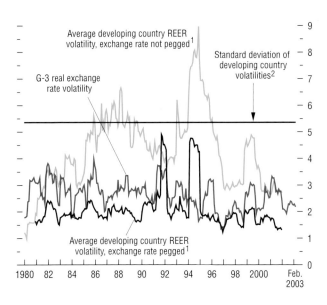

Sources: IMF, *Direction of Trade Statistics;* and World Bank, *Global Development Finance.*
[1] Simple average of volatility measure across all countries in group for each month.
[2] Standard deviation of volatility measure for all developing countries over all periods.

Table 2.7. Impact of Exchange Rate Volatility on Trade and on Emerging Market Capital Inflows[1]
(Percent change)

Impact on	Of	Full Sample	Exchange Rate Pegs	Emerging Markets
Exports	Increase in G-3 RER volatility[2]	−0.28	−0.70	0.79
	Increase in REER volatility[3]	**−3.01***	**−1.65***	5.59
	Memorandum: indirect impact of eliminating all G-3 RER volatility, through lower REER volatility[4]	**0.95****	**1.48****	−2.90
Imports	Increase in G-3 RER volatility[2]	0.21	0.50	**0.77***
	Increase in REER volatility[3]	**−3.75***	0.38	**−1.69***
	Memorandum: indirect impact of eliminating all G-3 RER volatility, through lower REER volatility[4]	**1.18****	−0.34	**0.88***
Total capital inflows	Increase in G-3 RER volatility[2]	. . .	. . .	**−4.27***
	Increase in REER volatility[3]	. . .	. . .	**−6.52****
	Memorandum: indirect impact of eliminating all G-3 RER volatility, through lower REER volatility[4]	. . .	. . .	**3.44****
Foreign direct investment	Increase in G-3 RER volatility[2]	. . .	. . .	2.56
	Increase in REER volatility[3]	. . .	. . .	**−5.48***
	Memorandum: indirect impact of eliminating all G-3 RER volatility, through lower REER volatility[4]	. . .	. . .	**2.93****

Source: IMF staff calculations.

[1]The results for exports, imports, total capital flows, and foreign direct investment (FDI) are based on panel regressions for, respectively, 133, 131, 132, and 124 developing countries, over 1980–2001, using monthly data. All coefficients are computed using procedures that allow for nonstationarity. Standard errors are corrected for autocorrelation and groupwise-heteroscedasticity. Statistically significant results are reported in bold type. The symbols *, **, and *** denote statistical significance at the 10 percent, 5 percent, and 1 percent level, respectively. In the export regression, the dependent variable is exports/GDP. Controls include the REER, a trade-share-weighted index of trade partners' real GDP, and a time trend. In the import regression, the dependent variable is imports/GDP. Controls include the REER, real GDP, and a time trend. In the total capital flow regression, the dependent variable is total capital flows/GDP. In the FDI regression, the dependent variable is FDI/GDP. In both of these last regressions, controls include world real GDP, the LIBOR, capital account openness, and a time trend.

[2]Given by a one-standard-deviation increase in our measure of G-3 RER volatility. The latter is defined as the standard deviation of the monthly percentage growth rate of a weighted average of the U.S. dollar/deutsche mark and U.S. dollar/yen RER (with weights as described in Appendix 2.2) over the preceding 12 months.

[3]Given by a one-standard-deviation increase in our measure of REER volatility. The latter is defined as the standard deviation of the monthly percentage REER growth rate over the preceding year.

[4]This calculation uses the results of the above regressions, but focuses on the indirect impact of G-3 RER volatility on trade and capital inflows through REER volatility. Specifically, we estimate separately the correlation between REER volatility and G-3 RER volatility, multiply this correlation coefficient by the mean G-3 RER volatility in the sample, and then multiply by the impact of a one-unit-increase in REER volatility.

enjoy greater access to international financial markets.[51]

Our analysis suggests that the direct impact of G-3 exchange rate volatility on trade is probably small but that indirect effects through a country's own REER volatility are significant (Table 2.7). The direct link between G-3 RER volatility and trade is statistically weak, occasionally incorrectly signed, and minor in magnitude, even in countries on an exchange rate peg. For instance, a one standard deviation increase in G-3 RER volatility is associated with at most a 0.7 percent

reduction in exports.[52] In contrast, a one standard deviation increase in REER volatility is associated with reductions in exports and imports of 3 percent and 4 percent, respectively. The impact on exports remains significant when one focuses on those countries with exchange rate pegs, although its magnitude falls by about half, as the REER is less volatile under such regimes. The effects are harder to detect when examining only emerging markets, possibly because of the small sample. Overall, these results suggest that increased G-3 RER volatility reduces developing

[51]Results for the sample of developing countries excluding these 21 emerging markets are very similar to the results for the full sample. Differences between the full sample and the countries on an exchange rate peg roughly mirror, although with the opposite sign, those between the full sample and the countries not on a peg.

[52]The estimated impact is weaker than found by Esquivel and Larraín (2002), largely because we control for own-currency REER volatility.

Table 2.8. Determinants of Exchange Rate Crises[1]
(Change in percentage points)

	Probability of Exchange Rate Crises		
	Full Sample	Exchange Rate Pegs	Emerging Markets
Increase in G-3 RER volatility[2]	1.41	1.14	−0.42
Increase in real effective exchange rate (REER) overvaluation[3]	8.58***	7.28***	6.42***
Increased correlation between geographical structure of trade and currency composition of debt[3]	−1.28***	−1.22***	−4.73***
Increase in external debt/GDP[3]	3.75***	3.75***	6.80***
Increase in exports/GDP[3]	−3.97***	−3.17***	−6.70***
Regional contagion[4]	2.94***	0.36*	2.45***
Memorandum			
Indirect impact of eliminating all G-3 RER volatility, through lower likelihood of REER overvaluation[5]	−1.12**	−2.38***	−1.13**

Source: IMF staff calculations.

[1]The results are based on a panel probit regression for 88 developing countries, over 1980–2001, using monthly data. The dependent variable is whether an exchange rate crisis occurred in the subsequent 24 months. Standard errors are corrected for autocorrelation and groupwise-heteroscedasticity. Statistically significant results are reported in bold type. The symbols *, **, and *** denote statistical significance at the 10 percent, 5 percent, and 1 percent level, respectively.

[2]Given by a one-standard-deviation increase in our measure of G-3 RER volatility. The latter is defined as the standard deviation of the monthly percentage growth rate of a weighted average of the U.S. dollar/deutsche mark and U.S. dollar/yen RER (with weights as described in Appendix 2.2) over the preceding year.

[3]Given by a one-standard-deviation increase in the relevant variable.

[4]Defined as a crisis occurring in at least one other country in the region.

[5]This calculation uses the results of the panel regression above, but focuses on the indirect impact of G-3 RER volatility on the probability of a crisis through the likelihood of REER overvaluation. Specifically, we estimate separately the correlation between REER overvaluation and G-3 volatility, multiply this correlation coefficient by the mean G-3 RER volatility in the sample, and then multiply by the impact of a one unit increase in REER overvaluation.

countries' trade levels principally through its impact on their own REER volatility.

Own REER volatility also matters for capital flows to emerging markets. In our broad sample, total capital inflows display no clear link with volatility, whether in a country's REER or in G-3 real exchange rates. However, it may be more relevant to focus on the emerging markets, which account for the bulk of private sector capital inflows. In these countries, the direct impact of G-3 RER volatility remains statistically weak but own REER volatility is associated with significantly lower capital inflows (see Table 2.7). Among the various components of the financial account, foreign direct investment (FDI) is most clearly affected by REER volatility, perhaps because returns on FDI projects often require a long time horizon, with correspondingly limited hedging opportunities.

The connection between G-3 exchange rate volatility and exchange rate crises in developing countries is also indirect, this time coming through misalignments and trade/finance mismatches. We analyzed whether G-3 RER volatility

increases the likelihood of exchange rate crises in developing countries, using a probit regression of a type familiar from the literature on Early Warning Systems (reviewed in Berg, Borensztein, and Pattillo, 2003; see also Berg and Pattillo, 1999a, 1999b; and Kaminsky, Lizondo, and Reinhart, 1998). Again, the results indicate no robust direct link between G-3 RER volatility and the probability of a crisis (Table 2.8). However, if the degree of REER overvaluation increases by one standard deviation, then the probability that an exchange rate crisis will occur over the subsequent two years rises by almost 9 percentage points. As increases in the volatility of developing countries' REER are associated with larger misalignments, this provides an indirect link to G-3 volatility. Simply put, these results indicate that pegging becomes more difficult and less meaningful when G-3 exchange rate volatility is high. Greater trade-finance mismatches also significantly increase the probability of an exchange rate crisis. At the extreme, going from no mismatch to a complete mismatch would increase average crisis probabilities by 8 percentage points. Of course, the decision on where to finance also depends on other factors, such as the depth and efficiency of alternative markets.

Overall, our results then suggest that G-3 RER volatility mainly affects developing countries indirectly, by increasing the variability of their own REER or the chance of misalignment. These indirect effects through own REER volatility or misalignment depend on countries' exchange rate regimes so that the impact of G-3 exchange rate volatility is partly reflected through the prism of their own policy choices. To quantify the indirect effects of G-3 RER volatility, one possible thought experiment is to assume that all volatility in G-3 real exchange rates could be costlessly eliminated. Then, given the estimated correlation between volatility in G-3 real exchange rates and both volatility in developing countries' REER and our measure of developing countries' overvaluation:

- exports and imports would increase on average by about 1 percent, and perhaps slightly more in countries on an exchange rate peg;
- capital flows to emerging markets would increase by 3½ percent; and
- the average probability of crises would decrease, but by less than 2½ percentage points.

These numbers clearly represent an upper limit, given that industrial countries' exchange rates did in fact display some volatility also under the Bretton Woods system and that any reduction in such volatility might be associated with greater G-3 interest rate instability. Even so, the effects are small, compared with other feasible policy changes. To put matters into perspective, it has been estimated that limited increases in trade barriers, as measured by a one unit increase in the IMF's 1–10 index of the restrictiveness of trade policy, reduce trade levels by 5 percent (Chapter III of the September 2002 *World Economic Outlook*). Conversely, full trade liberalization in developing countries would increase North-South trade by over 20 percent, and South-South trade by about 50 percent. Similarly, as regards crisis probabilities, the

impact of eliminating all G-3 RER volatility is roughly equivalent to that of reducing the average degree of overvaluation by 2 percent. The relatively weak effects of G-3 RER volatility may not be surprising, given that it is only one of many factors behind volatility and misalignment in developing countries' REER.

Which Vulnerabilities Matter Most?

While for the "average" developing country the estimated spillovers from G-3 exchange rate volatility may be limited, such exchange rate fluctuations may be a much more serious concern for some specific countries. The Asian crises, for instance, represent a situation where G-3 exchange rate volatility, together with inflexible domestic exchange rate regimes, contributed to extremely costly crises. Most emerging markets in east Asia de facto pegged to the U.S. dollar until 1997 (possibly out of concern that their liabilities had become increasingly dollarized), even while trading significantly with Japan. Given these pegs, the dollar's sharp real appreciation against the yen from 1995 onward led directly to significant REER appreciations in Korea, Thailand, Indonesia, and Malaysia, among others (Figure 2.22). As discussed earlier, such appreciations increased the likelihood of a crisis. In addition, given the importance of intraregional trade, the end of the (often informal) dollar pegs after 1997 lowered the share of trade linked to the dollar, increased trade-finance mismatches, and hence further raised the likelihood of crises in the region.

Macroeconomic model simulations can help analyze what structural characteristics or policy actions would exacerbate or reduce vulnerabilities. Simulations can also provide some insight into whether industrial country policy cooperation, aimed at reducing exchange rate volatility across the major economies, would create more or less instability in real activity. Accordingly, this section reports simulations using the IMF's Global Economy Model (GEM) to examine the impact of industrial-country exchange rate volatility. [53] GEM is the IMF's new macroeconomic model, explicitly based on rigorous microeconomic foundations and on the "new open-economy macroeconomics" literature (see Chapter IV, Box 4.3, of the April 2003 *World Economic Outlook*, and Pesenti, forthcoming, for an overview of GEM). For the purposes of this essay, a three-country version of GEM was constructed, comprising two large industrial countries (which will be called the euro area and the United States) and a smaller, relatively open emerging market. In the baseline, the developing country trades equally with the euro area and the United States, has a steady-state debt to GDP ratio of 40 percent, borrows exclusively from the United States, and pursues an inflation target. The rest of the model is calibrated based on earlier work by Hunt and Rebucci (2003) and Laxton and Pesenti (2003).

In the baseline, the spillover effects of industrial country exchange rate volatility generate a volatility of emerging market GDP of slightly over 0.1 percent (Table 2.9). This cost varies depending on the structure of the developing country. An increase in its external debt renders it more vulnerable to exchange rate or interest rate shocks, increasing its output volatility. Analogously, if the economy were less open to trade, it would be less vulnerable to external shocks, and its output less volatile—although underlying growth might of course be lower.[54] For a given trade ratio, if the emerging market were to trade mainly with the United States, and given that its debt is dollar denominated, the greater match between the currency composi-

Figure 2.22. Yen/Dollar Real Exchange Rate, and Real Effective Exchange Rates (REERs) in East Asia

(REER unless otherwise noted; 1995 = 100)

East Asian emerging markets de facto pegged to the U.S. dollar until 1997, even while trading significantly with Japan. As a result, the dollar's sharp real appreciation against the yen from 1995 through 1997 led directly to a significant REER appreciation in Korea, Thailand, Indonesia, and Malaysia.

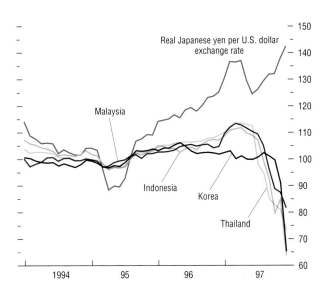

Source: IMF staff calculations.

[53]This volatility is modeled as shocks to the risk premium between euro- and dollar-denominated assets. The shocks were parameterized to produce realistic levels of exchange rate instability between the two industrial countries.

[54]Our results only hold for small disturbances around a stable equilibrium, and are therefore not applicable to large shocks, such as would arise in a crisis-type situation. In particular, the above result might not hold in crises, when lack of openness to trade can limit a country's ability to adjust (Chapter III of the September 2002 *World Economic Outlook*).

Table 2.9. Global Economy Model Simulations: How Various Emerging Market Characteristics Increase or Reduce the Impact of G-3 Real Exchange Rate (RER) Volatility[1]
(Standard deviation, percent, on an annual basis)

	Volatility of Developing Country Real GDP
Baseline[2]	0.14
Changes in structure:	
Emerging market debt doubles to 80 percent of GDP	0.22
Emerging market trades less	0.08
Emerging market trades mostly with United States	0.09
Emerging market trades mostly with euro area	0.22
Emerging market faces lower exchange rate pass-through into domestic prices	0.05
Changes in monetary regime:	
Emerging market pegs to U.S. dollar . . .	0.38
. . . and trades mostly with United States	0.26
Industrial countries conduct monetary policy to stabilize their exchange rate	0.14

Source: IMF staff calculations.

[1]Volatility in G-3 RER is modeled as shocks to the risk premium in the Uncovered Interest Parity condition between euro-denominated and U.S. dollar-denominated assets.

[2]The developing country is modeled as smaller and more open than the two large countries (euro area and United States), trades equally with the euro area and United States, has debt equal to 40 percent of GDP in the stochastic steady state, faces higher transaction costs in international borrowing, and faces higher exchange rate pass-through into domestic prices. The euro area and United States are modeled as identical, except that all internationally traded financial assets are denominated in U.S. dollars.

tion of its trade and of its debt would lower the induced macroeconomic instability. The converse holds if the emerging market trades mainly with the euro area. Finally, if the degree of exchange rate pass-through into domestic prices in the developing country were reduced to industrial country levels, its producers would be better insulated from exchange rate shocks and its output volatility would be correspondingly lower.

The impact of changes in developing countries' exchange rate regimes is generally larger. Pegging the exchange rate to one of the industrial country currencies increases interest rate volatility significantly. For our parameterization, emerging market output volatility also increases. The effect is smallest when the emerging market

trades and borrows largely with the country to which it pegs, but even in this case output volatility would be almost three times as large as under inflation targeting (although clearly the results depend on the structure of the country and parameterization of the model).

Finally, we analyze what would happen if the euro area and the United States changed their monetary policy objectives and acted to stabilize their bilateral exchange rate. In the simulations, this reduces exchange rate volatility, but only at the cost of a significant increase in interest rate volatility in the industrial countries. For our parameterization, this has little net effect on the emerging market, while the volatility of industrial country output increases significantly. That said, it should be noted that those who advocate reducing G-3 exchange rate volatility generally believe such a policy shift would reduce the magnitude of the underlying shocks to exchange rates, for instance by preventing the buildup of speculative bubbles, and hence help stabilize all countries (Bergsten, 2003).

Overall, and consistent with the earlier empirical work, the simulations suggest that the impact of industrial country exchange rate volatility on emerging markets is likely small relative to other disturbances. For instance, the results in Table 2.9 are small compared with actual developing-country output volatility of about 5 percent (see, for instance, Chapter III, Table 3.4 of the April 2003 *World Economic Outlook*). In addition, the estimated changes to developing country macroeconomic stability coming from G-3 exchange rate volatility are of a similar magnitude to those found in GEM for minor adjustments to inflation targeting rules in developing countries (Laxton and Pesenti, 2003).

Conclusions

This essay examined the potential spillover effects of industrial country exchange rate volatility on developing countries' trade, capital inflows, and the likelihood of exchange rate crises. Such volatility was found to have negative effects on developing country economic performance. These effects come mainly through indirect channels, as G-3 volatility increases the instability of developing countries' own real effective exchange rate and the chance of developing country exchange rate misalignments and overvaluations. The degree of mismatch between trade and financial links was also found to influence the likelihood of crises. In addition, simulations were used to explore which factors might amplify or dampen the effects and whether acting to reduce G-3 exchange rate volatility would benefit emerging markets.

That said, the magnitude of the estimated effects appears to be quite limited. On average, the estimates presented here suggest that even a complete elimination of all volatility in G-3 real exchange rates would boost developing country trade by a modest 1 percent, increase capital flows to emerging markets by 3 percent, and reduce the probability of exchange rate crises by up to 2½ percentage points. These indirect effects partly depend on the exchange rate policy being followed by the developing country, suggesting that more flexible exchange rate regimes and the use of various hedging instruments may help lower existing costs. Still, overall, the significant variation across developing countries in the extent of REER volatility and misalignment suggests that these can only be explained to a limited degree by factors that are more or less common to all developing countries, such as the extent of industrial country real exchange rate volatility. In addition, the reported policy simulations found that the beneficial impact on developing countries of any attempt to stabilize G-3 exchange rates could easily be offset by the induced fluctuations in G-3 interest rates and output.

Finding limited costs of industrial country exchange rate volatility is in a sense quite comforting, given recent moves in G-3 exchange rates and given that the size of current international imbalances raises the possibility of further significant exchange rate swings. Nevertheless, the analysis does not provide grounds for complacency. While G-3 exchange rate volatility might have small effects *on average*, it raises more

significant issues for certain types of developing countries. For instance, while the decision on what exchange rate regime to adopt depends on many factors not discussed in this essay, policymakers should be particularly concerned about such volatility when their country is pegged to a specific industrial country currency. In addition, countries may become especially vulnerable to G-3 exchange rate volatility when their debt ratios are relatively high and when external trade and external debt are mismatched, so that a peg that stabilizes competitiveness may be associated with a volatile debt service. Indeed, G-3 volatility and misalignments, combined with inflexible exchange rate regimes, appear to have played a role in the buildup to the Argentine and Asia crises and the associated large losses in output.

Appendix 2.1. Economic Growth in the Middle East and North Africa Region: Definitions, Data Sources, and Country Coverage

The main author of this appendix is Dalia Hakura.

This appendix defines variables, provides data sources, and specifies country coverage for the essay on economic growth in the MENA region.

Data Definitions and Sources

Economic growth is measured as the average growth rate of real per capita GDP over 1980–2000 (reflecting the availability of reliable data). The source of the data is the WEO database.

Inflation is the average of the logarithm of annual inflation rates in the Consumer Price Index over 1980–2000 (reflecting the availability of reliable data). The source of the data is the World Bank's *World Development Indicators* (WDI).

Initial level of income is measured as the natural logarithm of per capita GDP in purchasing power parity terms in 1980. The source of the data is the WEO database.

Government consumption is the average of the ratio of government "consumption" expenditure to GDP from 1980 to 2000 (reflecting the availability of reliable data). The source of the data is the WDI.

Trade openness is defined as the sum of imports and exports of goods and services (from balance of payments statistics), divided by GDP. The source of the data is the WDI.

Exchange rate overvaluation is based on purchasing-power-parity comparisons, using the Summers-Heston measure, where 100 signifies parity and higher (lower) values indicate over- (under-) valuation, following the methodology of Dollar (1992). The average degree of overvaluation over 1980–2000 is used. Since this index is not available for the GCC countries (except for Bahrain), exchange rate misalignment for these countries is calculated using the percentage difference between the actual real effective exchange rate (REER, reported in the IMF's Information Notice System) and a Hodrik-Prescott filter of the REER.

Institutional quality is constructed as the average of four indices reported by the International Country Risk Guide (ICRG) over 1984–2000. The indices are (1) corruption—the degree of all forms of corruption such as patronage, nepotism, and suspiciously close ties between politics and business; (2) rule of law—the strength and impartiality of the legal system and the extent of popular observance of the law; (3) bureaucracy quality—the strength and expertise of the bureaucracy to govern without drastic changes in policy or interruptions in government services; and (4) government stability—the ability of the government to carry out its declared program and to stay in office. The indices are re-scaled from 1 to 12, where high values indicate good institutions. For an alternative regression specification, the institutional quality index is constructed as the average of the four indices above as well as two indicators of internal and external conflict reported by the ICRG. The internal conflict indicator refers to the extent of political violence in the country, and the external conflict indicator refers to the

risk to the government arising from foreign action ranging from nonviolent external pressure (e.g., trade restrictions, territorial disputes, and diplomatic pressures) to cross-border conflicts and war.

Terms of trade volatility is measured as the standard deviation of the annual change in the terms of trade over 1980–2000 weighted by the share of natural resource exports in total exports in 1980 to capture the volatility of income flows that is associated with exports of natural resources. Natural resource exports are defined as the sum of exports of fuel, ores and metals, agricultural and raw materials, and food products. The data to measure the share of natural resources in total exports come from the WDI, while the terms of trade data are from the WEO database.

Secondary education is measured as the number enrolled in secondary school as a percent of the secondary-school-age population. The source of these data is the WDI.

The demographic burden is defined as the difference between the growth rate of the economically active population and the total population growth rate. The economically active population is defined as the population aged 15–64. The data to calculate the growth rates of the economically active population and total population are obtained from the WDI.

Female labor force participation is calculated as the ratio of females in the labor force to female working-age population (defined as the female economically active population aged 15–64). The data to calculate female participation ratios are obtained from the WDI.

Country Coverage

This section specifies all the countries used in the essay. Owing to data constraints, the regression analysis in the essay is limited to a sample of 74 countries, including 21 advanced economies and 53 developing countries, of which 10 were MENA countries—5 non-oil MENA countries, 3 GCC countries, and 2 other oil-exporting MENA countries.

Advanced Economies

Australia, Austria, Canada, Cyprus, Finland, France, Greece, Iceland, Ireland, Israel, Italy, Japan, the Netherlands, New Zealand, Norway, Portugal, Spain, Sweden, Switzerland, the United Kingdom, and the United States.

East Asia

China, Indonesia, Korea, Malaysia, the Philippines, Singapore, Thailand, Taiwan Province of China, and Papua New Guinea.

Other Developing Countries

Argentina, Bangladesh, Barbados, Bolivia, Botswana, Brazil, Burkina Faso, Burundi, Cameroon, Central African Republic, Chad, Chile, Colombia, Congo, Costa Rica, Côte d'Ivoire, Dominican Republic, Ecuador, El Salvador, Ethiopia, Gabon, Gambia, Ghana, Guatemala, Guyana, Haiti, Honduras, India, Jamaica, Kenya, Madagascar, Malawi, Mauritania, Mexico, Mozambique, Nepal, Nicaragua, Niger, Nigeria, Pakistan, Panama, Paraguay, Peru, Rwanda, Senegal, Sierra Leone, South Africa, Sri Lanka, Tanzania, Togo, Trinidad and Tobago, Turkey, Uganda, Uruguay, Venezuela, Zambia, and Zimbabwe.

Middle East and North Africa

This group is divided into non-oil MENA countries and oil-exporting MENA countries—GCC oil-exporting countries and other oil-exporting MENA countries. Following WEO convention, a country is classified as an oil exporter if its oil export earnings over 1994–98 constituted more than 50 percent of total export earnings.

Non-oil MENA countries. Egypt, Jordan, Lebanon, Morocco, Syria, Tunisia, and Yemen.

GCC countries. Bahrain, Kuwait, Oman, Qatar, Saudi Arabia, and United Arab Emirates.

Other oil-exporting MENA countries. Algeria, Iran, and Libya.

Appendix 2.2. How Concerned Should Developing Countries Be About G-3 Exchange Rate Volatility? Data and Modeling Strategy

The main author of this appendix is Nikola Spatafora.

This appendix provides further details on the data and the modeling strategy regarding the impact of G-3 exchange rate volatility on developing countries.

Data

The empirical work analyzes a broad panel of up to 133 developing countries,[55] representing all major geographic regions, over 1980–2001. Monthly data were used for exchange rates, and quarterly or annual data for other variables. Two subsamples were also analyzed. The first covers 21 large emerging markets.[56] The second covers all observations when countries are on an exchange rate peg, according to the Reinhart and Rogoff (2002) classification. This classification is based on de facto exchange rate performance, including in parallel markets, rather than on the de jure exchange rate regimes officially reported by countries. The Reinhart and Rogoff measure is available for three-fourths of the full sample. Exchange rate pegs account for 58 percent of these observations; 88 countries are reported as having been on a peg for some fraction (on average, over one-half) of the sample period.

The analysis focuses on the impact of G-3 real exchange rate (RER) volatility on the following measures of macroeconomic performance:

- *Exports; imports; net total capital inflows; and net FDI inflows.* These are all measured as the loga-

---

[55]The regressions for exports, imports, capital inflows, FDI, and exchange rate crises use, respectively, 133, 131, 132, 124, and 88 countries.

[56]Argentina, Brazil, Chile, China, Colombia, Czech Republic, Egypt, Hungary, India, Indonesia, Malaysia, Mexico, Pakistan, Peru, the Philippines, Poland, Russia, South Africa, Thailand, Turkey, and Venezuela.

rithm of the ratio of the relevant variable to GDP (all variables being measured in dollar terms).

- *Exchange rate crisis.* This is an indicator variable, equal to unity if (1) the country's nominal exchange rate against the U.S. dollar depreciated by at least 12.5 percent in that month; and (2) the depreciation rate exceeded its value in the previous month by at least 10 percentage points; and (3) the country had not experienced any crisis in the previous six months. It is equal to zero in all other cases.

A key issue is measuring G-3 RER volatility. Here it is defined as a weighted average of the volatilities of the real U.S. dollar/yen and U.S. dollar/deutsche mark exchange rates, where

- the volatility of any individual exchange rate is defined as the standard deviation of its monthly percentage growth rate over the previous year;[57] and
- the above weights are region-specific, and are based on a panel regression for each region of real effective exchange rate (REER) volatility on the volatilities of the real U.S. dollar/yen and U.S. dollar/deutsche mark exchange rates. The resulting coefficients are then scaled to add up to unity.

The analysis also measures the indirect impact of G-3 RER volatility on economic performance through its impact on REER volatility, misalignment, and overvaluation. REER volatility has been defined. REER misalignment is defined as the absolute percentage deviation of the 12-month moving average of the REER from its equilibrium level, as proxied by a country-specific exponential time trend. Similarly, REER overvaluation is defined as the percentage deviation of the REER from its equilibrium level, as proxied by a country-specific exponential time trend. Throughout, we use relative-CPI-based measures of real exchange rates.

The analysis also makes use of a novel variable: the correlation between the geographical structure of trade and the currency composition of debt, or "trade-finance mismatch." This is measured as follows. For each country, at each date, two sets of weights are constructed. The first is based on the currency composition of debt, using the major currencies: U.S. dollar, yen, deutsche mark, British pound, French franc, Swiss franc, and others. The second set of weights gives the geographical composition of total trade, broken down in an analogous way, with the exception that all trade with any trade partner that is pegged to, say, the U.S. dollar is for these purposes counted as part of the trade with the United States. The trade-finance mismatch is then computed as unity minus the correlation between these two sets of weights.

Summary statistics for the key variables used in the analysis are shown in Table 2.10.

Modeling Strategy

To examine the importance of G-3 RER volatility as a determinant of developing country trade or capital inflows, the following equations were estimated:

$$Y_{it} = \alpha_i + \beta \cdot Vol_t(REER_i) + \gamma \cdot Vol_t(G\text{-}3\_RER_i) + \delta \cdot Z_{it} + \varepsilon_{it}; \qquad (1)$$

$$Vol_t(REER_i) = a_i + b \cdot Vol_t(G\text{-}3\_RER_i) + e_{it}, \qquad (2)$$

where Y is the specific macroeconomic outcome of interest; $Vol(REER)$ is the measure of REER volatility; $Vol(G\text{-}3\_RER)$ is the measure of G-3 real exchange rate volatility; Z is a set of control variables; and the subscripts i and t denote, respectively, the country and the time period. Equation (1) captures the direct impact of G-3 real exchange rate volatility on the country's macroeconomic outcomes, while equation (2) allows us to estimate the indirect impact through

---

[57]Various alternative measures of perceived volatility are possible, including some based on high-frequency data. For instance, daily observations on exchange rates could be used to estimate perceived monthly exchange rate volatilities (see Andersen and others, 2001, for technical details; Baum, Caglayan, and Ozkan, 2003, or Klaassen, 1999, for applications). Such data, however, are difficult to obtain for such a wide range of countries.

Table 2.10. Selected Summary Statistics[1]
(Percent)

Variable	All Sample Countries	Exchange Rate Pegs	Emerging Markets
Economic outcomes			
Exports/GDP	25.8 (29.8)	22.8 (18.2)	22.1 (18.0)
Imports/GDP	35.9 (30.8)	34.0 (24.8)	23.4 (16.8)
Net capital inflows/GDP	5.9 (12.2)	7.1 (16.9)	4.4 (3.7)
Net FDI/GDP	2.5 (4.1)	3.2 (5.3)	1.4 (1.6)
Volatility measures[2]			
Volatility (REER)	3.3 (5.4)	2.1 (2.9)	2.8 (3.4)
Volatility (G-3 RER)	2.5 (0.6)	2.4 (0.6)	2.6 (0.6)
REER overvaluation[3]	5.7 (11.8)	6.0 (9.6)	5.4 (9.5)

Sources: IMF, *International Financial Statistics;* World Bank, *Global Development Finance;* and IMF staff estimates.
[1]Values are means, with panel standard deviations provided in parentheses next to each value.
[2]Volatility of an exchange rate is defined as the standard deviation of its monthly percentage growth rate over the previous year.
[3]Defined as the percentage deviation of the REER from a country-specific exponential time trend, subject to a minimum value of zero.

its effect on the country's REER volatility. In principle, a correlation between G-3 and developing country RER volatility need not imply causality from the former to the latter. For instance, it might instead reflect the presence of common RER shocks. Such arguments would strengthen our finding that reductions in G-3 RER volatility would only have a limited impact on developing countries. Equations (1) and (2) are estimated using the panel fixed-effects estimator.

When analyzing the impact of G-3 RER volatility on the probability of exchange rate crises, a slightly different model was adopted:

$$Y_{it} = \alpha + \beta \cdot Overvaluation_{it} + \gamma \cdot Vol_t(G\text{-}3\_RER_i) + \delta \cdot Z_{it} + \varepsilon_{it}; \quad (3)$$

$$Overvaluation_{it} = a_i + b \cdot Vol_t(G\text{-}3\_RER_i) + e_{it}, \quad (4)$$

where *Y* indicates whether an exchange rate crisis occurred over the subsequent two years; and *Overvaluation* is the measure of overvaluation, with any negative values treated as being equal to zero, so as to capture the nonlinearity of its impact on crisis probabilities. Equation (3) is estimated using the panel probit estimator, while equation (4) is estimated using the panel fixed-effects estimator.

In each regression, we also allow for a standard set of additional explanatory variables.

- In the *exports* regression, the controls include the REER; a weighted average of the trading partners' real GDP indices, with the weights given by each trading partner's trade share; and a time trend, to capture the impact of reductions over time in trade barriers and transport costs.
- In the *imports* regression, the controls include the REER; real GDP; and a time trend.
- In the *total capital inflows* regression and in the *net FDI inflows* regression, the controls include an index of real GDP in industrial countries; the six-month LIBOR, as a proxy for industrial country interest rates; capital-account openness, as measured by the proportion of years in which a country did not have restrictions on its capital account; and a time trend.
- In the *exchange rate crisis* regression, the controls include the ratio of external debt to GDP; the ratio of exports to GDP; a contagion indicator, equal to unity if a crisis occurred in at least one other country in the region, and equal to zero in all other cases; and our measure of trade-finance mismatch.

All these controls broadly have the expected sign. In each regression, the volatility of industrial country interest rates, as proxied by the volatility of the six-month LIBOR, was initially also controlled for. However, when the results were significant, the sign was consistently the opposite of what was expected. This variable was therefore omitted.

References

Abed, George T., 2003, "Unfulfilled Promise: Why the Middle East and North Africa Region Has Lagged in Growth and Globalization," *Finance & Development*, Vol. 40 (March), pp. 10–14.

Acemoglu, Daron, Simon Johnson, James Robinson, and Yunyong Thaicharoen, 2002, "Institutional Causes, Macroeconomic Symptoms: Volatility, Crises and Growth," NBER Working Paper No. 9124 (Cambridge, Massachusetts: National Bureau of Economic Research).

Aizenman, Joshua, and Nancy Marion, 2002a, "International Reserve Holdings with Sovereign Risk and Costly Tax Collection," NBER Working

Paper No. 9154 (Cambridge, Massachusetts: National Bureau of Economic Research).

———, 2002b, "The High Demand of International Reserves in the Far East: What's Going On?" NBER Working Paper No. 9266 (Cambridge, Massachusetts: National Bureau of Economic Research).

Alonso-Gamo, Patricia, Annalisa Fedelino, and Sebastian Paris Horvitz, 1997, "Globalization and Growth Prospects in Arab Countries," IMF Working Paper 97/125 (Washington: International Monetary Fund).

Andersen, Torben G., Tim Bollerslev, Francis X. Diebold, and Paul Labys, 2001, "The Distribution of Realized Exchange Rate Volatility," *Journal of the American Statistical Association*, Vol. 96 (March), pp. 42–55.

Baig, Taimur, 2001, "Characterizing Exchange Rate Regimes in Post-Crisis East Asia," IMF Working Paper 01/152 (Washington: International Monetary Fund).

Barro, Robert, 1991, "Economic Growth in a Cross Section of Countries," *Quarterly Journal of Economics*, Vol. 106 (May), pp. 407–43.

———, 1996, "Determinants of Economic Growth: A Cross-Country Empirical Study," NBER Working Paper No. 5698 (Cambridge, Massachusetts: National Bureau of Economic Research).

———, and Xavier Sala-i-Martin, 1995, *Economic Growth* (New York: McGraw-Hill, Inc.).

Baum, Christopher, Mustafa Caglayan, and Neslihan Ozkan, 2003, "Nonlinear Effects of Exchange Rate Volatility on the Volume of Bilateral Exports," *Journal of Applied Econometrics* (forthcoming).

Belke, Angsar, and Daniel Gros, 2002, "Monetary Integration in the Southern Cone: Mercosur Is Not Like the EU?" Central Bank of Chile Working Paper No. 188 (Santiago: Central Bank of Chile). Available via the Internet: *http://www.bcentral.cl/eng/studiesandpublications/studies/workingpaper/188.htm*.

Berg, Andrew, Eduardo Borensztein, Gian Maria Milesi-Ferretti, and Catherine Pattillo, 1999, *Anticipating Balance of Payments Crises: The Role of Early Warning Systems*, IMF Occasional Paper No. 186 (Washington: International Monetary Fund).

Berg, Andrew, Eduardo Borensztein, and Catherine Pattillo, 2003, "Assessing Early Warning Systems: How Have They Worked in Practice?" IMF Working Paper (Washington: International Monetary Fund, forthcoming).

Berg, Andrew, and Anne Krueger, 2003, "Trade, Growth, and Poverty: A Selective Survey," IMF

Working Paper 03/30 (Washington: International Monetary Fund).

Berg, Andrew, and Catherine Pattillo, 1999a, "Are Currency Crises Predictable? A Test," *IMF Staff Papers*, Vol. 46 (June), pp. 107–38.

———, 1999b, "Predicting Currency Crises: The Indicators Approach and an Alternative," *Journal of International Money and Finance*, Vol. 18 (August), pp. 561–86.

Bergin, Paul R., and Ivan Tchakarov, 2002, "Does Exchange Rate Risk Matter for Welfare? A Quantitative Investigation" (unpublished; Davis, California: University of California at Davis).

Bergsten, C. Fred, 2003, Letter to the Editor, *Finance & Development*, Vol. 40 (June), pp. 2–3.

Bloom, David E.M., and Jeffrey G. Williamson, 1998, "Demographic Transitions and Economic Miracles in Emerging Asia," *World Bank Economic Review*, Vol. 12 (September), pp. 419–55.

Bosworth, Barry, and Susan Collins, 2003, "The Empirics of Growth: An Update" (unpublished; Washington: Brookings Institution and Georgetown University).

Bussière, Matthieu, and Christian Mulder, 1999, "External Vulnerability in Emerging Market Economies: How High Liquidity Can Offset Weak Fundamentals and the Effects of Contagion," IMF Working Paper 99/88 (Washington: International Monetary Fund).

Calvo, Guillermo A., 1996, "Capital Flows and Macroeconomic Management: Tequila Lessons," *International Journal of Finance and Economics*, Vol. 1 (July), pp. 207–23.

———, and Carmen M. Reinhart, 2000, "Fixing for Your Life," in *Brookings Trade Forum 2000*, ed. by Susan M. Collins and Dani Rodrik (Washington: Brookings Institution), pp. 1–58.

———, 2002, "Fear of Floating," *Quarterly Journal of Economics*, Vol. 117 (May), pp. 379–408.

Cashin, Paul, and C. John McDermott, 2002, "The Long-Run Behavior of Commodity Prices: Small Trends and Big Variability," *IMF Staff Papers*, Vol. 49 (July), pp. 175–99.

Coe, David T., Elhanan Helpman, and Alexander W. Hoffmaister, 1997, "North-South R&D Spillovers," *Economic Journal*, Vol. 107 (January), pp. 134–49.

Côté, Agathe, 1994, "Exchange Rate Volatility and Trade: A Survey," Bank of Canada Working Paper No. 94–5 (Ottawa: Bank of Canada).

Cuddington, John T., and Hong Liang, 1999, "Commodity Price Volatility Across Exchange Rate

Regimes" (unpublished; Washington: Department of Economics, Georgetown University).

Dasgupta, Dipak, Jennifer Keller, and T.G. Srinivasan, 2002, "Reform and Elusive Growth in the Middle East—What Has Happened in the 1990s?" World Bank Working Paper No. 25 (Washington: World Bank).

Davoodi, Hamid, and Ulric Erikson von Allmen, 2001, "Demographics and Long-Term Growth in the Palestinian Economy," in *West Bank and Gaza Economic Performance, Prospects, and Policies*, ed. by R. Valdivieso, U. Erickson von Allmen, G. Bannister, H. Davoodi, F. Fischer, E. Jenker, and M. Said (Washington: International Monetary Fund).

Dollar, David, 1992, "Outward-Oriented Developing Countries Really Do Grow More Rapidly: Evidence from 95 LDCs, 1976–85," *Economic Development and Cultural Change*, Vol. 40 (April), pp. 523–24.

Easterly, William, Michael Kremer, Lant Pritchett, and Lawrence Summers, 1993, "Good Policy or Good Luck? Country Growth Performance and Temporary Shocks," *Journal of Monetary Economics* (Netherlands), Vol. 32 (December), pp. 459–83.

Easterly, William, and Ross Levine, 1997, "Africa's Growth Tragedy: Policies and Ethnic Divisions," *Quarterly Journal of Economics*, Vol. 112 (November), pp. 1203–50.

Edison, Hali J., 2000, "Do Indicators of Financial Crises Work? An Evaluation of an Early Warning System," International Finance Discussion Paper No. 675 (Washington: U.S. Board of Governors of the Federal Reserve System).

———, Ross Levine, Luca Antonio Ricci, and Torsten Sløk, 2002, "International Financial Integration and Economic Growth," *Journal of International Money and Finance*, Vol. 21 (November), pp. 749–76.

Edwards, Sebastian, 1983, "The Demand for International Reserves and Exchange Rate Adjustments: The Case of LDCs, 1964–72," *Economica*, Vol. 50 (August), pp. 269–80.

———, 1985, "On the Interest-Rate Elasticity of the Demand for International Reserves: Some Evidence from Developing Countries," *Journal of International Money and Finance*, Vol. 4 (June), pp. 287–95.

Esquivel, Gerardo, and Felipe Larraín B., 2002, "The Impact of G-3 Exchange Rate Volatility on Developing Countries," UNCTAD, G-24 Discussion Paper Series No. 16 (Geneva: United Nations Conference on Trade and Development).

Fischer, Stanley, 1993, "The Role of Macroeconomic Factors in Growth," NBER Working Paper No. 4565

(Cambridge, Massachusetts: National Bureau of Economic Research).

Flood, Robert, and Nancy Marion, 2002, "Holding International Reserves in an Era of High Capital Mobility," IMF Working Paper 02/62 (Washington: International Monetary Fund).

Frankel, Jeffrey, and David Romer, 1999, "Does Trade Cause Growth?" *American Economic Review*, Vol. 89 (June), pp. 379–99.

Frenkel, Jacob, and Boyan Jovanovic, 1981, "Optimal International Reserves: A Stochastic Framework," *Economic Journal*, Vol. 91 (June), pp. 507—14.

Gardner, Edward, 2003, "Wanted: More Jobs—High Unemployment in the MENA Region Presents Formidable Challenges for Policymakers," *Finance & Development*, Vol. 40 (March), pp. 18–21.

Goldstein, Morris, Graciela L. Kaminsky, and Carmen M. Reinhart, 2000, *Assessing Financial Vulnerability: An Early Warning System for Emerging Markets* (Washington: Institute for International Economics).

Hall, Robert, and Charles Jones, 1999, "Why Do Some Countries Produce So Much More Output per Worker Than Others?" *Quarterly Journal of Economics*, Vol. 114 (February), pp. 83–116.

Hausmann, Ricardo, and Roberto Rigobon, 2002, "An Alternative Interpretation of the 'Resource Curse': Theory and Policy Implications," NBER Working Paper No. 9424 (Cambridge, Massachusetts: National Bureau of Economic Research).

Heller, H. Robert, 1966, "Optimal International Reserves," *Economic Journal*, Vol. 76 (June), pp. 296–311.

———, and Mohsin Khan, 1978, "The Demand for International Reserves Under Fixed and Floating Exchange Rates," *Staff Papers*, International Monetary Fund, Vol. 25 (December), pp. 623–49.

Hernández, Leonardo, and Peter Montiel, 2001, "Post-Crisis Exchange Rate Policy in Five Asian Countries: Filling in the 'Hollow Middle'?" IMF Working Paper 01/170 (Washington: International Monetary Fund).

Hunt, Benjamin, and Alessandro Rebucci, 2003, "The U.S. Dollar and Trade Deficit: What Accounts for the Late 1990s?" (unpublished; Washington: International Monetary Fund).

International Monetary Fund, 1993, *Balance of Payments, Fifth Edition* (Washington: International Monetary Fund).

———, 1996, "Building on Progress: Reform and Growth in the Middle East and North Africa" (Washington: International Monetary Fund).

————, 2000, "Debt- and Reserve-Related Indicators of External Vulnerability" (Washington: International Monetary Fund). Available via the Internet: www.imf.org/external/np/sec/pn/2000/PN0037.htm.

————, 2001, "International Reserves and Foreign Currency Liquidity: Guidelines for a Data Template" (Washington: International Monetary Fund). Available via the Internet: http://dsbb.imf.org/vgn/images/pdfs/opguide.pdf.

Jbili, Abdelali, and Vitali Kramarenko, 2003, "Should MENA Countries Float or Peg?" *Finance & Development*, Vol. 40 (March), pp. 30–33.

Kaminsky, Graciela, Saul Lizondo, and Carmen M. Reinhart, 1998, "Leading Indicators of Currency Crises," *Staff Papers*, International Monetary Fund, Vol. 45 (March), pp. 1–48.

Kaufmann, Daniel, Aart Kraay, and Pablo Zoido-Lobatón, 1999, "Aggregating Governance Indicators," World Bank Policy Research Working Paper No. 2196 (Washington: World Bank).

Keller, Jennifer, and Mustapha K. Nabli, 2002, "The Macroeconomics of Labor Market Outcomes in MENA over the 1990s: How Growth Has Failed to Keep Pace with a Burgeoning Labor Market," ECES Working Paper No. 71 (Cairo: Egyptian Center for Economic Studies).

Khan, Mohsin S., and Carmen M. Reinhart, 1995, "Macroeconomic Management in APEC Economies: The Response to Capital Inflows," in *Capital Flows in the APEC Region*, IMF Occasional Paper No. 122, ed. by Mohsin Khan and Carmen Reinhart (Washington: International Monetary Fund).

Khan, Mohsin S., and Abdelhak S. Senhadji, 2000, "Threshold Effects in the Relationship Between Inflation and Growth," IMF Working Paper 00/110 (Washington: International Monetary Fund).

Klaassen, Frank, 1999, "Why Is It So Difficult to Find an Effect of Exchange Rate Risk on Trade?" Center for Economic Research Discussion Paper No. 73 (unpublished; Tilburg, The Netherlands: Tilburg University).

Klasen, Stephan, 1999, "Does Gender Inequality Reduce Growth and Development? Evidence from Cross-Country Regressions," Policy Research Report on Gender and Development Working Paper No. 7 (Washington: World Bank). Available via the Internet: http://www.worldbank.org/gender/prr.

Kletzer, Kenneth, and Ashoka Mody, 2000, "Will Self-Protection Policies Safeguard Emerging Markets from Crises?" in *Managing Financial and Corporate Distress: Lessons from Asia*, ed. by Charles Adams,

Robert E. Litan, and Michael Pomerleano (Washington: Brookings Institution Press), pp. 413–46.

Knack, Stephen, and Philip Keefer, 1995, "Institutions and Economic Performance: Cross-Country Tests Using Alternative Institutional Measures," *Economics and Politics*, Vol. 7, No. 3, pp. 207–27.

Lane, Philip R. and Dominic Burke, 2001, "The Empirics of Foreign Reserves," *Open Economies Review*, Vol. 12 (October), pp. 423–34.

Laxton, Douglas, and Paolo Pesenti, 2003, "Monetary Rules for Small, Open, Emerging Economies," NBER Working Paper No. 9568 (Cambridge, Massachusetts: National Bureau of Economic Research).

Lee, Jaewoo, 2003, "Option-Pricing Approach to Reserve Adequacy" (unpublished; Washington: International Monetary Fund).

Levy-Yeyati, Eduardo, and Federico Sturzeneger, 2002, "Classifying Exchange Rate Regimes: Deeds vs. Words" (unpublished; Buenos Aires, Argentina: Universidad Torcuato Di Tella).

Lizondo, José Saúl, and Donald J. Mathieson, 1987, "The Stability of the Demand for International Reserves," *Journal of International Money and Finance*, Vol. 6 (September), pp. 251–82.

Ljungqvist, Lars, and Thomas J. Sargent, 2000, *Recursive Macroeconomic Theory* (Cambridge, Massachusetts: MIT Press).

MacDonald, Ronald, 2000, "The Role of the Exchange Rate in Economic Growth: A Euro-Zone Perspective," National Bank of Belgium Working Paper No. 9 (Brussels: National Bank of Belgium).

Makdisi, Samir, Zeki Fattah, and Imed Limam, 2000, "Determinants of Growth in the MENA Countries," Arab Planning Institute Working Paper Series No. 03/01 (Kuwait: Arab Planning Institute).

McKenzie, Michael D., 1999, "The Impact of Exchange Rate Volatility on International Trade Flows," *Journal of Economic Surveys*, Vol. 13 (February), pp. 71–106.

Obstfeld, Maurice, and Kenneth Rogoff, 1999, *Foundations of International Macroeconomics* (Cambridge, Massachusetts: MIT Press).

————, 2002, "Global Implications of Self-Oriented National Monetary Rules," *Quarterly Journal of Economics*, Vol. 117 (May), pp. 503–35.

Page, John, 1998, "From Boom to Bust—and Back? The Crisis of Growth in the Middle East and North Africa," in *Prospects for Middle Eastern and North African Economies From Boom to Bust and Back?* ed. by Nemat Shafik (London: Macmillan).

Parsley, David, and Shang-Jin Wei, 2001, "Limiting Currency Volatility to Stimulate Goods Market Integration: A Price Based Approach," NBER Working Paper No. 8468 (Cambridge, Massachusetts: National Bureau of Economic Research).

Pesenti, Paolo A., forthcoming, "The Global Economy Model (GEM): Theoretical Framework," IMF Working Paper (Washington: International Monetary Fund).

Reinhart, Carmen M., and Vincent Raymond Reinhart, 2001, "What Hurts Most? G-3 Exchange Rate or Interest Rate Volatility," NBER Working Paper No. 8535 (Cambridge, Massachusetts: National Bureau of Economic Research).

———, 2002, "Is a G-3 Target Zone on Target for Emerging Markets?" *Finance & Development*, Vol. 39 (March), pp. 17–19.

Reinhart, Carmen M., and Kenneth S. Rogoff, forthcoming, "The Modern History of Exchange Rate Arrangements: A Reinterpretation," *Quarterly Journal of Economics*.

Rodrik, Dani, Arvind Subramanian, and Francesco Trebbi, 2002, "Institutions Rule: The Primacy of Institutions Over Integration and Geography in Economic Development," IMF Working Paper 02/189 (Washington: International Monetary Fund).

Rogoff, Kenneth, 2003, "A Vote Against Grandiose Schemes: Trying to Regiment Coordination of Dollar, Yen and Euro Monetary Policy Isn't Worth the Risks and Costs," *Finance & Development*, Vol. 40 (March), pp. 56–57.

Rose, Andrew K., 2000, "One Money, One Market: Estimating the Effect of Common Currencies on Trade," *Economic Policy: A European Forum* (U.K.), No. 30 (April), pp. 9–45.

———, 2001, "Currency Unions and Trade: The Effect Is Large," *Economic Policy*, Vol 16, No. 33, pp. 449–61.

———, 2002, "The Effect of Common Currencies on International Trade: Where Do We Stand?" (unpublished; Berkeley, California: University of California, Berkeley).

Sachs, Jeffrey, 2003, "Institutions Don't Rule: Direct Effects of Geography on Per Capita Income," NBER Working Paper No. 9490 (Cambridge, Massachusetts: National Bureau of Economic Research).

———, and Andrew Warner, 1995, "Natural Resource Abundance and Economic Growth," NBER Working Paper No. 5398 (Cambridge, Massachusetts: National Bureau of Economic Research).

———, 1997, "Sources of Slow Growth in African Economies," *Journal of African Economies*, Vol. 6 (October), pp. 335–76.

Sala-i-Martin, Xavier, and Elsa V. Artadi, 2002, "Economic Growth and Investment in the Arab World," Columbia University Department of Economics Discussion Paper No. 0203–08 (New York: Columbia University).

Slavov, Slavi Trifonov, 2002, "Should Small Open Economies Keep All Their Eggs in One Basket: The Role of Balance Sheet Effects" (unpublished; Stanford, California: Stanford University).

United Nations Development Program (UNDP), 2002, *Arab Human Development Report* (New York).

Wijnholds, J. Onno de Beaufort, and Arend Kapteyn, "Reserve Adequacy in Emerging Market Economies," IMF Working Paper 01/143 (Washington: International Monetary Fund).

CHAPTER III

PUBLIC DEBT IN EMERGING MARKETS: IS IT TOO HIGH?

The potential risks associated with high public debt have long been a concern of economic policymakers around the globe. In the industrial countries, the need to strengthen fiscal positions and reduce public debt to accommodate the pressures that population aging will put on government budgets in the future has received considerable attention in recent years (see, for example, the May 2001 *World Economic Outlook;* Economic Policy Committee, 2001; and Turner and others, 1998). For emerging market economies, high public debt has often had more immediate consequences for economic performance, with debt crises—and the resulting painful periods of economic adjustment—having been a recurring feature of the histories of many of these countries.

Following a period of relative calm in the first half of the 1990s, during which public debt in many countries declined, recent developments have once again brought to the fore the issue of public debt in emerging market economies. Public debt has increased quite sharply in recent years across a broad range of emerging market economies; there have been high profile and costly debt defaults or distressed debt restructurings in Argentina, Ecuador, Pakistan, Russia, Ukraine, and Uruguay; and other countries—Turkey, for example—have experienced severe fiscal difficulties. These developments have led to the suggestion that—despite the currently benign environment in global financial markets—emerging market economies may once again be on the verge of serious public debt problems.

Discussions of the economic impact of public debt go back at least as far as the eighteenth century, when debt problems in France and Great Britain began to mount. More recently, the political economy aspects of public debt have also received increasing attention.[1] There are of course valid reasons why a government may choose to borrow and accumulate debt. The debt may be used to fund spending that contributes to broader economic and social objectives. Financing public investment—for example, by improving physical infrastructure—might raise the rate of return on private capital or provide something that the private sector would not provide because of externalities, while higher spending on education or health care may enhance a nation's human capital. Further, if government spending has to be temporarily high today because of, say, a war or a natural disaster, debt could be used as a buffer to limit the need to immediately raise taxes (see Barro, 1979). Financing countercyclical fiscal policy also has an important role in helping stabilize economies and smooth business cycles.

High public debt can, however, have a significant negative effect on economic activity. It requires high taxes to finance and puts upward pressure on real interest rates, "crowding out" private investment. When a government is no longer able to finance its deficits, it is forced to contract spending or raise revenues, often at a time when fiscal policy is needed to help stabilize the economy (fiscal policy becomes procyclical rather than countercyclical). When it cannot take these actions, a debt crisis ensues and the government is forced to default or inflate the debt away (an implicit default), both of which entail large economic and welfare costs.

Note: The main authors of this chapter are Tim Callen (lead), Marco Terrones, Xavier Debrun, James Daniel, and Celine Allard, with consultancy support from Enrique Mendoza. Nathalie Carcenac, Carolina Gutierrez, and Bennett Sutton provided able research assistance.

[1]In this literature, debt is seen in a strategic context where the government can use it to finance higher expenditures or tax cuts to boost its reelection prospects, or to try to constrain the actions of successor regimes (see Rogoff, 1990, and Persson and Svenson, 1989).

Box 3.1. Data on Public Debt in Emerging Market Economies

Obtaining reliable and comparable cross-country time-series data on public debt and its key components for emerging market economies is not an easy task. Indeed, the considerable difficulties indicate the need for concerted efforts to improve the quality of the data in this important area.

Some of the major issues that arise in putting together a data set on public debt in emerging market economies are as follows.

- *Data availability.* Many countries have only recently started producing reasonably comprehensive measures of public debt, and they have only a limited time series that typically does not go back beyond the early 1990s on a consistent basis. Sometimes a longer time series is available for a narrower definition of debt—usually central government—although this is not always the case. Information on external public debt is typically more readily available than that for domestic public debt. Data on other key aspects of public debt—including its foreign/local currency denomination and average maturity—are rare (although improving).
- *Coverage of the data.* For an analysis of fiscal sustainability, it is important to have as broad a coverage as possible of public sector liabilities. Preferably, in addition to the liabilities of the central government, the liabilities of subnational governments and public sector enterprises should be included, as well as the contingent liabilities of the government (which may include loan guarantees, public sector pension liabilities, and even the potential costs of bank recapitalization). In reality, however, it is not possible to put together data on contingent liabilities for a large sample of countries. Even obtaining a comprehensive measure of explicit debt is difficult. For example, some countries only have data available on a central or general government basis, while even when public sector data is available, its coverage varies between countries.

Some countries include public sector banks and the central bank in the definition of the public sector; others do not. Coverage of extrabudgetary institutions also varies. For example, South Africa's data exclude extrabudgetary funds, while for Korea and Thailand the data include the debt of bank restructuring agencies. In general, data for Latin American countries tend to have the widest coverage of the public sector, and data for Middle Eastern countries the narrowest.

- *Other definitional issues.* Definitions, even for a given coverage, also vary greatly between countries. A major difference is in the use of gross or net data, and which assets are netted out. Brazil, because of its experience with high inflation, also uses a nonstandard ("valorized") definition of GDP, where adjustment for the effect of inflation on GDP is made. These adjustments can be substantial. For example, Brazil's general government debt at end-2002 was 55 percent of valorized GDP on a net basis, but 86 percent of standard GDP on a gross basis (with two-thirds of the increase due to the different GDP definition). Another related statistical issue is the comparability of public debt and fiscal data. While this is generally less of a problem when central or even general government debt data are used, when public sector debt is considered it is sometimes not possible to get fiscal revenues, expenditures, and balance data on a comparable basis. In such cases, inconsistencies between the debt and the fiscal flows data are inevitable.

Because of the limitations with currently available public debt data for emerging market economies, the approach that has been taken in this chapter is to construct two separate databases. Data on contingent liabilities, implicit debt, and arrears are not included for either industrialized or emerging market economies.

The first database focuses on obtaining the most comprehensive measure of public sector debt that is available, and contains data for 34 emerging market and 20 industrial countries covering the period 1990–2002 (although for some

Note: The main author of this box is James Daniel.

emerging market economies, data are not available for the whole period). The data for emerging market economies were collected from IMF staff reports and country economists. Of these 34 countries, 19 had data for the public sector, 10 for the general government, and 5 for the central government. For most countries, data are on a gross basis (i.e., financial assets are not netted out), with Brazil, Egypt, Jordan, Pakistan, and Turkey being exceptions. For the industrial countries, data are on a general government basis and are taken from the World Economic Outlook and OECD Analytical databases.

The second data set focuses on constructing a longer time series of data—which is essential for some of the econometric exercises and event analyses conducted in the chapter—for a broader sample of countries. This has data from 1970 to 2002 for 79 countries (20 industrial, 32 emerging market, and 27 other developing) and was constructed from the World Bank's Global Development Finance database, the IMF's Government Finance Statistics database, the OECD Analytical database, and country-specific sources. For industrial countries, data are again on a general government basis. For emerging market economies, total public debt is constructed as the sum of separately constructed series for external and domestic public debt. The external debt data are a comprehensive public sector debt measure, but the domestic debt data are on a central government basis.

Given the recent rise in public debt in emerging market economies, two increasingly important questions are at what point does public debt become too high?[2] and what policy actions does a government need to take to ensure that its debt is sustainable? A recent paper by Reinhart, Rogoff, and Savastano (2003) has investigated the "intolerance" of some emerging market economies to external debt, and has examined episodes of large external debt reductions in these economies. To date, however, few studies have empirically examined *public* debt sustainability or large *public* debt reductions in emerging market economies, partly because of the difficulties in constructing a data set on public debt in these countries. This chapter seeks to address this gap, and build on the work of Reinhart, Rogoff, and Savastano. In particular, it compiles a comprehensive cross-country database on public debt in emerging market economies, and then applies a number of different approaches to assess sustainability and analyze past instances in which countries have undertaken large public debt reductions.

Innovative aspects of the analysis include an investigation of how fiscal policy in emerging market economies responds to public debt, and the implications of the greater inherent volatility of emerging market economies for the sustainability of their public debt.

As already discussed, compiling a data set is a major challenge for any study of public debt in emerging market economies. The availability and coverage of public debt data vary considerably between countries, and there is no single source from which the data can be obtained. For the purposes of this chapter, two new data sets were constructed. They both focus on gross public sector debt, rather than net debt (i.e., where public sector assets are netted out) or the net present value of the debt, because of data limitations. The first data set contains a broad measure of public debt for the period 1990–2002, and the second a narrower definition of public debt, but over a longer time period (1970–2002). The reasons for creating two separate data sets, and the strengths and weaknesses of each, are discussed in Box 3.1.

[2]Economic theory provides little practical guidance on the optimum level of public debt as it is dependent on the specification of the model (see Aiyagari and McGrattan, 1998).

Public Debt and Fiscal Policy in Emerging Market Economies

Figure 3.1. Public Debt in Emerging Market Economies[1]
(Percent of GDP)

Public debt has risen across a broad range of emerging market economies since the mid-1990s. This rise has been due to domestic debt, which now accounts for nearly one-half of total debt.

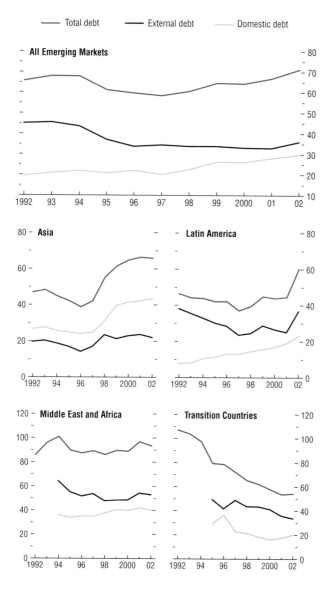

Source: IMF staff estimates.
[1]Unweighted averages. Only countries for which continuous data are available are included. For some countries, continuous data are available for total public debt, but not for the external and domestic subcomponents. Hence, external and domestic public debt do not always sum to total public debt.

Public debt in emerging market economies has risen quite sharply since the mid-1990s, and currently averages about 70 percent of GDP (Figure 3.1).[3] This increase in debt has more than reversed the decline that took place in the first half of the 1990s, so that despite the Brady debt restructuring initiative and large-scale privatization programs in many countries, public debt in emerging markets is higher than it was at the beginning of the 1990s. This is not to say there have not been success stories—Bulgaria, for example, has reduced its public debt ratio from close to 160 percent of GDP in the early 1990s to less than 60 percent of GDP in 2002—but many other countries have experienced very large increases in their debt ratios. In Argentina, public debt has risen from 30 percent of GDP in the early 1990s to 150 percent of GDP at end-2002, while in Lebanon it has increased from 50 percent of GDP to close to 180 percent of GDP over the same period.

The increase in public debt in emerging market economies in recent years has been concentrated in Latin America and Asia, with the latter seeing the most notable rise owing to the impact of the financial crisis in the region in the late 1990s. In contrast, debt ratios in the transition countries in Europe have fallen sharply as a number of these economies have implemented significant economic and fiscal reforms while they move toward accession to the European Union. In the Middle East and Africa, debt has remained broadly unchanged, but at uncomfortably high levels. The rise in public debt has been accounted for by increased issuance of domestic debt, spurred by domestic financial liberalization, the decline in inflation (particularly in

[3]Emerging market economies are here defined as those that were in the EMBI global index at the beginning of 2002 plus Costa Rica, Indonesia, India, Israel, and Jordan. Data are for nonfinancial public sector debt (external and domestic) where available, or the broadest definition of public sector that is otherwise available. Average figures are unweighted and only include countries for which continuous data are available for the sample period.

Latin America), and bank restructuring debt.[4] In contrast, the share of external public debt has declined, and now accounts for about one-half of the total, compared to about two-thirds at the beginning of the 1990s.

The increase in public debt in emerging market economies stands in contrast to developments among the industrial countries, where debt ratios have generally declined in recent years (with the notable exception of Japan) (Figure 3.2). Strikingly, after being well below industrial country levels during the 1990s, the average public debt ratio in emerging market economies is now higher than the average ratio in industrial countries (and much higher as a percent of government revenues).[5] It is also noticeable that despite the decline in the share of external debt in total public debt to about 50 percent in emerging market economies, it still remains well above the 25 percent share in industrial countries. The difference in debt denominated in, or indexed to, foreign currency is even larger. Based on a limited sample of emerging market economies, the foreign currency component is about 60 percent of total debt because some domestic government debt is linked to foreign currencies.

What have been the main factors behind the increase in public debt in emerging markets since the mid-1990s? The rise appears to be largely accounted for by interest and exchange rate movements and the recognition of off-balance-sheet and contingent liabilities (all captured in the "other" item in Figure 3.3). In a number of countries, the costs of recapitalizing banking systems have been particularly high.[6] Growth, on the other hand, has acted to reduce the public debt ratio. The primary fiscal balance

---

[4]Reinhart, Rogoff, and Savastano (2003) similarly note these trends, but across a much smaller subset of countries.

[5]The median public debt ratio is also higher in emerging market economies—66 percent in 2002 compared with 62 percent of GDP in industrial countries—and has shown the same upward trend since the mid-1990s.

[6]Burnside, Eichenbaum, and Rebelo (2001) model the impact of contingent financial sector liabilities in the context of the Asian financial crisis.

Figure 3.2. Comparison of Public Debt Levels in Emerging Market and Industrial Economies[1]

Public debt in emerging market economies is now higher than in industrial countries when compared to GDP, and is significantly higher in relation to government revenues. External debt also accounts for a higher proportion of public debt in emerging markets.

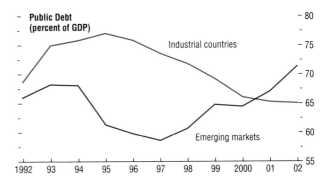

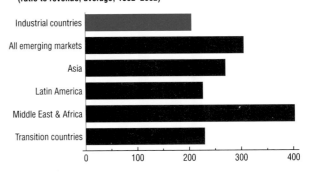

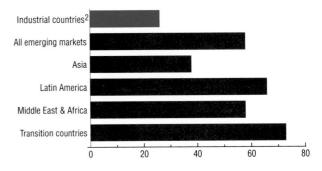

Source: IMF staff estimates.
[1]Unweighted averages.
[2]G-7 only.

(revenues less noninterest expenditures) has not itself added to the debt stock during this period, but it has not acted in any significant way to off-set the increase in debt that has been caused by other factors. Indeed, primary fiscal balances have weakened somewhat since the mid-1990s in all regions except the Middle East and Africa at a time when a strong fiscal effort was needed (Figure 3.4).

The increase in public debt to high levels in many emerging market economies in recent years has once again raised concerns about debt sustainability and whether there could be a repeat of the 1980s debt crisis. The long history of debt crises in many emerging market economies suggests that such concerns are not unfounded. Indeed, the fact that some emerging market economies have a long history of default-ing on their sovereign debt raises the question of why international investors continue to lend to these countries. Evidence, however, suggests that investors may not have lost by investing in these economies, although the ex post risk pre-mia earned on their investment has been small. For example, Klingen, Weder, and Zettelmeyer (2003) find that during 1970–2002 the rate of return on lending to emerging markets was the same as the return on U.S. government bonds. Over a more recent sample, the ex post risk pre-mium was found to be small, but positive.

Casual observation of sovereign debt default episodes in emerging markets over the past 30 years indicates that while the level of public debt at the time of a default has varied substan-tially, in many cases it has been quite low. In 55 percent of the defaults recorded, public debt was below 60 percent of GDP—the benchmark established for European Union members in the Maastricht treaty—in the year before the default, and in 35 percent of the cases the default actually occurred at a debt ratio of less than 40 percent of GDP (Figure 3.5).[7] Indeed,

Figure 3.3. Emerging Market Economies: Contributions to the Change in the Public Debt Stock Since 1997[1]
(Percent of GDP)

The recognition of contingent liabilities and interest and exchange rate developments—captured in the "other" category—have largely been responsible for the rise in public debt.

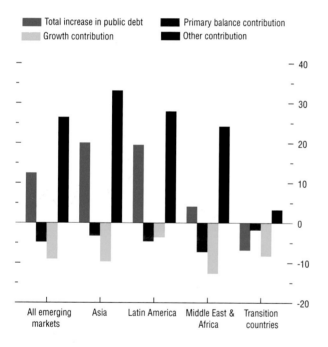

Source: IMF staff estimates.
[1]Unweighted averages.

---

[7]Looking at external debt at the time of sovereign debt default over the same period, Reinhart, Rogoff, and Savastano (2003) find that external debt was less than 60 percent of GNP in 47 percent of cases, but less than

the median public debt-to-GDP ratio in the year before a default was about 50 percent of GDP. Governments in emerging markets have also defaulted on their domestic debt through high inflation, particularly in the 1980s and early 1990s when several of these economies had triple-digit annual inflation rates (and a few experienced hyperinflation).[8]

Not all emerging market economies, however, have experienced debt crises or very high inflation rates, indicating that it is difficult to make generalizations about these economies as a group. Indeed, a number of emerging market economies—such as India and Malaysia—have managed to maintain relatively high public debt for a long period without a default. A comparison between emerging market country defaulters (since 1998) and nondefaulters points to a number of noticeable differences between the two groups.[9] The countries that have defaulted have, on average, a higher ratio of public debt to GDP, a higher debt-to-revenue ratio, a higher proportion of external debt in total public debt, and a lower ratio of broad money to GDP than those that did not default (Figure 3.5).[10] Indeed, in a number of cases it bears noting that debt ratios prior to the crisis were held down by overvalued exchange rates, given the importance of foreign currency–denominated debt in such cases.

The default experience of many emerging market economies stands in stark contrast to that of industrial countries, where there has been no

---

40 percent of GNP in only 17 percent of cases. For the calculations reported here, the default data are taken from Standard & Poor's (2002b) and refer to default events on both external and domestic government debt. Default episodes were matched with available data on total public debt to generate the 38 defaults that underlie the chart. Periods of severe fiscal stress that do not result in default are not captured.

[8]See the May 2001 *World Economic Outlook*.

[9]Hemming, Kell, and Schimmelpfennig (2003) provide a detailed analysis of the role of fiscal policy in 11 recent crisis episodes in emerging market economies.

[10]There may of course be other differences between the defaulters and nondefaulters. In particular, differences in the maturity structure of the debt may also have played a role. Data limitations, however, precluded examining this issue in this chapter.

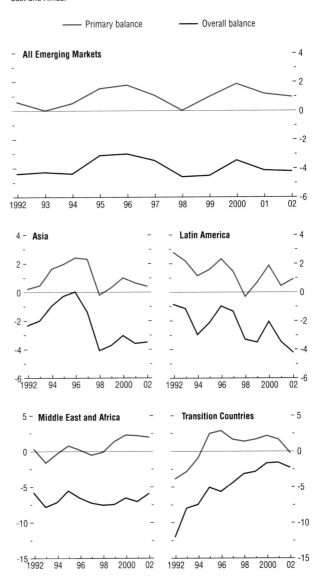

Figure 3.4. Fiscal Balances in Emerging Market Economies[1]
(Percent of GDP)

Primary balances have weakened slightly since the mid-1990s, except in the Middle East and Africa.

Source: IMF staff estimates.
[1]Unweighted averages. Only countries for which continuous data are available are included.

Figure 3.5. Debt Default and Public Debt Ratios

Public debt ratios are often quite low at the time of a default. There are, however, noticeable differences between defaulters and nondefaulters.

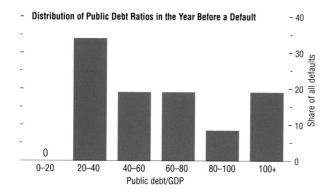

Distribution of Public Debt Ratios in the Year Before a Default

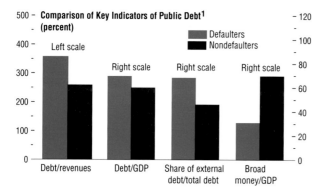

Comparison of Key Indicators of Public Debt[1] (percent)

Source: IMF staff estimates.
[1]Data are an average of 1998–2002. Defaulters refer to countries that have defaulted since 1998.

explicit public debt default since World War II (although inflation in many industrial countries has eroded the real value of debt, particularly during the 1970s). These differences in default history have led to the view that because of the characteristics of emerging market economies—including their inherent volatility, weaker institutions, and poor credit history—the level of public debt that they can sustain is much lower than for industrial countries (see Reinhart, Rogoff, and Savastano, 2003, and IMF, 2002).

Certainly, there are a number of features of the fiscal structure in emerging market economies that have an important bearing on the level of public debt that they can sustain. These include the following.

- *Revenue ratios in emerging market economies are low.* On average, the revenue-to-GDP ratio is about 27 percent of GDP, compared with 44 percent of GDP in industrial countries (Figure 3.6). There are, however, considerable differences among emerging market economies, with, for example, many of the transition economies and Israel having ratios on par with industrial countries. Effective tax rates in emerging market economies are generally much lower than in industrial countries.[11] The difference is particularly striking for direct tax rates, where industrial countries generally have effective direct tax rates of 30 percent or more and emerging markets outside eastern Europe, often only about 10 percent. This low effective tax rate is the result of inefficient tax systems, significant tax

[11]Estimates of effective direct and indirect tax rates were computed for a subset of industrial and emerging market economies for which data were available. Data were taken from the United Nations *National Accounts Statistics* and the IMF's *Government Finance Statistics*, and the calculations use a simplified version of the methodology proposed by Mendoza, Razin, and Tesar (1994). The length of the sample varied across countries depending on data availability. The effective direct tax rate was calculated as the ratio of total tax and nontax revenue net of domestic taxes on goods and services divided by the sum of compensation to employees and total operating surplus. The effective indirect tax rate was calculated as the ratio of all domestic taxes on goods and services divided by private consumption.

Figure 3.6. Revenue Ratios and Effective Tax Rates in Emerging Market and Industrial Economies[1]
(Percent)

Emerging market economies generally have lower revenue ratios and effective tax rates than industrial countries.

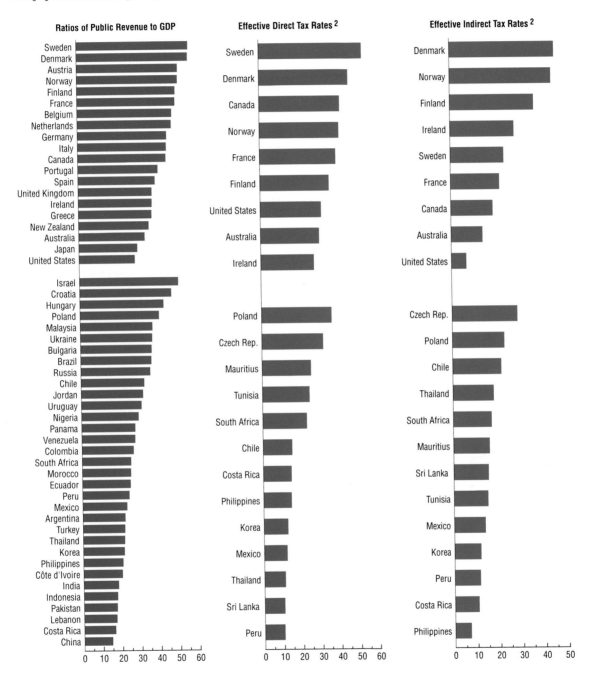

Source: IMF staff estimates.
[1]Calculations for the ratios of public revenue to GDP are generally for 1990–2002. Data for emerging market economies are on a nonfinancial public sector basis where available; otherwise, data are on the broadest basis available. For industrial countries, data are for the general government. Effective tax rate calculations are for country-specific periods for which detailed tax and national account data are available.
[2]To generate a larger sample of countries, Czech Republic, Sri Lanka, Mauritius, and Tunisia—which have detailed tax and national accounts data available—were included in the calculations.

exemptions, and a large informal sector. The difference in effective indirect tax rates between industrial and emerging market economies is also noticeable.

- *Revenues are volatile in emerging market economies.* The volatility of revenues—measured by the coefficient of variation—in emerging market economies is generally much higher than in industrial countries, although there are exceptions (Figure 3.7). This is partly due to the greater underlying volatility of the economy; income, consumption, and the terms of trade (which are often driven by the prices of a few commodities) are more volatile in emerging markets (see Kose, Prasad, and Terrones, 2003).[12] There is also a considerable difference in the volatility of effective tax rates (measured by the coefficient of variation).

- *Interest costs account for a high proportion of government expenditure in emerging market economies and are volatile.* At 5 percent of GDP, interest expenditures are almost twice as high in emerging market economies as in industrial countries, and account for an average of about 17 percent of expenditures (compared with 10 percent in industrial countries). Interest expenditures are also more volatile in emerging markets because of the structure of public debt. With a large proportion of debt either external or denominated in foreign currency, and revenues in domestic currency, high exchange rate volatility can result in large spikes in interest (and principal) payments relative to government income. Further, domestic debt is often of a short maturity, so interest costs are more sensitive to changes in the domestic interest rate environment.

These differences in the budget and public debt structures between emerging and industrial countries are striking and, as will be discussed in the next section, they have important implications for debt sustainability.

Assessing the Sustainability of Public Debt in Emerging Market Economies

Before proceeding, it is first necessary to define the related concepts of government solvency and public debt sustainability. A government is said to be solvent if it is expected to be able to generate sufficient future primary budget surpluses to be able to repay its outstanding debt (in more technical terms, the present discounted value of future primary fiscal surpluses must be at least equal to the value of the existing stock of public debt).[13] This criterion, however, is not very practical or demanding because, for example, it would permit a government to run large primary deficits for a period of time if it could commit to running primary surpluses of a sufficient size thereafter and so satisfy the solvency condition. In reality, a government cannot commit to such action—running large primary surpluses for a long period of time would be costly and politically very difficult.

So solvency needs to be viewed in relation to a fiscal adjustment path that is both economically and politically feasible, and a given debt level is usually thought of as being sustainable if it implies that the government's budget constraint (in present value terms) is satisfied without an unrealistically large future correction in the primary balance (see IMF, 2002). Liquidity conditions are also important. Even if a government satisfies its present value budget constraint, it may not have sufficient assets and financing available to meet or roll over its maturing liabilities. Unfortunately, there is no simple rule for determining whether, in practice, a government's debt is sustainable or not.[14] This section therefore

---

[12]The impact of commodity prices and commodity exports on government revenues is important even for those emerging market economies that have diversified their exports away from primary commodities. In Mexico, for example, oil exports are less than 15 percent of total exports, but oil-related revenues still account for about one-third of public sector revenue. Regression results reported in Appendix 3.1 confirm the importance of commodity price developments for the primary budget balance in emerging market economies.

[13]Appendix 3.1 shows why the government's primary fiscal balance, rather than the overall fiscal balance, is the key for the analysis of public debt sustainability.

[14]See Chalk and Hemming (2000) for a survey of methods for assessing fiscal sustainability.

Figure 3.7. Volatility of Revenues and Effective Tax Rates in Emerging Market and Industrial Economies[1]
(Coefficient of variation)

Emerging market economies generally have more volatile revenue ratios and effective tax rates than industrial countries.

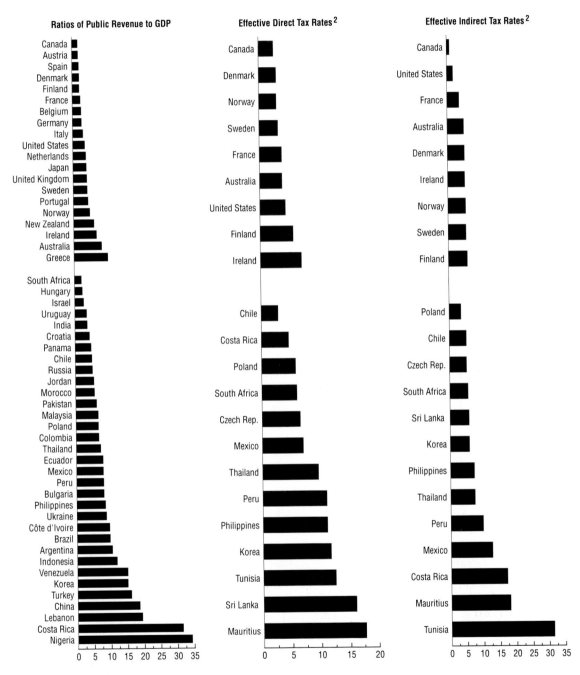

Source: IMF staff estimates.

[1]Calculations for the ratios of public revenue to GDP are generally for 1990–2002. Data for emerging market economies are on a nonfinancial public sector basis where available; otherwise, data are on the broadest basis available. For industrial countries, data are for the general government. Effective tax rate calculations are for country-specific periods for which detailed tax and national account data are available.

[2]To generate a larger sample of countries, Czech Republic, Sri Lanka, Mauritius, and Tunisia—which have detailed tax and national accounts data available—were included in the calculations.

applies a number of different approaches that have been developed in the economics literature to look at the issue of public debt sustainability in emerging market economies, and how the situation compares with industrial countries. The aim of the analysis is to look at trends across a broad range of countries, rather than to focus on the situation in any one country.

It should be noted up front that the following analysis does not take account of the risks that governments face from contingent and other off-balance-sheet liabilities. This is because of the difficulties in compiling cross-country data on such liabilities. The recent experience in many countries, however, has shown that the recognition of contingent or implicit liabilities—particularly those associated with the recapitalization of financial sectors—can add significantly to public debt, and in some cases push a situation that had previously appeared to be sustainable into one that is clearly not. Box 3.2 provides a discussion of the main contingent and other off-budget liabilities that are faced by governments in emerging and industrial countries, and the risks that these may present to the fiscal outlook. IMF (2003) also discusses contingent liabilities and public debt sustainability.

A Simple Approach to Public Debt Sustainability

Methods for assessing public debt sustainability usually start from the basic accounting identity that links public sector revenues and expenditures to the change in the debt stock. One commonly used approach is to view fiscal policy as sustainable if it delivers a ratio of public debt to GDP that is stable, and then to calculate the primary budget balance that would achieve

that (known as the "debt stabilizing primary balance").[15] If the actual primary balance is less than the debt stabilizing balance, current fiscal policy implies an increasing ratio of public debt to GDP, and is therefore viewed as unsustainable. The difference between the actual and debt stabilizing primary balance indicates the degree of fiscal adjustment that is needed to achieve a constant debt-to-GDP ratio. A judgment can then be made as to whether such an adjustment is attainable in the political and economic environment of the country concerned.

Over the past few years, only a small number of emerging market economies (mainly in Asia) appear to have been running primary budget surpluses consistent with what is required to stabilize or reduce the ratio of public debt to GDP (Figure 3.8).[16] For others—particularly countries in Latin America—there has been a significant difference between the actual and debt stabilizing primary balance. Of course, a number of emerging market economies have recently made considerable efforts to increase their primary fiscal surpluses, and such actions, if sustained, could address such sustainability concerns. Further, were growth to be stronger or real interest rates lower than in the past, a smaller primary surplus would be needed to stabilize the debt ratio. Among the industrial countries, only Japan has had a large gap between its actual and debt stabilizing primary balance in recent years.

While these types of indicators of debt sustainability are useful because they are quite simple to construct and have a straightforward interpretation, their drawback is that they are based on an arbitrary definition of sustainability (i.e., stabilize the debt-to-GDP ratio). Incurring temporarily high deficits and debt levels, however,

---

[15]See Buiter (1985), Blanchard (1990), and Blanchard and others (1990). This method is based on long-run, perfect foresight considerations that transform the government's budget constraint into an equation that maps the long-run primary fiscal balance as a share of GDP into a "sustainable" debt-to-GDP ratio that remains constant over time. The debt stabilizing primary balance depends on the debt-to-GDP ratio, the real growth rate, and the real interest rate on government debt. The real interest rate on debt is in practice difficult to measure accurately, and requires, among other factors, a breakdown of debt and interest payments into local and foreign currency that is not always available. Here, an emerging market country's real interest rate is taken as the U.S. long-term real interest rate plus its average EMBI spread. For industrial countries, the real 10-year bond yield is used.

[16]The figure is based on the average primary balance and ratio of public debt to GDP for 2000–02, the average real interest rate for 1998–2002, and the average real growth rate for 1990–2002 (1997–2002 for transition economies).

may be appropriate in some circumstances, and it is certainly unlikely that a country should try and maintain a stable debt-to-GDP ratio at all times. Further, it may be of little practical policy use to know what is needed to stabilize the debt ratio when it is already at a high level and leaves a country vulnerable to shocks, such as a sudden stop in capital flows.

How Does Fiscal Policy Respond to Public Debt Accumulation?

A more flexible approach to assessing debt sustainability is to look at it within the context of the broader objectives and constraints of the fiscal policy decision-making process. One way to do this is to look at the relationship between fiscal policy instruments (the variables deemed to reflect the actions of policymakers) and the objectives of fiscal policy (such as stabilizing output fluctuations and maintaining debt sustainability). Such "reaction functions" or "policy rules" are well established in the analysis of monetary policy, but they are much less developed in studies of fiscal policy, and to date have not been applied to emerging market economies.[17]

Fiscal policy reaction functions were separately estimated for both industrial and emerging market economies, with the primary fiscal balance being considered the key operating target of the fiscal authorities. The primary fiscal balance is assumed to respond to public debt, but it is also affected by temporary factors such as the level of economic activity.[18] Within this

---

[17]Such fiscal policy studies for industrial countries include Bohn (1998) for the United States; Mélitz (1997) for OECD countries; Debrun and Wyplosz (1999) for euro area countries; and Gali and Perotti (2003) for European countries. Favero (2002) makes joint estimates of monetary and fiscal policy rules.

[18]For emerging market economies, four temporary factors that affect the primary balance were considered (all of which were found to significantly affect the primary surplus in the estimated fiscal policy reaction function): the business cycle, inflation, commodity prices, and debt restructuring or default. For industrial economies, the temporary factors considered were limited to the business cycle and inflation. Appendix 3.1 contains details of the sample selection and econometric methodology used in this section.

Figure 3.8. Emerging Market and Industrial Economies: Actual and Debt Stabilizing Primary Balances[1]
(Percent of GDP)

Primary balances in many emerging market economies have fallen short of what has been needed to stabilize the public debt ratio in recent years. This stands in contrast to most industrial countries.

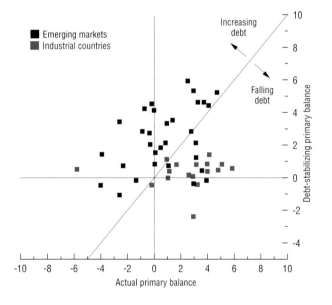

Source: IMF staff estimates.
[1]Calculated using the average primary surplus and public debt during 2000–02, the average real interest rate during 1998–2002, and the average real growth rate during 1990–2002 (1997–2002 for transition countries).

Box 3.2. Fiscal Risk: Contingent Liabilities and Demographics

Conventional approaches to fiscal sustainability, such as those discussed in the main text, focus on obligations *explicitly* recognized as liabilities in the budgetary system—that is, in practice, the total public debt and the financing of present expenditures. These, however, make up only a fraction of a government's potential obligations. As has been clearly illustrated in recent years, the recognition of *off-budget* obligations can significantly alter a government's debt position. Therefore, sustainability analysis needs to pay due attention to the government's off-budget obligations, which consist of two main categories.

- First, governments face a moral or *implicit* commitment to provide public goods and services in the future.[1] These depend on a series of interrelated factors such as future potential growth, demography, and specific pressures on health expenditures, such as those related to HIV-AIDS.

- Second, governments face obligations that will only come due if a specific event occurs.[2] These *contingent* liabilities may be the result of contractual or legal commitments such as loan guarantees and state insurance schemes, or stem from implicit understandings that, for example, the government should provide relief in the event of natural disasters, that it

should honor the financial commitments of institutions involved in quasi-fiscal activities, and that it should intervene beyond its explicit obligations under deposit insurance or other guarantees if the stability of the financial system is at risk.

Estimating off-budget items is subject to considerable uncertainty both because of the notorious unreliability of long-run projections and because of the very nature of contingent liabilities. As a consequence, implicit and contingent liabilities are generally interpreted as a source of risk affecting the "core" fiscal outlook resulting from conventional debt sustainability analysis. Of course, that fiscal risk comes in addition to the impact of macroeconomic risk—also discussed extensively in the main text. In recent years, events in a number of countries indicate that these two sources of risk can combine to produce full-blown financial and fiscal crises.

Among the many potential sources of fiscal risk, obligations related to adverse demographic trends—mainly population aging, but also the impact of HIV-AIDS on life expectancy in a number of developing countries—and implicit contingent liabilities—mainly associated with the preservation of financial system stability—stand out as the greatest threats to fiscal sustainability in both industrial and emerging market economies.

Impact of Aging

The consequences of population aging for fiscal sustainability are particularly significant in industrial economies, where demographic pressures combine with extensive social security systems. The problem is especially acute when pay-as-you-go (unfunded) pension systems and public health insurance prevail. A recent study by the European Commission (forthcoming) concluded that by 2050, age-related increases in pension and health care outlays would range between 2.6 percent of GDP in the United Kingdom and 11.8 percent of GDP in Greece, bearing "clear risks" to fiscal sustainability in at least six member states of the European Union. Other studies attempt to estimate the broad

Note: The main author of this box is Xavier Debrun. A recent and comprehensive coverage of fiscal risk can be found in Polackova Brixi and Schick (2002).

[1]If these implicit obligations exceed the future revenues implied by current tax policy (in net present value terms), the current policy amounts to shifting the payment of the government's bills to future generations. In a context of population aging, such intergenerational transfers raise particularly difficult issues—not discussed here—and have recently attracted a lot of attention (see Auerbach, Kotlikoff, and Leibfritz, 1999).

[2]Guidance on accounting treatment and disclosure of various kinds of contingent liabilities is provided in the *International Public Sector Accounting Standard* (IPSAS), paragraph 19, as released by the International Federation of Accountants in October 2002, and in paragraphs 62–66 of the IMF's *Manual on Fiscal Transparency.*

stock of implicit liabilities that would be implied by a continuation of current tax and expenditure policies, including unfunded pension liabilities and age-related increases in expenditures. For example, in a comparative analysis of 19 OECD countries, Frederiksen (2001) found that the stock of net implicit government liabilities varied between 84 percent of GDP in the United Kingdom and almost 400 percent of GDP in Spain, well above the respective public debt stocks in those countries. Such estimates are inevitably imprecise, and much higher numbers can be found elsewhere in the literature.

Implicit Contingent Liabilities

Although much harder to measure, contingent liabilities also constitute a significant risk to the fiscal outlook, with the implicit guarantees extended to the financial system and large nonfinancial enterprises being the most important sources of such liabilities. In recent years, a string of banking crises have dramatically illustrated the vulnerability of the fiscal position to contingent liabilities. Emerging market economies were particularly exposed, with an average estimated fiscal cost of almost 20 percent of GDP being incurred; in some cases this cost exceeded 50 percent of GDP (for example, Indonesia at the end of the 1990s). The realization of obligations vis-à-vis the financial sector has also affected industrial economies, although the average fiscal impact of banking crises has generally been much smaller than in emerging markets.

Today, a number of countries remain highly exposed to contingent financial sector obligations. Despite their inevitable imprecision, estimated ranges of financial sector liabilities suggest potentially very large fiscal costs in some countries in the event of future banking crises. For example, across a sample of 80 industrial

and emerging market economies, Standard & Poor's (2002a) most conservative estimates of these liabilities range from 3 percent of GDP (Mexico) to 64 percent of GDP (China).

How to Deal With Fiscal Risk?

Contingent liabilities and the growing pressures on expenditures from population aging present significant fiscal risks in many countries. Consequently, it is essential for fiscal decision makers—and for those to whom they are accountable—to be fully aware of these risks and the alternative fiscal strategies that may be needed to deal with them. Awareness implies the need for realistic long-run projections—an aspect especially important for countries facing large age-related obligations—and the complete disclosure of explicit contingent liabilities.[3] Budget documents should also provide a detailed discussion of the risks such liabilities imply for fiscal sustainability. A better grasp of fiscal risk, as well as greater public awareness about it, would encourage governments to adopt more prudent fiscal policies, including lower medium-term public debt objectives (which require structurally stronger fiscal positions in the short to medium run), provisions for impending expenditure shocks, and, last but not least, reforms of pension systems, social security, and other entitlements. Along with measures to make labor and product markets more competitive, those reforms would also help boost productivity (see the April 2003 *World Economic Outlook*), with direct feedback effects on the speed and the credibility of the fiscal consolidation process.

---

[3]It is understandably difficult to disclose implicit liabilities, if only because of the moral hazard problem such disclosure might create.

framework, the connection between policy actions and long-run debt sustainability—the key issue of interest here—lies in the fact that a positive response of the primary balance to public debt generally implies the consistency of fiscal

policy with long-run solvency (see Bohn, 1998, for a formal demonstration, and Appendix 3.1). As discussed earlier, however, long-run solvency (satisfying the present-value budget constraint) is a relatively undemanding criterion as it only

Figure 3.9   Relationship Between Public Debt and the Primary Balance[1]
(Percent of GDP; 1990–2002)

Primary surpluses respond much more strongly to debt in industrial countries than in emerging market economies. Indeed, fiscal policy in emerging market economies stops responding to an increase in public debt when debt is above 50 percent of GDP. This stands in contrast to industrial countries, where fiscal policy responds more aggressively when debt is above 80 percent of GDP.

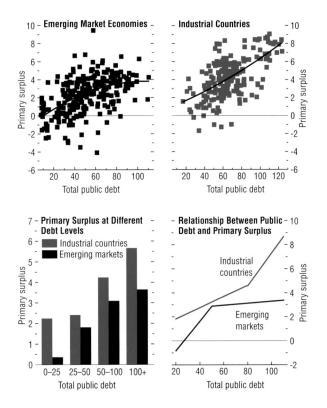

Source: IMF staff estimates.
[1]Primary balance adjusted for the impact of transitory shocks.

requires a commitment to adjust policy in the (possibly distant) future.

Two conclusions follow from examining the link between the adjusted primary balance (i.e., after the impact of temporary factors has been accounted for) and public debt.[19] First, emerging market economies as a group exhibit a lower average adjusted primary balance than industrial countries at any level of public debt (Figure 3.9). Second, the response of the primary surplus weakens as the debt-to-GDP ratio rises in emerging market economies, and this response stops altogether when debt exceeds 50 percent of GDP. This suggests that—on average—the conduct of fiscal policy in emerging market economies is not consistent with ensuring sustainability once public debt exceeds a threshold of 50 percent of GDP. In contrast, industrial countries respond strongly to rising debt when debt is at a high level. Indeed, when debt is above 80 percent of GDP, the estimated adjustment in the primary surplus is almost three times as large as that at lower debt levels. These estimates of course are for a large sample of emerging and industrial countries, and the reported results are an average for each sample. Therefore, this behavior is not true for every country in either the emerging market or industrial country group; some emerging market economies have acted quite strongly to maintain a sustainable debt position.

The analysis also indicates clear differences between emerging market and industrial countries in terms of the cyclicality of fiscal policy (Figure 3.10). While a 1 percentage point improvement in the output gap is estimated to result in an average improvement in the primary balance of only 0.04 percentage point of GDP in Latin America and 0.23 percentage point of GDP in non–Latin American emerging markets, it leads to a 0.87 percentage point of

---

[19]The figures and econometric results discussed in this section refer to the association between the primary surplus adjusted for the influence of temporary factors (as a percent of GDP) and the ratio of public debt to GDP observed at the end of the preceding year.

GDP improvement in industrial countries.[20] These differences are primarily driven by the behavior of expenditures, which, as a percent of GDP, are unreactive to cyclical fluctuations in emerging markets (in Latin American countries, expenditures actually appear to be slightly procyclical). In cyclical upswings, outlays expand at the same pace as economic activity (or faster in Latin America), but when economic growth weakens, revenues decline and lending conditions tighten, and outlays fall.[21] This behavior contrasts to that in industrial countries, where expenditures increase by less than economic growth in an upturn and fall by less than activity in a downturn, thus exerting a stabilizing influence on the economy. This behavior likely reflects the significant automatic stabilizers at work through the extensive social security systems in industrial countries, giving to government expenditure an insurance role against macroeconomic volatility (see Rodrik, 1998, and Fatàs and Mihov, forthcoming). Interestingly, better institutional quality is found to be associated with a more countercyclical policy in emerging market economies, suggesting that the ability to control expenditures (and raise revenues) is less of a problem in countries with better institutions (see Appendix 3.1).

These results are suggestive of a link between debt sustainability and the short-term conduct of fiscal policy. Because their behavior indicates a strong commitment to debt sustainability, industrial countries can run countercyclical fiscal policies without lenders becoming concerned about sustainability issues. In many emerging market economies, however, the ability to adjust fiscal

Figure 3.10. Emerging Market and Industrial Economies: Sensitivity of Fiscal Policy to the Business Cycle[1]
(Percent of GDP; 1990–2002)

Fiscal policy is much more countercyclical in industrial countries than in emerging market economies. Most of the cyclical sensitivity of the primary balance is due to the cyclical response of primary expenditure.

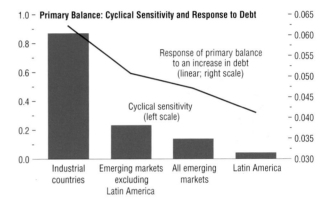

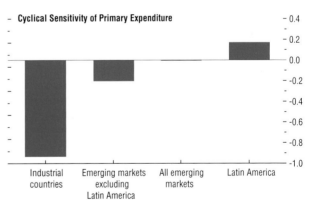

Source: IMF staff estimates.
[1]Response, in percent of GDP, to a percentage point improvement in the output gap.

---

[20]A number of other studies have found evidence of procyclical fiscal policies. For example, Talvi and Végh (2000) argue that fiscal policy is procyclical in most countries outside the G-7, while the April 2002 *World Economic Outlook* found that fiscal policy was procyclical in a number of Latin American countries.

[21]Procyclical fiscal policy in Latin America has implications for social spending and the poor. Braun and Di Grescia (2003) find that social spending in the region is procyclical (although less so than total government spending), and that in crisis situations governments often reduce social spending, which adversely affects the poor.

policy to maintain debt sustainability is often in doubt. Lenders therefore quickly become concerned when deficits widen, and the tight resource constraint forces governments to cut expenditures during a downturn, further adding to the economic weakness.

Do Governments in Emerging Market Economies Overborrow?

A third approach to assessing public debt sustainability is to see if a government is "overborrowing" in the sense of whether its debt stock exceeds the present discounted value of its expected future primary surpluses. To operationalize such a calculation, expected future primary balances are here approximated by the average primary balance achieved during the sample period, on the assumption that a government's fiscal policy track record is the best guide to what it can be expected to achieve in the future. A benchmark level of public debt (as a percent of GDP) is then calculated and compared with actual debt. The extent of over- or underborrowing is measured by the ratio of actual public debt to the benchmark level of debt, with a ratio greater than 1 suggesting that a government is overborrowing relative to what is justified by its fiscal policy track record.[22] The discount rate—the difference between the real interest rate and real output growth—is proxied by the difference between the real LIBOR interest rate plus a country-specific spread and the average real GDP growth.[23]

The benchmark debt-to-GDP ratio was calculated for 50 countries (14 industrial, 21 emerging market, and 15 developing) using data for the 1985–2002 period.[24] The median value of the ratio for industrial countries is estimated at 75 percent of GDP, three times higher than the 25 percent of GDP estimate for emerging market economies (Figure 3.11). Comparing the actual and benchmark public debt levels suggests that many emerging market economies have indeed been overborrowing as the typical (median) emerging market economy has a ratio of public debt to GDP that is 2½ times larger than its fiscal policy track record would suggest is warranted.[25] While this is lower than for the "other developing countries" group, it compares unfavorably with the typical industrial country, where the ratio is less than 1. There are differences, however, among emerging market regions. Asian countries have a similar ratio to industrial countries, while countries in Latin America and other regions have a ratio of 2½ and 6, respectively, suggesting significant overborrowing. Further, the typical emerging market economy with a default history has an overborrowing ratio of 3½, compared with a ratio of less than 1 for a nondefaulter. These results convey the same message as before: many emerging market economies need to generate larger primary surpluses than they have done in the past to be able to sustain their public debt levels.

The fact that many countries overborrow raises the question of whether there are any common features that help to explain this behavior. An econometric analysis suggests that

---

[22]This overborrowing ratio is closely related to the public debt sustainability measure discussed earlier, but it does not provide a quantitative estimate of the primary balance adjustment needed to stabilize the debt-to-GDP ratio. For a country that has undertaken significant fiscal reforms in recent years and is now achieving a higher sustained primary surplus than it has historically, the assumption that its past track record provides a good guide to future primary surpluses may of course not be valid.

[23]If future growth rates are expected to be higher, or real interest rates lower, than their historic average, this will affect the estimated overborrowing ratio. Because data on spreads are not available for the whole sample period or for all countries, the Institutional Investor rating—which is highly correlated with spreads—is used to derive a proxy (see Appendix 3.1).

[24]The calculation was not made for those countries where the average primary balance was negative or the discount factor was negative in the sample period.

[25]Because of a number of outliers, the mean overborrowing ratio for emerging market economies at 16 is much higher than the median.

the following policy variables are important determinants of overborrowing.[26]

- *Government revenues.* Governments with low revenues will often have difficulty meeting their desired expenditures from revenues, increasing the pressure on them to borrow. The econometric results suggest that an increase in emerging market economies' revenue ratio to the industrial country average would, other things remaining unchanged, reduce the overborrowing ratio by about 35 percent.

- *Trade openness.* Openness has a positive effect on economic growth, which helps mitigate the existing debt burden. Further, more open economies are able to generate the larger trade surpluses needed to service foreign debt after an exchange rate depreciation, and are therefore less likely to experience difficulties with external public debt.[27] The estimates suggest that reducing foreign exchange rate restrictions for current transactions—the proxy used here for trade openness—to industrial country levels would, other things remaining unchanged, reduce the overborrowing ratio in emerging markets by 60 percent.[28]

- *The quality of domestic institutions and the nature of the political system.* A number of studies have found a relationship between the quality of fiscal institutions—the rules and regulations by which budgets are constructed and implemented—and fiscal outcomes.[29] Further,

---

[26]Other factors not directly under the control of policymakers—macroeconomic volatility and relative (to the U.S.) per capita income—were also included in the regressions, as was an industrial country dummy variable (see Appendix 3.1 for details).

[27]On openness and economic growth, see the survey by Berg and Krueger (2003), and on openness and external debt difficulties, see Sachs (1985).

[28]The index of exchange rate restrictions for current transactions is used here because it is available for the countries during the full sample period of the analysis. The reported results, however, remain broadly unchanged when alternative measures of trade openness—such as that developed by Sachs and Warner (1995)—are used.

[29]See, for example, von Hagen (1992) and von Hagen and Harden (1995). Alesina and others (1998) find the nature of the budget process strongly influences fiscal outcomes in Latin America.

Figure 3.11. Do Governments in Emerging Market Economies Overborrow?
(Median values)

Governments in emerging market countries have a tendency to overborrow; however, there are important regional differences.

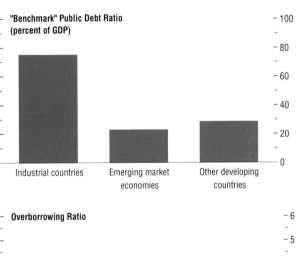

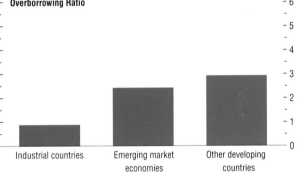

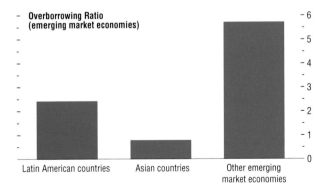

Source: IMF staff estimates.

good institutions are associated with stronger growth, which boosts revenues and eases the debt servicing burden.[30] On the other hand, political systems that deliver weak (minority or coalition) governments often delay fiscal adjustment and accumulate public debt based on short-term needs.[31] Simple correlations suggest that good institutions are associated with less overborrowing. In the econometric analysis, however, only the protection of property rights was found to be a significant explanatory variable, with the estimated coefficient suggesting that were the protection of property rights in emerging market economies to be raised to the level of industrial countries, the overborrowing ratio would be reduced by about 50 percent.

Uncertainty and Public Debt Sustainability

One of the problems with the three approaches to debt sustainability that have been discussed so far in this chapter is that they do not take account of the uncertainties that face governments in emerging market economies.[32] As outlined earlier, government revenues in emerging market economies are more variable than in industrial economies, and a government could find itself in a situation where it is faced with low revenues for an extended period of time because of, say, a collapse in the price of the country's primary commodity export. Further, emerging market governments also face considerable uncertainty from interest and exchange rate movements. There have recently been a number of attempts to incorporate such uncertainties into the analysis of public debt sustainability. One approach has been to apply the Value-at-Risk (VaR) methodology that is com-

monly used in the assessment of financial institution risk to look at the risks faced by the government—see Box 3.3 for a discussion of this methodology. A different approach has been to use economic models that incorporate uncertainty to derive estimates of sustainable public debt ratios (see Mendoza and Oviedo, 2003).

One way to look at the impact of uncertainty on public debt sustainability is to consider the case of a government that is credibly committed to servicing its debts in all circumstances. Such a government would need to take into account the fact that its future revenues—and consequently primary balance outcomes—are uncertain, and that it could be faced with the possibility of a long period of low revenues in the future. To be credibly committed to servicing its debt in all circumstances, the government cannot borrow more than the debt that it would be able to sustain with the primary balances that would occur with these low revenue outcomes.[33] This is not to say that the government could not borrow at all: if actual debt were below the maximum sustainable debt level, the government would be able to borrow until the threshold was reached, at which point it would need to reduce expenditures to maintain the credibility of its commitment.

The requirement that a government should only borrow up to the debt level that it could sustain in the face of a long period of low revenues may seem a stringent one. Emerging markets, however, have faced long periods of low revenue realizations in the past when the price of their main commodity export has fallen. For example, governments in oil-exporting countries faced this situation after the collapse of oil prices in the 1980s.[34] In such circumstances, the government is suddenly confronted with a debt stock that it had believed was sustainable when revenues

---

[30]See the April 2003 *World Economic Outlook* for an analysis of the relationship between growth and institutions.

[31]Alesina, Perotti, and Tavares (1998) find that coalition governments often have a harder time consolidating fiscal policy than do single party governments.

[32]See Gavin and others (1996) for an extensive discussion of the effects of volatility on fiscal policies in Latin America.

[33]Revenue volatility can also create liquidity problems even if long-run public debt is sustainable.

[34]Indeed, slumps in commodity prices—particularly oil—are generally quite long lasting. For example, Cashin, McDermott, and Scott (2002) find that slumps in commodity prices typically last for about three and a half years, with slumps in oil prices on average lasting over four years.

related to commodity exports were high, but which is not sustainable with the new reality of lower revenues from commodity exports.

To implement these ideas, it is first necessary to determine what constitutes a low revenue outcome, and in such circumstances, what fiscal adjustment the government could make. Here, a low revenue outcome is characterized by a revenue-to-GDP ratio that is two standard deviations below the average level, and the range of primary expenditure reductions that emerging markets have made in the past is taken as an indication of the fiscal adjustment that a government could potentially achieve. Using these assumptions, Figure 3.12 shows the maximum sustainable public debt ratios for two "typical" emerging market economies and an industrial economy for different assumptions about the possible variability of their future revenues (measured by the coefficient of variation) and their commitment to adjust expenditures if a low revenue outcome occurs. In the calculations, both emerging market economies are assumed to have revenue and primary expenditure ratios of 20 percent of GDP on average— broadly the averages seen in non-European emerging markets—while one (a "low-risk" country—Case A) has a real interest rate on public debt that is 5 percentage points higher than its growth rate, and the other (a "high-risk" country—Case B) has a real interest rate that exceeds its growth rate by 10 percentage points.[35] The industrial country (Case C) has revenue and primary expenditure ratios of 40 percent of GDP on average, and a real interest rate that is 2.5 percentage points higher than its growth rate.

Looking at the first emerging market country example (Case A), the more stable its revenues— i.e., the smaller the coefficient of variation of the revenue ratio—the higher is the maximum ratio

[35]While these assumed differences between the real interest rate and the real growth rate may seem high, they are intended to capture a situation where a country has been hit by a shock and spreads have increased sharply and growth weakened.

Figure 3.12. Maximum Ratios of Sustainable Public Debt to GDP[1]

Countries with more variable tax revenues, less ability to adjust expenditures, and a larger difference between the real interest rate and the real growth rate are able to sustain lower public debt ratios.

Low-Risk Emerging Market Economy (Case A)

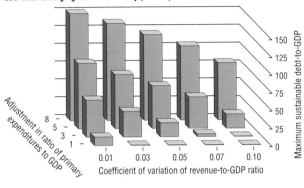

High-Risk Emerging Market Economy (Case B)

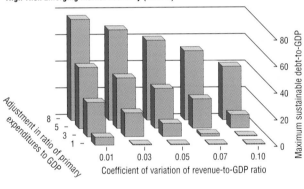

Industrial Economy (Case C)

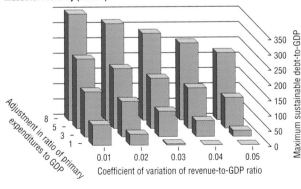

Source: IMF staff estimates.
[1]Based on the Mendoza-Oviedo Model. Zeros indicate that the government can not sustain a positive debt-to-GDP ratio under these conditions.

Box 3.3. Assessing Fiscal Sustainability Under Uncertainty

Conventional approaches to assessing fiscal sustainability and vulnerability—such as scenario analysis or summary indicators—are subject to a number of weaknesses. Besides limitations in coverage (they usually focus only on debt, and therefore exclude a range of contingent assets and liabilities and other components of the public sector balance sheet), they do not adequately address the downside risk of adverse future economic and financial outcomes. Attempts to correct this deficiency—particularly critical for emerging market economies that typically face a volatile economic environment—have usually focused on sensitivity (or stress) tests with respect to arbitrary changes in selected variables.

A recent extension of the Value-at-Risk (VaR) methodology—which is commonly used in the assessment of financial institution risk—to the public sector balance sheet provides a more comprehensive assessment of a country's fiscal sustainability. In this approach, the fiscal risks that are faced by the government and the potential impact that these may have on its net worth position (assets minus liabilities, which are defined to include the present value of contingent assets and liabilities) can be explicitly modeled.[1] Among other things, such fiscal risks may include interest and exchange rate movements, commodity price changes, and output fluctuations. The VaR analysis assesses the effect that movements in such variables, and their co-movements—for example, between oil prices and exchange rates—have on a government's net worth position, and it summarizes the worst possible position that the government could be in after a given time period for a given level of confidence. Put a different way, the VaR presents a numerical estimate of the potential loss in net worth the government could face over a given period of time if a "worst-case" scenario were to develop.

The VaR analysis proceeds broadly as follows. The first step is to calculate the government's current net worth from its balance sheet. But this net worth position in the future is uncertain, and will be strongly affected by the outcomes of key variables that affect the value of the government's assets and liabilities. For example, in a country that is a large oil exporter, the value of the government's assets will be influenced by the future price of oil, which is uncertain. Likewise, the value of both assets and liabilities may be affected by future exchange rate movements. To capture these uncertainties, the possible future movements of the main risk variables that affect the balance sheet, and any co-movements between these variables, are estimated. Based on these estimates, an overall probability distribution of the government's net worth is calculated, and the overall risks to the government's balance sheet can then be assessed. For example, while the estimated net worth may currently be, say, 100 percent of GDP, the calculations may suggest that because of the risks the government faces there is a 5 percent chance that in one year its net worth will only be 60 percent of GDP. In this case, the government's "value-at-risk" is said to be 40 percent of GDP.

From the VaR analysis, the government can identify the factors that present the most significant risks to its net worth position, and the potential size of these risks. To the extent possible, it can then act to mitigate or limit these risks, while also pursuing other fiscal reforms that could strengthen its overall balance sheet position and make it more resilient to such shocks if they occur.

While in principle the VaR approach could be applied to any country, incorporating the specific behavioral and institutional features of that country, at present the absence of data on the public sector balance sheet in most emerging market countries precludes the widespread application of the technique. A stylized applica-

Note: The main authors of this box are George Kopits and Tim Callen.
[1]See Barnhill and Kopits (2003). In a similar spirit, IMF (2003) reports the results of a stochastic simulation exercise that looked at the probability distribution of future public debt outcomes for a sample of 41 emerging market countries.

tion of the VaR approach has, however, recently been conducted for Ecuador, a country where the necessary data are available (see Barnhill and Kopits, 2003). The results from this exercise, which are briefly discussed below, are broadly illustrative of some of the fiscal risks that many emerging market countries face, and should not be taken to imply that these risks are greater in Ecuador than elsewhere.

The VaR calculations—which were carried out on the balance sheet for the year 2000—suggest that the public sector in Ecuador faces a number of important fiscal risks. The government's net worth position was found to be vulnerable to shocks that could affect the present value of its future income from petroleum reserves, the profits of its state-owned enterprises, the net liabilities of the public pension system, and its external liabilities. The VaR analysis was also used to look at the relative importance of spe-

cific fiscal risks in Ecuador by separately assessing the potential impact of interest and exchange rate movements and oil prices on the government's net worth position. Interest rate volatility was found to be the single most important source of risk facing the government in Ecuador. If, hypothetically, the government was able to eliminate the interest rate risk it faced, it would significantly reduce the potential erosion in net worth that it could experience in a worst-case scenario. Exchange rate movements were also an important source of risk at the time, and Ecuador's move to dollarization—which was actually introduced in early 2000—consequently reduced the risks to the government's balance sheet. Finally, if oil prices—the only truly exogenous source of risk—had been hypothetically stabilized, this would also have limited the downside to net worth, but by less than eliminating interest or exchange rate risk.

of sustainable public debt to GDP for any given level of expenditure adjustment that it can commit to. The rationale for this is that when the government is faced with a low revenue outcome, the actual revenue-to-GDP ratio will be higher, and consequently the primary surplus larger, than if the variability of revenues is greater. For example, if this country has a coefficient of variation on its revenue ratio of 5 percent and can commit to adjust primary expenditures by 5 percent of GDP, then its maximum sustainable public debt ratio is 60 percent of GDP. For the "high-risk" emerging market country (Case B) with similar revenue and expenditure characteristics, the maximum sustainable debt ratio is just 30 percent of GDP. But, if the coefficient of variation for this country is 7 percent, then the maximum debt level is only 22 percent of GDP. For the industrial country (Case C), the combination of a higher average revenue ratio, low revenue volatility, and a smaller difference between the real interest rate and the real growth rate means its maximum

sustainable debt ratio is higher than for the emerging market economies even if it can only commit to a modest cut in expenditures. For example, with a commitment to cut primary expenditures by 3 percent of GDP and revenue volatility of 3 percent, the maximum sustainable debt ratio for the industrial country is about 85 percent of GDP.

These calculations illustrate the link between revenue generation capacity, revenue variability, and primary expenditure adjustment—all of which affect the primary balance—and debt sustainability. If a country has low and variable government revenues, it will be able to sustain a lower public debt level than a country with a higher and more stable revenue base. This means that the sustainable debt level may vary—potentially by a considerable amount—between countries (it will also depend on real interest rates and growth). The implication is that differences in sustainable debt levels can be expected not only between industrial and emerging market economies, but also among emerging market economies themselves. For example, India—which has relatively stable government revenues—could be expected to sustain a higher debt level than Venezuela, where revenues are much more variable. (Of course, there may also be other reasons why India could sustain a higher public debt ratio, including the maturity profile and interest costs of the debt, the size of the domestic bond market, and its relatively strong growth rate.) Indeed, countries with higher average revenue ratios and lower revenue variability do in general have higher public debt ratios (Figure 3.13). Because revenue variability has important implications for debt sustainability, proposals have been made to create debt instruments that could help cushion emerging markets from changing economic conditions (Box 3.4).

Can Governments in Emerging Markets Economies Sustain Their Current Debt Levels?

A common theme running through the results presented in this section is that historically many emerging market economies have not generated large enough primary budget surpluses to ensure the sustainability of their public debt. This stands in contrast to industrial countries. This inability to generate adequate primary surpluses is both a function of weak revenue bases (which generally have low yields and are volatile) and an inability to control expenditures during economic upswings (this appears to be particularly important in Latin America). These factors suggest that emerging market economies can generally sustain lower public debt ratios than industrial countries. Although this sustainable debt level will certainly vary—and potentially by a considerable amount—the calculations based on past fiscal performance suggest that for the typical emerging market economy it is quite low. Of course, industrial countries face considerable pressures from population aging going forward, so this analysis should not be taken as suggesting that public debt levels in these countries are currently at a comfortable level.

Figure 3.13. Ratios of Revenue and Public Debt to GDP

Countries with higher and less volatile revenue ratios tend to have higher public debt levels.

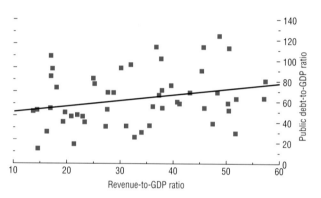

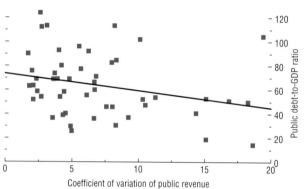

Source: IMF staff estimates.

How Can High Public Debt Levels Be Reduced?

If governments face high public debt levels, what can they do to reduce them? Governments have a number of potential policy options available to them to reduce their debt: (1) they can adjust fiscal policy and run primary budget surpluses sufficient to reduce the debt; (2) they can seek to grow or inflate their way out of their debt difficulties; (3) they can sell assets to retire debt; or (4) they can explicitly default on the debt.

While reducing the public debt ratio through strong economic growth would generally be a government's preferred option, growth is beyond the direct control of the government. Of course, the government can play an important role by creating an environment conducive to growth through the implementation of sound macroeconomic and structural policies (including by not accumulating excess debt that could adversely affect private sector activity).[36] The other options each have advantages and disadvantages. Reducing public debt by running primary budget surpluses, for example, maintains the fiscal credibility of the government, but is often difficult politically—particularly if high primary surpluses need to be maintained for any length of time—and may involve decisions that,

at least in the short run, have a detrimental effect on activity.[37] An explicit default or high inflation provide ways of reducing debt without having to run larger primary surpluses, but they both entail costs. If it defaults, a government is likely to suffer a loss of reputation that could prevent or limit its future borrowing, and hence constrain its future fiscal policy options, while high inflation has significant negative effects on economic activity and welfare.[38] Finally, a policy of selling government assets is only likely to be successful in reducing debt if accompanied by responsible fiscal policy (so the proceeds are not simply spent), and the policy does not change the underlying net worth position of the government although it reduces debt.

To examine how large public sector debt reductions have occurred in practice, data for 79 industrial, emerging market, and other developing countries for the period 1970–2002 were used, and a sample of large public debt reductions was constructed as follows. Cases were identified where public debt was reduced over a three-year period, and then the top 15 percent of these episodes (in terms of the size of the debt reduction, which in the sample corresponded to a drop in public debt of at least 18 percent of GDP) were chosen. Lastly, cases in which the debt stock at the end of the three-year

[36]A simple correlation between public debt and growth in emerging market economies since 1990 shows a clear negative relationship. More formally, Pattillo, Poirson, and Ricci (2002) find that external debt begins to have a negative effect on growth once it exceeds 35–40 percent of GDP.

[37]Assessing the impact of fiscal consolidation on economic activity is not straightforward. While most evidence points to the conclusion that fiscal multipliers are positive—i.e., that a fiscal consolidation will have a negative impact on growth in the short run—this appears not always to be the case (see Hemming, Kell, and Mahfouz, 2002). Recent studies in advanced countries have shown that if fiscal consolidation is mainly achieved through a reduction in current spending it may be expansionary (see Alesina, Perotti, and Tavares, 1998). For emerging market economies where there is a public debt sustainability problem and the risk premia on interest rates are high, a credible fiscal consolidation could result in a large fall in interest rates, spurring private activity and more than offsetting the withdrawal of fiscal stimulus. Hemming and Ter-Minassian (2003) discuss the impact of fiscal tightening during crisis episodes.

[38]The costs of an explicit default and/or high inflation are difficult to measure. For an extensive discussion of reputation and sovereign debt, see Obstfeld and Rogoff (1996) and the references therein. A default affects a country's access to capital markets, its borrowing costs, and its trade relations with its debtors. Empirical evidence on the size of the costs of default, however, is mixed. For example, Lindert and Morton (1989) argue that investors pay little attention to the past repayment record of a borrowing government. Özler (1993), however, finds that countries with default histories faced higher commercial bank interest rates in the 1970s. In terms of costs through the trade channel, Rose (2002) finds that a sovereign debt default is associated with a decline in bilateral trade between a debtor and its creditors of about 8 percent a year and this persists for about fifteen years. With regard to the costs of high inflation, Lucas (2003) estimates that the gains from eliminating an inflation rate of 200 percent—a level observed in many Latin American countries during the 1980s—are in excess of 5 percent of income in the long run.

Box 3.4. The Case for Growth-Indexed Bonds

Highly leveraged emerging market economies are heavily exposed to volatility in economic conditions, resulting in increased risk of financial distress and even debt crises. Debt instruments with repayments linked to key macroeconomic variables could help cushion emerging markets from unexpected changes in economic conditions. In particular, the idea of creating bonds indexed to GDP—or, equivalently, GDP growth—has recently regained attention (see Borensztein and Mauro, 2002).

Growth-indexed bonds could work as follows. Consider a country whose real GDP has been growing for many years at 3 percent, and is expected to continue doing so. Assume that this country can issue regular bonds at 7 percent interest. That country could contemplate issuing growth-indexed bonds whose yearly coupon payments will be increased by, for example, 1 percentage point for every percentage point by which GDP growth exceeds its 3 percent trend, with a symmetric reduction in the coupon rate when growth falls short of the reference growth rate (the contract could specify that coupon payments cannot fall below zero). In years when growth turns out to be 1 percent, the coupon will be 5 percent, and in years when growth turns out to be 5 percent, the coupon will be 9 percent.

Such growth indexation results in a number of advantages. First, growth-indexed bonds would help to reduce the volatility of debt-to-GDP ratios, thereby reducing the likelihood of crises. When GDP growth turns out lower than usual, interest payments due will also be lower than in the absence of indexation, and vice versa. Second, growth-indexed bonds provide an "automatic-stabilizer"-type mechanism, thus reducing the need for procyclical policies. These bonds would help avoid politically difficult adjustments in the primary balance at times of weak economic performance and, conversely, they would help avoid excessive fiscal expan-

sions in times of strong growth. This is especially important for emerging market economies, where economic downturns often lead to waning confidence in international financial markets, forcing them into untimely fiscal tightening to defend credibility. But interest savings, and the corresponding room for a somewhat lower primary fiscal surplus, in times of weak economic growth might also prove appealing for advanced countries—particularly those with limits on their overall fiscal deficits, such as the EMU countries. Finally, growth-indexed bonds would improve risk sharing at the international level. Indeed, individual GDP risk has relatively low correlation with global risk and can be largely diversified in a financial portfolio; global investors holding growth-indexed bonds issued by a variety of countries might thus be willing to accept a relatively low risk premium (see Borensztein and Mauro, 2002).

While focusing on GDP risk has intrinsic appeal, there are also other sources of risk affecting the debt-service capacity of emerging markets. Terms of trade risk has been stressed in this regard, supporting the idea of debt instruments with repayments adjusted to the world price of some key commodity, for example. However, the economic structure of many emerging market countries is becoming increasingly more diversified. Indexing bond payments to the prices of one or two key commodities may provide significant insurance only to a handful of countries. Indexing to the growth of GDP—the broadest measure of how the economy is doing—would provide far greater insurance benefits.

Similar proposals have been on the table for some time. In particular, the idea of linking debt payments to growth, exports, or export prices generated considerable interest in the aftermath of the debt crisis in the 1980s. In the event, a few of the Brady bonds that were issued to restructure syndicated bank loans included "value recovery rights" (VRRs) that occasionally provided for a higher payoff to bondholders in the event that GDP (or GDP per capita) of

Note: The main authors of this box are Eduardo Borensztein and Paolo Mauro.

the debtor country rose above a certain level. Precedents of countries that have used elements of GDP indexation in debt restructurings include Bosnia and Herzegovina, Bulgaria, and Costa Rica. For example, a portion of Bulgaria's Brady bonds provided for a GDP "kicker" such that, once real GDP exceeded 125 percent of its 1993 level, creditors would be entitled to an additional 0.5 percent in interest for every 1 percent of real GDP growth in the year prior to interest payment. A more recent precedent is a bond issued by the City of Buenos Aires in 2003 as part of a debt restructuring operation, which includes indexation of principal repayments to the city's tax revenues.

Still, creating markets for new financial instruments is by no means easy, and there are many practical and conceptual difficulties with the implementation of a growth-indexed bond market. Would investors find growth-indexed bonds too complicated or risky? Could countries misreport their growth rates or lose incentive to grow rapidly?

International investors already invest heavily in stocks of emerging market countries, whose prices are much more volatile than the GDP growth rates of the same countries. Moreover, international investors are already highly exposed to GDP risk under standard debt contracts, though implicitly, as growth slowdowns cause drops in bond prices, and may even prompt defaults. While some investors may be turned away by instruments that are difficult to understand and price, the indexation mechanism is not alien to financial markets, as inflation-indexed bonds are well established in several sovereign debt markets in both advanced and developing countries. In addition, as noted above, a few emerging market countries have already issued bonds that include payment conditions that are contingent on GDP.

If growth-indexed bonds were to constitute a large fraction of a country's external debt, that country's authorities might be tempted to understate its growth rate or even reduce the growth orientation of its policies. How strong that temptation would be, and whether it could

be resisted, are open questions, but they might reasonably make some investors reluctant to hold growth-indexed bonds. Nevertheless, one should note that it is high growth rather than low growth that typically gets politicians reelected. Data revisions could present another obstacle for investors. The bond contracts would therefore need to establish a clear method for dealing with revisions: for example, coupon payments for each date x could be based on GDP as estimated on date y, ignoring any subsequent data revision. Of course, the contract should specify that, for the purposes of the bond payment, the methodology used to estimate GDP data cannot be changed in midcourse.

Beneficial financial innovation is often hindered by the need to coordinate the actions of many potential market participants before a new instrument can be launched. As a result, historically, innovations in sovereign borrowing have been limited and have often seemed to emerge from a combination of historical accident, special circumstances, and strong official intervention. For example, a forceful case has been made for the introduction of inflation-indexed bonds by distinguished economists since the nineteenth century. Yet, inflation-indexed bonds represent a large share of debt in only a few countries. Moreover, the timing of introduction and the popularity of these bonds present no obvious regularities in terms of economic circumstances such as inflation history or the level of development. Similarly, financial flows to emerging markets switched from the bond format—the historical norm—to syndicated bank loans in the 1970s, and back to bonds in the 1990s largely on account of official encouragement and guarantees, regulations in financial markets, and the international financing needs that originated from the oil price shock in 1973. The episodes of financial turbulence that prompted the efforts under way to rethink the international financial architecture might thus also help bring about a new era of innovation in sovereign finance instruments.

Figure 3.14. How Do Emerging Market Countries Reduce Their Public Debt?[1]

(Percent of GDP)

Strong growth and fiscal consolidation were key factors behind the decline in the debt-to-GDP ratio. Fiscal consolidation was largely achieved through a reduction in the ratio of current expenditures to GDP.

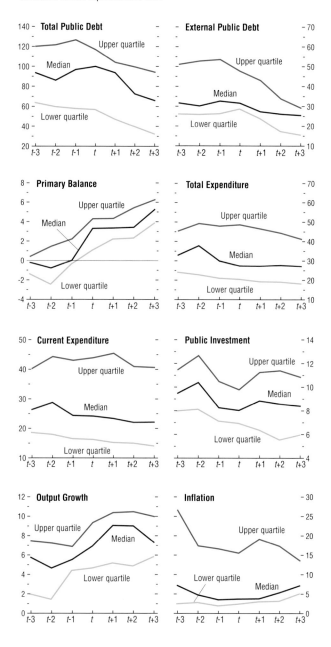

Source: IMF staff estimates.
[1]Only includes debt reduction episodes that do not involve debt defaulter countries.

period was still above the level three years prior to the event were eliminated. This selection process highlighted 26 debt reduction episodes in the emerging market economies in the sample.[39]

A large majority (19 out of 26) of these episodes were associated with a debt default. While it is not possible to identify the exact impact that the restructuring had on the outstanding debt, it appears to have generally been an important factor behind the decline in the debt ratio. The seven remaining episodes (which took place in five different countries) were then examined to understand the principal factors behind the debt reductions that have not involved a restructuring.[40] In these seven cases, the median decline in the public sector debt ratio was 34 percent of GDP over the three-year period (Figure 3.14). Strong growth appears to have been a significant contributing factor to the decline in the debt ratio, with real GDP growth averaging 8.5 percent a year. Fiscal consolidation played an important role as well, with a significant improvement in the primary balance beginning immediately before the debt began to fall. The fiscal consolidation was largely the result of expenditure restraint—with current expenditure being reduced and capital spending remaining constant—although the revenue ratio also increased somewhat. Moderate inflation of about 5 percent also helped, while exchange rate appreciation acted to reduce outstanding external public debt.

This analysis suggests that while large debt reductions have often occurred in conjunction with debt defaults, there are cases where they have been brought about by a combination of strong economic growth and fiscal consolidation. Interestingly, in all five of the countries where debt was reduced without a restructuring, the public debt ratio is still below the level at the

[39]This exercise is roughly parallel to the analysis of major reductions in external debt in Reinhart, Rogoff, and Savastano (2003).

[40]These occurred in Hungary, Israel (twice), Korea, Malaysia (twice), and Thailand.

beginning of the identified debt reduction episode (although in the Asian countries, the ratio has again risen in recent years following the financial crisis in the region). The outcome is more mixed in the cases where debt reduction was associated with a default. While in 10 of these countries debt has remained below the level prevailing at the beginning of the debt reduction episode, in 5 cases the country has either defaulted again and/or debt is currently above the level at the beginning of the debt reduction episode. This suggests that default does not always provide a long-term solution to public debt problems, and that, unless it is accompanied by complementary changes in fiscal and other economic policies, it will not be successful in fostering sustainably lower debt levels.

Whether it is achieved with or without a debt restructuring, a substantial and sustained reduction in public sector debt requires the implementation of sound economic and fiscal policies over a number of years. For example, Chile has implemented strong and sustained fiscal (and other economic) reforms since it defaulted on its external public debt in the 1980s, and the government has reduced its debt from 54 percent of GDP in 1990 to 21 percent of GDP in 2002. Several elements have contributed to this successful adjustment, including expenditure restraint, improved revenue collection, and state enterprise reform that transformed losses into significant profit transfers to the government. Privatization proceeds have also been used to reduce debt, and real exchange rate appreciation has reduced external debt in relation to GDP. Chile did not impose specific rules for the fiscal balance, but other institutional factors played useful roles in maintaining fiscal discipline, including giving more power to the finance ministry than to other ministries or the legislature; prohibiting the central bank from extending credit to the government; and preventing lower levels of government from borrowing. Since 2001, the government has committed to an annual target—a surplus of 1 percent of GDP—for the central government structural bal-

ance (adjusted for cyclical effects and copper price movements), thus allowing automatic stabilizers to work.

The benefits of these sustained policy actions are clear. The financial markets have confidence in Chile's fiscal policies, and spreads on government debt are well below those of other governments in the region. Further, uninterrupted access to the capital markets has enabled the Chilean government to avoid the forced procyclical fiscal policies seen in other countries in the region, reinforcing confidence in its economic management.

A number of other countries have also made progress in reducing high levels of public debt. In Hungary, public debt has fallen from about 85 percent of GDP in the mid-1990s to less than 60 percent now as a result of strong growth, a period of sustained primary budget surpluses (which, however, ended in 2002), and the proceeds from the sale of government assets. Bulgaria has reduced its public debt from about 160 percent of GDP in the early 1990s to less than 60 percent of GDP in 2002 as a result of debt restructuring, a fiscal consolidation program that has seen primary budget surpluses sustained since 1994, and high inflation (up to 1997). Lastly, in Mexico, public debt was reduced in the early 1990s as the country emerged from its Brady debt restructuring. Despite the Tequila crisis in 1995, which entailed a costly restructuring of the banking system, debt is currently about 50 percent of GDP, and the last of Mexico's Brady debt has recently been repaid.

Conclusions

High public debt is a cause for concern in many emerging market economies. At about 70 percent of GDP, the average public debt ratio in emerging market economies now exceeds that in industrial countries. Not only does this high level of public debt raise the risk of a fiscal crisis in some countries, but it also imposes costs on the economy by keeping borrowing costs high, discouraging private investment, and constraining the flexibility of fiscal policy. Lower public debt levels would likely enable governments in emerging markets to run a more countercyclical fiscal policy, with benefits for economic stability.

The analysis in this chapter suggests that, historically, many emerging market economies have not generated large enough primary budget surpluses to ensure the sustainability of their public debt. This stands in contrast to industrial countries. The inability to generate adequate primary surpluses appears to stem from the characteristics of the fiscal systems: governments in emerging market countries generally have weak revenue bases (with lower yields and higher volatility) and are less effective at controlling expenditures during economic upswings (this is particularly the case in Latin America).

While the sustainable level of public debt varies between countries—depending on the characteristics of each country—for the typical emerging market economy it is often quite low. For example, the analysis of overborrowing suggested that, based on past fiscal performance, the sustainable public debt level for a typical emerging market economy may only be about 25 percent of GDP, while the estimates of the fiscal policy reaction functions indicated that emerging market economies as a group have failed in the past to respond in a manner consistent with ensuring fiscal sustainability once public debt exceeds 50 percent of GDP.[41] There are, however, regional differences, with Asian countries generally doing more to ensure debt sustainability than countries in other regions.

What can policymakers do to reduce public debt and cushion themselves against the risks that high debt presents? It is important to recognize that the past does not necessarily condition the future—policies and institutions do change. The example of Chile, in particular, shows that strong fiscal and structural policy reforms—sometimes in combination with an initial debt

restructuring—can be effective in putting public debt on a firm and lasting downward path. To be successful, however, a broad and sustained package of reforms is needed that encompasses the following.

- *Tax and expenditure reforms.* Reforms to strengthen and broaden the tax base are needed so that governments have access to higher and less variable revenues. Effective tax rates in emerging market economies are generally low, suggesting that tax avoidance—through either legal or illegal means—and weak tax administration are serious issues that need to be addressed. The continued reliance on taxes and transfers related to commodity exports is a weakness of many current tax systems, and efforts are needed to broaden the tax base to reduce its variability. Better control of expenditures during economic upswings is also essential to ensure that periods of strong revenue growth result in higher primary surpluses rather than increased spending.

- *Steps to improve the credibility of fiscal policy.* Governments need to be able to demonstrate that their overall debt burden is manageable, and that it is likely to remain so under most circumstances. Building this credibility requires not only the implementation of effective fiscal reforms, but also a record of adhering to these reforms through upturns and downturns. The strengthening of fiscal institutions has a very important role to play in this regard. Fiscal rules—broadly defined as a permanent constraint on fiscal performance—in some cases may play a useful role in strengthening fiscal policy credibility if appropriately designed and obeyed. For example, the Fiscal Responsibility Law introduced in Brazil in 2000—which established policy rules consisting of limits and targets for selected fiscal indicators for all levels of government, including debt ceilings and transparency requirements—

---

[41]These thresholds are not dissimilar from those found in recent studies on external debt crises in emerging markets. For example, IMF (2002) estimates a threshold of 40 percent of GDP, Manasse, Roubini, and Schimmelpfennig (2003) estimate a threshold of 50 percent of GDP, and Reinhart, Rogoff, and Savastano (2003) derive country-specific thresholds in the range of 15–20 percent of GDP for countries that have repeatedly defaulted on their sovereign debt.

appears to have helped strengthen the government's credibility in financial markets.[42] Poland has also introduced a constitutional limit on public debt of 60 percent of GDP (including the risk-weighted stock of outstanding government guarantees) and corrective procedures that kick in when public debt exceeds 50 percent of GDP.

- *Steps to reduce exposure to exchange rate and interest rate movements.* Given the structure of their public debt, many emerging market economies are exposed to considerable interest rate and foreign exchange risk. Steps are needed to reduce the reliance on domestically issued foreign currency and short-term debt. Policies to promote more open economies would help reduce the risks from external debt as exchange rate depreciations would then provide more of a boost to exports and government revenues to mitigate the impact on the budget of higher debt servicing costs. Recent proposals to create GDP-linked bonds could also provide some cushion during times of economic stress.

- *Structural reforms to boost growth prospects.* Historic experience suggests that it is difficult to bring public debt ratios down without robust economic growth. In this context, the implementation of a broad-based agenda of structural reforms is a crucial complement to fiscal consolidation efforts. As emphasized in the April 2003 *World Economic Outlook*, the strengthening of institutions could be expected to provide a significant boost to growth over the medium term. Addressing corporate and financial sector weaknesses will also be a key, while further steps to liberalize trade and promote long-term foreign investment will have lasting growth benefits.

- *Addressing the risks from contingent and implicit liabilities.* It is also important that governments act to minimize the risks they face from contingent and implicit liabilities. This applies not only to countries trying to reduce high debt levels, but also to those that currently have relatively low debt. The experience of many countries in recent years has shown that the recognition of such liabilities can significantly add to public debt and quickly raise questions about sustainability. The recapitalization of banking systems, in particular, has proved costly, while government guarantees on private sector projects are a further source of risk. Governments need to be fully aware of the contingent and implicit liabilities they face—in this regard, improving fiscal transparency would help—and act to reduce them to the extent possible. Improving financial sector supervision is an essential step toward this goal.

More generally, the mechanisms for the restructuring of sovereign debt also need to be strengthened. Defaults on external public debt have been common among emerging market economies, and certainly cannot be ruled out in the future. It is therefore important that mechanisms are in place to deal with such events in an orderly manner to minimize, to the extent possible, the costs and disruptions to all the involved parties. To this end, current efforts to promote the inclusion of collective action clauses in debt contracts and, more generally, to find ways to improve arrangements for sovereign debt restructuring within the existing legal framework are important.

Appendix 3.1. Assessing Fiscal Sustainability: Data and Econometric Methods

The main authors of this appendix are Marco Terrones and Xavier Debrun.

This appendix provides further details on the data and the econometric methodology and results discussed in the main text.

---

[42]Kopits (2001) contains a detailed discussion of fiscal policy rules. For more detail on fiscal policy rules in Brazil, see Goldfajn and Guardia (forthcoming).

Data Issues

The main issues related to the two data sets used in the chapter have been discussed in Box 3.1. The emerging market and other developing countries in the data sets are as follows.

Data set 1: 1990–2002: Argentina, Brazil, Bulgaria, Chile, China, Colombia, Costa Rica, Côte d'Ivoire, Croatia, Ecuador, Egypt, Hungary, India, Indonesia, Israel, Jordan, Korea, Lebanon, Malaysia, Mexico, Morocco, Nigeria, Pakistan, Panama, Peru, the Philippines, Poland, Russia, South Africa, Thailand, Turkey, Ukraine, Uruguay, and Venezuela.

Data set 2: 1970–2002: Algeria, Argentina, Bangladesh, Benin, Bolivia, Botswana, Brazil, Burkina Faso, Burundi, Cameroon, Chile, China, Colombia, Costa Rica, Côte d'Ivoire, Czech Republic, Dominican Republic, Ecuador, Egypt, El Salvador, Gabon, Ghana, Guatemala, Haiti, Honduras, Hungary, India, Indonesia, Israel, Jamaica, Jordan, Korea, Malaysia, Mauritius, Mexico, Morocco, Niger, Nigeria, Pakistan, Papua New Guinea, Panama, Paraguay, Peru, the Philippines, Poland, Russia, Singapore, South Africa, Sri Lanka, Syrian Arab Republic, Tanzania, Togo, Thailand, Tunisia, Turkey, Ukraine, Uruguay, Venezuela, and Zimbabwe.

The industrial economies common to both data sets are Australia, Austria, Belgium, Canada, Denmark, Finland, France, Germany, Greece, Ireland, Italy, Japan, the Netherlands, New Zealand, Norway, Portugal, Spain, Sweden, the United Kingdom, and the United States.

Estimating Fiscal Policy Reaction Functions

A major issue in the specification of fiscal reaction functions is the choice of the policy instrument or operational target. Given this chapter's focus, it is important to choose a policy variable directly related to debt dynamics. The budget identity (1) indicates that the stock of public debt at the beginning of period $t + 1$ (B_{t+1}) results from the inherited debt, B_t, to which the period t financing requirements (the overall balance) F_t is added:

$$B_{t+1} = B_t + F_t. \tag{1}$$

Since F_t depends on interest payments (in principle not a choice variable of the fiscal authorities), and thereby on B_t itself (which reflects *past* policies), interest payments can be separated from other expenditures, and the identity rewritten as:

$$B_{t+1} = (1 + r)B_t + S_t - R_t = (1 + r)B_t - P_t, \tag{2}$$

where S_t is noninterest (primary) government spending, R_t is total government revenues, and r is the interest rate paid on existing debt. The variable $P_t \equiv R_t - S_t$ is the primary balance (surplus). To account for the effect of growth on borrowing capacity, (2) can be rewritten in terms of ratios to GDP (denoted by lowercase letters):

$$\frac{B_{t+1}}{Y_{t+1}}\frac{Y_{t+1}}{Y_t} = (1 + r)\frac{B_t}{Y_t} - \frac{P_t}{Y_t}$$
$$\Updownarrow$$
$$(1 + g)b_{t+1} = (1 + r)b_t - p_t, \tag{3}$$

where Y_t is the level of GDP and g is the nominal growth rate. From equation (3), the primary balance that stabilizes the debt ratio (that is, b_{t+1}) is given by $\bar{p}_t = b_t(r - g)$, where r and g can also be measured in real terms as the effect of inflation disappears with the use of ratios. Since the real interest rate is generally higher than real growth, the primary surplus consistent with a constant debt-to-GDP ratio increases with the initial debt stock and the difference between the real interest rate and the real growth rate.

With these identities in mind, and in line with Bohn (1998) and other studies, the primary balance is used as the operational target in the fiscal reaction function:

$$p_{i,t} = \alpha_i + \sum_{j=1}^{J}\beta_j X_{j,i,t} + \rho b_{i,t-1} + \varepsilon_{i,t}, \tag{4}$$

where $p_{i,t}$ is the primary balance in country i at time t; α_i is a country-specific intercept (fixed effect) accounting for heterogeneity in the group of countries under consideration; $b_{i,t-1}$ is the debt level at the end of the previous period; $\varepsilon_{i,t}$ is an error term; and X_j is a vector of macroeconomic variables explaining changes in the primary balance unrelated to the long-run solvency requirement. In the spirit of Barro's (1979) "tax smoothing" theory, these variables reflect transitory shocks to expenditure and revenues, such as business cycle fluctuations and exceptional events such as wars or natural disasters. That conjecture conveniently limits the number of potential explanatory variables while remaining consistent with a well-specified theory of fiscal policy.[43] Finally, as discussed in the main text, the connection between current policy actions and long-run solvency lies in the assumption that the primary balance systematically responds to past changes in the public debt, an aspect captured by the coefficient ρ in equation (4). While Bohn (1998) demonstrates that a positive value for ρ is sufficient to ensure long-run solvency under very weak technical assumptions, it is interesting to see how the dynamics of the debt-to-GDP ratio are affected by assuming (as in equation (4)) that $p_t = \rho b_t + x_t$, where x_t summarizes the determinants of the primary surplus unrelated to debt sustainability concerns. Equation (3) can then be rewritten as

$$b_{t+1} - b_t = -\left[1 - \left(\frac{1 + r - \rho}{1 + g}\right)\right]b_t - \frac{x_t}{1 + g}. \qquad (5)$$

Assuming that x_t is "stationary" (which in practice excludes a downward trend in the non-debt-related surplus), the sign of the term in square brackets determines whether the debt ratio is mean reverting, in the sense of converging toward some finite level pinned down by the average of x_t. A positive sign implies mean reversion and will be observed if $r - \rho < g$. Hence, ρ can be interpreted as the largest difference between the real interest rate and real growth that remains consistent with a mean-reverting debt ratio.

Equation (4) was separately estimated for panels of emerging market and industrial economies for the period 1990–2002. Four transitory determinants of fiscal policy were incorporated, with

the latter two only being included for emerging markets: the output gap, defined as the relative deviation of real GDP from its Hodrick-Prescott (HP)-filtered trend (to capture the impact of the business cycle on the primary balance); the CPI inflation rate (to account for shocks to seigniorage revenues); an indicator to capture the years in which a country experienced a debt default or restructuring (to account for the lack of financing that generally accompanies such situations); and the deviation of oil and non-oil commodity price cycles from their respective HP-filtered trends (to capture the direct effect of commodity price swings on government revenues in commodity exporting countries).

Commodity price data (oil price index and an index of food and metal commodities) are from the Commodity Price System database. All other data, including budgetary series in industrial countries, come from the World Economic Outlook database. For the econometric exercise, countries in a state of war or an extended period of default or restructuring during the sample period were eliminated on the grounds that unusual events were affecting the primary surplus. Countries in which there were clear trends in the fiscal series were also excluded.[44] The results reported in the main text refer to this restricted sample. As confirmed by the last column in Table 3.1, the exact country composition of the sample does not qualitatively affect the results for emerging market countries, although there is now a statistically significant positive, but very weak, reaction of the primary surplus to debt. For industrial countries, however, the inclusion of Japan in the sample does mean that the 80 percent of GDP threshold reported in Table 3.2 (and discussed below) could no longer be found.

Tables 3.1 and 3.2 present different variants of equation (4) for emerging market and industrial economies respectively. A key dimension of the empirical investigation was to capture statistically the nonlinear relationship between debt and

---

[43]See Favero (2002), Galí and Perotti (2003), and Fatàs and Mihov (forthcoming) for detailed discussions of the issues related to the specification of fiscal reaction functions.

[44]Of course, the short time-series dimension of the panel prevents formal stationarity tests.

Table 3.1. Emerging Market Economies: Fiscal Policy Reaction Functions, 1990–2002
(Dependent variable: primary surplus, percent of GDP)

Explanatory Variables	No Controls	Controls	Regional	Spline	Openness	Institutions	Full Sample
Output gap (YG)	. . .	0.141***	. . .	0.134***	0.057	−0.098	0.128***
Total public debt (TD)-lagged	0.039***	0.047***	. . .	0.123***	0.134***	0.132***	0.091***
Controls							
Inflation	. . .	0.001***	0.001***	0.001***	0.001***	0.001***	0.001***
Oil price cycles (if oil producer)	. . .	0.054**	0.050***	0.071***	0.071***	0.071***	0.088***
Non-oil commodity price cycles (if commodity producer)	. . .	0.069	0.067	0.078*	0.081*	0.066	0.105**
Default/restructuring	. . .	0.715***	0.541***	0.654***	0.493***	0.686***	0.822***
Nonlinearities and interactions							
Interaction of YG with:							
Trade openness	. . .	. . .	. . .	. . .	0.131**	. . .	. . .
Institutional quality	. . .	. . .	. . .	. . .	. . .	0.078***	. . .
Regional dummies	. . .						
Latin American	. . .	. . .	0.044*	. . .	. . .	. . .	. . .
Non–Latin American	. . .	. . .	0.235***	. . .	. . .	. . .	. . .
Interaction of TD with:							
Trade openness	. . .	. . .	. . .	. . .	−0.018**	. . .	. . .
Institutional quality	. . .	. . .	. . .	. . .	. . .	−0.003**	. . .
Regional dummies							
Latin American	. . .	. . .	0.041***	. . .	. . .	. . .	. . .
Non–Latin American	. . .	. . .	0.051***	. . .	. . .	. . .	. . .
Nonlinearities							
Spline regression coefficient							
Break at 50 percent	. . .	. . .	. . .	−0.115***	−0.113***	−0.111***	−0.072***
Test if slope equal to 0 (Wald χ^2)	. . .	. . .	. . .	1.641	. . .	. . .	8.601***
Adjusted R^2	0.497	0.578	0.562	0.630	0.578	0.623	0.682
Number of observations	249	249	249	249	249	249	362

Note: All equations have been estimated with Generalized Least Squares allowing for fixed effects and using a heteroscedasticity-consistent variance-covariance matrix for statistical tests. The symbols *, **, and *** indicate that the estimated coefficient is significantly different from zero at the 10, 5, and 1 percent level, respectively. Except for the full sample column, the following countries have been excluded for one of the reasons explained in the text: Bulgaria, China, Côte d'Ivoire, Croatia, Egypt, India, Israel, Jordan, Lebanon, Nigeria, and Pakistan.

the primary balance suggested by Figure 3.9. Although various powers (quadratic and cubic) of the debt variable were added to the basic specification (4) to test the statistical significance of a nonlinear relationship, spline regressions—that is, models allowing for a kink in the regression line—were found to fit the data very well, suggesting that the reaction of the primary surplus to the debt was indeed contingent on the debt level itself. A variety of debt thresholds were tested (from 30 percent of GDP to 90 percent of GDP by increments of 5 percentage points). For emerging market economies, the 50 percent of GDP threshold provided the best fit to the data (highest adjusted R^2), and this was also the lowest debt-to-GDP ratio beyond which the positive debt feedback effect disappeared (in the sense of not being statistically different from zero).

For industrial countries, spline regressions confirmed the visual impression from Figure 3.9, and indicated that the debt feedback effect was statistically larger when the debt-to-GDP ratio was above 80 percent.

In addition to the discussion in the main text, it is worth noting that all transitory determinants of fiscal policy have the expected signs and are generally highly significant in the regressions. Interestingly, whereas higher inflation is generally associated with a larger primary surplus in emerging market economies (in line with the effect on seigniorage revenues), inflation appears to have a strongly negative effect on the surplus in industrial economies, perhaps reflecting contemporaneous efforts to reduce inflation and to adjust the fiscal balance in a number of countries in the 1990s.

Table 3.2. Industrial Economies: Fiscal Policy Reaction Functions, 1990–2002
(Dependent variable: primary surplus, percent of GDP)

Explanatory Variables	No Controls	Controls	Spline	Full Sample
Output gap (*YG*)	. . .	0.971***	0.960***	0.961***
Total public debt (*TD*) – lagged	0.057***	0.060***	0.045***	0.039***
Inflation	. . .	−0.407***	−0.349***	−0.416***
Spline regression coefficient	. . .	. . .	. . .	. . .
Break at 80 percent	. . .	. . .	0.086***	−0.042
Adjusted R^2	0.367	0.691	0.702	0.621
Number of observations	191	191	191	227

Note: All equations have been estimated with Generalized Least Squares allowing for fixed effects and using a heteroscedasticity-consistent variance-covariance matrix for statistical tests. The symbols *, **, and *** indicate that the estimated coefficient is significantly different from zero at the 10, 5, and 1 percent level, respectively. Except for the full sample column, the following countries have been excluded for one of the reasons explained in the text: Germany (effect of reunification), Norway (effect of oil revenues), and Japan (increasing primary deficits).

The impact of broader economic and institutional factors on fiscal policy in emerging market economies was also investigated. Two points emerged from the econometric analysis (see Table 3.1).

- First, *trade openness* and *institutional quality* (defined as a combination of lower corruption, better bureaucracy, greater democratic accountability and a more effective rule of law according to indicators from *International Country Risk Guide*) tend to be associated with a much more countercyclical response of fiscal policy. The effect of trade openness may partly reflect the generally bigger size of governments in more open economies and the consequently larger automatic stabilizers (Rodrik, 1998). The effect of institutions is consistent with the conjecture that good institutions are associated with a better ability to raise revenues, more fiscal policy credibility, and correspondingly looser resource constraint, allowing the government to run more countercyclical policies.

- Second, governments in open emerging market economies tend to behave more like industrial countries as they post higher average primary surpluses and react less strongly to debt sustainability concerns at low debt levels. Countries with better institutions have on average lower public debt, which explains why their governments need to react less to debt sustainability concerns.

Finally, Table 3.3 shows strong evidence of a procyclical expenditure policy in Latin America, in contrast to other emerging markets and, even

Table 3.3. Expenditure Equations, 1990–2002
(Dependent variable: Primary expenditure, percent of GDP)

Explanatory Variables	Emerging Markets			Industrial Countries			
	Restricted sample		Full sample	Restricted sample		Full sample	
Output gap	. . .	. . .	. . .	−0.968***	−0.318***	−0.953***	−0.331***
Latin America	0.156***	0.121***	0.122***	. . .	. . .	. . .	. . .
Emerging markets excluding Latin America	−0.231***	−0.113***	−0.064***	. . .	. . .	. . .	. . .
Inflation	−0.003***	−0.002**	−0.001***	0.149**	0.023	0.196***	0.039
Total public debt lagged	0.002	−0.012**	−0.005	−0.006	−0.056***	0.015**	−0.039***
Default/restructuring	−0.851***	−0.718***	−0.711***	. . .	. . .	. . .	. . .
Lagged dependent variable	. . .	0.428***	0.535***	. . .	0.769***	. . .	0.759***
Adjusted R^2	0.926	0.939	0.940	0.928	0.972	0.925	0.970
Number of observations	242	242	350	191	191	227	227

Note: All equations have been estimated with Generalized Least Squares allowing for fixed effects and using a heteroscedasticity-consistent variance-covariance matrix for statistical tests. The symbols *, **, and *** indicate that the estimated coefficient is significantly different from zero at the 10, 5, and 1 percent level, respectively.

Table 3.4. Overborrowing and Institutions: Bivariate Regression Results

	Regression					
	(1)	(2)	(3)	(4)	(5)	(6)
Corruption	−0.75 (0.18)***	. . .	. . .	. . .	. . .	. . .
Property rights	. . .	−0.69 (0.20)***	. . .	. . .	. . .	. . .
Constraint on the executive	. . .	. . .	−0.15 (0.06)**	. . .	. . .	. . .
Quality of bureaucracy	. . .	. . .	. . .	−0.79 (0.18)***	. . .	. . .
Democratic accountability	. . .	. . .	. . .	. . .	−0.55 (0.16)***	. . .
Law and order	. . .	. . .	. . .	. . .	. . .	−0.84 (0.22)***
Constant	1.1 (0.26)***	3.2 (0.80)***	1.55 (0.33)***	2.91 (0.60)***	3.21 (0.80)***	1.18 (0.28)***
R^2	0.18	0.18	0.07	0.19	0.13	0.17
Number of observations	50	46	50	49	49	50

Notes: Robust standard errors are in brackets. The symbols *, **, and *** indicate statistical significance at 10, 5, and 1 percent levels, respectively. The dependent variable is the logarithm of the ratio of overborrowing. For definitions and sources of the three first measures of institutions, see Appendix 3.1 of the April 2003 *World Economic Outlook*. For definitions and sources of the three last measures of institutions see the International Country Risk Guide.

more so, to industrial economies, in which primary expenditures have a stabilizing influence on the business cycle. The results also suggest that industrial countries react to debt accumulation through a contraction in expenditure that appears stronger than in emerging market economies.

Determinants of Overborrowing

Following the literature on the determinants of debt default and fiscal crises, the role of a country's economic and institutional structure on public sector overborrowing was investigated.[45] The analysis assumes a linear cross-section regression model of the form

$$y = \alpha + \mathbf{X}\beta + u, \tag{6}$$

where y is a $(n \times 1)$ vector of the overborrowing ratio; $\mathbf{X}$ is a $(n \times K)$ matrix of economic and

institutional characteristics; β is a $(K \times 1)$ vector of parameters; and n is the number of countries in the sample. The model was estimated using both ordinary least squares (OLS) and instrumental variables (IV) techniques.

As discussed in the main text, the overborrowing ratio is measured as the ratio of actual public debt to the benchmark level of debt (both as percent of GDP). The benchmark debt level is calculated as the present discounted value of future primary balances (here proxied by the average historical primary balance), with the discount factor being the difference between the average real interest rate (measured by the real LIBOR rate plus a spread proxied from a country's Institutional Investor rating) and the average real GDP growth rate.[46] It was possible to calculate the benchmark debt-to-GDP ratio for 50 countries (14 industrialized countries and 36 develop-

---

[45]See, for instance, Manasse, Roubini, and Schimmelpfennig (2003).

[46]The benchmark debt-to-GDP ratio, v, is calculated using the following present value formula:

$$v = \int_0^\infty p_s \exp\left\{-\left[(r-g)s\right]\right\} ds \approx \frac{p}{r-g},$$

where p is the average primary balance as percent of GDP, r is the real interest rate, g is output growth, and s is time. The average primary balance is used to predict future fiscal policies under the premise of no major change in policies. Of course, if there is a structural break in the conduct of fiscal policy, this assumption may not be valid. Data on spreads are not available for all countries or all years in the sample. Therefore, the spread was proxied by (100 − the Institutional

ing countries, of which 21 were emerging market economies) using data for 1985–2002.[47]

The following economic factors were considered in the analysis: trade openness, the ratio of government revenue to GDP, economic volatility, and relative (to the United States) income per capita. Trade openness is measured as the average of the foreign exchange restrictions for current account transactions as compiled by the *Annual Report on Exchange Arrangements and Exchange Restrictions;* government revenue is calculated as the average ratio of total government revenue to nominal GDP, obtained from *Government Finance Statistics* and *International Finance Statistics*, respectively. Output volatility is measured as the standard deviation of the growth rate of real GDP, and relative income is measured as the ratio of the PPP-adjusted real per capita income of each country relative to United States using the WEO database.

A number of different measures of institutional quality were used in the analysis.[48] Simple bivariate regressions suggest that measures of institutional quality are inversely related to overborrowing (Table 3.4). Two institutional measures were found to be important in the regression analysis: an index of property rights and a measure of corruption. The property rights index, obtained from Heritage Foundation's Index of Economic Freedom, measures the extent of protection of private property, while the measure of corruption is the freedom from graft index—see Kaufmann, Kray, and Zoido-Lobatón (1999)—which measures the extent public investiture is used for corruption or private benefit.

The main results are reported in Table 3.5. In addition to the variables reported in the main

Table 3.5. Determinants of Overborrowing

	Ordinary Least Squares	Instrumental Variable
Openness (trade restrictions)	1.64 (0.59)***	1.65 (0.55)***
Government revenues (percent of GDP)	−0.05 (0.02)**	−0.04 (0.02)**
Property rights (index)	−0.62 (0.35)*	−0.64 (0.33)**
Volatility of growth rate of output	25.15 (11.16)**	25.50 (10.40)**
Relative (to the U.S.) income per capita	−0.57 (1.35)	−0.62 (1.21)
Constant	2.21 (1.15)*	2.11 (1.02)**
R^2	0.48	. . .
Number of observations	46	46
Wu-Hausman *F* test	. . .	0.29
P-value	. . .	(0.59)
Sargan test	. . .	0.77
P-value	. . .	(0.86)

Notes: Robust standard errors are in brackets. The symbols *, **, and *** indicate statistical significance at 10, 5, and 1 percent levels, respectively. The dependent variable is the logarithm of the ratio of overborrowing. The regressions also included an industrial country dummy. The following variables were used as instruments: government revenues as percent of GDP for the 1970–85 period, average terms of trade growth, an index of corruption, and an emerging market country dummy. The null hypothesis under the Wu-Hausman test is that the ratio of government revenues to GDP is exogenous. The null hypothesis under the Sargan test is that the instruments are uncorrelated with the error term and correctly excluded from the estimated equation.

text, the regression also included output volatility, relative income per capita, and an industrial country dummy. The first and the last regressors were statistically significant. One concern about the OLS results—reported in the first column—is that the revenue-to-GDP ratio may be endogenously determined as the degree of overborrowing could influence a government's policy response, including its tax policy. Although the Wu-Hausman test does not reveal strong evidence of such endogeneity, in view of

Investor (II) index); the II index is based on international banks' risk assessment of individual countries and has a scale of 0–100, with 100 representing the least chance of a debt default. Reinhart, Rogoff, and Savastano (2003) find a strong correlation between the Institutional Investor index—which is available for a large number of countries since 1979—and external debt, and between external debt and spreads. A simple regression on a subsample of countries where spreads data are available confirms a strong positive relationship between actual spreads and those constructed from the II index.

[47]The calculations were not made for those countries where the average primary balance or the discount factor was negative during the sample period. The ratios were calculated for 1985–2002 so that data for 1970–84 could be used to instrument variables in the regressions.

[48]Different measures of institutions are discussed in Appendix 3.1 of the April 2003 *World Economic Outlook*.

earlier results—whereby governments improve their primary balances in response to increased debt—this remains a concern. To deal with this possibility, instrumental variables analysis was employed, with the following variables used as instruments: the average ratio of government revenues to GDP during 1970–1984; average terms of trade for 1985–2002; the corruption index; and a Latin American country dummy. These instruments seem adequate, as the Sargan test fails to reject the null hypothesis that they are uncorrelated with the error term and correctly excluded from the estimated equations. The results from the first-stage regression suggest that the ratio of government revenues to GDP is strongly positively correlated with terms of trade growth and the freedom from graft index. In other words, high terms of trade growth and less corruption have a positive impact on the ratio of revenues to GDP, which in turn affects overborrowing.

References

Alesina, Alberto, Roberto Perotti, and José Tavares, 1998, "The Political Economy of Fiscal Adjustment," *Brookings Papers on Economic Activity: 1*, Brookings Institution, pp. 197–248.

Alesina, Alberto, Ricardo Hausmann, Rudolf Hommes, and Ernesto Stein, 1998, "Budget Institutions and Fiscal Performance in Latin America," IADB Working Paper No. 394 (Washington: Inter-American Development Bank).

Aiyagari, Rao S., and Ellen R. McGrattan, 1998, "The Optimum Quantity of Debt," *Journal of Monetary Economics*, Vol. 42 (December), pp. 447–69.

Auerbach, Alan J., Laurence J. Kotlikoff, and Willi Leibfritz, eds., 1999, *Generational Accounting Around the World* (Chicago: University of Chicago Press).

Barnhill Jr., Theodore M., and George Kopits, 2003, "Assessing Fiscal Sustainability Under Uncertainty," IMF Working Paper 03/79 (Washington: International Monetary Fund).

Barro, Robert J., 1979, "On the Determination of Public Debt," *Journal of Political Economy*, Vol. 87 (October), pp. 940–71.

Berg, Andrew, and Anne Krueger, 2003, "Trade, Growth, and Poverty: A Selective Survey," IMF Working Paper 03/30 (Washington: International Monetary Fund).

Blanchard, Olivier J., 1990, "Suggestions for a New Set of Fiscal Indicators," OECD Working Paper No. 79 (Paris: Organization for Economic Cooperation and Development).

———, Jean-Claude Chouraqui, Robert P. Hagemann, and Nicola Sartor, 1990, "The Sustainability of Fiscal Policy: New Answers to an Old Question," *OECD Economic Studies*, No. 15 (Autumn), pp. 7–36.

Bohn, Henning, 1998, "The Behavior of U.S. Public Debt and Deficits," *Quarterly Journal of Economics*, Vol. 113 (August), pp. 949–63.

Borensztein, Eduardo, and Paolo Mauro, 2002, "Reviving the Case for GDP-Indexed Bonds," IMF Policy Discussion Paper 02/10 (Washington: International Monetary Fund).

Braun, Miguel, and Luciano Di Grescia, 2003, "Toward Effective Social Insurance in Latin America: The Importance of Countercyclical Fiscal Policy," IADB Working Paper No. 487 (Washington: Inter-American Development Bank).

Buiter, Willem H., 1985, "Guide to Public Sector Debt and Deficits," *Economic Policy: A European Forum*, Vol. 1 (November), pp. 13–79.

Burnside, Craig, Martin Eichenbaum, and Sergio Rebelo, 2001, "Prospective Deficits and the Asian Currency Crisis," *Journal of Political Economy*, Vol. 109 (December), pp. 1155–97.

Cashin, Paul, C. John McDermott, and Alasdair Scott, 2002, "Booms and Slumps in World Commodity Prices," *Journal of Development Economics*, Vol. 69 (October), pp. 277–96.

Chalk, Nigel, and Richard Hemming, 2000, "Assessing Fiscal Sustainability in Theory and Practice," IMF Working Paper 00/81 (Washington: International Monetary Fund).

Debrun, Xavier, and Charles Wyplosz, 1999, "Onze Gouvernements et une Banque Centrale," *Revue d'Economie Politique*, Vol. 109 (May–June), pp. 387–424.

Economic Policy Committee, 2001, "Budgetary Challenges Posed by Ageing Populations," EPC/ECFIN/655/01-EN final (Brussels: European Commission, October).

European Commission, forthcoming, "Public Finances in EMU," in *European Economy*, No. 3/2003.

Fatàs, Antonio, and Ilian Mihov, forthcoming, "The Case for Restricting Fiscal Policy Discretion," *Quarterly Journal of Economics*.

Favero, Carlo A., 2002, "How Do European Monetary and Fiscal Authorities Behave?" CEPR Discussion Paper No. 3426 (London: Center for Economic Policy Research).

Frederiksen, Niels, 2001, "Fiscal Sustainability in the OECD: A Simple Method and Some Preliminary Results," Working Paper No. 3/2001 (Copenhagen: Finansministeriet).

Galí, Jordi, and Roberto Perotti, 2003, "Fiscal Policy and Monetary Integration in Europe," CEPR Discussion Paper No. 3933 (London: Center for Economic Policy Research).

Gavin, Michael, Ricardo Hausman, Roberto Perotti, and Ernesto Talvi, 1996, "Managing Fiscal Policy in Latin America and the Caribbean: Volatility, Procyclicality, and Limited Creditworthiness," IADB Working Paper No. 326 (Washington: Inter-American Development Bank).

Goldfajn, Ilan, and Eduardo Refinetti Guardia, forthcoming, "Fiscal Rules and Debt Sustainability in Brazil," in *Rules-Based Fiscal Policy in Emerging Markets: Background, Analysis, and Prospects*, ed. by George Kopits (London: Palgrave).

Hemming, Richard, Michael Kell, and Selma Mahfouz, 2002, "The Effectiveness of Fiscal Policy in Stimulating Economic Activity—A Review of the Literature," IMF Working Paper 02/208 (Washington: International Monetary Fund).

Hemming, Richard, Michael Kell, and Axel Schimmelpfennig, 2003, *Fiscal Vulnerability and Financial Crises in Emerging Market Economies*, IMF Occasional Paper No. 218 (Washington: International Monetary Fund).

Hemming, Richard, and Teresa Ter-Minassian, 2003, "Public Debt Dynamics and Fiscal Adjustment," Chapter 6 in *Managing Financial Crises: Recent Experience and Lessons for Latin America*, ed. by Charles Collyns and G. Russell Kincaid, IMF Occasional Paper No. 217 (Washington: International Monetary Fund), pp. 65–84.

International Monetary Fund, 2002, "Assessing Sustainability" (Washington). Available via the Internet: http://www.imf.org/external/np/pdr/sus/2002/eng/052802.htm.

———, 2003, "Sustainability—Review of Application and Methodological Refinements" (Washington). Available via the Internet: http://www.imf.org/external/np/pdr/sustain/2003/061003.htm.

Kaufmann, Daniel, Aart Kraay, and Pablo Zoido-Lobatón, 1999, "Aggregating Governance Indicators," World Bank Policy Research Working Paper No. 2195 (Washington: World Bank).

Klingen, Christoph, Beatrice Weder, and Jeromin Zettelmeyer, 2003, "How Private Creditors Fared in Emerging Debt Markets: 1970–2000" (unpublished; Washington: International Monetary Fund).

Kopits, George, 2001, "Fiscal Rules: Useful Policy Framework or Unnecessary Ornament?" IMF Working Paper 01/145 (Washington: International Monetary Fund).

Kose, M. Ayhan, Eswar S. Prasad, and Marco E. Terrones, 2003, "Financial Integration and Macroeconomic Volatility," *IMF Staff Papers*, Vol. 50 (Special Issue), pp. 119–42.

Lindert, Peter, and Peter Morton, 1989, "How Sovereign Debt Has Worked," in *Developing Country Debt and Economic Performance*, ed. by Jeffrey Sachs (Chicago: University of Chicago Press for the National Bureau of Economic Research), pp. 39–106.

Lucas, Robert E. Jr., 2003, "Macroeconomic Priorities," *American Economic Review*, Vol. 93 (March), pp. 1–14.

Manasse, Paolo, Nouriel Roubini, and Axel Schimmelpfennig, 2003, "Predicting Sovereign Debt Crises" (unpublished; Washington: International Monetary Fund).

Mélitz, Jacques, 1997, "Some Cross-Country Evidence about Debt, Deficits and the Behaviour of Monetary and Fiscal Authorities," CEPR Discussion Paper No. 1653 (London: Center for Economic Policy Research).

Mendoza, Enrique G., and Pedro Marcelo Oviedo, 2003, "Public Debt Sustainability under Uncertainty," Research Department, IADB (unpublished; Washington: Inter-American Development Bank).

Mendoza, Enrique G., Assaf Razin, and Linda L. Tesar, 1994, "Effective Tax Rates in Macroeconomics: Cross-Country Estimates of Tax Rates on Factor Incomes and Consumption," *Journal of Monetary Economics*, Vol. 34 (December), pp. 297–323.

Obstfeld, Maurice, and Kenneth Rogoff, 1996, *Foundations of International Macroeconomics* (Cambridge, Massachusetts: MIT Press).

Özler, Sule, 1993, "Have Commercial Banks Ignored History?" *American Economic Review*, Vol. 83 (June), pp. 608–20.

Pattillo, Catherine, Helene Poirson, and Luca Ricci, 2002, "External Debt and Growth," IMF Working Paper 02/69 (Washington: International Monetary Fund).

Persson, Torsten, and Lars E.O. Svensson, 1989, "Why a Stubborn Conservative Would Run a Deficit: Policy with Time-Inconsistent Preferences," *Quarterly Journal of Economics*, Vol. 104 (May), pp. 325–45.

Polackova Brixi, Hana, and Allen Schick, 2002, *Government at Risk: Contingent Liabilities and Fiscal Risk* (Washington: World Bank).

Ramey, Garey, and Valerie A. Ramey, 1995, "Cross-Country Evidence on the Link Between Volatility and Growth," *American Economic Review*, Vol. 85 (December), pp. 1138–51.

Reinhart, Carmen, Kenneth Rogoff, and Miguel Savastano, 2003, "Debt Intolerance," in *Brookings Papers on Economic Activity: 1*, Brookings Institution, pp. 1–62.

Rodrik, Dani, 1998, "Why Do More Open Economies Have Bigger Governments?" *Journal of Political Economy*, Vol. 106 (October), pp. 997–1032.

Rogoff, Kenneth, 1990, "Equilibrium Political Budget Cycles," *American Economic Review*, Vol. 80 (March), pp. 21–36.

Rose, Andrew, 2002, "One Reason Countries Pay Their Debts: Renegotiation and International Trade," NBER Working Paper No. 8853 (Cambridge, Massachusetts: National Bureau of Economic Research).

Sachs, Jeffrey D., 1985, "External Debt and Macroeconomic Performance in Latin America and East Asia," *Brookings Papers on Economic Activity: 2*, Brookings Institution, pp. 523–64.

———, and Andrew Warner, 1995, "Economic Reform and the Process of Global Integration," *Brookings Papers on Economic Activity: 1*, Brookings Institution, pp. 1–118.

Standard & Poor's, 2002a, "Global Financial Systems Stress."

———, 2002b, "Sovereign Defaults: Moving Higher Again in 2003?"

Talvi, Ernesto, and Carlos Végh, 2000, "Tax Base Variability and Procyclical Fiscal Policy," NBER Working Paper No. 7499 (Cambridge, Massachusetts: National Bureau of Economic Research).

Turner, Dave, Claude Giorno, Alain De Serres, Ann Voutc'h, and Pete Richardson, 1998, "The Macroeconomic Implications of Ageing in a Global Context," OECD Economics Department Working Paper No. 193 (Paris: Organization for Economic Cooperation and Development).

von Hagen, Jurgen, 1992, "Budgeting Procedures and Fiscal Performance in the European Communities," Directorate General for Economic and Financial Affairs, Economic Papers No. 96 (Brussels: European Commission), pp. 1–74.

———, and Ian Harden, 1995, "Budget Processes and Commitment to Fiscal Discipline," *European Economic Review*, Vol. 39 (April), pp. 771–79.

SUMMING UP BY THE ACTING CHAIR

The following remarks by the Acting Chair were made at the conclusion of the Executive Board's discussion of the World Economic Outlook on August 27, 2003.

Executive Directors were encouraged that recent economic data in some countries and forward-looking indicators, particularly in financial markets, point to a strengthening of global growth during the second half of 2003 and in 2004, up from the generally weak level of economic activity in the first half of this year. The prospects for a gradual—albeit moderate—recovery are underpinned by reduced geopolitical tensions, the projected decline in oil prices, and—for some countries—additional policy stimulus.

Directors observed that, among the major industrial countries, the recovery will likely be led by the United States, where recent data have generally been the strongest and where there is the most policy stimulus in the pipeline. They were also encouraged by the strength of second quarter GDP data for Japan, while noting that ongoing deflation, combined with banking and corporate sector weaknesses, continue to weigh on the outlook. With the subdued activity in the euro area, Directors expected the initial pace of recovery to be moderate, and largely dependent on developments in the rest of the world. Directors noted that growth among emerging markets has, on the whole, held up reasonably well, being supported—to varying degrees—by improvements in policy performance and external financing conditions, lower oil prices, increases in non-oil commodity prices, and the apparently short-lived impact of the SARS outbreak.

Directors considered that the balance of risks to the world economic outlook has improved in recent months, and the potential for upside shocks is beginning to offset the downside risks, albeit not yet fully. On the upside, developments in financial markets may be suggestive of the prospect that activity may pick up more quickly than currently projected—particularly in the United States, where productivity growth remains robust and corporate balance sheet restructuring is most advanced. At the same time, Directors noted the significant risks that continue to weigh on the downside. One such risk is the possibility of a continuing drag on investment in the aftermath of the equity price bubble. In addition, many Directors saw the continued heavy dependence of global growth on the United States—and the associated large current account imbalances among the major regions—as heightening the risk of potentially disorderly currency movements and resurgent protectionist pressures. The continued strength of housing prices in some countries may also be at risk if interest rates continue to rise sharply. Directors also pointed to the substantial vulnerabilities still confronting key emerging market economies, and several Directors observed that geopolitical tensions—while reduced since April—remain a significant concern.

Looking ahead, in light of this still fragile global recovery, Directors called for macroeconomic policies to remain appropriately supportive, and for reinvigorated structural reform efforts to strengthen confidence and reduce vulnerabilities over the medium term. In particular, monetary policies in industrial countries should remain supportive for the time being, and—with inflationary pressures very moderate—Directors considered that most regions have scope for further monetary easing if recovery falters or inflation significantly undershoots policy objectives.

The recent orderly depreciation of the dollar was generally welcomed. Going forward, most Directors were of the view that the cooperative approach, which will continue to need to underpin the global adjustment process, would be helped by currency adjustments that are more broadly spread, with several emerging Asian economies being relatively well placed to handle greater upward exchange rate flexibility.

Directors agreed that fiscal policy will have much less room for maneuver. While automatic stabilizers should generally be allowed to operate, they stressed that greater priority needs to be given to credible, high quality fiscal consolidation, in order to address both the recent deterioration in the fiscal outlook in the largest economies and the impending pressures of population aging. Directors also called on industrial and emerging market economies to make sustained further progress in vigorously implementing ongoing structural reforms to strengthen economic growth, support domestic demand, and reduce vulnerabilities. Directors underscored the particular importance at this juncture of a successful outcome of the WTO Cancún Ministerial meeting in September in curbing protectionist pressures and achieving further trade liberalization, as this will help strengthen confidence in the economic recovery. Progress with agricultural reforms—especially among the largest industrial economies—will be critical for boosting the growth prospects for developing economies and making progress with further poverty reduction. In this context, Directors expressed strong support for the initiatives being taken by the Fund and the World Bank to strengthen their assistance in support of developing countries' efforts to liberalize their trade regimes.

Major Currency Areas

Turning to the United States, Directors concurred that growth prospects appear to be firming, with generally encouraging trends in recent economic data and stronger forward-looking indicators. The substantial monetary and fiscal stimulus now in place, combined with the weaker dollar, will add support to this recovery, which, in the view of some Directors, could even be stronger than currently projected. At the same time, however, many Directors considered that the downdrafts to household and business spending implied by the still-stretched balance sheets, the substantial excess capacity, the continued labor market weakness, and the risk of a fall in housing prices, as well as the vulnerabilities arising from the large current account and fiscal deficits, call for continued caution in assessing the strength and durability of the U.S. recovery. Directors agreed that U.S. monetary policy should remain accommodative for the time being, with further easing not ruled out should activity falter or deflationary pressures rise. Directors acknowledged the important role U.S. fiscal policy has played in supporting activity during the current slowdown. However, most Directors emphasized the need to put in place a credible fiscal framework that would correct the recent significant deterioration in the medium-term fiscal outlook and support a gradual correction in global imbalances. They agreed with the view that the fiscal framework should aim at restoring fiscal balance (excluding social security) over the cycle, while putting the Social Security and Medicare systems on a sounder footing to help meet the impending costs of aging populations.

Notwithstanding the tentative signs of improvement in the outlook for the euro area, Directors observed that short-term prospects for the area remain generally subdued. Among the reasons for the persistent weakness of domestic demand, Directors highlighted the continued over-leveraging of corporate balance sheets and the impact of rising unemployment on consumer confidence and spending. Some Directors cautioned that the euro's recent appreciation might constrain the pace of recovery. Looking ahead, Directors expected the area's prospects to strengthen gradually, supported by a pickup in external demand, the winding down of corporate balance sheet adjustments, and continued low interest rates. They welcomed the ECB's interest rate cut in June, and saw scope for further easing if a sluggish recovery or further appreciation of the euro lead to an undershooting of inflation. Directors agreed that medium-term fiscal consolidation should remain a priority in the larger euro area economies. At the same time, many Directors acknowledged the challenge of striking an appropriate balance between short- and medium-term policy objectives. They agreed with the view that, where underpinned by tangible, credible, and high quality consolidation measures and structural reform efforts, a cumulative fiscal adjustment of 1½ percent of GDP over 2004–06—with the automatic stabilizers allowed to operate fully around this consolidation path—would strike such a balance. Some other Directors, however, cautioned against any departure from the commitment to achieve a steady underlying fiscal adjustment of ½ percent of GDP a year. Directors were encouraged by recent reforms in labor and product markets and pension arrangements. They emphasized that further efforts will be required to meet the Lisbon Summit targets, prepare for the economic and fiscal pressures of aging populations, and enhance Europe's contribution to balanced and sustained world growth.

Directors welcomed the pickup in economic activity in Japan since mid-2002. The outlook remains clouded, however, by entrenched deflation and weaknesses in the corporate, financial, and public sector balance sheets. While acknowledging progress in tackling the economic challenges facing Japan, Directors reiterated that a bold and broad-ranging strategy will remain key for laying a firm foundation for sustained medium-term growth. Priorities should include forceful measures to strengthen the banking sector—particularly through accelerated disposal of nonperforming loans and targeted use of public funds to recapitalize weak but systemically important banks—and rapid corporate restructuring—including through effective use of the new Industrial Revitalization Corporation. While welcoming the Bank of Japan's recent initiative to buy asset-backed securities, most Directors saw a need for a more aggressive monetary policy approach to tackle deflation effectively. This could include purchases of a wider array of assets, allowing monetary policy to work both through asset prices and through liquidity growth accompanied with a clear public communications strategy committing to end deflation in a limited time period. Many Directors were, however, concerned that extending such purchases to foreign currency assets might result in an unwarranted depreciation of the yen. To address the rapid buildup in public debt and impending pressures from population aging, Directors underscored the need for an ambitious and fully elaborated medium-term strategy to restore Japan's public finances to a sustainable basis.

Emerging Markets

Directors noted that growth has remained relatively robust in most emerging market regions, with stronger macroeconomic policies and structural reforms, as well as the strengthening in the major industrial countries contributing to improved prospects in an increasing number of countries. Nevertheless, prospects and vulnerabilities still vary widely among the emerging market economies, and policy efforts backed by measures to strengthen underlying institutions and reduce financial vulnerabilities need to be more widely deployed.

Directors welcomed the emerging recovery in Latin America, which has been helped by stronger global growth, substantial real exchange rate depreciations, and improved emerging bond market conditions. Directors were encouraged by the rebound in economic activity in Argentina, but stressed that sustained progress will require implementation of credible plans to restore solvency to the public finances and restructure the sovereign debt, strengthen the banking system and restructure the private corporate debt, and adequately protect the poor. In Brazil, steady policies have helped strengthen financial market confidence and reduce interest spreads, and the government's continued reform efforts and fiscal discipline will remain critical to underpin confidence and the recovery of domestic demand. For the region as a whole, Directors underscored the continued need for macroeconomic and structural reforms to enhance countries' ability to withstand economic shocks. The reforms should include, first and foremost, further steps to reduce public debt to more manageable levels, as well as measures to strengthen banking systems and central bank autonomy to pursue low inflation. In addition, trade, labor market, and regulatory, judicial, and institutional reforms will need to be pursued to improve productivity, equity, and governance. Directors considered that the current favorable financial market conditions provide a welcome opportunity for national authorities in the region to press ahead with ambitious reforms that they should not fail to seize.

Directors welcomed the quick recovery of emerging Asia from the slowdown in the first half of 2003 stemming largely from the war in Iraq and from SARS, and commended the appropriate and timely policy actions taken by a number of countries. Although domestic demand has been increasingly supportive of activity in many countries in recent years, the global cycle remains the preponderant determinant of cyclical developments in the region. Directors felt therefore that policies that promote stronger domestically sourced growth will remain a priority for the region. They welcomed the staff's analysis of the accumulation of foreign reserves in emerging Asia, which should help better inform the debate about desirable policy choices for the region going forward. The analysis suggests that for emerging Asia as a whole, reserve accumulation until 2001 had appeared broadly consistent with fundamentals. Directors noted the further increases in reserves in 2002–03. They acknowledged that these increases need to be assessed in light of country-specific characteristics, including the benefits perceived by many countries in holding high levels of reserves as insurance against crises in the context of continuing vulnerability to external shocks and an unfinished reform agenda. Some Directors looked forward, in this context, to further analysis of the level of reserve adequacy in

emerging market economies. Most Directors nevertheless supported the view that at this point some slowdown in the rate of accumulation of reserves in several countries in emerging Asia may be desirable, both from a domestic and a multilateral perspective. In these countries, allowing greater exchange rate flexibility would confer a number of benefits in support of ongoing reforms, by reducing risks of future crises, making domestic growth less dependent on the vagaries of the global cycle, and raising consumption opportunities for residents in cases where exchange rates may be undervalued. Several Directors acknowledged that the choice of exchange rate regimes and the timing of any changes in these are matters for national policy decisions.

Economic prospects for the countries in central and eastern Europe continue to be generally favorable, although growth will likely depend heavily on the pace of the euro area recovery. Directors agreed that early and substantial progress on fiscal consolidation will be essential in many countries, given already difficult fiscal positions and pressures arising from population aging and EU accession. Going forward, a key challenge facing EU accession countries will be to continue to make strong progress on the broad reform agenda to help ensure their successful EMU participation.

Growth in the CIS countries has been buoyed by robust consumption growth, and Directors agreed that prospects for the region remain generally favorable provided structural reforms are accelerated. Reform priorities should include measures to foster private sector development and strengthen financial regulation and supervision.

Directors observed that growth in the Middle East has picked up, largely on account of higher oil prices and production. The oil market outlook points, however, to potential risks to fiscal and growth prospects for the major oil exporters, while geopolitical tensions continue to affect the outlook for the region as a whole. Directors agreed that the key policy challenge facing the region will be to accelerate medium-term growth and absorb the rapidly growing labor force. They generally welcomed the staff's analysis of the growth performance in the Middle East and North Africa (MENA) region over the last two decades for its insights on how best to meet this challenge. The analysis suggests that efforts to reduce the relatively large size of government consumption and to strengthen institutions could, in many countries in the region, significantly contribute to a pickup in economic activity. The importance of policies aimed at broadening labor market participation and of strengthening the role of the financial sector in supporting private sector investments was also highlighted.

Directors were encouraged that growth in Africa has remained remarkably resilient during the global downturn, reflecting improved macroeconomic policies, higher commodity prices, and debt relief under the Heavily Indebted Poor Countries (HIPC) Initiative. Nevertheless, prospects for 2003 are likely to be dampened by adverse weather conditions and prevailing geopolitical uncertainties and civil unrest, although Directors acknowledged the progress being made with resolving conflicts in the region. Directors expressed concern that, on current projections, growth in Africa will remain far too low to meet the Millennium Development Goals. They saw the sustained implementation of the multifaceted strategy embedded in the New Partnership for Africa's Development (NEPAD) as key to strengthening the region's outlook. This should include policies aimed at reducing conflict and improving political governance; the promotion of competition, trade, and foreign investment, underpinned by measures to improve macroeconomic policy frameworks; and renewed efforts to develop the health care, education, infrastructure, and agriculture sectors. Directors underscored that the domestic reform efforts will need to be supported by additional external assistance, including higher aid flows, debt relief, and—most important of all—the opening of industrial country markets more fully to developing country exports.

Directors considered the staff's assessment and analysis of public debt in emerging market economies to be a timely contribution to ongoing efforts to identify key sources of vulnerability. The analysis notes that, after rising quite sharply in recent years, public debt in emerging market economies, at about 70 percent of GDP on average, now exceeds the average level in industrial countries. Directors recognized that the sustainable level of public debt varies among countries, depending on the characteristics of each country, and that generalizations based on debt thresholds should be avoided. Most Directors nevertheless shared the view that, for many emerging market economies, the level of debt that can prudently be held without giving rise to possible sustainability concerns is often quite low. Moreover, high public debt levels may adversely affect economic activity and constrain the flexibility to use fiscal policy as a policy tool. In highlighting some of the policy conclusions of the staff's analysis, Directors emphasized that strong and sustained fiscal and structural policy reforms—sometimes in combination with an initial debt restructuring—will be key to restoring public debt sustainability. These should include, in most cases, tax and expenditure reforms; steps to improve the credibility of fiscal policy; measures to limit fiscal risks—including from exchange rate and interest rate movements and contingent liabilities; improved debt management; and reforms to boost sustainable growth. Some Directors pointed to financial market inefficiencies that may help explain over-lending to governments accumulating rapidly rising public debts.

Directors also welcomed the staff analysis of the impact of industrial country exchange rate volatility on developing country economic performance. They generally endorsed the conclusion that the negative effects of this volatility on trade, capital inflows, and the likelihood of exchange rate crises in developing countries, appear on average to be quite limited. Nevertheless, the spillovers tend to be larger in countries where the currency is pegged to a specific industrial country currency, where external debt is high, and where there is a substantial mismatch between the currency composition of debt and of trade. In many cases, more flexible exchange rate regimes and steps to reduce external debt—together with access to effective hedging instruments in currency markets—will therefore need to be part of efforts to reduce vulnerabilities.

Finally, Executive Directors placed on record their strong appreciation for Kenneth Rogoff's contributions to the IMF's multilateral surveillance over the past two years, both through the World Economic Outlook and through his stimulating presentations on World Economic and Market Developments, which were highlights of the Board agenda.

STATISTICAL APPENDIX

The statistical appendix presents historical data, as well as projections. It comprises five sections: Assumptions, What's New, Data and Conventions, Classification of Countries, and Statistical Tables.

The assumptions underlying the estimates and projections for 2003–04 and the medium-term scenario for 2005–08 are summarized in the first section. The second section presents a brief description of changes to the database and statistical tables. The third section provides a general description of the data, and of the conventions used for calculating country group composites. The classification of countries in the various groups presented in the *World Economic Outlook* is summarized in the fourth section.

The last, and main, section comprises the statistical tables. Data in these tables have been compiled on the basis of information available through late August 2003. The figures for 2003 and beyond are shown with the same degree of precision as the historical figures solely for convenience; since they are projections, the same degree of accuracy is not to be inferred.

Assumptions

Real effective *exchange rates* for the advanced economies are assumed to remain constant at their average levels during the period July 1–28, 2003. For 2003 and 2004, these assumptions imply average U.S. dollar/SDR conversion rates of 1.389 and 1.388, respectively, U.S. dollar/euro conversion rate of 1.12 for both years, and U.S. dollar/yen conversion rates of 118.6 and 117.8, respectively.

Established *policies* of national authorities are assumed to be maintained. The more specific policy assumptions underlying the projections for selected advanced economies are described in Box A1.

It is assumed that the *price of oil* will average $28.50 a barrel in 2003 and $25.50 a barrel in 2004.

With regard to *interest rates*, it is assumed that the London interbank offered rate (LIBOR) on six-month U.S. dollar deposits will average 1.3 percent in 2003 and 2.0 percent in 2004; that the three-month interbank deposit rate for the euro will average 2.2 percent in 2003 and 2.4 percent in 2004; and that the three-month certificate of deposit rate in Japan will average 0.1 percent in 2003 and 0.2 in 2004.

With respect to *introduction of the euro*, on December 31, 1998 the Council of the European Union decided that, effective January 1, 1999, the irrevocably fixed conversion rates between the euro and currencies of the member states adopting the euro are:

1 euro	=	13.7603	Austrian schillings
	=	40.3399	Belgian francs
	=	1.95583	Deutsche mark
	=	5.94573	Finnish markkaa
	=	6.55957	French francs
	=	340.750	Greek drachma[1]
	=	0.787564	Irish pound
	=	1,936.27	Italian lire
	=	40.3399	Luxembourg francs
	=	2.20371	Netherlands guilders
	=	200.482	Portuguese escudos
	=	166.386	Spanish pesetas

See Box 5.4 in the October 1998 *World Economic Outlook* for details on how the conversion rates were established.

What's New

- No changes have been introduced for this issue of the *World Economic Outlook*.

---

[1]The conversion rate for Greece was established prior to inclusion in the euro area on January 1, 2001.

Box A1. Economic Policy Assumptions Underlying the Projections for Selected Advanced Economies

The short-term *fiscal policy assumptions* used in the *World Economic Outlook* are based on officially announced budgets, adjusted for differences between the national authorities and the IMF staff regarding macroeconomic assumptions and projected fiscal outturns. The medium-term fiscal projections incorporate policy measures that are judged likely to be implemented. In cases where the IMF staff has insufficient information to assess the authorities' budget intentions and prospects for policy implementation, an unchanged structural primary balance is assumed, unless otherwise indicated. Specific assumptions used in some of the advanced economies follow (see also Tables 14–16 in the Statistical Appendix for data on fiscal and structural balances).[1]

United States. The fiscal projections are based on the Administration's budget projections (July 15, 2003) adjusted to take into account (1) differences between macroeconomic assumptions; (2) the likelihood that additional Alternative Minimum Tax (AMT) relief would be provided; and (3) higher growth of discretionary and Medicare spending, in line with Congressional Budget Office projections. The 2001 and 2003 tax cuts are assumed to be made permanent, in line with Administration policy statements.

Japan. The medium-term fiscal projections assume implementation of planned policies in the social security system. For the rest of the general government (excluding social security),

expenditure and revenues are adjusted in line with the current government target to achieve a primary balance by the early 2010s.

Germany. Fiscal projections for 2002–06 are based on the updated Stability Program of December 2002, adjusted for (1) the Spring 2003 official estimates for tax revenue over the medium term; (2) the new fiscal measures announced in July in the content of the draft budget for the Bund for 2000; and (3) the IMF staff's macroeconomic projections.

France. The projections are based on the authorities' March 2003 estimates of the budget outturn, the 2004–06 structural adjustment envisaged in the Stability Report, and the IMF staff's macroeconomic assumptions. In addition, the projections assume that the structural balance will be broadly achieved in 2008. For 2007–08, the IMF staff assumes unchanged tax policies and real expenditure growth in line with the Stability Program (2004–06).

Italy. Fiscal projections for 2004 and beyond assume a constant structural primary balance.

United Kingdom. The fiscal projections are based on information provided in the 2003 Budget Report and incorporate the most recent data from the Office for National Statistics, including provisional budgetary outturns throughout June 2003.

Canada. Projections are based on the 2003 budget, released on February 18, 2003. After fiscal year 2002/03, it is assumed that new measures—aimed at reducing taxes and introducing new spending initiatives—are implemented such that the federal government maintains budget surpluses equivalent to the contingency reserve in the budget. The consolidated fiscal projections are assumed to be consistent with the provinces' stated medium-term targets.

Australia. The fiscal projections through the fiscal year 2005/06 are based on the *Mid-Year Economic and Fiscal Outlook 2002–03*, published by the Australian treasury in November 2002. For the remainder of the projection period, unchanged policies are assumed.

Austria. Fiscal projections for 2003–04 are based on the budget for 2003 and 2004,

---

[1]The output gap is actual less potential output, as a percent of potential output. Structural balances are expressed as a percent of potential output. The structural budget balance is the budgetary position that would be observed if the level of actual output coincided with potential output. Changes in the structural budget balance consequently include effects of temporary fiscal measures, the impact of fluctuations in interest rates and debt-service costs, and other noncyclical fluctuations in the budget balance. The computations of structural budget balances are based on IMF staff estimates of potential GDP and revenue and expenditure elasticities (see the October 1993 *World Economic Outlook*, Annex I). Net debt is defined as gross debt less financial assets of the general government, which include assets held by the social security insurance system. Estimates of the output gap and of the structural balance are subject to significant margins of uncertainty.

adjusted for the difference between budget assumptions and IMF staff projections. Projections for 2005–07 are based on the Austrian authorities' plans—set out in the updated Stability Program for 2003–07—to implement tax cuts in 2005 and gradually reduce the structural budget deficit thereafter, with the objective of maintaining a broadly balanced budget over the cycle. These plans are consistent with an initial widening of the structural budget deficit in 2005–06 and improvements thereafter.

Belgium. Fiscal projections for 2003 and 2004 assume unchanged policies. The projections for subsequent years are based on the deficit targets included in the government program of June 2003.

Denmark. Projections for 2003 and 2004 are aligned with the authorities' budget and latest projections, respectively, and adjusted for IMF staff's macroeconomic projections. For the years 2005 to 2008 the projections are in line with the authorities' medium-term framework—adjusted for IMF staff's macroeconomic projections—targeting an average budget surplus of 1.5–2.5 percent of GDP, supported by a ceiling real public consumption growth.

Korea. For 2003, it is assumed that the supplementary budget (0.7 percent of GDP) proposed by the government is approved by the National Assembly. Fiscal policy is consistent with achieving a balanced budget, excluding social security funds, in the medium term.

Netherlands. Projections for 2003 reflect the 2003 budget, adjusted for the IMF staff's macroeconomic assumptions. For 2004–07, the forecasts are based on the authorities' multiyear framework as laid out in the June 2003 update of the Stability Program. The framework is based on binding multiyear ceilings for real expenditure.

Portugal. Fiscal projections for 2003 build on the authorities' targets as published in their Stability Program (December 2002), taking into account actual fiscal outturns in 2003, as available. Projections for 2004 and beyond assume a constant structural primary balance.

Spain. Fiscal projections through 2006 are based on the policies outlined in the national authorities' updated Stability Program of December 2002, adjusted for the IMF staff's macroeconomic projections. In subsequent years, the fiscal projections assume no significant changes in these policies.

Sweden. The fiscal projections are based on information provided in the October 2002 Budget report. Additionally, the projections incorporate the most recent statistical releases from Statistics Sweden, including provisional budgetary outturns through November 2002.

Switzerland. Projections for 2003 are based on federal budget plans and IMF staff projections for lower levels of government. Projections for 2004–06 are based on the official financial plans (which include measures to strengthen the finances of social security), adjusted for the IMF staff's macroeconomic projections. Beyond 2006, the general government's balance is assumed to remain unchanged.

Monetary policy assumptions are based on the established policy framework in each country. In most cases, this implies a nonaccommodative stance over the business cycle: official interest rates will therefore increase when economic indicators suggest that prospective inflation will rise above its acceptable rate or range; and they will decrease when indicators suggest that prospective inflation will not exceed the acceptable rate or range, that prospective output growth is below its potential rate, and that the margin of slack in the economy is significant. On this basis, the London interbank offered rate (LIBOR) on six-month U.S. dollar deposits is assumed to average 1.3 percent in 2003 and 2.0 percent in 2004. The projected path for U.S. dollar short-term interest rates reflects the assumption implicit in prevailing forward rates that the U.S. Federal Reserve will begin to raise interest rates in late 2003. The interest rate on six-month Japanese yen deposits is assumed to average 0.1 percent in 2003 and 0.2 percent in 2004, with the current monetary policy framework being maintained. The rate on six-month euro deposits is assumed to average 2.2 percent in 2003 and 2.4 percent in 2004. Changes in interest rate assumptions compared with the April 2003 *World Economic Outlook* are summarized in Table 1.1.

Data and Conventions

Data and projections for 182 countries form the statistical basis for the *World Economic Outlook* (the World Economic Outlook database). The data are maintained jointly by the IMF's Research Department and area departments, with the latter regularly updating country projections based on consistent global assumptions.

Although national statistical agencies are the ultimate providers of historical data and definitions, international organizations are also involved in statistical issues, with the objective of harmonizing methodologies for the national compilation of statistics, including the analytical frameworks, concepts, definitions, classifications, and valuation procedures used in the production of economic statistics. The World Economic Outlook database reflects information from both national source agencies and international organizations.

The completion in 1993 of the comprehensive revision of the standardized *System of National Accounts 1993* (*SNA*) and the IMF's *Balance of Payments Manual* (*BPM*) represented important improvements in the standards of economic statistics and analysis.[2] The IMF was actively involved in both projects, particularly the new *Balance of Payments Manual,* which reflects the IMF's special interest in countries' external positions. Key changes introduced with the new *Manual* were summarized in Box 13 of the May 1994 *World Economic Outlook.* The process of adapting country balance of payments data to the definitions of the new *BPM* began with the May 1995 *World Economic Outlook.* However, full concordance with the *BPM* is ultimately dependent on the provision by national statistical compilers of revised country data, and hence the *World Economic Outlook* estimates are still only partially adapted to the *BPM.*

The members of the European Union have adopted a harmonized system for the compilation of the national accounts, referred to as ESA 1995. All national accounts data from 1995 onward are presented on the basis of the new system. Revision by national authorities of data prior to 1995 to conform to the new system has progressed, but has in some cases not been completed. In such cases, historical *World Economic Outlook* data have been carefully adjusted to avoid breaks in the series. Users of EU national accounts data prior to 1995 should nevertheless exercise caution until such time as the revision of historical data by national statistical agencies has been fully completed. See Box 1.2, *Revisions in National Accounts Methodologies,* in the May 2000 *World Economic Outlook.*

Composite data for country groups in the *World Economic Outlook* are either sums or weighted averages of data for individual countries. Unless otherwise indicated, multiyear averages of growth rates are expressed as compound annual rates of change. Arithmetically weighted averages are used for all data except inflation and money growth for the developing and transition country groups, for which geometric averages are used. The following conventions apply.

- Country group composites for exchange rates, interest rates, and the growth rates of monetary aggregates are weighted by GDP converted to U.S. dollars at market exchange rates (averaged over the preceding three years) as a share of group GDP.

- Composites for other data relating to the domestic economy, whether growth rates or ratios, are weighted by GDP valued at purchasing power parities (PPPs) as a share of total world or group GDP.[3]

- Composites for data relating to the domestic economy for the euro area (12 member coun-

---

[2]Commission of the European Communities, International Monetary Fund, Organization for Economic Cooperation and Development, United Nations, and World Bank, *System of National Accounts 1993* (Brussels/Luxembourg, New York, Paris, and Washington, 1993); and International Monetary Fund, *Balance of Payments Manual, Fifth Edition* (Washington: IMF, 1993).

[3]See Box A1 of the May 2000 *World Economic Outlook* for a summary of the revised PPP-based weights and Annex IV of the May 1993 *World Economic Outlook.* See also Anne-Marie Gulde and Marianne Schulze-Ghattas, "Purchasing Power Parity Based Weights for the *World Economic Outlook,*" in *Staff Studies for the World Economic Outlook* (International Monetary Fund, December 1993), pp. 106–23.

tries throughout the entire period unless otherwise noted) are aggregates of national source data using weights based on 1995 ECU exchange rates.

- Composite unemployment rates and employment growth are weighted by labor force as a share of group labor force.
- Composites relating to the external economy are sums of individual country data after conversion to U.S. dollars at the average market exchange rates in the years indicated for balance of payments data and at end-of-year market exchange rates for debt denominated in currencies other than U.S. dollars. Composites of changes in foreign trade volumes and prices, however, are arithmetic averages of percentage changes for individual countries weighted by the U.S. dollar value of exports or imports as a share of total world or group exports or imports (in the preceding year).

For central and eastern European countries, external transactions in nonconvertible currencies (through 1990) are converted to U.S. dollars at the implicit U.S. dollar/ruble conversion rates obtained from each country's national currency exchange rate for the U.S. dollar and for the ruble.

Classification of Countries

The country classification in the *World Economic Outlook* divides the world into three major groups: advanced economies, developing countries, and countries in transition.[4] Rather than being based on strict criteria, economic or otherwise, this classification has evolved over time with the objective of facilitating analysis by providing a reasonably meaningful organization of data. A few countries are presently not included in these groups, either because they are not IMF members, and their economies are not monitored by the IMF, or because databases have not yet been compiled. Cuba and the

Democratic People's Republic of Korea are examples of countries that are not IMF members, whereas San Marino, among the advanced economies, is an example of an economy for which a database has not been completed. It should also be noted that, owing to a lack of data, only three of the former republics of the dissolved Socialist Federal Republic of Yugoslavia (Croatia, the former Yugoslav Republic of Macedonia, and Slovenia) are included in the group composites for countries in transition.

Each of the three main country groups is further divided into a number of subgroups. Among the advanced economies, the seven largest in terms of GDP, collectively referred to as the major advanced countries, are distinguished as a subgroup, and so are the 15 current members of the European Union, the 12 members of the euro area, and the four newly industrialized Asian economies. The developing countries are classified by region, as well as into a number of analytical and other groups. A regional breakdown is also used for the classification of the countries in transition. Table A provides an overview of these standard groups in the *World Economic Outlook*, showing the number of countries in each group and the average 2002 shares of groups in aggregate PPP-valued GDP, total exports of goods and services, and population.

General Features and Compositions of Groups in the *World Economic Outlook* Classification

Advanced Economies

The 29 advanced economies are listed in Table B. The seven largest in terms of GDP—the United States, Japan, Germany, France, Italy, the United Kingdom, and Canada—constitute the subgroup of *major advanced economies,* often referred to as the Group of Seven (G-7) coun-

---

[4]As used here, the term "country" does not in all cases refer to a territorial entity that is a state as understood by international law and practice. It also covers some territorial entities that are not states, but for which statistical data are maintained on a separate and independent basis.

Table A. Classification by World Economic Outlook Groups and Their Shares in Aggregate GDP, Exports of Goods and Services, and Population, 2002[1]

(Percent of total for group or world)

	Number of Countries	GDP		Exports of Goods and Services		Population	
		← Share of total for →					
		Advanced economies	World	Advanced economies	World	Advanced economies	World
Advanced economies	**29**	**100.0**	**55.7**	**100.0**	**74.8**	**100.0**	**15.4**
United States		37.9	21.1	16.5	12.4	30.2	4.7
Euro area	12	28.2	15.7	41.7	31.2	32.2	5.0
Germany		8.0	4.4	12.2	9.1	8.7	1.3
France		5.7	3.2	6.8	5.1	6.4	1.0
Italy		5.5	3.0	5.4	4.0	6.1	0.9
Japan		12.8	7.1	7.8	5.8	13.4	2.1
United Kingdom		5.6	3.1	6.8	5.1	6.3	1.0
Canada		3.6	2.0	5.1	3.8	3.3	0.5
Other advanced economies	22	20.9	11.6	39.4	29.5	25.6	3.9
Memorandum							
Major advanced economies[2]	7	79.1	44.0	60.6	45.4	74.4	11.5
European Union	15	35.3	19.7	51.8	38.8	40.0	6.2
Newly industrialized Asian economies	4	6.1	3.4	13.0	9.7	8.6	1.3
		Developing countries	World	Developing countries	World	Developing countries	World
Developing countries	**125**	**100.0**	**38.1**	**100.0**	**20.3**	**100.0**	**78.2**
Regional groups							
Africa	51	8.5	3.2	9.2	1.9	16.0	12.5
Sub-Sahara	48	6.5	2.5	6.8	1.4	14.5	11.3
Excluding Nigeria and South Africa	46	3.8	1.5	3.6	0.7	10.7	8.4
Developing Asia	25	60.3	22.9	48.5	9.9	67.0	52.3
China		33.3	12.7	22.4	4.6	26.5	20.7
India		12.5	4.8	4.5	0.9	21.8	17.0
Other Asia	23	14.5	5.5	21.7	4.4	18.6	14.6
Middle East and Turkey	16	10.5	4.0	20.1	4.1	6.4	5.0
Western Hemisphere	33	20.8	7.9	22.2	4.5	10.7	8.4
Analytical groups							
By source of export earnings							
Fuel	18	9.1	3.5	19.3	3.9	7.5	5.8
Nonfuel	107	90.9	34.6	80.7	16.4	92.5	72.3
Of which, primary products	29	3.7	1.4	3.2	0.6	7.9	6.2
By external financing source							
Net debtor countries	108	59.1	22.5	61.9	12.6	70.0	54.7
Of which, official financing	34	12.1	4.6	10.6	2.2	25.2	19.7
Net debtor countries by debt-servicing experience							
Countries with arrears and/or rescheduling during 1997–2001	48	20.3	7.7	17.9	3.6	28.1	22.0
Other groups							
Heavily indebted poor countries	40	5.2	2.0	4.6	0.9	14.0	10.9
Middle East and north Africa	21	10.5	4.0	18.9	3.8	7.5	5.8
		Countries in transition	World	Countries in transition	World	Countries in transition	World
Countries in transition	**28**	**100.0**	**6.3**	**100.0**	**4.8**	**100.0**	**6.4**
Central and eastern Europe	15	37.0	2.3	53.2	2.6	28.8	1.9
CIS and Mongolia	13	63.0	3.9	46.8	2.3	71.2	4.6
Russia		42.8	2.7	32.1	1.5	36.4	2.3
Excluding Russia	12	20.2	1.3	14.7	0.7	34.8	2.2

[1]The GDP shares are based on the purchasing-power-parity (PPP) valuation of country GDPs.
[2]Advanced economies excluding major advanced economies.

Table B. Advanced Economies by Subgroup

Major Currency Areas	Other Subgroups					
	Euro area[1]/ European Union		Newly industrialized Asian economies	Major advanced economies	Other advanced economies	
United States	*Austria*	*Ireland*	Hong Kong SAR[2]	Canada	Australia	Korea
Euro area	*Belgium*	*Luxembourg*	Korea	France	Austria	Luxembourg
Japan	Denmark	*Netherlands*	Singapore	Germany	Belgium	Netherlands
	Finland	*Portugal*	Taiwan Province	Italy	Cyprus	New Zealand
	France	*Spain*	of China	Japan	Denmark	Norway
	Germany	Sweden		United Kingdom	Finland	Portugal
	Greece	United Kingdom		United States	Greece	Singapore
	Italy				Hong Kong SAR	Spain
					Iceland	Sweden
					Ireland	Switzerland
					Israel	Taiwan Province of China

[1]Italics indicate countries that are members of the euro area.
[2]On July 1, 1997, Hong Kong was returned to the People's Republic of China and became a Special Administrative Region of China.

tries. The current members of the *European Union* (15 countries), the euro area (12 countries), and the *newly industrialized Asian economies* are also distinguished as subgroups. Composite data shown in the tables for the European Union and the euro area cover the current members for all years, even though the membership has increased over time.

In 1991 and subsequent years, data for *Germany* refer to west Germany *and* the eastern Länder (i.e., the former German Democratic Republic). Before 1991, economic data are not available on a unified basis or in a consistent manner. Hence, in tables featuring data expressed as annual percent change, these apply to west Germany in years up to and including 1991, but to unified Germany from 1992 onward. In general, data on national accounts and domestic economic and financial activity through 1990 cover west Germany only, whereas data for the central government and balance of payments apply to west Germany through June 1990 and to unified Germany thereafter.

Developing Countries

The group of developing countries (125 countries) includes all countries that are not classified as advanced economies or as countries in transition, together with a few dependent territories for which adequate statistics are available.

The *regional breakdowns* of developing countries in the *World Economic Outlook* conform to the IMF's *International Financial Statistics (IFS)* classification—*Africa, Asia, Europe, Middle East,* and *Western Hemisphere*—with one important exception. Because all of the non-advanced countries in Europe except Malta and Turkey are included in the group of countries in transition, the *World Economic Outlook* classification places these two countries in a combined *Middle East and Turkey* region. In both classifications, Egypt and the Libyan Arab Jamahiriya are included in this region, not in Africa. Three additional regional groupings—two of them constituting part of Africa and one a subgroup of Asia—are included in the *World Economic Outlook* because of their analytical significance. These are *sub-Sahara, sub-Sahara excluding Nigeria and South Africa,* and *Asia excluding China and India.*

The developing countries are also classified according to *analytical criteria* and into *other groups.* The analytical criteria reflect countries' composition of export earnings and other income from abroad, a distinction between net creditor and net debtor countries, and, for the net debtor countries, financial criteria based on external financing source and experi-

Table C. European Union Accession Candidates

Bulgaria	Latvia	Slovak Rep.
Cyprus	Lithuania	Slovenia
Czech Rep.	Malta	Turkey
Estonia	Poland	
Hungary	Romania	

Table D. Developing Countries by Region and Main Source of Export Earnings

	Fuel	Nonfuel, of Which Primary Products
Africa		
Sub-Sahara	Angola Congo, Rep. of Equatorial Guinea Gabon Nigeria	Botswana Burkina Faso Burundi Chad Congo, Democratic Rep. of Côte d'Ivoire Ethiopia Ghana Guinea Guinea-Bissau Liberia Malawi Mali Mauritania Namibia Niger Rwanda Sierra Leone Somalia Togo Uganda Zambia Zimbabwe
North Africa	Algeria	
Developing Asia	Brunei Darussalam	Afghanistan, Islamic State of Papua New Guinea Solomon Islands
Middle East and Turkey	Bahrain Iran, Islamic Rep. of Iraq Kuwait Libya Oman Qatar Saudi Arabia United Arab Emirates Yemen, Rep. of	
Western Hemisphere	Venezuela	Bolivia Chile Guyana

ence with external debt servicing. Included as "other groups" are the heavily indebted poor countries (HIPCs), and Middle East and north Africa (MENA). The detailed composition of developing countries in the regional, analytical, and other groups is shown in Tables C through E.

The first analytical criterion, by *source of export earnings*, distinguishes between categories: *fuel* (Standard International Trade Classification—SITC 3) and nonfuel and then focuses on *nonfuel primary products* (SITC 0, 1, 2, 4, and 68).

The financial criteria focus on *net creditor* and *net debtor countries,* which are differentiated on the basis of two additional financial criteria: by *official external financing* and by *experience with debt servicing.*[5]

The *other groups* of developing countries constitute the HIPCs and MENA countries. The first group comprises the countries (except Nigeria) considered by the IMF and the World Bank for their debt initiative, known as the HIPC Initiative.[6] Middle East and north Africa, also referred to as the MENA countries, is a *World Economic Outlook* group, whose composition straddles the Africa and Middle East and Europe regions. It is defined as the Arab League countries plus the Islamic Republic of Iran.

Countries in Transition

The group of countries in transition (28 countries) is divided into two regional subgroups: *central and eastern Europe, and the Commonwealth of Independent States and Mongolia.* The detailed country composition is shown in Table F.

---

[5]During 1997–2001, 49 countries incurred external payments arrears or entered into official or commercial bank debt-rescheduling agreements. This group of countries is referred to as *countries with arrears and/or rescheduling during 1997–2001.*

[6]See David Andrews, Anthony R. Boote, Syed S. Rizavi, and Sukwinder Singh, *Debt Relief for Low-Income Countries: The Enhanced HIPC Initiative,* IMF Pamphlet Series, No. 51 (Washington: International Monetary Fund, November 1999)

Table E. Developing Countries by Region and Main External Financing Source

Countries	Net Debtor Countries		Countries	Net Debtor Countries	
	By main external financing source			By main external financing source	
	Net debtor countries	Of which, official financing		Net debtor countries	Of which, official financing
Africa			**North Africa**		
Sub-Sahara			Algeria		
Angola	●		Morocco	●	
Benin	●	●	Tunisia	●	
Botswana			**Developing Asia**		
Burkina Faso	●	●	Afghanistan, Islamic State of	●	●
Burundi	●	●	Bangladesh	●	●
Cameroon	●	●	Bhutan	●	●
Cape Verde	●		Brunei Darussalam		
Central African Rep.	●	●	Cambodia	●	●
Chad	●	●	China	●	
Comoros	●	●	Fiji	●	●
Congo, Democratic Rep. of	●	●	India	●	●
Congo, Rep. of	●	●	Indonesia	●	●
Côte d'Ivoire	●		Kiribati		
Djibouti	●	●	Lao People's Democratic Rep.	●	●
Equatorial Guinea	●		Malaysia	●	
Eritrea	●	●	Maldives	●	
Ethiopia	●	●	Myanmar	●	●
Gabon	●		Nepal	●	●
Gambia, The	●		Pakistan	●	●
Ghana	●	●	Papua New Guinea	●	●
Guinea	●	●	Philippines	●	
Guinea-Bissau	●	●	Samoa	●	
Kenya	●		Solomon Islands	●	●
Lesotho	●		Sri Lanka	●	
Liberia	●		Thailand	●	
Madagascar	●	●	Tonga	●	●
Malawi	●	●	Vanuatu	●	●
Mali	●	●	Vietnam	●	●
Mauritania	●	●	**Middle East and Turkey**		
Mauritius	●		Bahrain	●	
Mozambique, Rep. of	●	●	Egypt	●	
Namibia			Iran, Islamic Rep. of		
Niger	●	●	Iraq	●	
Nigeria	●	●	Jordan	●	●
Rwanda	●	●	Kuwait		
Sào Tomé and Príncipe	●	●	Lebanon	●	
Senegal	●		Libya		
Seychelles	●		Malta		
Sierra Leone	●		Oman	●	
Somalia	●		Qatar		
South Africa	●		Saudi Arabia		
Sudan	●		Syrian Arab Rep.	●	
Swaziland	●		Turkey	●	
Tanzania	●		United Arab Emirates		
Togo	●	●	Yemen, Rep. of	●	●
Uganda	●		**Western Hemisphere**		
Zambia	●		Antigua and Barbuda	●	
Zimbabwe	●	●	Argentina	●	
			Bahamas, The	●	

167

Table E *(concluded)*

| Countries | Net Debtor Countries | | Countries | Net Debtor Countries | |
| | By main external financing source | | | By main external financing source | |
	Net debtor countries	Of which, official financing		Net debtor countries	Of which, official financing
Barbados	•		Honduras	•	•
Belize	•		Jamaica	•	
Bolivia	•		Mexico	•	
Brazil	•		Netherlands Antilles	•	
Chile	•		Nicaragua	•	
Colombia	•		Panama	•	
Costa Rica	•		Paraguay	•	
Dominica	•		Peru	•	
Dominican Rep.	•		St. Kitts and Nevis	•	
Ecuador	•	•	St. Lucia	•	•
El Salvador	•	•	St. Vincent and the Grenadines	•	
Grenada	•	•	Suriname	•	
Guatemala	•		Trinidad and Tobago	•	
Guyana	•		Uruguay	•	
Haiti	•	•	Venezuela	•	

One common characteristic of these countries is the transitional state of their economies from a centrally administered system to one based on market principles. Another is that this transition involves the transformation of sizable industrial sectors whose capital stocks have proven largely obsolete. Although several other countries are also "in transition" from partially command-based economic systems toward market-based systems (including China, Cambodia, the Lao People's Democratic Republic, Vietnam, and a number of African countries), most of these are largely rural, low-income economies for whom the principal challenge is one of economic development. These countries are therefore classified in the developing country group rather than in the group of countries in transition.

Table F. Other Developing Country Groups

Countries	Heavily Indebted Poor Countries	Middle East and North Africa
Africa		
Sub-Sahara		
Angola	•	
Benin	•	
Burkina Faso	•	
Burundi	•	
Cameroon	•	
Central African Rep.	•	
Chad	•	
Comoros		
Congo, Democratic Rep. of	•	
Congo, Rep. of	•	
Côte d'Ivoire	•	
Ethiopia	•	
Gambia, The	•	
Ghana	•	
Guinea	•	
Guinea-Bissau	•	
Kenya	•	
Liberia	•	
Madagascar	•	
Malawi	•	
Mali	•	
Mauritania	•	•
Mozambique, Rep. of	•	
Niger	•	
Rwanda	•	
São Tomé and Príncipe	•	
Senegal	•	
Sierra Leone	•	
Somalia	•	•
Sudan	•	•

Countries	Heavily Indebted Poor Countries	Middle East and North Africa
Tanzania	•	
Togo	•	
Uganda	•	
Zambia	•	
North Africa		
Algeria		•
Morocco		•
Tunisia		•
Developing Asia		
Lao People's Democratic Rep.	•	
Myanmar	•	
Vietnam	•	
Middle East and Turkey		
Bahrain		•
Egypt		•
Iran, Islamic Rep. of		•
Iraq		•
Jordan		•
Kuwait		•
Lebanon		•
Libya		•
Oman		•
Qatar		•
Saudi Arabia		•
Syrian Arab Rep.		•
United Arab Emirates		•
Yemen, Rep. of		•
Western Hemisphere		
Bolivia	•	
Guyana	•	
Honduras	•	
Nicaragua	•	

Table G. Countries in Transition by Region

Central and Eastern Europe		Commonwealth of Independent States and Mongolia
Albania	Lithuania	Armenia
Bosnia and Herzegovina	Macedonia, former Yugoslav Republic of	Azerbaijan
Bulgaria	Poland	Belarus
Croatia	Romania	Georgia
Czech Republic	Serbia and Montenegro	Kazakhstan
Estonia	Slovak Republic	Kyrgyz Republic
Hungary	Slovenia	Moldova
Latvia		Mongolia
		Russia
		Tajikistan
		Turkmenistan
		Ukraine
		Uzbekistan

List of Tables

Table 1. Summary of World Output[1]

(Annual percent change)

	Ten-Year Averages		1995	1996	1997	1998	1999	2000	2001	2002	2003	2004
	1985–94	1995–2004										
World	**3.3**	**3.6**	**3.7**	**4.0**	**4.2**	**2.8**	**3.6**	**4.8**	**2.4**	**3.0**	**3.2**	**4.1**
Advanced economies	**3.0**	**2.7**	**2.8**	**3.0**	**3.5**	**2.7**	**3.4**	**3.9**	**1.0**	**1.8**	**1.8**	**2.9**
United States	2.9	3.2	2.7	3.6	4.4	4.3	4.1	3.8	0.3	2.4	2.6	3.9
Euro area	...	2.0	2.2	1.4	2.3	2.9	2.8	3.5	1.5	0.9	0.5	1.9
Japan[2]	3.4	1.3	1.8	3.5	1.9	−1.1	0.2	2.8	0.4	0.2	2.0	1.4
Other advanced economies	3.8	3.3	4.3	3.6	4.2	1.9	4.8	5.1	1.6	3.0	1.9	3.1
Developing countries	**5.2**	**5.1**	**6.1**	**6.6**	**5.9**	**3.5**	**3.9**	**5.7**	**4.1**	**4.6**	**5.0**	**5.6**
Regional groups												
Africa	1.9	3.6	3.0	5.6	3.0	3.2	2.7	3.0	3.7	3.1	3.7	4.8
Developing Asia	7.7	6.6	9.0	8.3	6.6	4.0	6.2	6.8	5.8	6.4	6.4	6.5
Middle East and Turkey[3]	3.0	4.2	4.0	5.3	6.1	3.7	0.9	6.0	2.0	4.8	5.1	4.6
Western Hemisphere	3.1	2.2	1.8	3.6	5.2	2.3	0.2	4.0	0.7	−0.1	1.1	3.6
Analytical groups												
By source of export earnings												
Fuel	2.4	3.7	2.9	4.2	5.2	3.0	1.0	5.2	4.4	2.7	3.1	5.2
Nonfuel	5.5	5.2	6.4	6.9	6.0	3.5	4.2	5.8	4.1	4.8	5.1	5.7
of which, primary products	3.3	3.7	6.6	6.1	4.2	2.8	1.4	2.3	2.6	2.3	2.5	5.8
By external financing source												
Net debtor countries	4.0	3.8	4.7	5.6	4.8	1.6	2.8	4.7	2.3	3.0	3.8	4.6
of which, official financing	4.6	3.7	6.2	6.2	4.2	−2.6	2.5	4.4	3.8	3.6	4.0	5.0
Net debtor countries by debt-servicing experience												
Countries with arrears and/or rescheduling during 1997–2001	3.7	3.4	5.0	5.1	4.2	−0.7	2.0	4.5	3.4	3.1	3.2	4.4
Countries in transition	**−2.1**	**2.8**	**−1.5**	**−0.6**	**1.9**	**−0.9**	**4.1**	**7.1**	**5.1**	**4.2**	**4.9**	**4.7**
Central and eastern Europe	...	3.4	5.5	4.0	2.5	2.5	2.3	3.9	3.1	3.0	3.4	4.1
Commonwealth of Independent States and Mongolia	...	2.4	−5.5	−3.5	1.4	−3.2	5.2	9.1	6.4	4.9	5.8	5.0
Russia	...	2.4	−4.1	−3.6	1.4	−5.3	6.3	10.0	5.0	4.3	6.0	5.0
Excluding Russia	...	2.5	−8.6	−3.1	1.5	1.4	2.7	6.9	9.2	5.9	5.4	5.0
Memorandum												
Median growth rate												
Advanced economies	3.1	2.9	2.9	3.5	3.8	3.6	3.9	4.2	1.4	1.9	1.4	2.6
Developing countries	3.5	3.9	4.5	4.6	4.7	3.6	3.5	4.0	3.2	2.7	3.6	4.2
Countries in transition	−1.9	3.9	0.4	3.2	3.7	3.9	3.3	5.2	5.0	4.8	5.0	4.6
Output per capita												
Advanced economies	2.4	2.1	2.1	2.3	2.8	2.1	2.8	3.4	0.5	1.4	1.4	2.5
Developing countries	3.2	3.5	4.4	4.9	4.2	1.9	2.3	4.1	2.5	3.1	3.5	4.1
Countries in transition	−2.6	3.0	−1.5	−0.6	1.9	−0.8	4.2	7.3	5.4	4.5	5.2	5.0
World growth based on market exchange rates	**2.7**	**2.8**	**2.8**	**3.3**	**3.5**	**2.2**	**3.0**	**4.0**	**1.3**	**1.9**	**2.3**	**3.2**
Value of world output in billions of U.S. dollars												
At market exchange rates	20,630	31,639	29,134	29,849	29,740	29,545	30,598	31,411	31,086	32,177	35,599	37,251
At purchasing power parities	25,626	43,507	33,989	36,024	38,249	39,724	41,735	44,581	46,616	48,443	51,149	54,562

[1]Real GDP.
[2]Annual data are calculated from seasonally adjusted quarterly data.
[3]Includes Malta.

Table 2. Advanced Economies: Real GDP and Total Domestic Demand
(Annual percent change)

	Ten-Year Averages		1995	1996	1997	1998	1999	2000	2001	2002	2003	2004	Fourth Quarter[1]		
	1985–94	1995–2004											2002	2003	2004
Real GDP															
Advanced economies	**3.0**	**2.7**	**2.8**	**3.0**	**3.5**	**2.7**	**3.4**	**3.9**	**1.0**	**1.8**	**1.8**	**2.9**	...	...	...
United States	2.9	3.2	2.7	3.6	4.4	4.3	4.1	3.8	0.3	2.4	2.6	3.9	2.9	3.3	3.8
Euro area	...	2.0	2.2	1.4	2.3	2.9	2.8	3.5	1.5	0.9	0.5	1.9	1.2	0.6	2.1
Germany	2.7	1.3	1.7	0.8	1.4	2.0	2.0	2.9	0.8	0.2	—	1.5	0.5	0.1	1.4
France	2.1	2.1	1.8	1.1	1.9	3.6	3.2	4.2	2.1	1.2	0.5	2.0	1.4	0.8	2.4
Italy	2.1	1.7	2.9	1.1	2.0	1.8	1.7	3.1	1.8	0.4	0.4	1.7	0.9	0.3	2.0
Spain	2.9	3.2	2.8	2.4	4.0	4.3	4.2	4.2	2.7	2.0	2.2	2.8	1.9	2.4	3.1
Netherlands	2.7	2.4	3.0	3.0	3.8	4.3	4.0	3.5	1.2	0.2	-0.5	1.4	0.3	-0.5	2.3
Belgium	2.3	2.0	2.3	0.8	3.9	2.1	3.2	3.7	0.8	0.7	0.8	1.9	1.7	0.7	2.2
Austria	2.6	1.9	1.6	2.0	1.6	3.9	2.7	3.5	0.7	1.0	0.7	1.5	1.1	1.0	2.0
Finland	1.2	3.5	3.8	4.0	6.3	5.3	4.1	5.6	0.7	1.6	1.3	2.6	2.4	2.2	1.1
Greece	1.7	3.5	2.1	2.4	3.6	3.4	3.6	4.2	4.1	4.0	4.0	3.9	3.4	3.2	3.9
Portugal	3.3	2.5	2.9	3.5	4.0	4.6	3.8	3.7	1.6	0.4	-0.8	1.6	-1.3	0.9	2.0
Ireland[2]	3.7	7.6	9.9	8.1	11.1	8.6	11.3	10.1	6.2	6.9	1.0	3.8	7.6	1.1	4.2
Luxembourg	6.1	4.4	3.5	3.7	7.7	7.5	6.0	8.9	1.0	0.5	1.5	4.0	...	...	...
Japan[3]	3.4	1.3	1.8	3.5	1.9	-1.1	0.2	2.8	0.4	0.2	2.0	1.4	2.5	1.4	1.6
United Kingdom	2.6	2.5	2.9	2.6	3.4	2.9	2.4	3.1	2.1	1.9	1.7	2.4	2.3	1.4	2.9
Canada	2.5	3.4	2.8	1.6	4.2	4.1	5.5	5.3	1.9	3.3	1.9	3.0	3.5	1.9	3.4
Korea	8.2	5.0	8.9	6.8	5.0	-6.7	10.9	9.3	3.1	6.3	2.5	4.7	6.8	1.7	5.4
Australia	3.2	3.7	3.5	4.3	3.8	5.3	4.5	2.8	2.7	3.6	3.0	3.5	2.7	4.3	2.4
Taiwan Province of China	8.0	4.3	6.4	6.1	6.7	4.6	5.4	5.9	-2.2	3.5	2.7	3.8	4.2	4.0	4.0
Sweden	1.7	2.7	4.0	1.3	2.4	3.6	4.6	4.4	1.1	1.9	1.4	2.0	1.3	1.1	2.4
Switzerland	1.6	1.1	0.5	0.3	1.7	2.4	1.5	3.2	0.9	0.1	-0.4	1.4	0.4	-0.3	2.2
Hong Kong SAR	6.2	2.8	3.9	4.3	5.1	-5.0	3.4	10.2	0.5	2.3	1.5	2.8	5.1	-0.8	4.5
Denmark	1.8	2.3	2.8	2.5	3.0	2.5	2.6	2.9	1.4	2.1	1.2	1.8	1.5	1.8	1.8
Norway	2.9	2.8	4.4	5.3	5.2	2.6	2.1	2.8	1.9	1.0	0.6	2.3	...	...	...
Israel	5.1	2.8	6.8	4.7	3.3	3.0	2.6	7.4	-0.9	-1.0	0.7	2.1	0.5	1.3	2.0
Singapore	7.8	4.3	8.0	8.1	8.5	-0.9	6.4	9.4	-2.4	2.2	0.5	4.2	3.0	3.1	3.7
New Zealand	2.2	3.0	4.3	4.0	2.0	-0.2	3.9	4.0	2.6	4.4	2.6	2.9	4.5	2.1	3.6
Cyprus	5.5	3.7	6.1	1.9	2.5	5.0	4.8	5.2	4.1	2.2	2.0	3.8	...	...	...
Iceland	2.0	3.3	0.1	5.2	4.7	5.5	3.9	5.5	2.9	-0.5	2.3	3.7	...	...	...
Memorandum															
Major advanced economies	2.8	2.5	2.4	2.7	3.2	2.8	3.0	3.5	0.8	1.6	1.8	2.8	2.3	2.1	2.9
European Union	2.4	2.2	2.5	1.7	2.6	3.0	2.8	3.6	1.7	1.1	0.8	2.0	...	...	...
Newly industrialized Asian economies	7.8	4.5	7.5	6.3	5.8	-2.4	8.0	8.4	0.8	4.8	2.3	4.2	5.8	2.5	5.1
Real total domestic demand															
Advanced economies	**3.1**	**2.7**	**2.7**	**3.0**	**3.3**	**3.0**	**4.0**	**3.8**	**0.8**	**1.8**	**2.1**	**2.7**	...	...	...
United States	2.8	3.6	2.5	3.7	4.7	5.4	5.0	4.4	0.4	3.0	2.8	3.8	3.7	3.1	3.7
Euro area	...	1.9	2.1	1.0	1.8	3.6	3.5	2.9	1.0	0.1	1.1	2.0	0.8	1.1	2.3
Germany	2.7	1.0	1.7	0.3	0.6	2.4	2.8	1.8	-0.8	-1.6	1.0	2.1	-0.8	1.3	2.1
France	2.1	2.1	1.7	0.7	0.6	4.2	3.7	4.5	2.0	1.1	1.1	1.8	1.2	1.4	2.2
Italy	2.0	2.0	2.0	0.9	2.7	3.1	3.2	2.3	1.8	1.1	1.2	1.7	1.8	0.6	2.2
Japan[3]	3.6	1.1	2.4	4.0	0.9	-1.5	0.3	2.3	1.1	-0.5	1.5	0.9	1.5	1.1	1.0
United Kingdom	2.7	3.2	2.0	3.1	3.9	5.0	3.7	4.0	2.6	2.9	2.4	2.4	3.7	1.3	2.6
Canada	2.4	3.2	1.2	0.9	5.7	2.4	4.1	5.0	1.7	3.4	4.3	3.1	5.4	3.8	3.2
Other advanced economies	4.2	3.0	4.6	3.7	3.7	1.1	5.2	4.5	0.9	2.2	1.4	2.6	...	...	...
Memorandum															
Major advanced economies	2.8	2.6	2.2	2.8	3.1	3.5	3.6	3.6	0.8	1.7	2.2	2.8	2.7	2.2	2.8
European Union	2.5	2.2	2.2	1.4	2.3	4.0	3.5	3.2	1.3	0.8	1.4	2.1	...	...	...
Newly industrialized Asian economies	8.4	2.9	7.6	6.7	4.1	-9.3	7.9	7.5	-0.9	3.0	0.8	3.0	3.1	1.5	4.7

[1]From fourth quarter of preceding year.
[2]Fourth-quarter data are calculated from seasonally adjusted data.
[3]Annual data are calculated from seasonally adjusted quarterly data.

Table 3. Advanced Economies: Components of Real GDP

(Annual percent change)

	Ten-Year Averages		1995	1996	1997	1998	1999	2000	2001	2002	2003	2004
	1985–94	1995–2004										
Private consumer expenditure												
Advanced economies	**3.2**	**2.8**	**2.6**	**2.8**	**2.8**	**2.9**	**4.0**	**3.6**	**2.3**	**2.2**	**1.9**	**2.4**
United States	3.1	3.5	3.0	3.2	3.6	4.8	4.9	4.3	2.5	3.1	2.9	3.2
Euro area	1.9	1.9	1.6	1.6	3.0	3.5	2.5	1.8	0.5	1.1	1.8	
Germany	2.9	1.4	2.1	1.0	0.6	1.8	3.7	2.0	1.4	–1.0	0.8	1.8
France	1.8	2.0	1.3	1.3	0.2	3.6	3.5	2.9	2.8	1.5	1.2	1.8
Italy	2.3	1.9	1.7	1.2	3.2	3.2	2.6	2.7	1.0	0.4	1.1	1.9
Japan[1]	3.5	1.1	1.8	2.3	1.1	–0.1	0.2	0.9	1.7	1.4	1.1	0.6
United Kingdom	3.2	3.5	1.9	3.8	3.8	3.8	4.5	5.2	4.1	3.7	2.2	2.1
Canada	2.6	3.3	2.1	2.6	4.6	2.8	3.8	4.0	2.6	3.4	3.6	3.6
Other advanced economies	4.0	3.1	3.8	3.9	3.7	1.6	5.1	4.5	2.3	2.5	0.9	2.3
Memorandum												
Major advanced economies	3.0	2.7	2.3	2.5	2.6	3.3	3.7	3.4	2.3	2.2	2.1	2.4
European Union	2.6	2.3	1.9	2.0	2.2	3.3	3.7	3.2	2.1	1.1	1.3	1.9
Newly industrialized Asian economies	8.1	3.7	6.9	6.3	5.2	–4.7	7.9	7.2	3.1	4.0	–0.7	2.7
Public consumption												
Advanced economies	**2.4**	**2.2**	**1.1**	**1.7**	**1.4**	**1.7**	**2.6**	**2.7**	**2.9**	**3.4**	**2.6**	**2.0**
United States	2.0	2.3	—	0.5	1.8	1.4	2.9	2.8	3.7	4.4	3.7	2.3
Euro area	1.7	0.7	1.7	1.2	1.4	2.0	2.1	2.2	2.8	1.6	1.0	
Germany	1.7	1.1	1.5	1.8	0.3	1.9	0.8	1.0	1.0	1.7	0.8	0.4
France	2.5	1.9	—	2.2	2.1	–0.1	1.5	3.0	2.9	4.1	1.6	1.6
Italy	1.8	1.0	–2.1	1.1	0.3	0.3	1.4	1.7	3.5	1.7	2.0	–0.2
Japan[1]	3.0	2.6	4.2	2.9	1.0	2.1	4.4	4.7	2.5	2.3	0.5	1.4
United Kingdom	0.9	2.3	1.7	1.2	0.1	1.5	3.1	2.1	2.5	3.3	3.8	4.0
Canada	2.1	1.8	–0.6	–1.2	–1.0	3.2	2.1	2.6	3.7	3.0	3.2	3.0
Other advanced economies	3.7	2.6	2.2	3.7	2.4	2.6	2.3	2.5	2.3	3.0	2.7	2.3
Memorandum												
Major advanced economies	2.1	2.1	0.8	1.2	1.2	1.5	2.7	2.8	3.1	3.5	2.6	1.9
European Union	2.1	1.8	0.9	1.5	1.0	1.6	2.1	2.1	2.4	2.9	1.9	1.4
Newly industrialized Asian economies	6.0	2.8	2.6	8.0	3.3	1.8	–0.5	1.8	1.7	1.9	4.3	3.8
Gross fixed capital formation												
Advanced economies	**3.4**	**3.2**	**4.0**	**5.7**	**5.6**	**5.6**	**5.1**	**5.0**	**–1.4**	**–1.7**	**1.4**	**2.8**
United States	2.8	4.6	5.4	8.4	8.8	10.2	7.9	5.5	–2.7	–1.8	2.1	2.9
Euro area	2.1	2.4	1.3	2.5	5.2	5.9	4.9	–0.6	–2.8	–0.5	3.1	
Germany	3.3	–0.1	–0.6	–0.8	0.6	3.0	4.1	2.7	–4.2	–6.7	–1.8	3.5
France	2.3	2.7	2.2	–0.1	–0.2	7.2	8.3	8.4	2.1	–1.4	–1.0	2.4
Italy	1.0	3.4	6.0	3.6	2.1	4.0	5.0	7.1	2.6	0.5	0.6	3.0
Japan[1]	4.3	0.3	0.5	6.9	0.7	–4.1	–0.7	2.7	–1.2	–4.7	1.6	1.2
United Kingdom	2.8	3.3	3.1	4.7	6.9	12.8	0.6	1.9	1.0	–1.0	1.3	2.2
Canada	3.1	4.6	–2.1	4.4	15.2	2.4	7.3	5.5	4.3	1.3	3.6	4.6
Other advanced economies	5.1	3.5	7.2	5.3	6.2	3.0	4.2	5.9	–1.9	0.7	1.7	3.3
Memorandum												
Major advanced economies	3.0	3.1	3.2	5.8	5.5	6.2	5.3	4.8	–1.3	–2.4	1.3	2.7
European Union	2.8	2.7	3.5	2.3	3.5	6.9	5.2	4.9	0.4	–2.1	–0.2	3.1
Newly industrialized Asian economies	10.3	2.0	10.3	7.3	4.4	–9.0	—	10.3	–7.1	0.7	2.2	2.7

Table 3 *(concluded)*

	Ten-Year Averages		1995	1996	1997	1998	1999	2000	2001	2002	2003	2004
	1985–94	1995–2004										
Final domestic demand												
Advanced economies	**3.1**	**2.7**	**2.6**	**3.2**	**3.1**	**3.1**	**3.9**	**3.8**	**1.6**	**1.6**	1.9	2.4
United States	2.8	3.6	3.0	3.7	4.3	5.3	5.2	4.3	1.6	2.4	2.9	3.0
Euro area	...	1.9	1.7	1.6	1.7	3.2	3.7	3.0	1.4	0.2	0.8	1.9
Germany	2.7	1.0	1.3	0.7	0.5	2.1	3.2	1.9	0.1	−1.7	0.3	1.8
France	2.1	2.1	1.2	1.3	0.6	3.4	4.0	4.0	2.7	1.5	0.9	1.8
Italy	2.0	2.0	1.7	1.7	2.4	2.8	2.9	3.4	1.8	0.7	1.2	1.7
Japan[1]	3.6	1.1	1.8	3.7	1.0	−0.9	0.6	2.0	1.1	−0.1	1.1	0.9
United Kingdom	2.6	3.2	2.1	3.5	3.6	4.9	3.5	4.0	3.3	2.9	2.3	2.5
Canada	2.6	3.2	0.7	2.1	5.4	2.8	4.2	4.0	3.2	2.9	3.5	3.6
Other advanced economies	4.4	3.1	4.5	4.2	3.9	1.5	4.2	4.7	1.2	2.3	1.5	2.6
Memorandum												
Major advanced economies	2.8	2.6	2.2	3.0	2.9	3.5	3.8	3.6	1.7	1.4	2.0	2.4
European Union	2.5	2.2	1.9	1.9	2.1	3.6	3.6	3.4	1.8	0.8	1.2	2.1
Newly industrialized Asian economies	8.4	3.1	7.5	7.0	4.6	−5.7	4.3	7.4	0.1	2.8	0.6	2.7
Stock building[2]												
Advanced economies	**—**	**—**	**0.1**	**−0.2**	**0.2**	**−0.1**	**—**	**—**	**−0.7**	**0.3**	0.1	—
United States	—	−0.1	−0.4	—	0.4	0.2	−0.2	0.1	−1.2	0.6	−0.1	—
Euro area	...	—	0.3	−0.5	0.1	0.4	−0.2	—	−0.4	−0.1	0.3	0.1
Germany	—	—	0.3	−0.5	—	0.3	−0.4	−0.1	−0.8	0.1	0.6	0.2
France	—	—	0.5	−0.6	0.1	0.8	−0.2	0.5	−0.7	−0.4	0.2	—
Italy	—	—	0.2	−0.7	0.3	0.3	0.3	−1.1	—	0.4	0.1	−0.1
Japan[1]	—	—	0.6	0.3	—	−0.6	−0.3	0.3	—	−0.4	0.4	—
United Kingdom	0.1	−0.1	—	−0.4	0.3	0.1	0.2	—	−0.7	—	—	−0.1
Canada	—	0.2	1.1	−0.7	0.7	−0.3	0.1	0.8	−1.6	1.8	0.3	−0.6
Other advanced economies	—	—	0.3	−0.3	−0.3	−0.7	0.8	−0.1	−0.4	—	0.1	0.1
Memorandum												
Major advanced economies	—	—	0.1	−0.2	0.3	0.1	−0.1	0.1	−0.8	0.4	0.1	—
European Union	—	—	0.3	−0.5	0.1	0.3	−0.1	−0.1	−0.5	0.1	0.2	—
Newly industrialized Asian economies	0.1	−0.2	0.2	−0.2	−0.5	−3.4	2.7	—	−0.8	0.1	0.2	0.2
Foreign balance[2]												
Advanced economies	**—**	**—**	**0.1**	**—**	**0.2**	**−0.4**	**−0.5**	**0.1**	**0.1**	**—**	−0.3	0.1
United States	0.1	−0.4	0.1	−0.2	−0.3	−1.2	−1.0	−0.8	−0.2	−0.6	−0.3	−0.1
Euro area	...	0.1	0.2	0.4	0.6	−0.6	−0.6	0.6	0.5	0.6	−0.6	−0.1
Germany	—	0.3	0.1	0.5	0.8	−0.4	−0.7	1.1	1.6	1.7	−1.0	−0.4
France	—	0.1	0.1	0.4	1.2	−0.5	−0.4	−0.2	0.1	0.1	−0.6	0.1
Italy	0.1	−0.3	1.0	0.2	−0.6	−1.2	−1.4	0.9	0.1	−0.7	−0.9	—
Japan[1]	−0.1	0.2	−0.5	−0.4	1.0	0.3	−0.1	0.5	−0.7	0.7	0.5	0.6
United Kingdom	−0.2	−0.7	0.9	−0.4	−0.5	−2.2	−1.4	−1.1	−0.6	−1.1	−0.9	−0.1
Canada	−0.1	0.1	1.0	0.3	−1.7	1.7	1.4	0.6	0.6	−0.3	−2.2	—
Other advanced economies	−0.2	0.6	—	0.1	0.9	1.3	0.3	1.1	0.9	0.7	0.4	0.6
Memorandum												
Major advanced economies	—	−0.2	0.2	−0.1	0.1	−0.7	−0.7	−0.2	—	−0.1	−0.4	—
European Union	−0.1	—	0.4	0.2	0.3	−1.0	−0.7	0.3	0.4	0.3	−0.6	−0.1
Newly industrialized Asian economies	−0.1	1.9	0.3	−0.2	1.9	6.5	1.5	2.0	1.8	2.4	1.8	1.6

[1]Annual data are calculated from seasonally adjusted quarterly data.
[2]Changes expressed as percent of GDP in the preceding period.

Table 4. Advanced Economies: Unemployment, Employment, and Real Per Capita GDP

(Percent)

	Ten-Year Averages[1]		1995	1996	1997	1998	1999	2000	2001	2002	2003	2004
	1985–94	1995–2004										
Unemployment rate												
Advanced economies	**6.8**	**6.6**	**7.0**	**7.1**	**6.9**	**6.8**	**6.4**	**5.8**	**5.9**	**6.4**	**6.7**	**6.6**
United States[2]	6.4	5.1	5.6	5.4	4.9	4.5	4.2	4.0	4.8	5.8	6.0	5.7
Euro area	9.4	9.5	10.6	10.8	10.8	10.2	9.4	8.5	8.0	8.4	9.1	9.2
Germany	6.3	8.7	8.0	8.7	9.6	9.1	8.4	7.8	7.9	8.6	9.5	9.8
France	10.2	10.3	11.4	11.9	11.8	11.4	10.7	9.3	8.5	8.8	9.5	9.7
Italy	11.0	10.5	11.6	11.6	11.7	11.8	11.4	10.6	9.5	9.0	9.0	9.0
Spain	19.8	15.9	22.9	22.2	20.8	18.7	15.7	13.9	10.5	11.4	11.4	11.0
Netherlands	7.1	4.2	7.1	6.6	5.5	4.2	3.2	2.6	2.0	2.3	4.2	4.5
Belgium	8.5	8.4	9.7	9.5	9.2	9.3	8.6	6.9	6.7	7.3	8.1	8.3
Austria	3.3	4.1	3.9	4.4	4.4	4.5	3.9	3.6	3.6	4.1	4.4	4.4
Finland	7.8	11.1	15.4	14.6	12.6	11.4	10.2	9.8	9.1	9.1	9.3	9.3
Greece	8.0	10.3	9.1	9.8	9.8	11.1	11.9	11.1	10.4	9.9	9.8	9.7
Portugal	6.1	5.7	7.2	7.3	6.7	5.0	4.4	4.0	4.1	5.1	6.5	6.7
Ireland	15.5	7.0	12.1	11.5	9.8	7.4	5.6	4.3	3.9	4.4	5.1	5.6
Luxembourg	1.7	3.0	3.0	3.3	3.3	3.1	2.9	2.6	2.6	2.8	3.2	3.3
Japan[3]	2.5	4.5	3.2	3.4	3.4	4.1	4.7	4.7	5.0	5.4	5.5	5.4
United Kingdom	9.1	6.2	8.7	8.1	7.1	6.3	6.0	5.5	5.1	5.2	5.2	5.2
Canada	9.6	8.1	9.4	9.6	9.1	8.3	7.6	6.8	7.2	7.6	7.9	7.7
Korea	2.9	3.8	2.1	2.1	2.6	7.0	6.4	4.2	3.8	3.1	3.4	3.3
Australia	8.4	7.1	8.2	8.2	8.2	7.7	7.0	6.3	6.7	6.3	6.1	6.0
Taiwan Province of China	1.8	3.6	1.8	2.6	2.7	2.7	2.9	3.0	4.6	5.2	5.3	5.0
Sweden	3.6	5.7	7.7	8.0	8.0	6.5	5.6	4.7	4.0	4.0	4.5	4.2
Switzerland	1.7	3.5	4.2	4.7	5.2	3.9	2.7	2.0	1.9	2.8	4.2	3.8
Hong Kong SAR	1.9	5.2	3.2	2.8	2.2	4.7	6.2	5.0	5.1	7.3	7.8	7.5
Denmark	9.7	6.4	10.0	8.5	7.7	6.4	5.5	5.1	4.9	4.9	5.7	5.6
Norway	4.3	4.1	5.0	4.9	4.1	3.2	3.2	3.4	3.6	3.9	4.6	4.7
Israel	8.4	8.8	6.8	6.6	7.7	8.5	8.9	8.8	9.4	10.3	10.8	10.6
Singapore	3.2	3.3	2.7	2.0	1.8	3.2	3.5	3.1	3.3	4.4	4.9	4.2
New Zealand	7.1	6.0	6.3	6.1	6.7	7.5	6.8	6.0	5.3	5.2	5.4	5.3
Cyprus	2.8	3.2	2.6	3.1	3.4	3.4	3.6	3.4	3.0	3.2	3.4	3.3
Iceland	2.0	2.9	5.0	4.4	3.9	2.8	1.9	1.3	1.4	2.5	3.0	2.5
Memorandum												
Major advanced economies	6.6	6.4	6.7	6.7	6.6	6.3	6.1	5.7	5.9	6.5	6.8	6.7
European Union	9.5	9.1	10.6	10.7	10.5	9.8	9.1	8.2	7.4	7.7	8.2	8.3
Newly industrialized Asian economies	2.5	3.8	2.1	2.3	2.6	5.4	5.3	3.9	4.1	4.1	4.4	4.2
Growth in employment												
Advanced economies	**1.5**	**1.1**	**1.1**	**1.2**	**1.5**	**1.0**	**1.4**	**2.0**	**0.7**	**0.2**	**0.7**	**1.1**
United States	1.6	1.4	1.5	1.5	2.3	1.5	1.5	2.5	—	-0.3	1.5	1.8
Euro area	...	1.0	0.5	0.5	0.8	1.8	1.7	2.0	1.3	0.5	—	0.5
Germany	3.5	0.2	0.1	-0.3	-0.2	1.1	1.2	1.8	0.4	-0.6	-1.1	-0.4
France	0.2	1.1	0.9	0.4	0.4	1.5	2.0	2.6	1.8	0.7	—	0.4
Italy	-0.2	0.9	-0.6	0.5	0.4	1.1	1.3	1.9	2.1	1.5	0.4	0.6
Japan[3]	1.1	-0.2	0.1	0.4	1.1	-0.7	-0.8	-0.3	-0.5	-1.3	-0.2	0.4
United Kingdom	0.3	0.9	1.1	0.9	1.7	0.9	1.3	1.1	0.8	0.7	0.6	0.5
Canada	1.5	2.0	1.9	0.8	2.3	2.7	2.8	2.6	1.1	2.2	1.9	1.9
Other advanced economies	1.5	1.8	2.1	2.3	1.7	1.0	2.3	3.0	1.6	1.3	1.0	1.3
Memorandum												
Major advanced economies	1.5	0.9	0.8	0.8	1.4	1.0	1.1	1.7	0.4	-0.1	0.6	1.0
European Union	1.2	1.1	0.8	1.0	1.0	1.9	1.9	2.1	1.4	0.5	0.1	0.5
Newly industrialized Asian economies	2.8	1.4	2.3	2.1	1.8	-2.9	1.5	3.5	1.0	2.0	1.4	1.6

Table 4 *(concluded)*

	Ten-Year Averages[1]		1995	1996	1997	1998	1999	2000	2001	2002	2003	2004
	1985–94	1995–2004										
Growth in real per capita GDP												
Advanced economies	**2.4**	**2.1**	**2.1**	**2.3**	**2.8**	**2.1**	**2.8**	**3.4**	**0.5**	**1.4**	**1.4**	**2.5**
United States	1.8	2.1	1.5	2.4	3.2	3.1	2.9	2.6	−0.8	1.4	1.5	2.9
Euro area	—	1.8	2.0	1.2	2.1	2.6	2.6	3.1	0.9	0.6	0.3	1.7
Germany	−0.1	1.2	1.4	0.5	1.1	1.8	2.1	2.8	0.7	—	—	1.5
France	1.5	1.7	1.5	0.7	1.5	3.2	2.8	3.7	1.5	0.7	0.1	1.5
Italy	1.9	1.5	2.7	0.9	1.8	1.7	1.6	2.9	1.5	0.2	0.2	1.5
Japan[3]	3.0	1.1	1.6	3.1	1.6	−1.4	—	2.6	0.2	—	1.8	1.3
United Kingdom	2.3	2.2	2.7	2.4	3.2	2.7	2.1	2.8	1.8	1.4	1.2	1.9
Canada	1.2	2.3	1.7	0.5	3.1	3.2	4.7	4.3	0.9	2.3	1.1	1.8
Other advanced economies	3.2	2.9	3.6	3.2	3.7	1.7	4.5	4.8	1.2	2.3	1.3	2.6
Memorandum												
Major advanced economies	2.2	1.9	1.7	2.1	2.6	2.2	2.4	3.0	0.3	1.1	1.4	2.4
European Union	2.1	2.0	2.1	1.4	2.4	2.8	2.7	3.4	1.6	1.0	0.7	1.9
Newly industrialized Asian economies	6.7	3.5	6.3	5.2	4.6	−3.5	6.9	7.4	−0.1	3.9	1.5	3.5

[1]Compound annual rate of change for employment and per capita GDP; arithmetic average for unemployment rate.
[2]The projections for unemployment have been adjusted to reflect the new survey techniques adopted by the U.S. Bureau of Labor Statistics in January 1994.
[3]Annual data are calculated from seasonally adjusted quarterly data.

Table 5. Developing Countries: Real GDP
(Annual percent change)

	Ten-Year Averages		1995	1996	1997	1998	1999	2000	2001	2002	2003	2004
	1985–94	1995–2004										
Developing countries	**5.2**	**5.1**	**6.1**	**6.6**	**5.9**	**3.5**	**3.9**	**5.7**	**4.1**	**4.6**	**5.0**	**5.6**
Regional groups												
Africa	1.9	3.6	3.0	5.6	3.0	3.2	2.7	3.0	3.7	3.1	3.7	4.8
Sub-Sahara	1.8	3.6	3.8	5.2	3.7	2.4	2.7	3.2	3.5	3.0	3.1	5.0
Excluding Nigeria and South Africa	1.9	4.1	4.4	5.4	4.4	3.7	3.3	2.5	4.0	3.5	3.3	6.4
Developing Asia	7.7	6.6	9.0	8.3	6.6	4.0	6.2	6.8	5.8	6.4	6.4	6.5
China	10.2	8.2	10.5	9.6	8.8	7.8	7.1	8.0	7.5	8.0	7.5	7.5
India	5.4	5.8	7.6	7.5	5.0	5.8	6.7	5.4	4.2	4.7	5.6	5.9
Other developing Asia	5.8	3.8	7.6	6.7	3.8	−5.1	3.6	5.3	3.3	4.4	4.5	4.8
Middle East and Turkey	3.0	4.2	4.0	5.3	6.1	3.7	0.9	6.0	2.0	4.8	5.1	4.6
Western Hemisphere	3.1	2.2	1.8	3.6	5.2	2.3	0.2	4.0	0.7	−0.1	1.1	3.6
Analytical groups												
By source of export earnings												
Fuel	2.4	3.7	2.9	4.2	5.2	3.0	1.0	5.2	4.4	2.7	3.1	5.2
Nonfuel	5.5	5.2	6.4	6.9	6.0	3.5	4.2	5.8	4.1	4.8	5.1	5.7
of which, primary products	3.3	3.7	6.6	6.1	4.2	2.8	1.4	2.3	2.6	2.3	2.5	5.8
By external financing source												
Net debtor countries	4.0	3.8	4.7	5.6	4.8	1.6	2.8	4.7	2.3	3.0	3.8	4.6
of which, official financing	4.6	3.7	6.2	6.2	4.2	−2.6	2.5	4.4	3.8	3.6	4.0	5.0
Net debtor countries by debt-servicing experience												
Countries with arrears and/or rescheduling during 1997–2001	3.7	3.4	5.0	5.1	4.2	−0.7	2.0	4.5	3.4	3.1	3.2	4.4
Other groups												
Heavily indebted poor countries	2.2	4.9	5.8	6.0	5.2	3.9	4.3	4.3	4.8	4.5	4.2	6.4
Middle East and north Africa	2.6	4.3	2.5	5.3	4.8	4.3	2.9	4.9	4.7	3.9	5.2	4.5
Memorandum												
Real per capita GDP												
Developing countries	3.2	3.5	4.4	4.9	4.2	1.9	2.3	4.1	2.5	3.1	3.5	4.1
Regional groups												
Africa	−0.9	1.1	0.4	3.1	0.5	0.7	0.2	0.6	1.2	0.7	1.3	2.4
Developing Asia	5.9	5.2	7.5	6.8	5.1	2.6	4.8	5.4	4.5	5.1	5.1	5.3
Middle East and Turkey	0.2	2.2	1.8	3.1	3.9	1.5	−1.2	3.9	−0.1	2.8	3.2	2.7
Western Hemisphere	1.2	0.7	0.1	2.0	3.6	0.7	−1.4	2.4	−0.9	−1.6	−0.4	2.2

Table 6. Developing Countries—by Country: Real GDP[1]
(Annual percent change)

	Average 1985–94	1995	1996	1997	1998	1999	2000	2001	2002	2003	2004
Africa	**1.9**	**3.0**	**5.6**	**3.0**	**3.2**	**2.7**	**3.0**	**3.7**	**3.1**	**3.7**	**4.8**
Algeria	0.5	3.8	3.8	1.1	5.1	3.2	2.2	2.6	4.1	5.9	3.8
Angola	−1.5	10.4	11.2	7.9	6.8	3.3	3.0	3.2	15.3	4.4	11.4
Benin	2.5	4.6	5.9	5.8	4.6	4.7	5.8	5.0	6.0	5.6	6.5
Botswana	8.1	4.5	5.7	6.7	5.9	6.3	8.6	4.9	2.6	3.7	3.6
Burkina Faso	4.2	4.6	7.1	5.2	1.0	6.7	1.6	4.6	4.6	3.2	4.0
Burundi	2.6	−7.9	−8.0	—	4.7	−0.9	−1.1	2.2	4.5	−0.5	5.4
Cameroon[2]	−1.7	3.3	5.0	5.1	5.0	4.4	4.2	5.3	6.5	4.0	4.4
Cape Verde	4.7	7.5	5.5	8.5	8.0	8.9	6.6	3.8	4.6	5.0	5.1
Central African Republic	1.1	4.9	−8.1	7.5	3.9	3.6	1.8	1.0	0.8	−0.7	5.8
Chad	4.6	0.4	3.1	4.2	7.7	2.3	1.0	8.5	9.7	10.9	42.7
Comoros	0.5	8.9	−1.3	4.2	1.2	1.9	−1.1	1.9	2.5	2.5	3.0
Congo, Dem. Rep. of	−3.7	0.7	−1.0	−5.6	−1.6	−4.3	−6.2	−2.1	3.0	5.0	6.0
Congo, Rep. of	4.6	4.0	4.3	−0.6	3.7	−3.0	8.2	3.6	3.5	2.0	7.0
Côte d'Ivoire	1.2	7.1	7.7	5.7	4.8	1.6	−2.5	0.3	−1.8	−3.0	3.0
Djibouti	−0.9	−3.5	−4.1	−0.7	0.1	2.2	0.7	1.9	2.6	3.0	3.1
Equatorial Guinea	2.9	14.3	31.8	80.7	14.6	30.6	15.2	45.3	13.3	15.6	10.2
Eritrea	...	2.9	9.3	7.9	1.8	—	−13.2	10.2	1.8	5.0	8.0
Ethiopia	1.4	6.2	10.6	4.7	−1.4	6.0	5.4	7.7	1.2	−3.8	6.7
Gabon	2.0	5.0	3.6	5.7	3.5	−8.9	−1.9	2.0	—	1.0	1.7
Gambia, The	3.7	−3.4	6.1	4.9	3.5	6.4	5.5	5.8	−3.1	7.4	5.5
Ghana	4.9	4.0	4.6	4.2	4.7	4.4	3.7	4.2	4.5	4.7	5.0
Guinea	4.1	4.7	5.1	5.0	4.8	4.6	1.9	3.8	4.2	3.6	5.0
Guinea-Bissau	3.0	4.4	4.6	5.5	−28.1	8.0	9.5	0.2	−7.2	2.4	2.9
Kenya	3.5	4.4	4.2	2.1	1.6	1.3	−0.1	1.2	1.0	1.3	2.6
Lesotho	5.1	5.9	9.5	4.8	−3.5	0.5	1.9	3.6	4.2	4.2	4.4
Liberia	...	...	...	...	...	...	...	...	...	...	...
Madagascar	1.2	1.7	2.1	3.7	3.9	4.7	4.8	6.0	−12.7	6.0	6.0
Malawi	1.5	16.7	7.3	3.8	3.3	4.0	1.1	−4.2	1.8	6.5	5.2
Mali	2.5	7.0	4.3	6.7	4.9	6.7	3.7	3.5	9.7	−1.1	5.7
Mauritania	2.9	4.6	5.7	2.8	3.9	5.2	5.2	4.0	3.3	5.4	6.1
Mauritius	7.2	3.5	5.2	6.0	6.0	5.3	2.6	7.2	4.0	3.3	5.5
Morocco	4.0	−6.6	12.2	−2.2	7.7	−0.1	1.0	6.3	3.2	5.5	3.4
Mozambique, Rep. of	4.0	4.3	7.1	11.1	12.6	7.5	1.5	13.0	8.3	7.0	8.0
Namibia	3.7	4.1	3.2	4.2	3.3	3.3	3.3	2.4	2.7	3.7	4.7
Niger	2.1	2.6	3.4	2.8	10.4	−0.6	−1.4	7.1	3.0	4.0	4.1
Nigeria	3.9	2.4	6.5	3.1	0.3	1.5	5.8	2.8	0.5	5.2	2.8
Rwanda	−7.0	35.2	12.7	13.8	8.9	7.6	6.0	6.7	9.4	3.2	6.0
São Tomé and Príncipe	0.8	2.0	1.5	1.0	2.5	2.5	3.0	4.0	4.1	5.0	5.0
Senegal	2.1	5.2	5.1	5.0	5.7	5.0	5.6	5.6	2.4	6.6	5.6
Seychelles	5.3	0.5	10.0	12.2	5.7	−1.3	4.8	−2.2	0.3	−5.1	−2.0
Sierra Leone	−1.1	−10.0	−24.8	−17.6	−0.8	−8.1	3.8	5.4	6.3	6.5	6.8
Somalia	...	...	...	...	...	...	...	...	...	...	...
South Africa	0.8	3.1	4.3	2.6	0.8	2.0	3.5	2.8	3.0	2.2	3.0
Sudan	3.3	3.0	6.3	9.3	5.7	6.9	6.9	5.3	5.0	5.8	6.5
Swaziland	6.5	3.8	3.9	3.8	3.3	3.5	2.0	1.8	1.6	1.5	1.6
Tanzania	3.8	3.6	4.5	3.5	3.7	3.7	5.6	6.1	6.3	5.5	6.3
Togo	1.1	6.9	9.7	4.3	−2.1	2.9	−0.8	0.6	2.9	3.5	3.9
Tunisia	3.7	2.4	7.1	5.4	4.8	6.1	4.7	4.9	1.7	5.5	5.8
Uganda	4.8	11.9	8.6	5.1	4.7	7.9	5.3	5.5	6.6	5.4	6.0
Zambia	−0.4	−2.5	6.5	3.4	−1.9	2.2	3.6	4.9	3.0	4.5	4.5
Zimbabwe	3.5	0.2	9.7	1.4	0.8	−4.1	−6.8	−8.8	−12.8	−11.0	5.1

Table 6 *(continued)*

	Average 1985–94	1995	1996	1997	1998	1999	2000	2001	2002	2003	2004
Developing Asia	**7.7**	**9.0**	**8.3**	**6.6**	**4.0**	**6.2**	**6.8**	**5.8**	**6.4**	**6.4**	**6.5**
Afghanistan, Islamic State of	. . .	. . .	. . .	. . .	. . .	. . .	. . .	. . .	. . .	. . .	. . .
Bangladesh	4.0	4.8	5.0	5.3	5.0	5.4	5.6	4.8	4.9	5.4	5.8
Bhutan	6.4	7.4	5.2	7.2	6.4	7.6	5.3	6.6	7.7	7.3	7.6
Brunei Darussalam	. . .	2.1	1.0	3.6	−4.0	2.6	2.8	0.8	3.0	5.1	0.1
Cambodia	. . .	5.9	4.6	4.3	2.2	6.9	7.7	6.3	5.5	4.7	5.8
China	10.2	10.5	9.6	8.8	7.8	7.1	8.0	7.5	8.0	7.5	7.5
Fiji	2.6	2.5	3.1	−0.9	1.5	9.5	−3.2	4.3	4.4	5.2	3.2
India	5.4	7.6	7.5	5.0	5.8	6.7	5.4	4.2	4.7	5.6	5.9
Indonesia	6.8	8.2	8.0	4.5	−13.1	0.8	4.9	3.4	3.7	3.5	4.0
Kiribati	0.7	5.2	3.8	1.9	12.6	9.5	1.6	1.8	1.0	2.5	1.8
Lao P.D. Republic	5.2	7.0	6.9	6.9	4.0	7.3	5.8	5.8	5.9	5.5	6.0
Malaysia	7.1	9.8	10.0	7.3	−7.4	6.1	8.6	0.3	4.1	4.2	5.3
Maldives	8.0	7.2	9.1	10.4	9.8	7.2	4.8	3.5	6.0	6.2	4.0
Myanmar	1.3	7.2	6.4	5.7	5.8	10.9	13.7	10.5	5.5	5.1	4.3
Nepal	5.7	3.3	5.3	5.3	2.9	4.5	6.1	4.8	−0.5	2.3	4.0
Pakistan	5.3	4.9	2.9	1.8	3.1	4.0	3.4	2.7	4.4	5.4	5.1
Papua New Guinea	5.6	−3.3	7.7	−3.9	−3.8	7.6	−1.3	−3.4	−3.3	2.5	2.3
Philippines	2.2	4.7	5.8	5.2	−0.6	3.4	4.4	4.5	4.4	4.0	4.0
Samoa	2.2	6.6	7.3	0.8	2.4	2.6	6.9	6.2	1.8	3.1	3.2
Solomon Islands	4.4	8.2	1.6	−1.4	1.3	−0.5	−14.2	−9.0	−2.0	1.9	3.1
Sri Lanka	4.3	5.5	3.8	6.4	4.7	4.3	6.0	−1.5	4.0	5.5	6.5
Thailand	9.0	9.2	5.9	−1.4	−10.5	4.4	4.6	1.9	5.3	5.0	5.1
Tonga	2.4	3.2	−0.4	0.2	2.4	2.9	6.5	0.5	1.6	2.5	−0.5
Vanuatu	2.4	7.4	2.5	2.4	3.0	−2.1	2.5	−2.1	−2.8	1.0	2.2
Vietnam	6.1	9.5	9.3	8.2	3.5	4.2	5.5	5.0	5.8	6.0	7.0
Middle East and Turkey	**3.0**	**4.0**	**5.3**	**6.1**	**3.7**	**0.9**	**6.0**	**2.0**	**4.8**	**5.1**	**4.6**
Bahrain	3.6	3.9	4.1	3.1	4.8	4.3	5.3	4.8	4.1	4.1	4.3
Egypt	3.0	4.5	4.9	5.9	4.5	6.3	5.1	3.5	2.0	2.8	3.0
Iran, Islamic Republic of	1.8	3.4	7.6	4.0	3.4	2.0	5.3	5.9	6.7	6.1	5.7
Iraq	. . .	. . .	. . .	. . .	. . .	. . .	. . .	. . .	. . .	. . .	. . .
Jordan	3.5	6.2	2.1	3.3	3.0	3.1	4.2	4.2	4.9	3.0	5.5
Kuwait	2.0	−2.0	5.1	2.3	2.4	−2.5	1.4	−1.1	−0.9	4.7	2.2
Lebanon	−2.1	6.5	4.0	4.0	3.0	1.0	−0.5	2.0	2.0	2.0	3.0
Libya	−1.0	−0.3	3.3	5.2	−3.6	0.7	2.3	0.5	−0.2	5.6	2.8
Malta	5.4	6.9	4.0	4.9	3.4	4.1	6.4	−1.2	1.2	2.8	3.8
Oman	5.3	4.8	2.9	6.2	2.7	−0.2	5.5	9.3	2.3	2.2	4.8
Qatar	−0.5	2.9	4.8	25.4	6.2	5.3	11.6	7.2	3.0	4.0	8.2
Saudi Arabia	2.9	0.5	1.4	2.6	2.8	−0.7	4.9	1.3	1.0	4.7	2.1
Syrian Arab Republic	4.5	7.3	4.7	4.1	6.3	−0.9	0.6	7.2	2.7	1.0	2.9
Turkey	4.2	6.9	6.9	7.6	3.1	−4.7	7.4	−7.5	7.8	5.3	5.0
United Arab Emirates	2.5	7.0	6.1	8.3	1.4	4.4	10.0	3.8	1.5	6.3	3.9
Yemen, Republic of	. . .	12.5	7.4	6.4	5.3	3.5	4.4	4.6	3.9	3.8	3.3

Table 6 *(concluded)*

	Average 1985–94	1995	1996	1997	1998	1999	2000	2001	2002	2003	2004
Western Hemisphere	**3.1**	**1.8**	**3.6**	**5.2**	**2.3**	**0.2**	**4.0**	**0.7**	**-0.1**	**1.1**	**3.6**
Antigua and Barbuda	6.2	-5.0	6.1	5.6	5.0	4.9	3.3	1.5	2.1	2.5	1.0
Argentina	2.3	-2.8	5.5	8.1	3.8	-3.4	-0.8	-4.4	-10.9	5.5	4.0
Bahamas, The	1.4	0.3	4.2	3.3	3.0	5.9	4.9	-2.0	0.7	0.9	2.5
Barbados	0.7	2.3	2.5	2.9	4.4	2.5	3.0	-2.7	-1.8	1.6	2.3
Belize	6.8	4.0	0.7	3.8	3.1	4.1	11.2	5.3	3.5	4.5	4.4
Bolivia	2.9	4.7	4.4	5.0	5.0	0.4	2.3	1.5	2.8	2.9	4.3
Brazil	2.9	4.2	2.7	3.3	0.1	0.8	4.4	1.4	1.5	1.5	3.0
Chile	7.0	10.8	7.4	6.6	3.2	-0.8	4.2	3.1	2.1	3.3	4.5
Colombia	4.3	5.2	2.1	3.4	0.6	-4.2	2.9	1.4	1.5	2.0	3.3
Costa Rica	4.6	3.9	0.9	5.6	8.4	8.2	1.8	1.1	2.8	3.0	2.5
Dominica	3.8	1.6	3.1	2.0	2.8	1.6	0.7	-4.6	-3.6	-1.0	0.5
Dominican Republic	2.8	4.7	7.2	8.3	7.3	8.0	7.3	3.2	4.1	-3.0	0.5
Ecuador	3.0	1.7	2.4	4.1	2.1	-6.3	2.8	5.1	3.4	3.1	5.0
El Salvador	2.3	6.4	1.7	4.2	3.7	3.4	2.2	1.8	2.3	2.5	3.0
Grenada	3.9	3.1	3.1	4.0	7.3	7.5	6.5	-3.3	-0.5	2.5	4.5
Guatemala	3.0	4.9	3.0	4.4	5.0	3.8	3.6	2.3	2.2	2.4	3.5
Guyana	2.3	5.0	7.9	6.2	-1.7	3.0	-1.3	2.3	1.1	-0.2	2.0
Haiti	-2.3	9.9	4.1	2.7	2.2	2.7	0.9	-1.1	-0.9	—	1.0
Honduras	3.3	4.1	3.6	5.0	2.9	-1.9	5.2	3.3	2.0	2.0	2.5
Jamaica	2.4	0.5	-1.2	-1.4	-0.4	-0.2	0.9	1.1	1.5	2.2	1.6
Mexico	2.5	-6.2	5.2	6.8	5.0	3.6	6.6	-0.2	0.7	1.5	3.5
Netherlands Antilles	1.9	0.3	1.3	-0.5	0.7	-0.7	-2.0	0.6	0.2	0.5	1.0
Nicaragua	-1.8	4.3	4.8	5.1	4.1	7.0	4.2	3.0	1.0	2.3	3.7
Panama	2.7	1.8	2.8	4.6	8.7	4.2	3.3	0.3	0.8	1.5	3.0
Paraguay	3.5	4.7	1.3	2.6	-0.4	0.5	-0.4	2.7	-3.9	0.6	1.0
Peru	1.4	8.6	2.5	6.7	-0.5	0.9	3.1	0.6	5.3	4.0	4.0
St. Kitts and Nevis	5.4	3.7	0.8	12.9	1.1	3.5	6.2	2.3	0.8	1.2	1.4
St. Lucia	6.4	4.1	1.4	0.6	2.6	3.1	0.2	-5.2	-0.5	1.5	2.0
St. Vincent and the Grenadines	4.9	6.8	1.4	3.9	5.2	3.0	1.3	0.9	1.1	2.2	2.8
Suriname	-2.7	7.2	12.3	7.0	4.1	-2.0	-1.0	4.9	2.7	3.8	4.3
Trinidad and Tobago	-1.2	4.0	3.8	2.8	7.8	4.4	6.1	3.3	2.7	3.8	4.0
Uruguay	4.2	-1.4	5.6	4.9	4.7	-2.8	-1.4	-3.4	-10.8	-1.0	4.5
Venezuela	2.6	4.0	-0.2	6.4	0.2	-6.1	3.2	2.8	-8.9	-16.7	7.7

[1]For many countries, figures for recent years are IMF staff estimates. Data for some countries are for fiscal years.
[2]The percent changes in 2002 are calculated over a period of 18 months, reflecting a change in the fiscal year cycle (from July–June to January–December).

Table 7. Countries in Transition: Real GDP[1]
(Annual percent change)

	Average 1985–94	1995	1996	1997	1998	1999	2000	2001	2002	2003	2004
Central and eastern Europe	...	**5.5**	**4.0**	**2.5**	**2.5**	**2.3**	**3.9**	**3.1**	**3.0**	**3.4**	**4.1**
Albania	−2.1	8.9	9.1	−10.5	12.7	8.9	7.7	6.8	4.7	6.0	6.0
Bosnia and Herzegovina	...	16.4	60.8	30.4	15.6	9.6	5.4	4.5	3.8	3.3	5.0
Bulgaria	−3.2	−1.8	−8.0	−5.6	4.0	2.3	5.4	4.1	4.8	5.0	5.5
Croatia	...	6.8	6.0	6.8	2.5	−0.9	2.9	3.8	5.2	4.6	4.5
Czech Republic	...	5.9	4.3	−0.8	−1.0	0.5	3.3	3.1	2.0	1.7	2.6
Estonia	...	4.3	3.9	9.8	4.6	−0.6	7.1	5.0	5.8	5.0	5.1
Hungary	−1.1	1.5	1.3	4.6	4.9	4.2	5.2	3.8	3.3	3.0	3.5
Latvia	...	−0.8	3.7	8.4	4.8	2.8	6.8	7.9	6.1	5.5	6.0
Lithuania	...	3.3	4.7	7.0	7.3	−1.8	4.0	6.5	6.7	5.8	6.2
Macedonia, former Yugoslav Rep. of	...	−1.1	1.2	2.0	3.4	4.4	4.5	−4.5	0.7	3.0	4.0
Poland	1.3	6.8	6.0	6.8	4.8	4.1	4.0	1.0	1.4	2.9	4.1
Romania	−2.5	8.0	3.9	−6.1	−4.8	−1.2	2.1	5.7	4.9	4.7	5.0
Serbia and Montenegro	...	...	...	...	2.5	−18.0	5.0	5.5	4.0	4.0	5.0
Slovak Republic	...	6.5	5.8	5.6	4.0	1.3	2.2	3.3	4.4	4.0	4.0
Slovenia	...	4.9	3.5	4.6	3.8	5.2	4.6	2.9	3.2	2.2	3.0
Commonwealth of Independent States and Mongolia	...	**−5.5**	**−3.5**	**1.4**	**−3.2**	**5.2**	**9.1**	**6.4**	**4.9**	**5.8**	**5.0**
Russia	...	−4.1	−3.6	1.4	−5.3	6.3	10.0	5.0	4.3	6.0	5.0
Excluding Russia	...	−8.6	−3.1	1.5	1.4	2.7	6.9	9.2	5.9	5.4	5.0
Armenia	...	6.9	5.9	3.3	7.3	3.3	6.0	9.6	12.9	7.0	6.0
Azerbaijan	...	−11.8	1.3	5.8	10.0	7.4	11.1	9.9	10.6	9.2	9.1
Belarus	...	−10.4	2.8	11.4	8.4	3.4	5.8	4.7	4.7	4.0	3.2
Georgia	...	2.6	10.5	10.6	2.9	3.0	1.9	4.7	5.3	4.8	4.5
Kazakhstan	...	−8.3	0.5	1.6	−1.9	2.7	9.8	13.5	9.5	9.0	8.0
Kyrgyz Republic	...	−5.8	7.1	9.9	2.1	3.7	5.3	5.4	−0.5	5.6	4.0
Moldova	...	−1.4	−5.9	1.7	−6.5	−3.4	2.1	6.1	7.2	6.0	5.0
Mongolia	0.4	6.3	2.4	4.0	3.5	3.2	1.1	1.0	3.9	5.0	5.3
Tajikistan	...	−12.5	−4.4	1.7	5.3	3.7	8.3	10.2	9.1	6.0	4.0
Turkmenistan	...	−7.2	−6.7	−11.3	7.0	16.5	18.0	20.5	...	...	...
Ukraine	...	−12.2	−10.0	−3.0	−1.9	−0.2	5.9	9.2	4.8	5.3	4.8
Uzbekistan	...	−0.9	1.6	2.5	2.1	3.4	3.3	4.1	3.2	0.3	2.5
Memorandum											
EU accession candidates	...	5.9	4.8	4.1	2.6	0.2	5.0	—	4.3	3.9	4.3

[1]Data for some countries refer to real net material product (NMP) or are estimates based on NMP. For many countries, figures for recent years are IMF staff estimates. The figures should be interpreted only as indicative of broad orders of magnitude because reliable, comparable data are not generally available. In particular, the growth of output of new private enterprises of the informal economy is not fully reflected in the recent figures.

Table 8. Summary of Inflation
(Percent)

	Ten-Year Averages		1995	1996	1997	1998	1999	2000	2001	2002	2003	2004
	1985–94	1995–2004										
GDP deflators												
Advanced economies	**3.7**	**1.5**	**2.3**	**1.9**	**1.7**	**1.3**	**0.8**	**1.4**	**1.8**	**1.2**	**1.3**	**1.0**
United States	3.0	1.7	2.2	1.9	1.9	1.2	1.4	2.1	2.4	1.1	1.5	1.2
Euro area	. . .	1.9	2.9	2.2	1.6	1.7	1.1	1.4	2.3	2.4	2.1	1.7
Japan[1]	1.4	−1.2	−0.5	−0.8	0.3	−0.1	−1.5	−1.9	−1.6	−1.7	−2.5	−2.0
Other advanced economies	5.4	2.0	3.1	2.9	2.4	1.9	0.8	1.9	1.8	1.4	2.0	1.7
Consumer prices												
Advanced economies	**3.8**	**1.9**	**2.6**	**2.4**	**2.1**	**1.5**	**1.4**	**2.2**	**2.2**	**1.5**	**1.8**	**1.3**
United States	3.6	2.3	2.8	2.9	2.3	1.5	2.2	3.4	2.8	1.6	2.1	1.3
Euro area[2]	. . .	1.9	2.7	2.2	1.6	1.1	1.1	2.1	2.4	2.3	2.0	1.6
Japan[1]	1.6	−0.1	−0.1	—	1.7	0.6	−0.3	−0.9	−0.7	−0.9	−0.3	−0.6
Other advanced economies	5.9	2.3	3.8	3.2	2.4	2.6	1.0	2.2	2.4	1.8	2.0	1.6
Developing countries	**49.9**	**9.2**	**23.3**	**15.3**	**9.9**	**10.4**	**6.5**	**5.8**	**5.8**	**5.3**	**5.9**	**4.9**
Regional groups												
Africa	28.1	15.5	35.5	30.3	14.5	10.7	12.2	14.3	12.9	9.3	10.6	7.7
Developing Asia	11.0	4.8	13.2	8.2	4.8	7.7	2.5	1.8	2.7	2.0	2.5	2.9
Middle East and Turkey	26.3	22.2	39.1	29.6	28.1	27.5	23.6	19.5	17.1	15.7	13.5	10.8
Western Hemisphere	190.7	12.3	36.1	20.9	12.4	9.2	7.4	6.8	6.4	8.7	10.9	7.0
Analytical groups												
By source of export earnings												
Fuel	19.8	19.5	43.1	35.4	19.8	17.3	16.8	13.4	11.7	12.3	14.8	14.4
Nonfuel	54.7	8.1	21.3	13.3	8.8	9.7	5.5	5.0	5.2	4.6	5.1	4.0
of which, primary products	49.2	18.3	34.7	31.1	16.8	13.8	17.1	22.5	18.6	8.2	13.0	10.3
By external financing source												
Net debtor countries	70.2	11.9	25.1	17.3	12.5	15.8	10.1	8.5	8.6	8.5	8.2	6.0
of which, official financing	22.4	13.4	22.0	15.6	10.2	26.5	13.2	8.0	12.8	10.2	9.3	7.9
Net debtor countries by debt-servicing experience												
Countries with arrears and/or rescheduling during 1997–2001	163.5	15.4	40.2	20.6	11.7	18.5	12.3	10.5	12.2	10.8	12.4	8.4
Countries in transition	**97.1**	**30.1**	**133.8**	**42.5**	**27.4**	**21.5**	**44.4**	**20.7**	**16.2**	**11.1**	**9.7**	**9.1**
Central and eastern Europe	. . .	15.0	24.7	23.3	42.0	17.2	11.0	12.9	9.7	5.6	4.0	4.8
Commonwealth of Independent States and Mongolia	. . .	40.1	235.7	55.9	19.1	24.5	71.2	25.8	20.3	14.5	13.1	11.7
Russia	. . .	38.6	198.0	47.9	14.7	27.8	85.7	20.8	20.6	16.0	14.4	12.9
Excluding Russia	. . .	43.7	338.9	75.5	29.7	17.9	43.5	37.4	19.8	11.5	10.4	9.4
Memorandum												
Median inflation rate												
Advanced economies	3.9	2.1	2.4	2.2	1.9	1.7	1.5	2.7	2.7	2.2	2.1	1.7
Developing countries	9.5	5.2	10.0	7.3	6.3	5.3	3.8	3.9	4.3	3.3	4.4	3.8
Countries in transition	146.4	12.9	41.4	24.1	14.8	9.9	8.0	10.0	7.1	4.5	4.6	4.7

[1]Annual data are calculated from seasonally adjusted quarterly data.
[2]Based on Eurostat's harmonized index of consumer prices.

Table 9. Advanced Economies: GDP Deflators and Consumer Prices
(Annual percent change)

	Ten-Year Averages		1995	1996	1997	1998	1999	2000	2001	2002	2003	2004	Fourth Quarter[1]		
	1985–94	1995–2004											2002	2003	2004
GDP deflators															
Advanced economies	**3.7**	**1.5**	**2.3**	**1.9**	**1.7**	**1.3**	**0.8**	**1.4**	**1.8**	**1.2**	**1.3**	**1.0**	...	...	...
United States	3.0	1.7	2.2	1.9	1.9	1.2	1.4	2.1	2.4	1.1	1.5	1.2	1.3	1.3	1.4
Euro area	...	1.9	2.9	2.2	1.6	1.7	1.1	1.4	2.3	2.4	2.1	1.7	2.1	2.0	1.6
Germany	2.9	1.0	2.0	1.0	0.7	1.1	0.5	−0.3	1.3	1.6	0.9	0.9	0.9	1.0	1.0
France	3.2	1.3	1.7	1.4	1.3	0.8	0.4	0.7	1.7	1.9	1.6	1.6	1.8	1.6	1.7
Italy	6.4	2.9	5.0	5.3	2.4	2.7	1.6	2.1	2.7	2.7	2.9	2.1	2.3	3.1	1.9
Spain	6.7	3.5	4.9	3.5	2.3	2.4	2.7	3.5	4.2	4.4	3.9	2.8	4.6	3.3	2.7
Netherlands	1.5	2.6	2.0	1.2	2.0	1.7	1.6	3.9	5.4	3.4	3.3	1.9	3.1	2.6	2.0
Belgium	3.1	1.5	1.3	1.2	1.2	1.6	1.4	1.3	1.9	1.9	1.8	1.6	1.5	1.7	1.5
Austria	2.9	1.3	2.5	1.3	0.9	0.5	0.7	1.4	1.6	1.3	1.3	1.2	1.4	1.2	1.4
Finland	4.1	1.7	4.1	−0.2	2.1	3.0	−0.2	3.2	2.2	1.3	1.0	0.6	...	...	...
Greece	15.9	5.1	11.2	7.4	6.8	5.2	3.0	3.4	3.4	3.7	4.0	2.8	3.9	4.5	2.8
Portugal	12.2	3.9	7.6	3.0	3.8	3.8	3.1	3.2	4.8	4.6	3.3	2.4	4.3	2.7	2.4
Ireland	3.3	3.9	3.0	2.1	4.0	6.3	3.8	4.3	5.1	5.4	2.1	2.9	...	...	...
Luxembourg	2.5	2.5	4.3	1.6	3.3	2.1	3.1	2.8	2.3	0.9	2.2	2.2	...	...	...
Japan[2]	1.4	−1.2	−0.5	−0.8	0.3	−0.1	−1.5	−1.9	−1.6	−1.7	−2.5	−2.0	−2.6	−1.8	−2.1
United Kingdom	5.0	2.7	2.6	3.3	2.9	2.9	2.5	2.2	2.3	3.1	2.8	2.7	3.1	2.8	2.7
Canada	3.0	1.8	2.3	1.6	1.2	−0.4	1.7	4.0	1.0	1.0	3.5	1.8	4.1	2.5	2.0
Korea	7.2	2.3	7.1	3.9	3.1	5.1	−2.0	−1.1	2.5	1.7	1.1	1.8	3.1	0.5	2.2
Australia	4.6	2.1	1.9	2.0	1.5	0.5	0.7	4.1	3.4	2.3	2.5	2.0	2.8	1.7	2.8
Taiwan Province of China	2.5	0.7	2.0	3.1	1.7	2.6	−1.4	−1.7	0.6	−1.1	0.7	0.7	−1.9	0.8	0.7
Sweden	5.4	1.7	3.4	1.2	1.5	0.8	0.7	1.3	2.0	1.3	2.3	2.0	1.0	2.5	2.0
Switzerland	3.1	0.5	1.1	0.4	−0.2	—	0.7	1.2	1.4	0.4	−0.1	0.6	0.4	−0.1	0.6
Hong Kong SAR	8.1	−0.9	2.5	5.9	5.7	0.2	−5.9	−6.2	−1.9	−3.0	−2.9	−2.1	−4.1	−0.4	−5.1
Denmark	3.5	1.9	1.8	2.5	2.2	1.0	1.8	3.1	2.0	0.9	1.7	2.1	0.9	2.2	1.9
Norway	2.8	3.2	2.9	4.1	2.9	−0.7	6.6	15.9	1.9	−1.3	2.2	−0.9	...	...	...
Israel	33.9	5.2	9.8	10.9	9.0	6.9	6.4	1.3	2.1	4.6	1.2	0.2	7.3	−0.5	1.3
Singapore	2.3	0.1	2.2	1.1	0.4	−2.4	−5.5	4.5	−1.2	0.2	0.4	1.2	1.1	0.7	1.2
New Zealand	6.0	1.6	2.1	1.9	1.5	1.3	0.6	2.3	4.0	—	0.4	1.9	−1.9	1.0	1.9
Cyprus	4.7	2.9	3.6	1.9	2.6	2.3	2.2	4.2	2.4	2.9	3.8	3.5	...	...	...
Iceland	14.7	3.7	2.8	2.0	3.3	4.9	2.8	2.9	9.3	5.0	1.9	2.1	...	...	...
Memorandum															
Major advanced economies	3.1	1.3	1.9	1.6	1.5	1.1	0.9	1.2	1.5	1.0	1.1	0.9	1.0	1.1	1.0
European Union	4.6	2.2	3.1	2.5	1.9	2.0	1.4	1.6	2.4	2.5	2.2	1.9	...	...	...
Newly industrialized Asian economies	5.6	1.3	4.7	3.7	2.8	3.1	−2.5	−1.5	1.1	0.2	0.5	1.0	0.6	0.5	0.9
Consumer prices															
Advanced economies	**3.8**	**1.9**	**2.6**	**2.4**	**2.1**	**1.5**	**1.4**	**2.2**	**2.2**	**1.5**	**1.8**	**1.3**	...	...	...
United States	3.6	2.3	2.8	2.9	2.3	1.5	2.2	3.4	2.8	1.6	2.1	1.3	2.2	1.7	1.6
Euro area[3]	...	1.9	2.7	2.2	1.6	1.1	1.1	2.1	2.4	2.3	2.0	1.6	2.3	1.6	1.6
Germany[3]	2.5	1.2	1.7	1.2	1.5	0.6	0.6	1.4	1.9	1.3	1.0	0.6	1.2	1.0	0.7
France[3]	3.1	1.6	1.8	2.1	1.3	0.7	0.6	1.8	1.8	1.9	1.9	1.7	2.0	1.7	2.3
Italy[3]	5.8	2.7	5.2	4.1	1.9	2.0	1.7	2.6	2.7	2.6	2.8	2.0	2.9	2.7	1.9
Japan[2]	1.6	−0.1	−0.1	—	1.7	0.6	−0.3	−0.9	−0.7	−0.9	−0.3	−0.6	−0.4	−0.3	−0.5
United Kingdom[4]	4.8	2.5	2.8	3.0	2.8	2.7	2.3	2.1	2.1	2.2	2.8	2.5	2.6	2.9	2.4
Canada	3.5	2.0	2.2	1.6	1.6	1.0	1.7	2.7	2.5	2.3	2.8	1.7	3.8	1.8	2.0
Other advanced economies	6.1	2.5	3.8	3.2	2.4	2.4	1.3	2.4	2.9	2.4	2.2	1.9	...	...	...
Memorandum															
Major advanced economies	3.3	1.8	2.3	2.2	2.0	1.3	1.4	2.2	2.0	1.3	1.8	1.1	1.8	1.5	1.3
European Union[3]	4.3	2.1	2.9	2.5	1.9	1.5	1.4	2.2	2.4	2.3	2.2	1.8	...	...	...
Newly industrialized Asian economies	4.8	2.4	4.6	4.3	3.4	4.4	—	1.1	1.9	1.0	1.5	1.7	1.2	1.4	1.9

[1]From fourth quarter of preceding year.
[2]Annual data are calculated from seasonally adjusted quarterly data.
[3]Based on Eurostat's harmonized index of consumer prices.
[4]Retail price index excluding mortgage interest.

Table 10. Advanced Economies: Hourly Earnings, Productivity, and Unit Labor Costs in Manufacturing
(Annual percent change)

	Ten-Year Averages		1995	1996	1997	1998	1999	2000	2001	2002	2003	2004
	1985–94	1995–2004										
Hourly earnings												
Advanced economies	**5.5**	**3.3**	**3.2**	**3.0**	**3.0**	**3.0**	**3.1**	**4.7**	**2.8**	**3.5**	**4.0**	**3.1**
United States	4.0	3.8	2.1	1.4	1.9	5.4	4.0	7.4	2.5	5.0	5.4	3.1
Euro area	...	3.3	4.2	4.2	3.1	1.7	2.6	3.4	3.8	3.7	3.2	3.5
Germany	5.5	3.3	4.3	4.2	4.0	—	3.8	3.7	3.6	3.4	3.0	3.0
France	4.3	2.5	2.3	2.3	2.1	0.5	1.1	4.7	2.5	3.2	2.6	3.7
Italy	7.5	2.9	4.7	5.8	4.2	−1.4	2.3	3.1	3.0	2.7	2.1	3.1
Japan	3.9	0.8	2.3	1.8	3.1	0.8	−0.8	−0.2	0.9	−1.2	1.3	0.1
United Kingdom	7.6	4.6	4.4	4.3	4.2	4.5	4.0	4.6	4.3	3.4	6.1	5.8
Canada	4.1	2.1	2.2	1.0	2.2	0.8	1.6	1.3	3.5	2.7	3.1	2.5
Other advanced economies	8.9	4.4	5.2	5.9	4.4	3.1	4.5	4.3	4.0	4.2	3.9	4.2
Memorandum												
Major advanced economies	4.7	3.1	2.8	2.3	2.7	3.0	2.7	4.8	2.5	3.3	4.0	2.8
European Union	6.4	3.4	4.2	4.1	3.8	1.6	3.0	3.8	3.6	3.4	3.4	3.6
Newly industrialized Asian economies	13.7	6.2	7.9	10.2	5.6	1.7	7.8	6.5	3.5	5.8	6.0	6.8
Productivity												
Advanced economies	**2.9**	**3.1**	**3.7**	**2.7**	**4.0**	**2.3**	**4.0**	**4.7**	**0.6**	**3.6**	**3.2**	**2.6**
United States	2.8	4.1	3.9	3.5	4.2	4.9	5.1	4.0	1.7	6.3	4.5	3.1
Euro area	...	3.3	4.9	2.9	5.5	3.7	2.8	5.1	1.2	1.8	2.1	2.6
Germany	3.3	2.7	3.3	3.2	3.1	3.0	—	5.9	—	2.8	3.0	2.8
France	3.5	3.9	6.0	1.0	5.6	5.5	2.9	7.7	2.2	2.5	2.0	3.8
Italy	3.2	1.2	3.7	−0.2	2.6	−0.4	1.6	3.4	1.0	−1.4	0.9	1.2
Japan	2.1	2.4	4.4	3.8	4.7	−4.0	2.9	6.4	−3.5	3.3	4.3	1.6
United Kingdom	4.3	2.1	−0.8	−0.6	1.3	1.0	3.5	5.6	2.2	1.1	4.1	4.0
Canada	2.1	1.1	1.4	−2.4	3.4	−0.4	2.6	2.1	−2.0	2.0	2.0	2.0
Other advanced economies	3.0	2.9	3.9	3.4	4.5	1.9	5.5	4.1	0.8	1.9	1.3	2.2
Memorandum												
Major advanced economies	2.9	3.2	3.6	2.5	3.9	2.4	3.6	4.8	0.5	4.1	3.7	2.8
European Union	3.5	2.5	3.2	1.3	3.6	2.6	2.1	4.8	1.1	1.4	2.1	2.5
Newly industrialized Asian economies	4.4	5.3	7.8	6.9	5.9	−0.4	14.0	9.6	0.3	3.5	2.0	4.3
Unit labor costs												
Advanced economies	**2.6**	**0.2**	**−0.3**	**0.4**	**−0.9**	**0.8**	**−0.8**	**—**	**2.2**	**−0.1**	**0.7**	**0.4**
United States	1.2	−0.3	−1.7	−2.1	−2.2	0.4	−1.1	3.2	0.7	−1.3	0.9	0.1
Euro area	...	0.1	−0.6	1.3	−2.3	−1.9	−0.3	−1.6	2.6	1.9	1.1	0.9
Germany	2.2	0.6	1.0	0.9	0.8	−2.9	3.8	−2.1	3.6	0.7	—	0.2
France	0.8	−1.4	−3.5	1.2	−3.2	−4.8	−1.8	−2.8	0.3	0.7	0.6	−0.1
Italy	4.2	1.7	1.0	6.1	1.6	−1.0	0.7	−0.3	2.0	4.1	1.2	1.9
Japan	1.7	−1.5	−2.1	−1.9	−1.6	5.0	−3.5	−6.2	4.5	−4.4	−2.9	−1.5
United Kingdom	3.1	2.4	5.2	5.0	2.9	3.4	0.5	−0.9	2.1	2.3	1.9	1.7
Canada	2.0	1.0	0.9	3.4	−1.2	1.1	−0.9	−0.7	5.5	0.7	1.1	0.5
Other advanced economies	6.0	1.5	1.5	2.7	0.1	1.5	−0.9	0.1	3.2	2.2	2.4	1.8
Memorandum												
Major advanced economies	1.8	−0.1	−0.8	−0.2	−1.2	0.6	−0.8	—	2.0	−0.7	0.3	0.1
European Union	2.9	1.0	1.0	2.8	0.3	−0.9	0.9	−0.9	2.5	2.0	1.2	1.1
Newly industrialized Asian economies	8.8	0.9	0.7	3.7	0.3	3.0	−5.2	−3.2	3.0	1.6	3.3	1.9

Table 11. Developing Countries: Consumer Prices

(Annual percent change)

| | Ten-Year Averages | | 1995 | 1996 | 1997 | 1998 | 1999 | 2000 | 2001 | 2002 | 2003 | 2004 |
	1985–94	1995–2004										
Developing countries	**49.9**	**9.2**	**23.3**	**15.3**	**9.9**	**10.4**	**6.5**	**5.8**	**5.8**	**5.3**	**5.9**	**4.9**
Regional groups												
Africa	28.1	15.5	35.5	30.3	14.5	10.7	12.2	14.3	12.9	9.3	10.6	7.7
Sub-Sahara	33.7	18.8	41.2	36.8	17.8	12.8	15.4	18.4	16.2	11.5	13.2	9.2
Excluding Nigeria and South Africa	48.0	26.5	58.3	59.7	25.5	16.8	23.3	28.9	22.0	12.5	16.4	11.3
Developing Asia	11.0	4.8	13.2	8.2	4.8	7.7	2.5	1.8	2.7	2.0	2.5	2.9
China	11.0	2.7	17.1	8.3	2.8	−0.8	−1.4	0.4	0.7	−0.8	0.8	1.5
India	9.0	6.5	10.2	9.0	7.2	13.2	4.7	4.0	3.8	4.3	4.0	4.8
Other developing Asia	12.2	7.9	9.3	7.5	6.8	22.0	9.0	3.0	6.2	6.5	5.1	4.7
Middle East and Turkey	26.3	22.2	39.1	29.6	28.1	27.5	23.6	19.5	17.1	15.7	13.5	10.8
Western Hemisphere	190.7	12.3	36.1	20.9	12.4	9.2	7.4	6.8	6.4	8.7	10.9	7.0
Analytical groups												
By source of export earnings												
Fuel	19.8	19.5	43.1	35.4	19.8	17.3	16.8	13.4	11.7	12.3	14.8	14.4
Nonfuel	54.7	8.1	21.3	13.3	8.8	9.7	5.5	5.0	5.2	4.6	5.1	4.0
of which, primary products	49.2	18.3	34.7	31.1	16.8	13.8	17.1	22.5	18.6	8.2	13.0	10.3
By external financing source												
Net debtor countries	70.2	11.9	25.1	17.3	12.5	15.8	10.1	8.5	8.6	8.5	8.2	6.0
of which, official financing	22.4	13.4	22.0	15.6	10.2	26.5	13.2	8.0	12.8	10.2	9.3	7.9
Net debtor countries by debt-servicing experience												
Countries with arrears and/or rescheduling during 1997–2001	163.5	15.4	40.2	20.6	11.7	18.5	12.3	10.5	12.2	10.8	12.4	8.4
Other groups												
Heavily indebted poor countries	61.1	21.4	49.8	47.2	22.0	17.6	18.3	19.3	17.0	10.9	11.6	8.0
Middle East and north Africa	17.4	11.2	24.2	16.8	11.7	10.6	10.6	8.1	6.9	7.2	8.5	8.5
Memorandum												
Median												
Developing countries	9.5	5.2	10.0	7.3	6.3	5.3	3.8	3.9	4.3	3.3	4.4	3.8
Regional groups												
Africa	10.9	6.0	12.4	7.5	7.9	5.8	3.9	5.4	4.9	3.3	5.3	4.0
Developing Asia	8.4	5.4	8.7	7.3	6.5	8.5	4.4	3.0	3.8	3.9	4.1	4.1
Middle East and Turkey	6.9	3.2	6.4	6.8	3.4	3.0	2.2	1.5	1.7	1.6	2.6	2.7
Western Hemisphere	13.4	5.3	10.1	7.1	6.9	4.6	3.5	4.6	3.7	4.2	4.6	3.4

Table 12. Developing Countries—by Country: Consumer Prices[1]
(Annual percent change)

	Average 1985–94	1995	1996	1997	1998	1999	2000	2001	2002	2003	2004
Africa	**28.1**	**35.5**	**30.3**	**14.5**	**10.7**	**12.2**	**14.3**	**12.9**	**9.3**	**10.6**	**7.7**
Algeria	15.8	29.8	18.7	5.7	5.0	2.6	0.3	4.2	1.4	2.3	3.5
Angola	104.5	2,672.2	4,146.0	221.5	107.4	248.2	325.0	152.6	108.9	95.2	30.1
Benin	4.6	14.5	4.9	3.8	5.8	0.3	4.2	4.0	2.4	2.5	2.4
Botswana	12.8	10.5	10.3	9.4	7.6	6.9	7.9	7.2	5.5	4.7	4.5
Burkina Faso	1.8	7.8	6.1	2.4	5.0	−1.1	−0.3	4.9	2.3	3.0	2.8
Burundi	7.4	19.4	26.4	31.1	12.5	3.4	24.3	9.3	−1.3	11.0	7.2
Cameroon[2]	2.6	25.8	6.6	5.1	—	2.9	0.8	2.8	6.3	2.5	2.1
Cape Verde	7.0	8.4	6.0	8.6	4.4	3.9	−2.4	3.8	1.8	2.8	2.0
Central African Republic	1.7	19.2	3.7	1.6	−1.9	−1.4	3.2	3.8	2.3	3.2	1.7
Chad	2.1	5.4	11.3	5.6	4.3	−8.4	3.8	12.4	5.2	4.3	4.0
Comoros	2.1	7.1	2.0	3.0	3.5	3.5	4.5	−3.5	3.3	2.5	2.0
Congo, Dem. Rep. of	534.5	541.8	617.0	199.0	107.0	270.0	553.7	357.9	27.7	9.1	6.0
Congo, Rep. of	2.2	8.6	10.2	13.2	1.8	3.1	0.4	0.8	3.3	2.0	2.0
Côte d'Ivoire	5.4	14.1	2.7	4.2	4.5	0.7	2.5	4.4	3.1	3.5	2.9
Djibouti	6.2	4.9	3.5	2.5	2.2	−20.8	2.4	1.8	0.6	2.0	2.0
Equatorial Guinea	6.5	11.4	6.0	4.5	3.7	6.0	6.5	6.0	12.0	10.0	8.0
Eritrea	...	12.0	10.3	3.7	9.5	8.4	19.9	14.6	16.9	18.8	12.4
Ethiopia	8.1	13.4	0.9	−6.4	3.6	3.9	4.2	−7.1	−7.2	14.6	5.5
Gabon	3.8	10.0	4.5	4.1	2.3	−0.7	0.4	2.1	0.2	2.0	2.0
Gambia, The	16.1	4.0	4.8	3.1	1.1	3.8	0.9	4.5	8.6	13.0	8.0
Ghana	24.3	59.5	46.6	27.9	14.6	12.4	25.2	32.9	14.8	26.4	8.6
Guinea	23.3	5.6	3.0	1.9	5.1	4.6	6.8	5.4	3.0	6.2	3.0
Guinea-Bissau	59.1	45.4	50.7	49.1	8.0	−2.1	8.6	3.3	3.3	3.0	3.0
Kenya	17.5	1.6	8.9	11.9	6.7	5.8	10.0	4.9	2.0	12.4	3.9
Lesotho	13.6	10.0	9.1	8.5	7.8	8.6	6.1	6.9	12.3	9.3	10.1
Liberia	...	...	...	...	...	...	...	...	...	...	...
Madagascar	15.6	49.0	19.8	4.5	6.2	9.9	11.9	5.0	4.5	3.5	3.5
Malawi	19.4	83.1	37.7	9.1	29.8	44.8	29.6	27.2	14.1	5.0	4.3
Mali	2.0	12.4	6.5	−0.7	4.1	−1.2	−0.7	5.2	2.4	3.8	2.5
Mauritania	7.5	6.5	4.7	4.5	8.0	4.1	3.3	4.7	3.9	6.4	3.7
Mauritius	7.4	6.0	5.9	7.9	5.4	7.9	5.3	4.4	6.4	5.0	5.0
Morocco	5.6	6.1	3.0	1.0	2.7	0.7	1.9	0.6	2.8	2.0	2.0
Mozambique, Rep. of	53.0	54.4	44.6	6.4	0.6	2.9	12.7	9.0	16.8	12.9	9.7
Namibia	12.7	10.0	8.0	8.8	6.2	8.7	9.3	9.3	11.3	9.5	8.5
Niger	1.2	10.9	5.3	2.9	4.5	−2.3	3.9	4.0	2.7	0.5	1.7
Nigeria	28.0	72.9	29.3	8.5	10.0	6.6	6.9	18.0	13.7	12.3	10.6
Rwanda	9.7	48.2	13.4	11.7	6.8	−2.4	3.9	3.4	2.0	4.7	3.0
Sâo Tomé and Príncipe	31.6	36.8	42.0	69.0	42.1	16.3	11.0	9.5	9.2	9.0	8.0
Senegal	3.9	8.1	2.8	1.8	−1.1	0.8	0.7	3.0	2.2	2.0	1.8
Seychelles	1.9	−0.3	−1.1	0.6	2.7	6.3	6.2	6.0	0.2	7.0	5.0
Sierra Leone	70.4	26.0	23.1	14.6	36.0	34.1	−0.9	2.2	−3.1	7.4	3.5
Somalia	...	...	...	...	...	...	...	...	...	...	...
South Africa	14.0	8.7	7.3	8.6	6.9	5.2	5.4	5.7	9.1	7.7	4.9
Sudan	75.5	68.4	132.8	46.7	17.1	16.0	8.0	4.9	8.3	7.0	5.0
Swaziland	13.1	12.3	6.4	7.9	7.5	5.9	9.9	7.5	11.8	9.5	6.7
Tanzania	30.3	26.5	21.0	16.1	9.8	9.0	6.2	5.2	4.6	5.3	5.0
Togo	3.5	15.7	4.7	8.2	2.2	−0.1	1.9	3.9	3.1	—	3.1
Tunisia	6.6	6.2	3.7	3.7	3.1	2.7	3.0	1.9	2.8	2.5	2.5
Uganda	78.5	6.1	7.5	7.8	5.8	−0.2	6.3	4.5	−2.0	5.9	5.9
Zambia	87.3	34.9	43.1	24.4	24.5	26.8	26.1	21.7	22.2	18.4	5.2
Zimbabwe	18.4	22.6	21.5	18.8	31.7	58.5	55.9	76.7	140.0	420.0	380.0

Table 12 *(continued)*

	Average 1985–94	1995	1996	1997	1998	1999	2000	2001	2002	2003	2004
Developing Asia	**11.0**	**13.2**	**8.2**	**4.8**	**7.7**	**2.5**	**1.8**	**2.7**	**2.0**	**2.5**	**2.9**
Afghanistan, Islamic State of	...	...	...	...	...	...	...	...	...	...	...
Bangladesh	8.1	10.8	2.5	5.0	8.6	6.2	2.2	1.5	3.8	4.5	4.1
Bhutan	9.3	9.5	7.4	9.0	9.2	3.6	3.6	2.7	5.0	5.0	5.0
Brunei Darussalam	...	6.0	2.0	1.7	−0.4	—	1.2	0.6	−2.0	1.0	1.3
Cambodia	...	1.3	7.1	8.0	14.8	4.0	−0.8	0.2	3.3	2.6	3.5
China	11.0	17.1	8.3	2.8	−0.8	−1.4	0.4	0.7	−0.8	0.8	1.5
Fiji	5.5	0.3	4.9	3.4	5.9	2.0	1.1	4.3	1.9	2.0	2.5
India	9.0	10.2	9.0	7.2	13.2	4.7	4.0	3.8	4.3	4.0	4.8
Indonesia	7.7	9.4	7.9	6.2	58.0	20.7	3.8	11.5	11.9	6.6	5.4
Kiribati	2.7	4.1	−1.5	2.2	3.7	1.8	0.4	6.0	3.2	1.4	2.3
Lao P.D. Republic	19.4	19.1	19.1	19.5	85.3	127.1	25.1	8.6	10.6	11.3	7.0
Malaysia	2.6	3.5	3.5	2.7	5.3	2.8	1.6	1.4	1.8	1.7	2.2
Maldives	8.1	3.0	6.2	7.6	−1.4	3.0	−1.2	0.7	0.9	−1.5	2.0
Myanmar	21.4	28.9	20.0	33.9	49.1	10.9	−1.7	34.5	46.9	40.0	43.0
Nepal	11.3	7.7	7.2	8.1	8.3	11.4	3.4	2.4	2.9	4.7	5.4
Pakistan	8.3	12.3	10.4	11.4	6.2	4.1	4.4	3.1	2.9	3.6	4.0
Papua New Guinea	4.8	17.3	11.6	3.9	13.6	14.9	15.6	9.3	11.8	17.2	8.0
Philippines	10.3	8.0	9.0	5.8	9.7	6.7	4.3	6.1	3.1	3.0	3.4
Samoa	1.8	−2.9	5.4	6.9	2.2	0.3	1.0	3.8	8.1	4.2	2.4
Solomon Islands	12.2	9.8	11.7	8.1	12.3	8.0	7.3	6.8	9.8	12.1	11.0
Sri Lanka	10.7	7.7	15.9	9.6	9.4	4.7	6.2	14.2	9.6	7.5	7.0
Thailand	4.0	6.3	5.6	5.9	7.8	—	1.7	1.5	0.6	1.4	0.1
Tonga	8.8	2.7	2.0	3.0	3.9	5.3	6.9	10.4	15.0	20.0	20.0
Vanuatu	5.9	2.2	0.9	2.8	3.3	2.2	2.5	3.7	2.2	4.0	3.2
Vietnam	112.0	16.9	5.7	3.2	7.7	4.2	−1.6	−0.4	4.0	4.0	3.5
Middle East and Turkey	**26.3**	**39.1**	**29.6**	**28.1**	**27.5**	**23.6**	**19.5**	**17.1**	**15.7**	**13.5**	**10.8**
Bahrain	−0.2	3.1	−0.1	4.6	−0.4	−1.3	−0.7	−1.2	−1.0	3.3	5.0
Egypt	17.2	9.4	7.1	6.2	4.7	3.8	2.8	2.4	2.5	3.2	4.2
Iran, Islamic Republic of	21.1	49.4	23.2	17.3	18.1	20.1	12.6	11.4	15.8	18.0	17.0
Iraq	...	...	...	...	...	...	...	...	...	...	...
Jordan	4.8	2.3	6.5	3.0	3.1	0.6	0.7	1.8	1.8	2.5	1.8
Kuwait	7.8	2.7	3.6	0.7	0.1	3.0	1.8	1.7	1.4	2.0	2.0
Lebanon	91.2	10.3	8.9	7.7	4.5	0.2	−0.4	−0.4	1.8	2.0	2.5
Libya	7.2	8.3	4.0	3.6	3.7	2.6	−2.9	−8.8	−9.8	2.8	2.9
Malta	1.9	4.0	2.0	3.1	2.4	2.1	2.4	2.9	2.2	2.0	2.0
Oman	2.5	−1.1	0.5	−0.5	−0.5	0.5	−1.2	−1.0	−0.7	1.0	1.1
Qatar	2.6	3.0	8.8	1.1	2.9	2.2	1.7	1.4	1.0	4.2	1.2
Saudi Arabia	−0.1	5.0	0.9	−0.4	−0.2	−1.3	−0.6	−0.8	−0.6	1.1	1.0
Syrian Arab Republic	21.8	7.7	8.9	1.9	−0.4	−2.1	−0.6	0.5	1.5	2.5	3.0
Turkey	61.3	93.6	82.3	85.7	84.6	64.9	54.9	54.4	45.0	26.0	13.4
United Arab Emirates	4.3	4.4	3.0	2.9	2.0	2.1	1.4	2.2	1.4	2.4	1.9
Yemen, Republic of	35.7	62.5	40.0	4.6	11.5	8.0	10.9	11.9	12.2	9.1	6.6

Table 12 *(concluded)*

	Average 1985–94	1995	1996	1997	1998	1999	2000	2001	2002	2003	2004
Western Hemisphere	**190.7**	**36.1**	**20.9**	**12.4**	**9.2**	7.4	6.8	**6.4**	**8.7**	**10.9**	**7.0**
Antigua and Barbuda	4.0	2.7	3.0	0.2	3.4	1.1	0.7	1.0	2.2	2.5	2.5
Argentina	267.7	3.4	0.2	0.5	0.9	−1.2	−0.9	−1.1	25.9	14.3	7.7
Bahamas, The	4.7	2.1	1.4	0.5	1.3	1.3	1.6	2.0	2.0	1.7	2.5
Barbados	3.6	1.9	2.4	7.7	−1.3	1.6	2.6	—	1.5	1.5	2.4
Belize	−2.7	2.6	2.9	6.4	1.0	−0.8	−1.3	0.7	1.2	1.5	1.5
Bolivia	104.4	10.2	12.4	4.7	7.7	2.2	4.6	1.6	0.9	2.6	3.1
Brazil	773.0	66.0	16.0	6.9	3.2	4.9	7.1	6.8	8.4	15.0	6.2
Chile	18.8	8.2	7.4	6.1	5.1	3.3	3.8	3.6	2.5	3.4	3.0
Colombia	25.3	20.8	20.8	18.3	18.6	10.2	9.3	7.8	6.3	6.9	5.3
Costa Rica	17.3	23.2	26.3	13.2	11.7	10.0	11.0	11.3	9.1	10.5	10.0
Dominica	3.5	1.3	1.7	2.4	1.0	1.2	0.9	1.8	−0.3	0.5	1.5
Dominican Republic	25.2	12.5	5.4	8.3	4.8	6.5	7.7	8.9	5.2	26.1	20.1
Ecuador	0.2	5.3	—	4.1	−0.6	−29.2	−7.7	37.7	12.6	8.2	4.4
El Salvador	19.4	10.1	9.8	4.5	2.5	0.5	2.3	3.7	1.9	2.9	2.7
Grenada	2.6	2.2	2.8	1.3	1.4	0.5	2.2	3.2	3.0	2.5	2.5
Guatemala	17.2	8.4	11.0	9.2	6.6	4.9	5.1	8.9	6.3	5.0	4.0
Guyana	36.6	12.2	7.1	3.6	4.6	7.5	6.1	2.7	5.3	5.8	4.6
Haiti	13.7	30.2	21.9	16.2	12.7	8.1	11.5	16.8	8.7	32.3	20.0
Honduras	12.1	29.5	23.8	20.2	13.7	11.6	11.0	9.7	7.7	8.4	7.9
Jamaica	28.6	21.7	21.5	9.1	8.1	6.3	7.7	8.0	6.5	7.0	7.0
Mexico	43.4	35.0	34.4	20.6	15.9	16.6	9.5	6.4	5.0	4.6	3.4
Netherlands Antilles	2.4	2.8	3.4	3.1	1.2	0.8	5.0	1.8	0.5	2.0	2.5
Nicaragua	879.0	11.2	11.6	9.2	13.0	11.2	11.5	7.4	4.0	5.2	5.2
Panama	0.8	0.9	1.3	1.3	0.6	1.5	1.2	0.3	1.0	1.7	1.4
Paraguay	24.3	13.4	9.8	7.0	11.6	6.8	9.0	7.3	10.5	17.4	12.1
Peru	319.0	23.8	11.5	8.5	7.3	3.5	3.8	2.0	0.2	2.5	2.5
St. Kitts and Nevis	2.3	3.0	2.0	8.7	3.7	3.4	2.1	2.1	2.1	1.4	1.5
St. Lucia	3.2	5.9	1.2	0.3	2.8	3.5	3.6	1.9	0.9	2.0	2.0
St. Vincent and the Grenadines	3.1	1.7	4.4	0.5	2.1	1.0	0.2	0.8	1.0	0.3	2.0
Suriname	49.3	235.5	−0.8	7.3	19.0	112.8	80.4	4.9	28.3	20.0	18.0
Trinidad and Tobago	8.3	5.3	3.3	3.6	−0.5	3.4	3.5	5.5	4.2	3.5	2.8
Uruguay	72.6	42.2	28.3	19.8	10.8	5.7	4.8	4.4	14.0	21.6	18.9
Venezuela	35.6	59.9	99.9	50.0	35.8	23.6	16.2	12.5	22.4	34.0	40.8

[1]For many countries, figures for recent years are IMF staff estimates. Data for some countries are for fiscal years.
[2]The percent changes in 2002 are calculated over a period of 18 months, reflecting a change in the fiscal year cycle (from July–June to January–December).

Table 13. Countries in Transition: Consumer Prices[1]

(Annual percent change)

	Average 1985–94	1995	1996	1997	1998	1999	2000	2001	2002	2003	2004
Central and eastern Europe	...	**24.7**	**23.3**	**42.0**	**17.2**	**11.0**	**12.9**	**9.7**	**5.6**	**4.0**	**4.8**
Albania	25.9	7.8	12.7	33.2	20.9	0.4	—	3.1	5.4	3.0	3.0
Bosnia and Herzegovina	...	4.7	−11.8	5.8	−0.2	2.8	4.9	3.2	0.3	1.1	1.6
Bulgaria	44.3	62.1	123.0	1,061.2	18.8	2.6	10.4	7.5	5.8	2.6	4.2
Croatia	...	2.0	3.5	3.6	5.7	4.1	6.2	6.2	2.2	2.0	3.5
Czech Republic	...	9.1	8.8	8.5	10.6	2.1	3.9	4.8	1.8	0.6	3.5
Estonia	...	29.0	23.1	11.2	8.2	3.3	4.0	5.8	3.6	1.7	2.0
Hungary	17.8	28.3	23.5	18.3	14.3	10.0	9.8	9.2	5.3	4.7	5.5
Latvia	...	25.2	17.6	8.4	4.6	2.4	2.6	2.5	1.9	3.0	3.0
Lithuania	...	39.5	24.7	8.8	5.1	0.8	1.0	1.3	0.3	—	2.5
Macedonia, former Yugoslav Rep. of	...	15.8	2.3	2.5	−0.1	−0.7	5.8	5.3	2.4	2.5	3.0
Poland	76.0	27.9	19.9	14.9	11.8	7.3	10.1	5.5	1.9	0.8	2.2
Romania	66.5	32.3	38.8	154.8	59.1	45.8	45.7	34.5	22.5	15.1	12.0
Serbia and Montenegro	...	...	...	...	29.5	42.1	69.9	91.1	21.2	12.2	7.6
Slovak Republic	...	9.9	5.8	6.1	6.7	10.7	12.0	7.3	3.3	8.5	8.1
Slovenia	...	13.5	9.9	8.4	7.9	6.2	8.9	8.4	7.5	5.9	5.0
Commonwealth of Independent States and Mongolia	...	**235.7**	**55.9**	**19.1**	**24.5**	**71.2**	**25.8**	**20.3**	**14.5**	**13.1**	**11.7**
Russia	...	198.0	47.9	14.7	27.8	85.7	20.8	20.6	16.0	14.4	12.9
Excluding Russia	...	338.9	75.5	29.7	17.9	43.5	37.4	19.8	11.5	10.4	9.4
Armenia	...	176.7	18.7	14.0	8.6	0.6	−0.8	3.1	1.1	2.2	3.0
Azerbaijan	...	411.8	19.8	3.7	−0.8	−8.5	1.8	1.5	2.8	2.7	2.5
Belarus	...	709.3	52.7	63.8	73.0	293.7	168.6	61.1	42.6	29.0	24.1
Georgia	...	162.7	39.3	7.0	3.6	19.1	4.0	4.7	5.6	4.4	5.0
Kazakhstan	...	176.3	39.1	17.4	7.3	8.4	13.3	8.3	5.9	6.4	5.9
Kyrgyz Republic	...	43.4	32.0	23.4	10.5	35.9	18.7	6.9	2.0	3.3	3.8
Moldova	...	30.2	23.5	11.8	7.7	39.3	31.3	9.8	5.3	8.1	4.5
Mongolia	37.9	56.8	46.8	36.6	9.4	7.6	11.6	6.3	0.9	5.0	5.0
Tajikistan	...	610.0	418.2	88.0	43.2	27.5	32.9	38.6	12.2	14.5	5.0
Turkmenistan	...	1,005.2	992.4	83.7	16.8	23.5	8.0	11.6	...	...	...
Ukraine	...	376.4	80.2	15.9	10.6	22.7	28.2	12.0	0.8	5.5	5.3
Uzbekistan	...	304.6	54.0	70.9	16.7	44.6	50.7	48.9	38.7	21.9	20.7
Memorandum											
EU accession candidates	...	42.7	39.4	55.6	35.6	25.3	24.7	21.1	15.8	10.1	7.3

[1]For many countries, inflation for the earlier years is measured on the basis of a retail price index. Consumer price indices with a broader and more up-to-date coverage are typically used for more recent years.

Table 14. Summary Financial Indicators

(Percent)

	1995	1996	1997	1998	1999	2000	2001	2002	2003	2004
Advanced economies										
Central government fiscal balance[1]										
Advanced economies	−3.4	−2.8	−1.6	−1.0	−1.1	0.2	−0.9	−2.3	−3.3	−3.1
United States	−2.6	−1.8	−0.6	0.5	1.2	2.1	0.7	−2.2	−4.3	−4.2
Euro area	−4.1	−3.8	−2.6	−2.4	−1.6	−0.4	−1.5	−2.0	−2.4	−2.3
Japan	−4.6	−4.6	−4.2	−4.0	−8.7	−7.2	−6.7	−6.3	−6.1	−5.4
Other advanced economies	−2.4	−1.5	−0.2	—	0.4	2.4	0.6	−0.3	−1.1	−0.7
General government fiscal balance[1]										
Advanced economies	−4.1	−3.3	−1.8	−1.3	−1.0	−0.1	−1.5	−3.3	−4.4	−4.0
United States	−3.3	−2.4	−1.3	−0.1	0.5	1.2	−0.7	−3.8	−6.0	−5.6
Euro area	−5.0	−4.3	−2.6	−2.3	−1.3	0.1	−1.7	−2.3	−3.0	−2.8
Japan	−4.7	−5.0	−3.8	−5.5	−7.2	−7.4	−6.1	−7.5	−7.4	−6.5
Other advanced economies	−3.1	−1.7	—	0.6	1.2	2.5	0.5	−0.7	−1.2	−0.9
General government structural balance[2]										
Advanced economies	−3.8	−3.0	−1.7	−1.3	−1.1	−1.0	−1.4	−2.8	−3.5	−3.2
Growth of broad money[3]										
Advanced economies	5.0	4.9	5.1	6.6	5.8	4.9	8.7	5.7	...	...
United States	3.9	4.6	5.6	8.5	6.3	6.1	10.2	6.8	...	...
Euro area[4]	5.5	4.0	4.7	4.8	5.3	4.2	11.1	6.7	...	...
Japan	3.2	3.0	3.9	4.0	2.7	1.9	3.3	1.8	...	...
Other advanced economies	8.6	9.5	6.0	9.2	9.0	6.7	7.3	6.0	...	...
Short-term interest rates[5]										
United States	5.7	5.1	5.2	4.9	4.8	6.0	3.5	1.6	1.1	1.6
Euro area[4]	7.1	5.2	4.4	4.1	3.0	4.5	4.2	3.3	2.5	2.7
Japan	0.8	0.3	0.3	0.2	0.0	0.2	0.0	0.0	0.0	0.0
LIBOR	6.1	5.6	5.9	5.6	5.5	6.6	3.7	1.9	1.3	2.0
Developing countries										
Central government fiscal balance[1]										
Weighted average	−2.6	−2.1	−2.5	−3.7	−3.8	−3.2	−3.8	−3.8	−3.3	−3.1
Median	−3.3	−2.5	−2.6	−2.7	−3.3	−3.2	−3.8	−3.8	−3.3	−2.9
General government fiscal balance[1]										
Weighted average	−3.2	−2.8	−3.3	−4.7	−4.8	−4.0	−4.7	−4.8	−4.1	−3.6
Median	−3.3	−2.8	−2.5	−3.3	−3.5	−3.3	−3.7	−4.3	−3.1	−2.6
Growth of broad money										
Weighted average	24.4	29.5	17.3	16.4	14.8	9.3	12.6	15.3	15.4	11.9
Median	16.2	15.6	14.7	10.5	12.2	11.8	11.8	12.3	9.9	9.3
Countries in transition										
Central government fiscal balance[1]	−4.8	−4.7	−4.9	−3.7	−2.1	−0.3	−0.1	−0.9	−0.7	−0.6
General government fiscal balance[1]	−4.9	−6.1	−5.6	−5.0	−2.2	−0.1	−0.4	−1.7	−1.4	−1.1
Growth of broad money	75.4	32.1	33.2	19.6	38.5	37.2	28.5	20.1	20.3	16.5

[1]Percent of GDP.

[2]Percent of potential GDP.

[3]M2, defined as M1 plus quasi-money, except for Japan, for which the data are based on M2 plus certificates of deposit (CDs). Quasi-money is essentially private term deposits and other notice deposits. The United States also includes money market mutual fund balances, money market deposit accounts, overnight repurchase agreements, and overnight Eurodollars issued to U.S. residents by foreign branches of U.S. banks. For the euro area, M3 is composed of M2 plus marketable instruments held by euro-area residents, which comprise repurchase agreements, money market fund shares/units, money market paper, and debt securities up to two years.

[4]Excludes Greece prior to 2001.

[5]For the United States, three-month treasury bills; for Japan, three-month certificates of deposit; for the euro area, a weighted average of national three-month money market interest rates through 1998 and three-month EURIBOR thereafter; for LIBOR, London interbank offered rate on six-month U.S. dollar deposits.

Table 15. Advanced Economies: General and Central Government Fiscal Balances and Balances Excluding Social Security Transactions[1]

(Percent of GDP)

	1995	1996	1997	1998	1999	2000	2001	2002	2003	2004
General government fiscal balance										
Advanced economies	**−4.1**	**−3.3**	**−1.8**	**−1.3**	**−1.0**	**−0.1**	**−1.5**	**−3.3**	**−4.4**	**−4.0**
United States	−3.3	−2.4	−1.3	−0.1	0.5	1.2	−0.7	−3.8	−6.0	−5.6
Euro area	−5.0	−4.3	−2.6	−2.3	−1.3	0.1	−1.7	−2.3	−3.0	−2.8
Germany	−3.3	−3.4	−2.7	−2.2	−1.5	1.3	−2.8	−3.5	−3.9	−3.9
France[2]	−5.5	−4.1	−3.0	−2.7	−1.8	−1.4	−1.4	−3.1	−4.0	−3.5
Italy	−7.6	−7.1	−2.7	−2.8	−1.7	−0.6	−2.6	−2.3	−2.8	−2.6
Spain	−7.0	−4.9	−3.2	−2.7	−1.1	−0.6	−0.1	−0.1	−0.2	−0.2
Netherlands	−4.5	−1.8	−1.1	−0.8	0.7	2.2	—	−1.6	−2.4	−2.4
Belgium	−4.3	−3.8	−2.0	−0.7	−0.5	0.1	0.4	—	−0.5	−0.2
Austria[3]	−5.2	−3.8	−2.0	−2.5	−2.4	−1.6	0.1	−0.4	−1.5	−1.3
Finland	−3.7	−3.2	−1.5	1.3	1.9	7.0	5.0	4.6	2.0	0.9
Greece	−10.2	−7.4	−4.0	−2.5	−1.8	−1.9	−1.4	−1.2	−1.4	−1.1
Portugal	−4.5	−4.0	−3.0	−2.6	−2.4	−2.9	−4.2	−2.7	−4.0	−4.4
Ireland[4]	−2.2	−0.3	1.2	2.4	4.1	4.3	1.1	−0.1	−1.1	−1.7
Luxembourg	2.6	2.0	2.8	3.1	3.6	5.6	6.1	−0.3	−0.1	0.2
Japan	−4.7	−5.0	−3.8	−5.5	−7.2	−7.4	−6.1	−7.5	−7.4	−6.5
United Kingdom	−5.8	−4.4	−2.2	0.2	1.1	4.0	0.9	−1.3	−2.5	−2.7
Canada	−5.3	−2.8	0.2	0.1	1.6	3.0	1.4	0.8	1.5	1.5
Korea[5]	0.3	—	−1.7	−4.3	−3.3	1.3	0.6	2.7	0.8	1.0
Australia[6]	−2.1	−0.9	−0.1	0.3	0.9	0.9	0.2	0.1	0.4	0.5
Taiwan Province of China	2.7	2.3	2.3	3.7	0.8	−4.5	−6.4	−6.0	−6.5	−5.3
Sweden	−7.4	−2.9	−1.7	2.3	1.3	3.4	4.6	1.1	0.4	1.0
Switzerland	−1.9	−2.0	−2.4	−0.4	−0.2	2.6	0.2	−1.1	−2.2	−2.3
Hong Kong SAR	−0.3	2.1	6.5	−1.8	0.8	−0.6	−5.0	−4.9	−6.3	−3.1
Denmark	−2.3	−1.0	0.4	1.1	3.2	2.5	2.8	2.0	1.4	1.5
Norway	3.4	6.5	7.8	3.5	6.1	15.0	13.7	10.0	8.3	7.6
Israel	−4.3	−5.8	−4.4	−3.7	−4.2	−2.0	−4.0	−4.4	−6.8	−4.8
Singapore	12.2	9.3	9.2	3.6	4.6	8.1	5.7	3.1	1.9	3.4
New Zealand[7]	3.3	2.7	2.2	2.1	1.5	1.3	1.6	1.5	2.0	3.0
Cyprus	−1.0	−3.4	−5.3	−5.5	−4.0	−2.7	−2.8	−3.5	−5.4	−4.9
Iceland	−3.0	−1.6	—	0.5	2.4	2.5	0.5	−0.3	−0.1	0.7
Other advanced economies	−3.1	−1.8	−0.5	−0.2	0.3	0.8	−0.1	−0.6	−1.3	−1.0
Memorandum										
Major advanced economies	−4.3	−3.6	−2.1	−1.6	−1.2	−0.3	−1.8	−3.8	−5.1	−4.7
European Union	−5.4	−4.3	−2.5	−1.7	−0.8	0.8	−1.0	−1.9	−2.6	−2.5
Newly industrialized Asian economies	3.3	3.3	4.4	2.4	1.4	−1.7	−4.3	−4.4	−5.2	−3.5
Fiscal balance excluding social security transactions										
United States	−3.7	−2.7	−1.7	−0.7	−0.6	—	−1.6	−4.3	−6.4	−6.0
Japan	−7.0	−7.2	−6.0	−7.2	−8.7	−8.5	−6.3	−7.8	−7.6	−6.3
Germany	−2.9	−3.1	−2.8	−2.4	−1.8	1.3	−2.7	−3.2	−3.8	−3.9
France	−4.8	−3.6	−2.6	−2.5	−2.0	−2.0	−1.7	−3.2	−3.5	−3.2
Italy	−5.6	−5.3	−0.7	1.3	2.7	3.4	1.3	2.1	1.7	2.0
Canada	−2.7	—	3.0	2.7	3.9	4.9	3.0	2.3	2.9	2.9

Table 15 *(concluded)*

	1995	1996	1997	1998	1999	2000	2001	2002	2003	2004
Central government fiscal balance										
Advanced economies	**-3.4**	**-2.8**	**-1.6**	**-1.0**	**-1.1**	**0.2**	**-0.9**	**-2.3**	**-3.3**	**-3.1**
United States[8]	-2.6	-1.8	-0.6	0.5	1.2	2.1	0.7	-2.2	-4.3	-4.2
Euro area	-4.1	-3.8	-2.6	-2.4	-1.6	-0.4	-1.5	-2.0	-2.4	-2.3
Germany[9]	-1.4	-2.2	-1.7	-1.5	-1.3	1.3	-1.1	-1.5	-1.9	-1.7
France	-4.1	-3.7	-3.6	-3.9	-2.5	-2.4	-2.2	-3.7	-3.8	-3.7
Italy	-8.0	-7.0	-2.9	-2.7	-1.6	-1.0	-2.8	-2.6	-2.9	-2.7
Japan[10]	-4.6	-4.6	-4.2	-4.0	-8.7	-7.2	-6.7	-6.3	-6.1	-5.4
United Kingdom	-5.5	-4.6	-2.2	0.3	1.2	4.1	0.9	-1.4	-2.6	-2.8
Canada	-3.9	-2.0	0.7	0.8	0.9	1.8	1.2	1.0	0.7	0.7
Other advanced economies	-2.6	-1.7	-1.0	-1.2	-0.7	0.8	-0.2	-0.5	-1.2	-0.8
Memorandum										
Major advanced economies	-3.6	-3.1	-1.8	-1.0	-1.2	0.1	-1.1	-2.7	-3.9	-3.7
European Union	-4.6	-4.1	-2.6	-1.9	-1.1	0.3	-1.1	-1.9	-2.3	-2.3
Newly industrialized Asian economies	1.0	1.0	0.8	-1.3	-1.2	1.0	-0.6	-0.7	-2.1	-1.1

[1]On a national income accounts basis except as indicated in footnotes. See Box A1 for a summary of the policy assumptions underlying the projections.

[2]Adjusted for valuation changes of the foreign exchange stabilization fund.

[3]Based on ESA95 methodology, according to which swap income is not included.

[4]To maintain comparability, data excludes the impact of discharging future pension liabilities of the formerly state-owned telecommunications company at a cost of 1.8 percent of GDP in 1999.

[5]Data cover the consolidated central government including the social security funds but excluding privatization.

[6]Data exclude net advances (primarily privatization receipts and net policy-related lending).

[7]Government balance is revenue minus expenditure plus balance of state-owned enterprises, excluding privatization receipts. Data from 1992 onward are accrual based and are not strictly comparable with prior cash-based data.

[8]Data are on a budget basis.

[9]Data are on an administrative basis and exclude social security transactions.

[10]Data are on a national income basis and exclude social security transactions.

Table 16. Advanced Economies: General Government Structural Balances[1]
(Percent of potential GDP)

	1995	1996	1997	1998	1999	2000	2001	2002	2003	2004
Structural balance										
Advanced economies	**−3.8**	**−3.0**	**−1.7**	**−1.3**	**−1.1**	**−1.0**	**−1.4**	**−2.8**	**−3.5**	**−3.2**
United States	−2.7	−1.9	−1.1	−0.2	—	0.6	−0.5	−3.2	−5.1	−4.9
Euro area[2,3]	−4.4	−3.2	−1.6	−1.8	−1.2	−1.5	−2.0	−2.0	−1.7	−1.4
Germany[2,4]	−3.6	−3.0	−2.0	−1.7	−1.2	−1.6	−2.9	−2.9	−2.3	−2.3
France[2]	−3.7	−1.9	−1.0	−1.6	−1.1	−1.8	−1.8	−2.8	−2.7	−2.1
Italy[2]	−7.0	−6.3	−1.9	−2.8	−1.8	−2.4	−3.1	−2.7	−2.1	−1.7
Spain[2]	−5.1	−3.0	−1.7	−1.9	−1.0	−1.0	−0.4	0.5	0.7	0.9
Netherlands[2]	−4.0	−1.4	−1.1	−1.4	−0.7	−0.2	−0.9	−1.9	−1.5	−1.0
Belgium[2]	−4.1	−2.9	−1.9	−0.7	−0.9	−1.2	−0.4	0.4	0.8	1.3
Austria[2]	−5.0	−3.7	−1.7	−2.5	−2.6	−2.8	0.2	0.5	0.1	0.5
Finland	0.3	0.3	0.1	2.0	1.1	6.0	5.1	5.4	3.5	2.4
Greece	−9.5	−6.9	−3.9	−2.5	−2.0	−2.5	−2.5	−2.1	−2.4	−2.4
Portugal[2]	−3.2	−2.9	−2.4	−2.7	−2.9	−4.2	−4.7	−2.3	−2.3	−2.2
Ireland[2]	−1.3	0.6	0.8	1.9	2.6	1.9	−0.8	−2.0	−1.2	−1.2
Japan	−4.4	−5.4	−4.2	−5.0	−6.2	−7.0	−5.4	−6.5	−6.7	−5.9
United Kingdom[2]	−5.4	−4.2	−2.1	—	1.0	1.7	0.8	−1.2	−2.1	−1.9
Canada	−5.4	−2.0	0.8	0.5	1.4	2.1	1.2	0.8	2.1	2.0
Other advanced economies	−3.9	−2.0	−1.0	−0.8	−0.4	−0.1	—	—	0.1	0.3
Australia[5]	−2.9	−1.0	0.1	0.2	0.5	0.8	0.3	0.2	0.7	0.8
Sweden	−5.5	0.6	1.6	4.3	2.3	3.9	3.3	1.0	1.5	1.8
Denmark	−2.1	−1.0	0.2	0.7	2.8	2.0	2.6	2.3	2.0	1.7
Norway[6]	−4.2	−3.1	−2.6	−3.9	−3.1	−1.8	−1.8	−3.0	−3.0	−1.9
New Zealand[7]	2.2	1.8	1.9	1.9	1.0	1.4	2.1	2.6	2.9	3.0
Memorandum										
Major advanced economies	−3.8	−3.1	−1.8	−1.4	−1.2	−1.1	−1.7	−3.3	−4.2	−3.8
European Union[2,3]	−4.7	−3.4	−1.6	−1.3	−0.7	−0.8	−1.4	−1.7	−1.6	−1.3

[1]On a national income accounts basis. The structural budget position is defined as the actual budget deficit (or surplus) less the effects of cyclical deviations of output from potential output. Because of the margin of uncertainty that attaches to estimates of cyclical gaps and to tax and expenditure elasticities with respect to national income, indicators of structural budget positions should be interpreted as broad orders of magnitude. Moreover, it is important to note that changes in structural budget balances are not necessarily attributable to policy changes but may reflect the built-in momentum of existing expenditure programs. In the period beyond that for which specific consolidation programs exist, it is assumed that the structural deficit remains unchanged.

[2]Excludes one-off receipts from the sale of mobile telephone licenses equivalent to 2.5 percent of GDP in 2000 for Germany, 0.1 percent of GDP in 2001 and 2002 for France, 1.2 percent of GDP in 2000 for Italy, 2.4 percent of GDP in 2000 for the United Kingdom, 0.1 percent of GDP in 2000 for Spain, 0.7 percent of GDP in 2000 for the Netherlands, 0.2 percent of GDP in 2001 for Belgium, 0.4 percent of GDP in 2000 for Austria, 0.3 percent of GDP in 2000 for Portugal, and 0.2 percent of GDP in 2002 for Ireland. Also excludes one-off receipts from sizable asset transactions.

[3]Excludes Luxembourg.

[4]The estimate of the fiscal impulse for 1995 is affected by the assumption by the federal government of the debt of the Treuhandanstalt and various other agencies, which were formerly held outside the general government sector. At the public sector level, there would be an estimated withdrawal of fiscal impulse amounting to just over 1 percent of GDP.

[5]Excludes commonwealth government privatization receipts.

[6]Excludes oil.

[7]Government balance is revenue minus expenditure plus balance of state-owned enterprises, excluding privatization receipts. Data from 1992 onward are accrual based and are not strictly comparable with prior cash-based data.

Table 17. Advanced Economies: Monetary Aggregates

(Annual percent change)[1]

	1995	1996	1997	1998	1999	2000	2001	2002
Narrow money[2]								
Advanced economies	**5.2**	**4.9**	**4.7**	**5.7**	**8.1**	**2.5**	**8.9**	**9.1**
United States	−1.5	−4.5	−1.2	2.1	1.9	−1.7	6.8	3.2
Euro area[3]	5.8	8.0	8.0	10.5	10.9	5.3	6.6	10.0
Japan	13.1	9.7	8.6	5.0	11.7	3.5	13.7	23.5
United Kingdom	5.6	6.7	6.4	5.3	11.6	4.5	8.3	5.6
Canada	7.6	18.9	10.9	8.0	7.9	14.4	15.1	5.1
Memorandum								
Newly industrialized Asian economies	10.4	5.9	−3.8	0.9	19.7	4.5	11.3	13.1
Broad money[4]								
Advanced economies	**5.0**	**4.9**	**5.1**	**6.6**	**5.8**	**4.9**	**8.7**	**5.7**
United States	3.9	4.6	5.6	8.5	6.3	6.1	10.2	6.8
Euro area[3]	5.5	4.0	4.7	4.8	5.3	4.2	11.1	6.7
Japan	3.2	3.0	3.9	4.0	2.7	1.9	3.3	1.8
United Kingdom	9.9	9.6	5.6	8.5	4.2	8.4	6.5	6.9
Canada	4.1	2.1	−1.3	0.8	5.1	6.5	5.9	4.9
Memorandum								
Newly industrialized Asian economies	13.0	12.6	11.5	19.7	16.9	14.0	7.0	5.4

[1]Based on end-of-period data.

[2]M1 except for the United Kingdom, where M0 is used here as a measure of narrow money; it comprises notes in circulation plus bankers' operational deposits. M1 is generally currency in circulation plus private demand deposits. In addition, the United States includes traveler's checks of nonbank issues and other checkable deposits and excludes private sector float and demand deposits of banks. Canada excludes private sector float.

[3]Excludes Greece prior to 2001.

[4]M2, defined as M1 plus quasi-money, except for Japan, and the United Kingdom, for which the data are based on M2 plus certificates of deposit (CDs), and M4, respectively. Quasi-money is essentially private term deposits and other notice deposits. The United States also includes money market mutual fund balances, money market deposit accounts, overnight repurchase agreements, and overnight Eurodollars issued to U.S. residents by foreign branches of U.S. banks. For the United Kingdom, M4 is composed of non-interest-bearing M1, private sector interest-bearing sterling sight bank deposits, private sector sterling time banks deposits, private sector holdings of sterling bank CDs, private sector holdings of building society shares and deposits, and sterling CDs less building society of banks deposits and bank CDs and notes and coins. For the euro area, M3 is composed of M2 plus marketable instruments held by euro-area residents, which comprise repurchase agreements, money market fund shares/units, money market paper, and debt securities up to two years.

Table 18. Advanced Economies: Interest Rates

(Percent a year)

	1995	1996	1997	1998	1999	2000	2001	2002	August 2003
Policy-related interest rate[1]									
United States	5.6	5.3	5.5	4.7	5.3	6.4	1.8	1.2	1.0
Euro area[2]	...	...	...	...	3.0	4.8	3.3	2.8	2.0
Japan	0.4	0.4	0.4	0.3	0.0	0.2	0.0	0.0	0.0
United Kingdom	6.4	5.9	7.3	6.3	5.5	6.0	4.0	4.0	3.5
Canada	5.8	3.0	4.3	5.0	4.8	5.8	2.3	2.8	3.0
Short-term interest rate[3]									
Advanced economies	**5.4**	**4.2**	**4.1**	**4.1**	**3.4**	**4.4**	**3.2**	**2.0**	**1.8**
United States	5.7	5.1	5.2	4.9	4.8	6.0	3.5	1.6	0.9
Euro area[2]	7.1	5.2	4.4	4.1	3.0	4.5	4.2	3.3	2.1
Japan	0.8	0.3	0.3	0.2	0.0	0.2	0.0	0.0	0.0
United Kingdom	6.8	6.1	6.9	7.4	5.5	6.1	5.0	4.0	3.5
Canada	7.0	4.3	3.2	4.7	4.7	5.5	3.9	2.6	2.7
Memorandum									
Newly industrialized Asian economies	9.1	8.6	9.2	10.4	4.6	4.6	3.3	0.9	6.2
Long-term interest rate[4]									
Advanced economies	**6.8**	**6.1**	**5.5**	**4.5**	**4.7**	**5.0**	**4.4**	**4.2**	**3.7**
United States	6.6	6.4	6.4	5.3	5.6	6.0	5.0	4.6	4.0
Euro area[2]	8.6	7.3	6.1	4.8	4.7	5.5	5.0	5.0	3.7
Japan	3.3	3.0	2.1	1.3	1.7	1.7	1.3	1.3	1.5
United Kingdom	8.1	7.8	6.8	5.1	5.2	5.0	5.0	4.8	4.1
Canada	8.1	7.2	6.1	5.3	5.6	5.9	5.5	5.3	5.0
Memorandum									
Newly industrialized Asian economies	8.9	8.1	9.0	9.3	6.8	6.7	5.3	5.3	4.4

[1]Annual data are end of period. For the United States, federal funds rate; for Japan, overnight call rate; for the euro area, main refinancing rate; for the United Kingdom, base lending rate; and for Canada, overnight money market financing rate.

[2]Excludes Greece prior to 2001.

[3]Annual data are period average. For the United States, three-month treasury bill market bid yield at constant maturity; for Japan, three-month bond yield with repurchase agreement; for the euro area, a weighted average of national three-month money market interest rates through 1998 and three-month EURIBOR thereafter; for the United Kingdom, three-month London interbank offered rate; and for Canada, three-month treasury bill yield.

[4]Annual data are period average. For the United States, 10-year treasury bond yield at constant maturity; for Japan, 10-year government bond yield; for euro area, a weighted average of national 10-year government bond yields through 1998 and 10-year euro bond yield thereafter; for the United Kingdom, 10-year government bond yield; and for Canada, government bond yield of 10 years and over.

Table 19. Advanced Economies: Exchange Rates

	1995	1996	1997	1998	1999	2000	2001	2002	Exchange Rate Assumption[1] 2003
U.S. dollar nominal exchange rates					*U.S. dollars per national currency unit*				
Euro	...	...	...		1.067	0.924	0.896	0.944	1.119
ECU	1.308	1.269	1.134	1.120	...	...	...		
Pound sterling	1.578	1.562	1.638	1.656	1.618	1.516	1.440	1.501	1.615
Irish pound	1.604	1.601	1.518	1.426	1.355	1.173	1.137	...	...
					National currency units per U.S. dollar				
Deutsche mark	1.433	1.505	1.734	1.760	1.833	2.117	2.184	...	...
French franc	4.991	5.116	5.837	5.900	6.149	7.101	7.324	...	...
Italian lira	1,628.9	1,542.9	1,703.1	1,736.2	1,815.0	2,096.2	2,161.8	...	...
Spanish peseta	124.7	126.7	146.4	149.4	156.0	180.1	185.8	...	...
Netherlands guilder	1.606	1.686	1.951	1.984	2.066	2.386	2.460	...	...
Belgian franc	29.480	30.962	35.774	36.299	37.813	43.671	45.039	...	...
Austrian schilling	10.081	10.587	12.204	12.379	12.898	14.897	15.363	...	...
Finnish markka	4.367	4.594	5.191	5.344	5.573	6.437	6.638	...	...
Greek drachma	231.7	240.7	273.1	295.5	305.1	360.9	380.4	...	...
Portuguese escudo	151.1	154.2	175.3	180.1	187.9	217.0	223.8	...	...
Japanese yen	94.1	108.8	121.0	130.9	113.9	107.8	121.5	125.4	118.6
Canadian dollar	1.372	1.363	1.385	1.483	1.486	1.485	1.549	1.569	1.417
Swedish krona	7.133	6.706	7.635	7.950	8.262	9.162	10.329	9.737	8.225
Danish krone	5.602	5.799	6.604	6.701	6.976	8.083	8.323	7.895	6.670
Swiss franc	1.182	1.236	1.451	1.450	1.502	1.689	1.688	1.559	1.363
Norwegian krone	6.335	6.450	7.073	7.545	7.799	8.802	8.992	7.984	7.235
Israeli new sheqel	3.011	3.192	3.449	3.800	4.140	4.077	4.206	4.738	4.530
Icelandic krona	64.69	66.50	70.90	70.96	72.34	78.62	97.42	91.66	77.45
Cyprus pound	0.452	0.466	0.514	0.518	0.543	0.622	0.643	0.611	0.526
Korean won	771.3	804.5	951.3	1,401.4	1,188.8	1,131.0	1,291.0	1,251.1	1,200.0
Australian dollar	1.349	1.277	1.344	1.589	1.550	1.717	1.932	1.839	1.566
New Taiwan dollar	26.486	27.458	28.703	33.456	32.270	31.234	33.813	34.579	34.658
Hong Kong dollar	7.736	7.734	7.742	7.745	7.758	7.791	7.799	7.799	7.799
Singapore dollar	1.417	1.410	1.485	1.674	1.695	1.724	1.792	1.791	1.750
									Percent change from previous assumption[2]
Real effective exchange rates[3]				*Index, 1990 = 100*					
United States	87.6	90.6	95.3	101.0	99.1	106.3	116.2	115.5	1.5
Japan	145.2	123.5	117.7	109.9	125.3	135.3	120.7	111.1	0.3
Euro[4]	101.3	101.6	91.3	88.1	83.9	74.8	74.6	76.3	−1.4
Germany	123.7	122.0	114.3	110.7	106.6	99.9	98.7	98.5	−0.5
France	96.7	93.7	90.0	89.8	89.3	86.1	85.3	86.1	−0.5
United Kingdom	92.2	96.8	116.8	125.1	127.4	134.0	132.9	134.7	1.7
Italy	73.5	84.4	86.7	85.5	85.6	82.9	82.4	83.6	−0.5
Canada	85.8	87.0	90.1	85.3	84.9	85.2	81.7	81.0	−0.4
Spain	92.1	94.7	92.9	95.4	96.3	95.7	98.1	100.8	−0.5
Netherlands	103.5	100.2	95.9	97.5	97.3	95.5	97.6	100.6	−0.5
Belgium	103.1	98.2	94.4	93.8	90.5	88.0	89.3	88.5	−0.5
Sweden	81.0	91.4	89.0	87.5	84.7	84.0	76.1	77.8	−0.8
Austria	90.5	85.9	81.7	80.5	79.1	77.7	77.7	78.3	−0.2
Denmark	100.5	98.5	95.8	97.3	97.0	93.9	95.2	96.7	−0.4
Finland	73.0	67.7	63.9	63.1	60.7	57.8	58.2	57.7	−0.4
Greece	104.2	107.0	110.9	107.3	108.1	104.8	105.4	108.6	−0.4
Portugal	119.9	118.6	116.8	117.9	118.9	118.7	122.5	126.3	−0.4
Ireland	75.0	70.5	64.8	57.4	52.7	47.2	46.7	46.7	−1.1
Switzerland	112.3	111.7	107.8	113.7	113.3	113.3	119.3	126.2	−2.3
Norway	103.2	106.0	111.1	112.9	118.8	121.5	128.4	143.4	−5.4
Australia	92.7	108.8	113.4	101.7	103.3	97.2	91.6	96.8	2.0
New Zealand	100.9	112.5	116.4	100.7	98.2	86.8	84.2	93.1	1.7

[1]Average exchange rates for the period July 1–28, 2003. See "Assumptions" in the Introduction to the Statistical Appendix.
[2]In nominal effective terms. Average May 14–June 5, 2003 rates compared with July 1–28, 2003 rates.
[3]Defined as the ratio, in common currency, of the normalized unit labor costs in the manufacturing sector to the weighted average of those of its industrial country trading partners, using 1989–91 trade weights.
[4]A synthetic euro for the period prior to January 1, 1999 is used in the calculation of real effective exchange rates for the euro. See Box 5.5 in the *World Economic Outlook*, October 1998.

Table 20. Developing Countries: Central Government Fiscal Balances
(Percent of GDP)

	1995	1996	1997	1998	1999	2000	2001	2002	2003	2004
Developing countries	**−2.6**	**−2.1**	**−2.5**	**−3.7**	**−3.8**	**−3.2**	**−3.8**	**−3.8**	**−3.3**	**−3.1**
Regional groups										
Africa	−3.9	−2.2	−2.8	−3.9	−3.2	−1.3	−2.1	−2.7	−2.1	−2.0
Sub-Sahara	−4.1	−2.8	−3.4	−3.9	−3.7	−2.2	−2.5	−3.0	−2.3	−1.8
Excluding Nigeria and South Africa	−5.0	−2.8	−3.6	−3.5	−4.4	−4.1	−3.0	−3.6	−3.1	−2.4
Developing Asia	−2.5	−2.1	−2.6	−3.6	−4.2	−4.3	−4.1	−4.0	−3.9	−3.7
China	−2.1	−1.6	−1.9	−3.0	−4.0	−3.6	−3.2	−3.3	−3.2	−2.9
India	−4.6	−4.2	−4.7	−5.3	−5.5	−5.7	−6.2	−6.1	−6.4	−6.3
Other developing Asia	−1.5	−1.2	−2.1	−3.1	−3.1	−4.5	−4.3	−3.5	−3.4	−3.1
Middle East and Turkey	−3.5	−3.1	−3.5	−5.5	−4.1	−0.6	−5.7	−5.6	−2.2	−2.8
Western Hemisphere	−1.9	−1.8	−1.8	−3.3	−2.9	−2.4	−2.8	−3.0	−2.7	−1.9
Analytical groups										
By source of export earnings										
Fuel	−3.3	0.3	−1.0	−5.5	−1.7	5.8	—	−2.1	1.5	0.2
Nonfuel	−2.5	−2.4	−2.7	−3.6	−4.0	−4.1	−4.2	−4.0	−3.8	−3.4
of which, primary products	−1.7	−1.3	−1.7	−2.4	−3.6	−4.3	−3.3	−3.5	−3.3	−2.7
By external financing source										
Net debtor countries	−2.8	−2.7	−3.1	−3.9	−4.0	−4.2	−4.7	−4.4	−4.1	−3.6
of which, official financing	−1.9	−1.6	−2.9	−3.7	−3.2	−3.6	−3.8	−3.0	−2.5	−2.3
Net debtor countries by debt-servicing experience										
Countries with arrears and/or rescheduling during 1997–2001	−2.3	−1.8	−2.8	−4.2	−3.0	−3.0	−3.0	−2.2	−2.8	−2.0
Other groups										
Heavily indebted poor countries	−4.2	−2.4	−3.7	−2.8	−3.9	−4.1	−3.5	−3.8	−3.5	−3.1
Middle East and north Africa	−3.4	−1.0	−1.7	−4.5	−1.7	3.1	−0.8	−2.5	−0.2	−1.7
Memorandum										
Median										
Developing countries	−3.3	−2.5	−2.6	−2.7	−3.3	−3.2	−3.8	−3.8	−3.3	−2.9
Regional groups										
Africa	−3.7	−3.7	−2.9	−3.0	−3.3	−2.8	−3.7	−3.8	−3.0	−2.4
Developing Asia	−3.5	−3.1	−2.8	−2.5	−3.9	−4.4	−4.4	−3.3	−4.0	−3.4
Middle East and Turkey	−4.0	−2.2	−2.5	−5.5	−2.4	1.9	−0.3	−2.1	0.1	−0.9
Western Hemisphere	−1.4	−1.9	−2.6	−2.2	−3.2	−2.7	−3.9	−5.3	−3.8	−3.1

Table 21. Developing Countries: Broad Money Aggregates
(Annual percent change)

	1995	1996	1997	1998	1999	2000	2001	2002	2003	2004
Developing countries	**24.4**	**29.5**	**17.3**	**16.4**	**14.8**	**9.3**	**12.6**	**15.3**	**15.4**	**11.9**
Regional groups										
Africa	23.5	18.4	21.5	18.0	17.9	19.0	22.1	20.0	15.7	13.2
Sub-Sahara	28.4	20.7	23.9	16.4	19.5	21.4	23.7	22.9	16.1	13.7
Developing Asia	22.2	20.8	18.2	18.3	14.4	12.3	12.9	14.2	14.8	13.0
China	29.5	25.3	19.6	14.8	14.7	12.3	14.4	16.8	17.0	14.0
India	13.7	16.9	17.6	20.2	18.6	16.2	13.9	15.2	14.8	14.6
Other developing Asia	19.9	18.4	17.1	21.1	11.6	9.9	9.7	9.2	11.2	10.0
Middle East and Turkey	32.5	36.7	28.0	25.5	29.4	18.9	23.8	18.6	13.3	10.4
Western Hemisphere	23.7	39.2	11.8	10.9	9.7	1.0	6.1	14.2	17.0	10.7
Analytical groups										
By source of export earnings										
Fuel	16.6	21.4	17.8	13.4	15.9	17.8	15.8	17.5	16.2	12.2
Nonfuel	25.7	30.8	17.2	16.8	14.7	8.2	12.1	15.0	15.3	11.8
of which, primary products	36.3	18.8	24.8	13.1	17.1	18.2	20.7	20.7	16.4	14.1
By external financing source										
Net debtor countries	25.3	32.1	16.9	17.3	15.2	7.8	11.8	14.8	15.0	11.3
of which, official financing	24.7	17.9	24.6	29.9	15.2	19.8	18.2	16.8	14.7	12.2
Net debtor countries by debt-servicing experience										
Countries with arrears and/or rescheduling during 1997–2001	27.7	40.4	5.6	15.0	11.5	9.9	16.2	21.0	17.4	12.4
Other groups										
Heavily indebted poor countries	42.1	33.2	30.9	19.3	32.5	30.9	26.7	26.9	17.8	16.1
Middle East and north Africa	12.0	12.9	10.9	11.0	11.3	12.4	14.7	15.0	12.9	8.2
Memorandum										
Median										
Developing countries	16.2	15.6	14.7	10.5	12.2	11.8	11.8	12.3	9.9	9.3
Regional groups										
Africa	16.3	15.7	14.2	8.6	13.3	14.0	14.9	14.6	10.9	10.0
Developing Asia	16.2	15.7	17.2	12.5	15.0	12.6	11.8	12.9	11.0	10.6
Middle East and Turkey	8.5	8.4	9.7	8.6	11.4	10.2	12.2	11.1	10.4	7.9
Western Hemisphere	19.2	17.3	14.0	11.5	11.6	8.4	8.9	7.1	8.1	7.9

Table 22. Summary of World Trade Volumes and Prices

(Annual percent change)

	Ten-Year Averages		1995	1996	1997	1998	1999	2000	2001	2002	2003	2004
	1985–94	1995–2004										
Trade in goods and services												
World trade[1]												
Volume	5.5	6.0	9.0	7.0	10.4	4.4	5.8	12.6	0.1	3.2	2.9	5.5
Price deflator												
In U.S. dollars	3.0	0.1	9.0	−1.5	−6.0	−5.4	−1.9	−0.7	−3.1	1.0	10.6	0.8
In SDRs	−0.4	0.4	2.9	2.9	−0.9	−4.1	−2.7	2.9	0.3	−0.7	3.1	0.9
Volume of trade												
Exports												
Advanced economies	5.8	5.5	8.8	6.1	10.6	4.2	5.5	12.0	−0.8	2.2	1.6	5.2
Developing countries	7.7	7.6	8.1	9.5	13.5	5.5	5.4	14.4	2.7	6.5	4.3	6.9
Imports												
Advanced economies	6.0	5.9	8.9	6.4	9.4	6.0	8.1	11.9	−1.0	2.2	2.8	4.8
Developing countries	4.8	6.7	9.6	9.9	10.5	−0.8	2.4	16.1	1.6	6.0	5.1	7.8
Terms of trade												
Advanced economies	0.9	—	−0.1	−0.1	−0.5	1.4	−0.3	−2.5	0.2	0.6	0.9	0.2
Developing countries	−3.3	0.3	2.4	2.8	−1.4	−7.4	4.5	6.8	−3.9	1.1	—	−1.4
Trade in goods												
World trade[1]												
Volume	5.7	6.1	9.7	6.6	10.9	4.7	5.8	13.3	−0.6	3.3	2.9	5.4
Price deflator												
In U.S. dollars	2.8	0.1	9.4	−1.4	−6.6	−6.3	−1.5	−0.1	−3.5	0.6	11.0	0.9
In SDRs	−0.6	0.4	3.2	3.0	−1.4	−4.9	−2.3	3.6	−0.1	−1.1	3.4	1.0
World trade prices in U.S. dollars[2]												
Manufactures	5.0	0.4	10.4	−3.2	−8.1	−1.7	−1.8	−4.7	−2.4	2.6	12.8	1.7
Oil	−5.7	4.8	7.9	18.4	−5.4	−32.1	37.5	57.0	−14.0	2.8	14.2	−10.5
Nonfuel primary commodities	1.1	−1.0	9.3	−1.8	−3.1	−14.3	−6.7	4.5	−4.0	0.6	5.0	2.4
World trade prices in SDRs[2]												
Manufactures	1.6	0.7	4.2	1.2	−3.0	−0.3	−2.6	−1.2	1.1	0.8	5.1	1.8
Oil	−8.8	5.1	1.8	23.7	−0.2	−31.2	36.5	62.8	−10.9	1.1	6.4	−10.4
Nonfuel primary commodities	−2.2	−0.7	3.2	2.6	2.2	−13.0	−7.5	8.3	−0.6	−1.1	−2.1	2.4
World trade prices in euros[2]												
Manufactures	0.8	1.0	0.3	−0.2	2.9	−0.5	3.1	10.0	0.7	−2.7	−4.8	1.8
Oil	−9.4	5.5	−2.0	22.0	5.8	−31.3	44.5	81.4	−11.3	−2.5	−3.6	−10.4
Nonfuel primary commodities	−3.0	−0.4	−0.7	1.2	8.4	−13.2	−2.1	20.7	−1.0	−4.6	−11.4	2.5

Table 22 *(concluded)*

	Ten-Year Averages		1995	1996	1997	1998	1999	2000	2001	2002	2003	2004
	1985–94	1995–2004										
Trade in goods												
Volume of trade												
Exports												
Advanced economies	5.9	5.4	9.4	5.7	11.1	4.4	5.3	12.6	−1.6	2.0	1.1	4.8
Developing countries	7.7	7.6	9.2	8.6	13.4	5.2	4.6	15.4	2.2	6.3	5.0	6.8
Fuel exporters	6.6	2.8	−1.2	7.1	7.2	1.5	−1.3	7.1	0.6	—	3.5	3.7
Nonfuel exporters	8.1	8.9	12.3	9.1	15.3	6.2	5.8	17.6	2.7	8.1	5.3	7.5
Imports												
Advanced economies	6.3	6.1	9.7	6.0	10.2	6.0	8.7	12.6	−1.7	2.4	2.9	4.8
Developing countries	5.2	6.9	10.6	9.4	10.3	0.4	1.7	17.1	1.2	6.2	5.3	8.0
Fuel exporters	−3.5	6.7	5.2	6.5	16.0	0.8	2.1	13.2	11.3	6.5	0.5	5.7
Nonfuel exporters	8.2	7.0	11.5	9.9	9.5	0.4	1.7	17.8	−0.3	6.1	6.1	8.4
Price deflators in SDRs												
Exports												
Advanced economies	0.2	0.2	3.2	1.8	−2.4	−3.6	−3.3	0.3	0.2	−0.9	5.0	1.6
Developing countries	−3.7	1.6	4.5	8.1	0.9	−11.1	5.3	13.8	−2.3	0.2	−0.4	−0.7
Fuel exporters	−8.7	4.8	9.0	18.4	0.1	−26.8	30.8	47.8	−8.7	1.3	1.4	−6.5
Nonfuel exporters	−1.3	0.7	3.1	5.3	1.2	−6.7	−0.1	5.0	−0.2	−0.1	−0.8	0.7
Imports												
Advanced economies	−1.0	0.1	2.8	2.4	−1.8	−5.0	−3.3	3.3	−0.3	−1.7	3.8	1.0
Developing countries	−0.1	1.0	1.6	5.0	1.9	−4.6	−0.4	6.1	1.7	−1.5	—	1.0
Fuel exporters	−0.1	0.3	1.4	1.8	−1.5	−0.2	−2.6	1.4	3.0	−1.1	−1.1	1.9
Nonfuel exporters	−0.3	1.2	1.6	5.6	2.5	−5.4	—	6.9	1.4	−1.6	0.2	0.8
Terms of trade												
Advanced economies	1.2	0.1	0.4	−0.6	−0.6	1.5	—	−2.9	0.4	0.8	1.1	0.6
Developing countries	−3.6	0.6	2.8	3.0	−1.0	−6.8	5.8	7.2	−3.9	1.8	−0.4	−1.7
Fuel exporters	−8.7	4.5	7.5	16.3	1.7	−26.7	34.3	45.8	−11.4	2.4	2.5	−8.2
Nonfuel exporters	−1.0	−0.5	1.4	−0.3	−1.3	−1.4	—	−1.8	−1.6	1.5	−1.1	−0.1
Memorandum												
World exports in billions of U.S. dollars												
Goods and services	3,849	7,513	6,276	6,606	6,865	6,759	6,994	7,786	7,533	7,876	8,938	9,494
Goods	3,072	5,998	5,051	5,287	5,488	5,370	5,568	6,272	6,009	6,262	7,119	7,557

[1]Average of annual percent change for world exports and imports. The estimates of world trade comprise, in addition to trade of advanced economies and developing countries (which is summarized in the table), trade of countries in transition.

[2]As represented, respectively, by the export unit value index for the manufactures of the advanced economies; the average of U.K. Brent, Dubai, and West Texas Intermediate crude oil spot prices; and the average of world market prices for nonfuel primary commodities weighted by their 1995–97 shares in world commodity exports.

Table 23. Nonfuel Commodity Prices[1]

(Annual percent change; U.S. dollar terms)

	Ten-Year Averages		1995	1996	1997	1998	1999	2000	2001	2002	2003	2004
	1985–94	1995–2004										
Nonfuel primary commodities	**1.1**	**−1.0**	**9.3**	**−1.8**	**−3.1**	**−14.3**	**−6.7**	**4.5**	**−4.0**	**0.6**	**5.0**	**2.4**
Food	−0.2	−0.9	6.2	8.2	−8.9	−11.0	−11.6	1.7	2.3	0.8	6.2	−0.9
Beverages	−1.9	−3.5	0.5	−14.8	31.1	−13.2	−21.3	−15.1	−16.1	16.5	6.1	3.3
Agricultural raw materials	5.4	−1.6	3.3	−3.7	−4.7	−16.7	1.2	4.6	−4.9	1.6	0.4	4.4
Metals	1.3	−0.2	21.0	−11.3	1.2	−17.7	−1.1	12.2	−9.8	−2.7	6.5	5.7
Advanced economies	**1.3**	**−1.1**	**10.7**	**−2.6**	**−4.3**	**−15.7**	**−5.9**	**5.3**	**−5.1**	**1.7**	**4.8**	**2.8**
Developing countries	**1.0**	**−1.5**	**9.3**	**−2.8**	**−1.3**	**−15.8**	**−8.8**	**3.0**	**−5.9**	**2.5**	**5.3**	**2.4**
Regional groups												
Africa	0.7	−1.3	8.9	−5.8	−0.5	−14.1	−9.1	1.8	−6.0	5.9	5.2	2.9
Sub-Sahara	0.7	−1.3	9.1	−6.5	—	−14.1	−9.3	1.7	−6.4	6.4	5.3	3.0
Developing Asia	1.3	−1.5	8.0	−1.9	−3.6	−13.6	−7.5	1.8	−5.6	2.4	4.5	2.6
Excluding China and India	1.1	−1.6	7.6	−2.1	−3.8	−12.6	−9.1	0.1	−5.4	3.7	4.8	2.2
Middle East and Turkey	1.0	−1.1	11.6	−3.2	−3.7	−15.2	−6.9	5.3	−5.1	0.8	5.4	2.8
Western Hemisphere	0.8	−1.6	10.3	−2.5	0.8	−18.3	−10.2	4.1	−6.4	1.8	5.9	2.1
Analytical groups												
By source of export earnings												
Fuel	1.2	−0.8	13.6	−6.1	−1.7	−16.0	−4.7	7.2	−6.7	0.1	5.4	3.8
Nonfuel	1.0	−1.5	9.2	−2.6	−1.3	−15.8	−8.9	2.9	−5.9	2.6	5.3	2.4
of which, primary products	1.3	−1.6	14.0	−10.4	—	−16.9	−10.8	3.8	−7.0	6.5	5.3	3.8
By external financing source												
Net debtor countries	1.0	−1.5	9.2	−2.8	−1.0	−16.0	−9.2	2.7	−6.0	2.7	5.3	2.4
of which, official financing	1.0	−1.8	8.7	−5.4	−0.6	−13.3	−11.1	−0.5	−6.4	5.3	5.1	2.7
Net debtor countries by debt-servicing experience												
Countries with arrears and/or rescheduling during 1997–2001	0.6	−1.6	8.5	−3.7	1.0	−15.6	−10.6	1.6	−6.7	4.1	5.8	2.1
Other groups												
Heavily indebted poor countries	−0.3	−1.8	9.0	−8.5	4.1	−10.6	−17.0	−5.1	−7.9	14.2	6.0	2.3
Middle East and north Africa	0.8	−1.2	10.7	−2.8	−3.6	−14.6	−7.9	4.5	−4.9	0.9	5.9	2.5
Memorandum												
Average oil spot price[2]	−5.7	4.8	7.9	18.4	−5.4	−32.1	37.5	57.0	−14.0	2.8	14.2	−10.5
In U.S. dollars a barrel	18.65	21.94	17.20	20.37	19.27	13.07	17.98	28.24	24.28	24.96	28.50	25.50
Export unit value of manufactures[3]	5.0	0.4	10.4	−3.2	−8.1	−1.7	−1.8	−4.7	−2.4	2.6	12.8	1.7

[1]Averages of world market prices for individual commodities weighted by 1995–97 exports as a share of world commodity exports and total commodity exports for the indicated country group, respectively.
[2]Average of U.K. Brent, Dubai, and West Texas Intermediate crude oil spot prices.
[3]For the manufactures exported by the advanced economies.

Table 24. Advanced Economies: Export Volumes, Import Volumes, and Terms of Trade in Goods and Services
(Annual percent change)

	Ten-Year Averages		1995	1996	1997	1998	1999	2000	2001	2002	2003	2004
	1985–94	1995–2004										
Export volume												
Advanced economies	**5.8**	**5.5**	**8.8**	**6.1**	**10.6**	**4.2**	**5.5**	**12.0**	**-0.8**	**2.2**	**1.6**	**5.2**
United States	8.2	4.4	10.3	8.2	12.3	2.1	3.4	9.7	-5.4	-1.6	0.3	6.3
Euro area	4.7	5.6	7.9	4.4	10.7	7.0	5.1	12.5	3.3	1.4	—	4.2
Germany	3.6	6.1	5.7	5.1	11.2	7.0	5.5	13.7	5.6	3.4	0.5	3.6
France	4.6	5.5	7.7	3.2	12.0	8.3	4.2	13.4	1.8	1.3	-1.6	5.2
Italy	5.4	3.9	12.6	0.6	6.4	3.4	0.1	11.7	1.1	-1.0	-1.2	6.2
Japan	3.2	5.0	4.1	6.4	11.3	-2.2	1.4	12.4	-6.0	8.1	7.7	8.6
United Kingdom	4.4	4.7	9.0	8.2	8.3	3.0	5.3	10.1	0.9	-0.9	-0.2	3.7
Canada	5.9	4.9	8.5	5.6	8.3	9.1	10.7	8.8	-3.1	-0.1	-1.8	3.6
Other advanced economies	6.9	6.4	10.1	6.5	10.6	4.7	7.8	13.1	—	3.9	3.0	4.8
Memorandum												
Major advanced economies	5.2	4.9	8.1	5.8	10.6	3.8	4.1	11.4	-1.4	1.2	0.7	5.4
European Union	4.7	5.5	8.1	4.9	10.3	6.4	5.4	12.1	2.8	1.2	0.2	4.1
Newly industrialized Asian economies	11.9	8.0	15.7	8.0	10.8	1.4	9.9	16.9	-3.5	10.0	6.0	6.7
Import volume												
Advanced economies	**6.0**	**5.9**	**8.9**	**6.4**	**9.4**	**6.0**	**8.1**	**11.9**	**-1.0**	**2.2**	**2.8**	**4.8**
United States	5.9	7.3	8.2	8.6	13.7	11.8	10.9	13.2	-2.9	3.7	2.6	4.9
Euro area	5.2	5.6	7.6	3.2	9.2	10.0	7.6	11.4	1.6	-0.1	1.7	4.6
Germany	3.9	5.3	5.6	3.1	8.3	9.1	8.4	10.5	0.9	-1.7	3.7	5.4
France	4.9	5.6	7.6	1.6	7.3	11.6	6.2	15.3	1.4	0.8	0.4	5.0
Italy	5.3	5.3	9.7	-0.3	10.1	8.9	5.6	8.9	1.0	1.5	1.8	6.2
Japan	5.6	4.3	12.8	13.2	1.3	-6.8	3.0	9.4	0.1	2.0	4.3	5.2
United Kingdom	4.8	6.4	5.4	9.6	9.7	9.6	8.7	11.7	2.3	2.1	2.0	3.3
Canada	6.5	4.9	5.8	5.1	14.2	5.1	7.8	8.0	-5.0	0.6	4.1	3.9
Other advanced economies	7.5	5.8	10.7	6.2	9.3	2.9	8.0	12.4	-1.4	3.1	3.0	4.6
Memorandum												
Major advanced economies	5.2	5.9	7.9	6.6	9.5	7.8	8.2	11.6	-0.8	1.8	2.7	4.9
European Union	5.0	5.7	7.3	4.1	9.5	9.9	7.6	11.4	1.6	0.2	1.9	4.5
Newly industrialized Asian economies	13.4	5.9	15.6	8.2	8.3	-8.7	8.8	16.8	-6.2	8.4	4.9	6.0
Terms of trade												
Advanced economies	**0.9**	**—**	**-0.1**	**-0.1**	**-0.5**	**1.4**	**-0.3**	**-2.5**	**0.2**	**0.6**	**0.9**	**0.2**
United States	-0.3	0.3	-0.5	0.6	1.6	3.5	-0.7	-3.1	2.7	-0.1	-2.0	1.6
Euro area	0.7	—	-0.1	0.2	-1.0	1.7	—	-3.6	0.8	1.0	0.9	0.3
Germany	-0.4	0.1	0.8	-0.7	-1.9	2.3	0.5	-4.3	0.4	1.0	3.1	0.2
France	0.8	-0.2	-0.3	-1.0	0.2	0.8	0.3	-3.8	1.0	0.9	-0.6	0.8
Italy	1.8	—	-2.3	4.3	-1.5	2.0	0.3	-7.4	1.5	1.6	1.4	0.3
Japan	3.0	-2.0	-0.1	-5.4	-3.7	3.2	-0.7	-4.7	-1.5	—	-2.6	-4.0
United Kingdom	1.3	1.1	-2.5	1.2	3.3	2.2	—	0.7	-1.2	2.1	3.8	2.1
Canada	-0.4	0.8	2.9	1.8	-0.7	-3.9	1.4	4.0	-1.5	-2.1	5.9	0.9
Other advanced economies	0.8	-0.3	—	0.1	-0.6	0.2	-0.6	-1.2	-0.2	0.4	-0.3	-0.4
Memorandum												
Major advanced economies	0.9	0.1	-0.1	-0.3	-0.4	2.1	-0.1	-3.3	0.5	0.7	1.6	0.6
European Union	0.8	0.2	-0.3	0.3	-0.3	1.6	-0.1	-2.9	0.5	0.9	1.4	0.6
Newly industrialized Asian economies	0.9	-1.1	-1.7	-0.2	-0.8	-0.2	-2.5	-3.6	-1.1	0.1	-0.4	-0.8
Memorandum												
Trade in goods												
Advanced economies												
Export volume	5.9	5.4	9.4	5.7	11.1	4.4	5.3	12.6	-1.6	2.0	1.1	4.8
Import volume	6.3	6.1	9.7	6.0	10.2	6.0	8.7	12.6	-1.7	2.4	2.9	4.8
Terms of trade	1.2	0.1	0.4	-0.6	-0.6	1.5	—	-2.9	0.4	0.8	1.1	0.6

Table 25. Developing Countries—by Region: Total Trade in Goods

(Annual percent change)

	Ten-Year Averages		1995	1996	1997	1998	1999	2000	2001	2002	2003	2004
	1985–94	1995–2004										
Developing countries												
Value in U.S. dollars												
Exports	6.1	8.6	20.4	11.9	8.2	−7.9	9.8	25.6	−3.7	8.1	12.3	5.8
Imports	7.7	7.5	19.0	9.5	6.5	−5.4	1.0	19.7	−0.8	6.4	13.5	9.0
Volume												
Exports	7.7	7.6	9.2	8.6	13.4	5.2	4.6	15.4	2.2	6.3	5.0	6.8
Imports	5.2	6.9	10.6	9.4	10.3	0.4	1.7	17.1	1.2	6.2	5.3	8.0
Unit value in U.S. dollars												
Exports	−0.4	1.3	10.7	3.5	−4.3	−12.4	6.2	9.8	−5.7	1.9	6.9	−0.8
Imports	3.3	0.7	7.6	0.5	−3.4	−6.0	0.4	2.4	−1.9	0.2	7.3	0.9
Terms of trade	−3.6	0.6	2.8	3.0	−1.0	−6.8	5.8	7.2	−3.9	1.8	−0.4	−1.7
Memorandum												
Real GDP growth in developing country trading partners	3.9	3.0	3.7	3.9	4.2	1.8	3.5	4.7	1.0	2.1	2.2	3.3
Market prices of nonfuel commodities exported by developing countries	1.0	−1.5	9.3	−2.8	−1.3	−15.8	−8.8	3.0	−5.9	2.5	5.3	2.4
Regional groups												
Africa												
Value in U.S. dollars												
Exports	1.9	6.3	17.8	11.1	3.4	−13.6	7.9	27.4	−7.0	3.6	17.1	1.5
Imports	3.0	5.6	19.9	0.9	4.1	−2.4	1.2	5.2	2.7	6.3	14.8	5.2
Volume												
Exports	2.4	4.6	7.9	8.0	6.7	0.1	4.2	8.0	0.2	1.7	4.9	5.0
Imports	1.1	5.4	11.0	3.4	8.0	3.8	4.4	2.9	5.4	4.3	5.8	5.6
Unit value in U.S. dollars												
Exports	0.2	1.6	9.4	3.0	−3.0	−13.7	3.9	16.9	−7.0	2.2	11.6	−3.1
Imports	2.8	0.6	8.2	−2.0	−3.4	−5.7	−2.2	2.8	−2.7	2.2	8.9	0.3
Terms of trade	−2.6	1.1	1.1	5.0	0.3	−8.5	6.3	13.7	−4.4	—	2.5	−3.4
Sub-Sahara												
Value in U.S. dollars												
Exports	2.2	5.7	17.6	10.4	3.5	−13.8	6.7	24.7	−7.4	4.4	14.8	2.1
Imports	2.5	5.7	21.0	3.2	6.7	−5.0	0.4	5.5	3.0	5.7	14.5	3.8
Volume												
Exports	2.8	4.6	8.7	9.6	6.7	−1.3	2.8	8.2	—	1.2	4.7	5.7
Imports	1.2	5.9	12.6	7.7	9.2	1.4	4.4	2.6	5.6	3.7	6.9	5.3
Unit value in U.S. dollars												
Exports	0.3	1.1	8.4	0.8	−3.0	−12.7	4.2	13.8	−7.1	3.6	9.5	−3.3
Imports	2.3	0.3	7.9	−3.9	−1.9	−6.0	−2.7	3.6	−2.7	2.4	7.6	−0.6
Terms of trade	−2.0	0.9	0.5	4.9	−1.1	−7.2	7.2	9.8	−4.6	1.2	1.7	−2.6

Table 25 *(concluded)*

	Ten-Year Averages		1995	1996	1997	1998	1999	2000	2001	2002	2003	2004
	1985–94	1995–2004										
Developing Asia												
Value in U.S. dollars												
Exports	12.8	10.7	23.2	10.1	12.2	−2.3	8.5	22.3	−1.8	13.8	14.1	9.6
Imports	12.6	9.3	23.7	10.3	1.0	−13.6	9.0	27.9	−0.8	13.0	18.3	10.7
Volume												
Exports	10.5	10.4	13.6	9.3	18.1	6.9	5.9	22.6	1.2	12.1	7.2	8.4
Imports	9.5	8.5	14.5	9.9	5.7	−5.8	6.5	23.7	1.7	12.7	8.5	10.0
Unit value in U.S. dollars												
Exports	2.4	0.5	8.4	1.1	−4.8	−8.4	4.4	—	−2.9	1.6	6.3	0.9
Imports	3.2	1.1	8.2	0.8	−4.2	−8.5	5.3	3.8	−2.2	0.4	8.7	0.4
Terms of trade	−0.7	−0.6	0.2	0.2	−0.6	0.1	−0.9	−3.6	−0.8	1.2	−2.2	0.5
Excluding China and India												
Value in U.S. dollars												
Exports	12.0	6.9	22.3	5.8	7.4	−4.0	10.4	18.8	−9.3	5.8	9.4	5.8
Imports	12.7	4.8	26.9	5.5	−0.9	−23.2	6.2	24.1	−6.7	6.2	11.2	7.9
Volume												
Exports	11.3	6.2	13.9	2.3	10.9	9.1	3.4	15.9	−6.5	5.3	3.7	5.5
Imports	10.7	3.7	18.9	3.7	1.5	−14.3	−0.6	20.2	−6.8	6.8	4.7	7.4
Unit value in U.S. dollars												
Exports	0.8	1.1	7.4	3.7	−3.1	−11.7	10.1	2.7	−3.0	0.6	5.4	0.2
Imports	2.1	1.7	6.9	2.2	−2.2	−10.3	12.1	3.3	0.2	−0.5	6.1	0.5
Terms of trade	−1.2	−0.6	0.4	1.4	−0.8	−1.6	−1.7	−0.6	−3.2	1.1	−0.7	−0.3
Middle East and Turkey												
Value in U.S. dollars												
Exports	1.7	7.1	14.3	17.0	1.2	−22.2	22.9	40.2	−6.1	5.1	13.4	−1.8
Imports	1.0	6.8	17.7	10.8	6.5	−1.6	−4.5	15.5	−1.5	10.3	10.9	6.6
Volume												
Exports	7.8	4.0	−0.5	8.2	7.7	2.0	−1.1	7.6	4.0	3.0	6.1	3.2
Imports	−1.8	6.9	8.5	13.7	13.8	2.3	−2.5	16.1	0.3	10.2	3.3	4.7
Unit value in U.S. dollars												
Exports	−5.2	3.5	15.9	9.5	−6.0	−23.5	24.2	31.3	−9.6	2.5	7.1	−4.4
Imports	3.3	0.1	8.4	−2.1	−6.2	−3.7	−2.1	−0.6	−1.7	0.4	7.4	1.9
Terms of trade	−8.2	3.4	6.9	11.9	0.2	−20.6	26.8	32.2	−8.1	2.1	−0.3	−6.2
Western Hemisphere												
Value in U.S. dollars												
Exports	5.2	6.9	22.4	11.3	9.8	−3.7	4.0	19.7	−3.8	1.0	5.1	6.1
Imports	11.2	5.2	11.1	11.2	18.1	4.6	−6.7	14.8	−1.6	−8.3	4.1	8.4
Volume												
Exports	6.9	6.4	10.8	8.2	13.2	6.8	6.2	10.6	3.4	−0.6	−0.8	7.0
Imports	9.4	4.5	5.0	8.2	17.9	8.3	−3.1	12.5	−0.6	−7.4	—	7.0
Unit value in U.S. dollars												
Exports	0.4	0.6	10.5	2.9	−2.6	−9.9	−1.8	8.8	−7.0	2.1	6.0	−0.6
Imports	3.2	0.6	5.8	3.0	0.3	−3.5	−3.9	2.0	−1.1	−1.0	3.9	1.4
Terms of trade	−2.7	—	4.5	−0.1	−3.0	−6.7	2.2	6.7	−5.9	3.1	2.0	−2.0

Table 26. Developing Countries—by Source of Export Earnings: Total Trade in Goods
(Annual percent change)

	Ten-Year Averages		1995	1996	1997	1998	1999	2000	2001	2002	2003	2004
	1985–94	1995–2004										
Fuel												
Value in U.S. dollars												
Exports	0.1	7.0	13.1	20.5	1.7	−27.2	30.2	52.2	−11.3	2.5	12.5	−3.9
Imports	−0.6	6.4	12.7	3.3	8.4	−1.0	−0.2	10.6	10.6	6.8	6.9	6.7
Volume												
Exports	6.6	2.8	−1.2	7.1	7.2	1.5	−1.3	7.1	0.6	—	3.5	3.7
Imports	−3.5	6.7	5.2	6.5	16.0	0.8	2.1	13.2	11.3	6.5	0.5	5.7
Unit value in U.S. dollars												
Exports	−5.6	4.5	15.5	13.3	−5.1	−27.9	31.9	42.6	−11.9	3.0	8.7	−6.6
Imports	3.3	—	7.4	−2.6	−6.7	−1.7	−1.8	−2.2	−0.6	0.6	6.1	1.8
Terms of trade	−8.7	4.5	7.5	16.3	1.7	−26.7	34.3	45.8	−11.4	2.4	2.5	−8.2
Nonfuel												
Value in U.S. dollars												
Exports	9.1	9.1	22.6	9.5	10.2	−2.5	5.5	18.8	−1.2	9.7	12.3	8.5
Imports	10.5	7.7	20.1	10.6	6.1	−6.2	1.2	21.2	−2.5	6.3	14.6	9.3
Volume												
Exports	8.1	8.9	12.3	9.1	15.3	6.2	5.8	17.6	2.7	8.1	5.3	7.5
Imports	8.2	7.0	11.5	9.9	9.5	0.4	1.7	17.8	−0.3	6.1	6.1	8.4
Unit value in U.S. dollars												
Exports	2.0	0.4	9.2	0.7	−4.1	−8.0	0.7	1.3	−3.7	1.6	6.4	0.6
Imports	3.1	0.8	7.7	1.0	−2.9	−6.7	0.8	3.1	−2.1	0.1	7.5	0.7
Terms of trade	−1.0	−0.5	1.4	−0.3	−1.3	−1.4	—	−1.8	−1.6	1.5	−1.1	−0.1
Primary products												
Value in U.S. dollars												
Exports	5.6	5.0	26.4	4.0	3.8	−8.3	2.3	4.3	−4.6	3.8	11.3	10.6
Imports	6.1	5.1	23.7	12.7	8.7	−4.2	−10.7	5.9	−0.9	1.2	11.6	7.2
Volume												
Exports	4.4	4.7	8.0	3.1	7.3	3.0	6.6	3.1	3.7	1.7	4.1	6.5
Imports	5.4	5.1	13.4	9.0	13.5	5.1	−6.7	0.7	3.2	3.1	4.2	7.2
Unit value in U.S. dollars												
Exports	2.1	0.3	17.1	1.3	−3.3	−10.4	−3.8	1.0	−7.6	2.2	7.2	2.6
Imports	2.0	0.3	9.6	3.8	−4.1	−8.9	−4.1	6.0	−3.8	−2.0	7.6	0.5
Terms of trade	0.1	0.1	6.9	−2.4	0.8	−1.7	0.3	−4.7	−3.9	4.2	−0.4	2.1

Table 27. Summary of Payments Balances on Current Account
(Billions of U.S. dollars)

	1995	1996	1997	1998	1999	2000	2001	2002	2003	2004
Advanced economies	**49.4**	**33.7**	**88.7**	**40.6**	**−94.8**	**−234.5**	**−190.9**	**−186.6**	**−245.2**	**−224.6**
United States	−105.8	−117.8	−128.4	−203.8	−292.9	−410.3	−393.7	−480.9	−553.3	−537.3
Euro area[1]	50.9	78.1	98.2	62.5	29.0	−28.7	11.8	61.2	62.4	65.7
Japan	111.4	65.7	96.6	119.1	114.5	119.6	87.8	112.7	121.1	120.1
Other advanced economies	−7.1	7.6	22.3	62.9	54.5	84.9	103.3	120.3	124.6	126.8
Memorandum										
Newly industrialized Asian economies	2.7	−2.1	8.5	66.8	60.1	43.5	54.6	68.0	76.0	81.0
Developing countries	**−97.2**	**−73.8**	**−55.6**	**−82.6**	**−9.6**	**67.8**	**25.9**	**74.0**	**65.7**	**28.0**
Regional groups										
Africa	−16.6	−6.2	−6.2	−18.6	−15.9	4.8	−2.2	−5.9	−3.8	−8.1
Developing Asia	−43.3	−39.3	8.1	47.8	46.8	43.6	35.6	65.4	42.4	34.9
Excluding China and India	−39.4	−40.5	−25.9	23.2	34.3	28.2	19.0	25.2	19.7	14.5
Middle East and Turkey	0.4	10.8	9.4	−22.1	15.0	65.3	45.0	29.3	40.6	22.2
Western Hemisphere	−37.6	−39.2	−66.8	−89.7	−55.6	−46.0	−52.5	−14.9	−13.5	−21.0
Analytical groups										
By source of export earnings										
Fuel	2.3	30.3	24.1	−26.5	18.7	106.2	54.0	40.0	63.7	40.2
Nonfuel	−99.3	−103.6	−78.8	−55.0	−26.8	−36.5	−25.9	36.8	5.5	−8.0
of which, primary products	−3.2	−5.4	−8.3	−8.6	−3.8	−4.2	−5.5	−4.2	−4.6	−5.1
By external financing source										
Net debtor countries	−104.6	−109.6	−114.9	−92.6	−48.5	−48.0	−42.3	−1.1	−14.7	−28.3
of which, official financing	−20.9	−18.5	−13.7	−10.6	−3.5	9.7	3.0	0.4	−1.5	−5.6
Net debtor countries by debt-servicing experience										
Countries with arrears and/or rescheduling during 1997–2001	−44.3	−43.7	−47.3	−51.1	−35.2	−17.5	−23.9	−9.5	−8.2	−16.4
Countries in transition	**−4.6**	**−11.6**	**−25.3**	**−29.5**	**−2.4**	**25.1**	**12.8**	**9.9**	**10.0**	**−2.9**
Central and eastern Europe	−5.0	−14.1	−16.4	−19.8	−23.0	−21.2	−19.8	−22.1	−26.0	−27.6
Commonwealth of Independent States and Mongolia	0.4	2.5	−8.9	−9.7	20.6	46.3	32.6	32.0	36.0	24.7
Russia	4.4	8.3	−2.6	−2.1	22.2	44.6	33.4	30.9	36.1	26.3
Excluding Russia	−4.0	−5.8	−6.3	−7.6	−1.6	1.7	−0.8	1.1	−0.1	−1.7
Total[1]	**−52.4**	**−51.7**	**7.8**	**−71.6**	**−106.8**	**−141.6**	**−152.2**	**−102.8**	**−169.5**	**−199.5**
In percent of total world current account transactions	−0.4	−0.4	0.1	−0.5	−0.8	−0.9	−1.0	−0.6	−0.9	−1.0
In percent of world GDP	−0.2	−0.2	—	−0.2	−0.3	−0.5	−0.5	−0.3	−0.5	−0.5
Memorandum										
European Union	46.9	77.4	106.3	62.6	10.7	−45.6	6.5	62.1	67.5	69.9
Emerging market countries, excluding Asian countries in surplus[2]	−79.6	−70.0	−104.5	−168.9	−60.1	48.3	6.4	29.4	38.9	−9.5

[1]Reflects errors, omissions, and asymmetries in balance of payments statistics on current account, as well as the exclusion of data for international organizations and a limited number of countries. Calculated as the sum of the balance of individual euro area countries. See "Classification of Countries" in the introduction to this Statistical Appendix.
[2]All developing and transition countries excluding China, Hong Kong SAR, Korea, Malaysia, the Philippines, Singapore, Taiwan Province of China, and Thailand.

Table 28. Advanced Economies: Balance of Payments on Current Account

	1995	1996	1997	1998	1999	2000	2001	2002	2003	2004
					Billions of U.S. dollars					
Advanced economies	**49.4**	**33.7**	**88.7**	**40.6**	**−94.8**	**−234.5**	**−190.9**	**−186.6**	**−245.2**	**−224.6**
United States	−105.8	−117.8	−128.4	−203.8	−292.9	−410.3	−393.7	−480.9	−553.3	−537.3
Euro area[1]	50.9	78.1	98.2	62.5	29.0	−28.7	11.8	61.2	62.4	65.7
Germany	−27.0	−13.8	−9.1	−12.3	−23.7	−26.3	0.9	46.1	57.0	51.3
France	10.9	20.5	39.5	38.6	42.0	18.0	23.0	25.9	21.4	28.2
Italy	25.1	40.0	32.4	20.0	8.1	−5.8	−0.7	−6.7	−16.0	−12.9
Spain	0.2	0.4	2.5	−2.9	−14.0	−19.4	−16.4	−15.7	−22.3	−23.2
Netherlands	25.8	21.4	25.1	13.0	15.7	7.7	8.1	5.3	19.2	17.4
Belgium	15.4	13.8	13.8	13.3	12.8	9.4	9.2	11.6	11.9	13.5
Austria	−6.1	−5.4	−6.5	−5.2	−6.8	−4.9	−4.2	1.5	0.4	−0.4
Finland	5.3	5.1	6.8	7.3	7.8	9.2	8.6	9.0	9.7	9.4
Greece	−2.9	−4.6	−4.8	−3.6	−5.1	−7.7	−7.2	−8.2	−11.3	−11.9
Portugal	−0.1	−4.1	−6.1	−7.9	−9.8	−11.1	−10.5	−8.9	−7.2	−6.5
Ireland	1.9	2.4	2.5	0.7	0.2	−0.4	−0.7	−0.9	−2.6	−1.8
Luxembourg	2.4	2.2	2.0	1.7	1.8	2.7	1.8	2.1	2.4	2.5
Japan	111.4	65.7	96.6	119.1	114.5	119.6	87.8	112.7	121.1	120.1
United Kingdom	−14.2	−13.6	−2.8	−8.0	−31.8	−29.0	−18.0	−14.4	−17.1	−16.1
Canada	−4.4	3.4	−8.2	−7.7	1.7	20.7	17.3	14.9	13.6	14.8
Korea	−8.5	−23.0	−8.2	40.4	24.5	12.2	8.2	6.1	8.2	10.1
Australia	−19.3	−15.8	−12.7	−18.0	−22.3	−15.0	−8.6	−17.6	−25.7	−25.7
Taiwan Province of China	5.5	10.9	7.1	3.4	8.4	8.9	17.9	25.7	24.4	25.9
Sweden	8.4	9.6	10.3	9.7	10.6	9.5	8.5	10.7	13.2	11.1
Switzerland	21.1	22.0	25.5	26.2	30.6	30.9	22.5	32.9	32.8	33.7
Hong Kong SAR	−9.1	−4.0	−5.3	4.4	12.0	9.1	12.3	17.5	22.1	22.9
Denmark	1.8	3.2	0.7	−1.5	2.9	2.5	4.2	4.6	8.9	9.2
Norway	5.2	11.0	10.0	0.1	8.5	26.0	26.5	25.1	27.0	23.8
Israel	−5.2	−5.4	−4.0	−1.3	−1.5	−0.7	−1.8	−1.2	−0.8	−0.9
Singapore	14.8	14.0	14.9	18.5	15.2	13.3	16.1	18.7	21.3	22.1
New Zealand	−3.1	−3.9	−4.3	−2.2	−3.5	−2.5	−1.3	−2.2	−2.7	−3.2
Cyprus	−0.2	−0.5	−0.3	−0.6	−0.2	−0.4	−0.4	−0.6	−0.6	−0.6
Iceland	0.1	−0.1	−0.1	−0.6	−0.6	−0.9	−0.3	—	−0.1	−0.2
Memorandum										
Major advanced economies	−4.1	−15.6	19.9	−54.2	−182.0	−313.2	−283.3	−302.4	−373.2	−351.8
European Union[2]	...	...	108.2	63.4	−3.2	−62.2	−19.0	44.9	46.8	49.3
Euro area[2]	...	...	64.3	29.7	−25.3	−60.9	−17.3	56.4	56.2	60.0
Newly industrialized Asian economies	2.7	−2.1	8.5	66.8	60.1	43.5	54.6	68.0	76.0	81.0

Table 28 *(concluded)*

	1995	1996	1997	1998	1999	2000	2001	2002	2003	2004
					Percent of GDP					
Advanced economies	**0.2**	**0.1**	**0.4**	**0.2**	**−0.4**	**−0.9**	**−0.8**	**−0.7**	**−0.9**	**−0.8**
United States	−1.4	−1.5	−1.5	−2.3	−3.2	−4.2	−3.9	−4.6	−5.1	−4.7
Euro area[1]	0.7	1.1	1.5	0.9	0.4	−0.5	0.2	0.9	0.8	0.8
Germany	−1.1	−0.6	−0.4	−0.6	−1.1	−1.4	—	2.3	2.4	2.1
France	0.7	1.3	2.8	2.7	2.9	1.4	1.7	1.8	1.2	1.6
Italy	2.3	3.2	2.8	1.7	0.7	−0.5	−0.1	−0.6	−1.1	−0.9
Spain	—	0.1	0.5	−0.5	−2.3	−3.4	−2.8	−2.4	−2.7	−2.7
Netherlands	6.2	5.2	6.6	3.3	3.9	2.1	2.1	1.3	3.8	3.3
Belgium	5.6	5.1	5.6	5.3	5.1	4.1	4.0	4.7	4.0	4.4
Austria	−2.6	−2.3	−3.2	−2.5	−3.2	−2.6	−2.2	0.7	0.1	−0.2
Finland	4.1	4.0	5.6	5.6	6.0	7.6	7.1	6.9	6.1	5.8
Greece	−2.4	−3.7	−4.0	−3.0	−4.0	−6.8	−6.2	−6.1	−6.6	−6.6
Portugal	−0.1	−3.6	−5.7	−7.0	−8.5	−10.4	−9.6	−7.3	−4.9	−4.2
Ireland	2.8	3.3	3.1	0.8	0.3	−0.4	−0.7	−0.7	−1.7	−1.1
Luxembourg	13.4	12.1	11.3	8.8	8.9	14.0	9.3	10.4	10.0	9.8
Japan	2.1	1.4	2.2	3.0	2.6	2.5	2.1	2.8	2.9	2.9
United Kingdom	−1.3	−1.1	−0.2	−0.6	−2.2	−2.0	−1.3	−0.9	−1.0	−0.9
Canada	−0.8	0.5	−1.3	−1.2	0.3	2.9	2.4	2.0	1.6	1.6
Korea	−1.7	−4.4	−1.7	12.7	6.0	2.7	1.9	1.3	1.6	1.8
Australia	−5.3	−3.9	−3.1	−4.9	−5.7	−4.0	−2.4	−4.4	−5.2	−4.8
Taiwan Province of China	2.1	3.9	2.4	1.3	2.9	2.9	6.4	9.1	8.5	8.8
Sweden	3.4	3.6	4.2	3.9	4.2	4.0	3.9	4.5	4.5	3.6
Switzerland	6.8	7.4	9.9	10.0	11.8	12.9	9.1	12.3	10.5	10.5
Hong Kong SAR	−6.4	−2.6	−3.1	2.7	7.5	5.5	7.5	10.8	13.9	14.3
Denmark	1.0	1.8	0.4	−0.9	1.7	1.6	2.6	2.7	4.2	4.2
Norway	3.5	6.9	6.3	—	5.4	15.6	15.6	13.2	12.5	11.4
Israel	−5.7	−5.5	−3.9	−1.3	−1.5	−0.6	−1.6	−1.2	−0.7	−0.8
Singapore	17.6	15.2	15.6	22.6	18.7	14.5	19.0	21.5	23.7	23.0
New Zealand	−5.2	−5.9	−6.5	−4.0	−6.3	−4.8	−2.6	−3.7	−3.7	−4.1
Cyprus	−1.8	−5.2	−4.0	−6.7	−1.7	−4.0	−4.3	−5.6	−4.9	−4.7
Iceland	0.8	−1.8	−1.8	−7.0	−7.0	−10.2	−4.0	−0.1	−0.9	−2.1
Memorandum										
Major advanced economies	—	−0.1	0.1	−0.3	−0.9	−1.5	−1.4	−1.4	−1.6	−1.5
European Union[2]	...	...	1.3	0.7	—	−0.8	−0.2	0.5	0.5	0.5
Euro area[2]	...	...	1.0	0.4	−0.4	−1.0	−0.3	0.8	0.7	0.7
Newly industrialized Asian economies	0.3	−0.2	0.8	8.0	6.4	4.2	5.7	6.8	7.2	7.3

[1]Calculated as the sum of the balances of individual euro area countries.
[2]Corrected for reporting discrepancies in intra-area transactions.

Table 29. Advanced Economies: Current Account Transactions
(Billions of U.S. dollars)

	1995	1996	1997	1998	1999	2000	2001	2002	2003	2004
Exports	3,975.4	4,092.9	4,205.4	4,174.8	4,283.1	4,661.6	4,437.4	4,558.6	5,184.2	5,510.6
Imports	3,880.2	4,030.1	4,131.2	4,113.9	4,359.4	4,890.2	4,628.6	4,737.0	5,420.6	5,731.6
Trade balance	95.2	62.7	74.2	60.9	−76.3	−228.6	−191.1	−178.4	−236.4	−221.0
Services, credits	1,010.9	1,073.9	1,105.7	1,128.8	1,175.3	1,239.5	1,237.6	1,311.4	1,494.8	1,585.2
Services, debits	955.7	1,003.8	1,017.7	1,055.1	1,106.4	1,167.5	1,171.2	1,228.0	1,386.6	1,459.3
Balance on services	55.2	70.0	88.0	73.7	68.9	72.0	66.4	83.4	108.2	125.9
Balance on goods and services	150.4	132.8	162.2	134.6	−7.4	−156.6	−124.7	−95.0	−128.2	−95.1
Income, net	−19.2	−7.2	12.8	−2.5	15.0	22.8	−57.5	−101.6	−115.7	−121.3
Current transfers, net	−81.8	−91.9	−86.3	−91.6	−102.4	−100.7	−8.7	10.0	−1.3	−8.2
Current account balance	**49.4**	**33.7**	**88.7**	**40.6**	**−94.8**	**−234.5**	**−190.9**	**−186.6**	**−245.2**	**−224.6**
Balance on goods and services										
Advanced economies	**150.4**	**132.8**	**162.2**	**134.6**	**−7.4**	**−156.6**	**−124.7**	**−95.0**	**−128.2**	**−95.1**
United States	−96.4	−101.8	−107.8	−166.9	−262.2	−378.7	−357.8	−418.0	−488.6	−478.1
Euro area[1]	123.3	151.5	157.8	143.9	96.6	41.8	97.0	162.2	171.6	178.2
Germany	11.6	18.9	22.8	25.6	12.0	2.1	34.8	77.5	91.8	84.5
France	28.9	31.2	45.8	42.3	36.3	16.5	21.4	27.2	23.1	30.0
Italy	45.3	62.2	47.6	39.8	24.5	10.5	15.5	13.2	10.0	11.9
Japan	74.7	21.2	47.3	73.2	69.2	69.0	26.5	51.8	59.3	59.2
United Kingdom	−5.6	−6.4	0.3	−15.2	−27.9	−32.3	−42.1	−48.2	−44.3	−34.2
Canada	18.4	24.4	12.1	11.8	23.8	41.3	40.4	31.6	34.0	38.0
Other advanced economies	73.4	83.1	93.9	124.1	117.0	114.9	136.8	169.9	186.5	193.7
Memorandum										
Major advanced economies	77.0	49.7	68.2	10.6	−124.5	−271.5	−261.5	−264.9	−314.7	−288.8
European Union	142.4	172.2	182.9	147.2	91.7	31.5	76.5	138.3	157.8	173.0
Newly industrialized Asian economies	1.2	−1.7	6.9	65.1	59.1	43.5	49.8	63.8	74.9	80.6
Income, net										
Advanced economies	**−19.2**	**−7.2**	**12.8**	**−2.5**	**15.0**	**22.8**	**−57.5**	**−101.6**	**−115.7**	**−121.3**
United States	24.6	24.1	20.2	7.6	18.1	21.8	−82.5	−121.7	−125.3	−117.9
Euro area[1]	−28.4	−27.0	−19.5	−33.1	−22.2	−24.7	−37.8	−54.1	−51.3	−51.4
Germany	0.1	1.2	−1.5	−7.6	−9.0	−2.2	−9.3	−6.3	−6.9	−4.5
France	−9.0	−2.7	2.6	8.7	19.0	15.5	16.5	12.8	13.9	12.6
Italy	−15.6	−15.0	−11.2	−12.3	−11.1	−12.0	−10.3	−14.6	−18.5	−16.7
Japan	44.4	53.5	58.1	54.7	57.4	60.4	69.2	65.8	69.7	69.8
United Kingdom	−20.6	−16.2	−12.6	−6.4	−14.7	−11.9	14.6	19.9	11.0	2.0
Canada	−22.7	−21.6	−20.9	−20.0	−22.6	−21.4	−24.1	−17.5	−20.6	−23.3
Other advanced economies	−20.4	−30.6	−21.9	−27.1	−22.2	−27.3	−31.4	−40.1	−39.0	−43.3
Memorandum										
Major advanced economies	1.2	23.4	34.7	24.7	37.2	50.1	−26.1	−61.5	−76.7	−78.0
European Union	−59.5	−53.9	−42.2	−45.8	−40.8	−40.9	−26.6	−37.8	−43.6	−52.7
Newly industrialized Asian economies	5.1	3.2	5.9	2.5	3.9	4.8	10.7	10.8	7.8	7.3

[1]Calculated as the sum of the of individual euro area countries.

Table 30. Developing Countries: Payments Balances on Current Account

	1995	1996	1997	1998	1999	2000	2001	2002	2003	2004
					Billions of U.S. dollars					
Developing countries	**−97.2**	**−73.8**	**−55.6**	**−82.6**	**−9.6**	**67.8**	**25.9**	**74.0**	**65.7**	**28.0**
Regional groups										
Africa	−16.6	−6.2	−6.2	−18.6	−15.9	4.8	−2.2	−5.9	−3.8	−8.1
Sub-Sahara	−12.4	−7.0	−9.0	−16.9	−15.3	−3.0	−10.0	−10.5	−11.5	−12.7
Excluding Nigeria and South Africa	−8.6	−7.5	−9.5	−12.7	−11.5	−6.7	−10.8	−7.8	−10.0	−10.2
Developing Asia	−43.3	−39.3	8.1	47.8	46.8	43.6	35.6	65.4	42.4	34.9
China	1.6	7.2	37.0	31.5	15.7	20.5	17.4	35.4	19.4	18.8
India	−5.6	−6.0	−3.0	−6.9	−3.2	−5.1	−0.8	4.8	3.2	1.6
Other developing Asia	−39.4	−40.5	−25.9	23.2	34.3	28.2	19.0	25.2	19.7	14.5
Middle East and Turkey	0.4	10.8	9.4	−22.1	15.0	65.3	45.0	29.3	40.6	22.2
Western Hemisphere	−37.6	−39.2	−66.8	−89.7	−55.6	−46.0	−52.5	−14.9	−13.5	−21.0
Analytical groups										
By source of export earnings										
Fuel	2.3	30.3	24.1	−26.5	18.7	106.2	54.0	40.0	63.7	40.2
Nonfuel	−99.3	−103.6	−78.8	−55.0	−26.8	−36.5	−25.9	36.8	5.5	−8.0
of which, primary products	−3.2	−5.4	−8.3	−8.6	−3.8	−4.2	−5.5	−4.2	−4.6	−5.1
By external financing source										
Net debtor countries	−104.6	−109.6	−114.9	−92.6	−48.5	−48.0	−42.3	−1.1	−14.7	−28.3
of which, official financing	−20.9	−18.5	−13.7	−10.6	−3.5	9.7	3.0	0.4	−1.5	−5.6
Net debtor countries by debt-servicing experience										
Countries with arrears and/or rescheduling during 1997–2001	−44.3	−43.7	−47.3	−51.1	−35.2	−17.5	−23.9	−9.5	−8.2	−16.4
Other groups										
Heavily indebted poor countries	−12.5	−12.9	−13.9	−14.7	−12.8	−7.8	−11.4	−9.7	−12.7	−13.2
Middle East and north Africa	−4.7	12.6	12.9	−27.4	14.1	81.4	47.2	33.9	53.9	30.1

Table 30 *(concluded)*

| | Ten-Year Averages | | 1995 | 1996 | 1997 | 1998 | 1999 | 2000 | 2001 | 2002 | 2003 | 2004 |
	1985–94	1995–2004										
	Percent of exports of goods and services											
Developing countries	**−9.8**	**1.5**	**−9.4**	**−6.4**	**−4.4**	**−7.1**	**−0.8**	**4.4**	**1.7**	**4.6**	**3.6**	**1.5**
Regional groups												
Africa	−11.2	−4.5	−14.0	−4.7	−4.6	−15.5	−12.4	3.1	−1.5	−3.8	−2.1	−4.5
Sub-Sahara	−10.6	−9.7	−13.7	−7.0	−8.7	−18.7	−16.0	−2.6	−9.3	−9.4	−9.0	−9.7
Excluding Nigeria and South Africa	−17.8	−14.9	−19.4	−15.5	−19.2	−28.1	−24.0	−12.6	−21.0	−13.8	−15.5	−14.9
Developing Asia	−5.3	3.6	−9.5	−7.8	1.4	8.9	8.1	6.2	5.1	8.3	4.8	3.6
China	6.4	3.9	1.1	4.2	17.8	15.2	7.2	7.3	5.8	9.7	4.6	3.9
India	−5.3	1.7	−14.6	−14.7	−6.7	−15.1	−6.3	−8.3	−1.2	6.5	3.7	1.7
Other developing Asia	−11.6	3.6	−14.6	−13.9	−8.3	8.1	11.2	7.9	5.8	7.2	5.3	3.6
Middle East and Turkey	−1.2	6.0	0.2	4.4	3.6	−10.1	6.0	19.4	14.2	8.9	10.9	6.0
Western Hemisphere	−25.2	−5.4	−15.3	−14.3	−22.2	−30.7	−18.4	−12.8	−15.2	−4.3	−3.7	−5.4
Analytical groups												
By source of export earnings												
Fuel	−1.4	11.5	1.1	12.7	9.8	−14.5	8.0	30.5	17.3	12.4	17.5	11.5
Nonfuel	−12.0	−0.5	−3.6	−2.7	1.2	3.8	3.1	1.9	1.1	3.3	1.7	1.1
of which, primary products	−9.4	−8.6	−6.9	−11.2	−16.6	−18.2	−8.0	−8.6	−11.6	−8.6	−8.4	−8.6
By external financing source												
Net debtor countries	−15.5	−2.5	−14.7	−14.1	−13.6	−11.5	−5.7	−4.9	−4.4	−0.1	−1.4	−2.5
of which, official financing	−13.4	−2.8	−16.2	−13.1	−8.8	−7.7	−2.5	5.4	1.8	0.2	−0.8	−2.8
Net debtor countries by debt-servicing experience												
Countries with arrears and/or rescheduling during 1997–2001	−10.5	−4.9	−22.3	−20.1	−19.7	−22.8	−15.0	−6.1	−8.5	−3.3	−2.6	−4.9
Other groups												
Heavily indebted poor countries	−28.8	−15.2	−28.4	−25.8	−26.7	−28.8	−23.5	−12.2	−18.1	−14.0	−15.9	−15.2
Middle East and north Africa	−6.2	8.6	−2.3	5.5	5.4	−14.5	6.1	25.2	15.5	10.8	15.1	8.6
Memorandum												
Median												
Developing countries	−14.0	−10.3	−13.2	−14.1	−12.4	−14.9	−11.4	−11.3	−11.3	−8.9	−9.8	−10.3

Table 31. Developing Countries—by Region: Current Account Transactions
(Billions of U.S. dollars)

	1995	1996	1997	1998	1999	2000	2001	2002	2003	2004
Developing countries										
Exports	861.7	964.3	1,043.5	960.7	1,054.8	1,325.3	1,276.3	1,379.3	1,549.4	1,638.5
Imports	864.6	947.0	1,008.3	953.7	963.0	1,152.6	1,143.6	1,216.5	1,380.3	1,504.1
Trade balance	−2.9	17.3	35.2	7.0	91.8	172.7	132.8	162.7	169.0	134.4
Services, net	−56.3	−56.2	−62.3	−53.8	−53.4	−57.9	−60.0	−56.6	−66.4	−66.8
Balance on goods and services	−59.2	−38.9	−27.0	−46.8	38.3	114.9	72.8	106.1	102.6	67.6
Income, net	−71.0	−72.7	−73.4	−76.4	−92.1	−94.2	−98.7	−97.7	−108.8	−108.3
Current transfers, net	32.9	37.8	44.9	40.6	44.1	47.1	51.8	65.6	71.9	68.8
Current account balance	**−97.2**	**−73.8**	**−55.6**	**−82.6**	**−9.6**	**67.8**	**25.9**	**74.0**	**65.7**	**28.0**
Memorandum										
Exports of goods and services	1,033.1	1,157.8	1,260.4	1,169.1	1,257.8	1,551.3	1,505.9	1,620.1	1,803.9	1,916.1
Interest payments	98.8	104.0	105.5	112.6	116.8	120.1	114.5	105.3	106.5	108.7
Oil trade balance	126.9	157.9	149.7	98.1	144.3	229.2	189.0	189.8	213.5	193.7
Regional groups										
Africa										
Exports	99.4	110.4	114.1	98.6	106.3	135.5	126.0	130.5	152.9	155.1
Imports	98.3	99.1	103.2	100.7	101.9	107.2	110.1	117.1	134.4	141.4
Trade balance	1.1	11.2	10.9	−2.1	4.4	28.3	15.9	13.4	18.5	13.7
Services, net	−11.6	−10.3	−10.4	−11.5	−11.5	−11.8	−12.6	−16.1	−17.8	−16.9
Balance on goods and services	−10.6	0.9	0.5	−13.6	−7.1	16.5	3.3	−2.6	0.6	−3.2
Income, net	−16.5	−18.0	−17.5	−16.4	−19.1	−23.6	−19.4	−18.6	−22.4	−22.9
Current transfers, net	10.5	10.9	10.8	11.4	10.3	12.0	13.9	15.3	18.0	18.0
Current account balance	**−16.6**	**−6.2**	**−6.2**	**−18.6**	**−15.9**	**4.8**	**−2.2**	**−5.9**	**−3.8**	**−8.1**
Memorandum										
Exports of goods and services	118.4	131.1	135.3	119.8	127.8	156.6	148.1	153.0	177.3	181.1
Interest payments	15.6	16.1	15.7	15.7	15.7	14.8	13.3	12.3	12.6	12.3
Oil trade balance	21.3	29.4	28.9	18.6	25.8	47.3	40.0	36.8	51.5	48.5
Developing Asia										
Exports	378.4	416.5	467.1	456.4	495.2	605.4	594.7	676.8	772.2	846.0
Imports	404.9	446.6	451.2	389.6	424.7	543.4	539.2	609.6	721.1	798.1
Trade balance	−26.5	−30.2	15.9	66.8	70.5	62.1	55.5	67.2	51.1	47.9
Services, net	−11.8	−6.9	−11.3	−12.5	−10.6	−10.3	−10.3	−5.6	−12.0	−11.4
Balance on goods and services	−38.3	−37.0	4.6	54.3	59.9	51.8	45.2	61.6	39.1	36.4
Income, net	−23.4	−24.7	−24.4	−28.0	−37.8	−35.4	−38.1	−33.7	−36.4	−37.6
Current transfers, net	18.4	22.4	27.9	21.4	24.8	27.2	28.5	37.5	39.7	36.1
Current account balance	**−43.3**	**−39.3**	**8.1**	**47.8**	**46.8**	**43.6**	**35.6**	**65.4**	**42.4**	**34.9**
Memorandum										
Exports of goods and services	455.2	505.2	565.3	539.2	577.8	699.5	694.8	789.1	889.1	977.7
Interest payments	27.4	30.5	27.9	32.0	33.5	33.1	30.2	28.4	29.2	30.3
Oil trade balance	−11.8	−18.1	−20.9	−12.5	−19.8	−37.9	−34.5	−37.5	−50.0	−50.5

Table 31 *(concluded)*

	1995	1996	1997	1998	1999	2000	2001	2002	2003	2004
Middle East and Turkey										
Exports	179.8	210.3	212.9	165.6	203.5	285.4	268.0	281.5	319.1	313.5
Imports	155.9	172.7	183.9	181.0	172.9	199.6	196.7	217.1	240.7	256.5
Trade balance	24.0	37.6	29.0	−15.4	30.6	85.8	71.2	64.4	78.4	56.9
Services, net	−24.3	−28.6	−25.4	−14.2	−20.7	−24.7	−23.9	−26.4	−27.9	−27.8
Balance on goods and services	−0.4	9.0	3.6	−29.6	9.9	61.0	47.3	38.0	50.5	29.2
Income, net	13.0	12.9	15.7	17.8	16.6	18.2	13.7	7.2	6.3	9.5
Current transfers, net	−12.3	−11.1	−10.0	−10.3	−11.5	−13.9	−16.1	−15.9	−16.2	−16.5
Current account balance	**0.4**	**10.8**	**9.4**	**−22.1**	**15.0**	**65.3**	**45.0**	**29.3**	**40.6**	**22.2**
Memorandum										
Exports of goods and services	213.8	247.2	259.4	217.4	249.5	336.5	317.1	331.4	373.0	370.9
Interest payments	10.7	11.1	11.9	12.2	12.1	13.3	13.5	12.3	14.2	15.3
Oil trade balance	98.3	121.2	117.4	76.7	114.4	180.2	153.8	157.8	180.2	165.2
Western Hemisphere										
Exports	204.1	227.1	249.4	240.1	249.8	299.0	287.7	290.4	305.1	323.8
Imports	205.5	228.5	269.9	282.4	263.5	302.4	297.5	272.8	284.1	308.0
Trade balance	−1.5	−1.4	−20.6	−42.3	−13.8	−3.4	−9.8	17.6	21.0	15.8
Services, net	−8.4	−10.4	−15.2	−15.6	−10.6	−11.1	−13.2	−8.5	−8.6	−10.7
Balance on goods and services	−9.9	−11.9	−35.7	−57.9	−24.3	−14.5	−23.0	9.1	12.4	5.1
Income, net	−44.1	−43.0	−47.2	−49.9	−51.8	−53.4	−54.9	−52.5	−56.3	−57.3
Current transfers, net	16.4	15.7	16.1	18.0	20.5	21.9	25.4	28.5	30.4	31.2
Current account balance	**−37.6**	**−39.2**	**−66.8**	**−89.7**	**−55.6**	**−46.0**	**−52.5**	**−14.9**	**−13.5**	**−21.0**
Memorandum										
Exports of goods and services	245.8	274.3	300.4	292.7	302.7	358.6	345.9	346.6	364.6	386.4
Interest payments	45.1	46.4	50.0	52.7	55.5	58.8	57.6	52.3	50.5	50.8
Oil trade balance	19.1	25.4	24.3	15.3	23.9	39.5	29.7	32.7	31.8	30.4

Table 32. Developing Countries—by Analytical Criteria: Current Account Transactions
(Billions of U.S. dollars)

	1995	1996	1997	1998	1999	2000	2001	2002	2003	2004
By source of export earnings										
Fuel										
Exports	187.7	226.3	230.1	167.5	218.0	331.7	294.1	301.4	338.9	325.6
Imports	125.1	129.2	140.1	138.7	138.4	153.0	169.2	180.8	193.2	206.0
Trade balance	62.6	97.1	90.0	28.8	79.6	178.7	124.9	120.6	145.7	119.6
Services, net	−43.3	−50.4	−51.9	−42.4	−43.1	−50.5	−48.2	−50.4	−49.9	−51.3
Balance on goods and services	19.3	46.7	38.1	−13.7	36.5	128.2	76.7	70.1	95.8	68.3
Income, net	4.8	3.6	5.5	8.4	5.3	3.4	2.9	−5.0	−7.5	−3.1
Current transfers, net	−21.8	−20.0	−19.5	−21.2	−23.1	−25.4	−25.6	−25.1	−24.5	−25.0
Current account balance	**2.3**	**30.3**	**24.1**	**−26.5**	**18.7**	**106.2**	**54.0**	**40.0**	**63.7**	**40.2**
Memorandum										
Exports of goods and services	199.3	238.1	244.9	182.9	233.4	348.0	312.0	323.0	363.3	350.4
Interest payments	13.8	13.9	15.5	15.5	14.4	15.0	13.6	13.2	13.1	13.3
Oil trade balance	140.0	177.3	174.2	116.3	165.8	266.5	224.6	228.5	261.8	244.8
Nonfuel exports										
Exports	673.2	737.1	812.5	792.2	835.6	992.4	980.8	1,076.4	1,208.8	1,310.9
Imports	738.2	816.5	866.7	813.3	822.8	997.6	972.2	1,033.4	1,184.6	1,295.3
Trade balance	−65.0	−79.3	−54.2	−21.2	12.8	−5.3	8.6	42.9	24.1	15.7
Services, net	−13.0	−5.7	−10.4	−11.3	−10.3	−7.4	−11.8	−6.2	−16.4	−15.4
Balance on goods and services	−78.0	−85.1	−64.6	−32.5	2.5	−12.7	−3.2	36.7	7.7	0.2
Income, net	−75.7	−76.3	−78.9	−84.8	−97.5	−97.5	−101.5	−92.4	−100.7	−104.3
Current transfers, net	54.4	57.8	64.7	62.3	68.1	73.7	78.8	92.4	98.5	96.2
Current account balance	**−99.3**	**−103.6**	**−78.8**	**−55.0**	**−26.8**	**−36.5**	**−25.9**	**36.8**	**5.5**	**−8.0**
Memorandum										
Exports of goods and services	833.0	918.8	1,014.5	985.1	1,023.2	1,201.9	1,192.4	1,295.5	1,438.9	1,563.7
Interest payments	85.0	90.0	90.0	97.1	102.3	105.1	100.9	92.1	93.4	95.4
Oil trade balance	−13.0	−19.3	−24.3	−18.0	−21.3	−37.0	−35.4	−38.4	−48.0	−50.8
Nonfuel primary products										
Exports	38.9	40.5	42.0	38.5	39.4	41.1	39.2	40.7	45.3	50.1
Imports	36.1	40.7	44.2	42.4	37.9	40.1	39.7	40.2	44.9	48.1
Trade balance	2.8	−0.2	−2.2	−3.9	1.5	1.0	−0.5	0.5	0.4	2.0
Services, net	−5.3	−3.9	−4.1	−4.4	−4.3	−4.1	−4.2	−5.0	−5.6	−6.1
Balance on goods and services	−2.4	−4.1	−6.3	−8.3	−2.7	−3.1	−4.7	−4.6	−5.2	−4.1
Income, net	−5.6	−6.3	−6.3	−5.0	−5.7	−6.3	−6.3	−5.6	−6.3	−7.7
Current transfers, net	4.8	5.0	4.3	4.7	4.6	5.1	5.5	6.0	6.9	6.6
Current account balance	**−3.2**	**−5.4**	**−8.3**	**−8.6**	**−3.8**	**−4.2**	**−5.5**	**−4.2**	**−4.6**	**−5.1**
Memorandum										
Exports of goods and services	46.2	48.4	50.3	47.0	47.7	49.3	47.8	49.2	54.6	60.0
Interest payments	4.6	4.8	4.7	4.7	4.8	5.2	4.9	4.5	4.2	4.6
Oil trade balance	−2.0	−2.7	−3.0	−2.8	−3.2	−5.1	−4.8	−4.7	−5.2	−3.6

Table 32 *(continued)*

	1995	1996	1997	1998	1999	2000	2001	2002	2003	2004
By external financing source										
Net debtor countries										
Exports	567.1	616.0	662.5	634.0	679.3	806.8	772.5	810.2	890.1	941.7
Imports	643.6	702.2	750.5	694.7	690.8	815.1	778.0	793.6	878.5	945.4
Trade balance	−76.4	−86.2	−88.1	−60.8	−11.4	−8.3	−5.5	16.7	11.6	−3.7
Services, net	−13.1	−10.2	−13.8	−16.2	−10.7	−9.9	−15.1	−10.2	−17.6	−15.7
Balance on goods and services	−89.5	−96.3	−101.9	−77.0	−22.2	−18.2	−20.5	6.5	−6.0	−19.4
Income, net	−69.2	−69.9	−74.2	−73.9	−87.4	−94.6	−90.7	−86.7	−94.4	−95.9
Current transfers, net	54.1	56.6	61.2	58.2	61.1	64.7	68.9	79.2	85.8	87.0
Current account balance	**−104.6**	**−109.6**	**−114.9**	**−92.6**	**−48.5**	**−48.0**	**−42.3**	**−1.1**	**−14.7**	**−28.3**
Memorandum										
Exports of goods and services	709.3	779.0	841.8	804.6	844.7	987.9	952.6	992.0	1,080.7	1,147.8
Interest payments	81.5	85.7	90.1	95.0	98.4	101.2	95.3	85.9	86.8	88.0
Oil trade balance	8.7	10.6	10.7	7.8	20.0	34.3	29.1	25.6	29.6	25.4
Official financing										
Exports	107.1	118.5	129.7	115.8	123.2	159.0	145.7	150.6	167.8	173.2
Imports	115.1	123.9	129.0	113.3	112.3	131.8	130.2	138.8	157.0	165.3
Trade balance	−8.0	−5.5	0.7	2.5	10.8	27.2	15.5	11.7	10.8	7.9
Services, net	−14.9	−16.7	−18.2	−20.0	−12.9	−15.5	−16.2	−17.3	−19.2	−19.1
Balance on goods and services	−22.9	−22.2	−17.6	−17.5	−2.0	11.7	−0.7	−5.6	−8.5	−11.2
Income, net	−14.0	−13.2	−14.4	−11.9	−21.6	−23.9	−20.1	−21.4	−23.0	−23.9
Current transfers, net	16.0	16.8	18.2	18.8	20.1	21.9	23.8	27.5	30.0	29.5
Current account balance	**−20.9**	**−18.5**	**−13.7**	**−10.6**	**−3.5**	**9.7**	**3.0**	**0.4**	**−1.5**	**−5.6**
Memorandum										
Exports of goods and services	128.7	141.5	155.1	138.4	144.4	181.3	168.9	175.4	192.4	199.1
Interest payments	14.6	15.7	16.3	18.1	19.1	19.1	15.9	14.8	14.7	15.0
Oil trade balance	15.5	19.7	18.7	12.2	15.8	26.1	20.1	16.5	20.3	18.5
Net debtor countries by debt-servicing experience										
Countries with arrears and/or rescheduling during 1997–2001										
Exports	167.7	181.9	200.7	186.5	198.4	249.8	239.9	250.3	277.8	288.8
Imports	178.5	190.8	204.6	190.3	185.4	215.1	216.6	219.8	243.8	259.3
Trade balance	−10.7	−8.8	−3.9	−3.9	13.0	34.7	23.3	30.4	34.0	29.5
Services, net	−19.5	−24.8	−28.8	−30.3	−19.2	−21.5	−23.5	−23.2	−26.5	−26.8
Balance on goods and services	−30.2	−33.6	−32.7	−34.2	−6.2	13.2	−0.3	7.2	7.5	2.6
Income, net	−32.9	−29.0	−33.2	−34.8	−46.1	−48.9	−45.6	−43.7	−46.2	−48.6
Current transfers, net	18.7	18.9	18.6	17.9	17.1	18.2	22.0	27.0	30.4	29.6
Current account balance	**−44.3**	**−43.7**	**−47.3**	**−51.1**	**−35.2**	**−17.5**	**−23.9**	**−9.5**	**−8.2**	**−16.4**
Memorandum										
Exports of goods and services	199.3	217.2	240.1	224.1	234.3	289.4	281.0	292.7	321.6	334.9
Interest payments	30.4	33.1	34.5	38.7	40.9	41.1	37.9	33.9	34.3	34.6
Oil trade balance	12.3	15.3	17.6	15.1	25.0	40.6	36.6	37.1	40.7	41.4

Table 32 *(concluded)*

	1995	1996	1997	1998	1999	2000	2001	2002	2003	2004
Other groups										
Heavily indebted poor countries										
Exports	34.5	39.5	41.7	40.4	43.5	52.2	51.7	57.5	66.6	72.4
Imports	40.1	44.4	47.2	48.0	49.2	52.8	55.6	60.8	71.8	77.7
Trade balance	−5.6	−5.0	−5.4	−7.6	−5.7	−0.7	−3.9	−3.4	−5.2	−5.3
Services, net	−6.4	−6.9	−7.4	−7.8	−7.5	−7.9	−9.3	−10.4	−11.7	−11.1
Balance on goods and services	−12.0	−11.8	−12.8	−15.4	−13.2	−8.5	−13.2	−13.8	−16.9	−16.5
Income, net	−7.5	−8.8	−8.0	−7.2	−7.6	−8.4	−7.9	−6.8	−8.2	−9.0
Current transfers, net	7.0	7.7	7.0	7.9	8.0	9.2	9.6	10.8	12.4	12.3
Current account balance	**−12.5**	**−12.9**	**−13.9**	**−14.7**	**−12.8**	**−7.8**	**−11.4**	**−9.7**	**−12.7**	**−13.2**
Memorandum										
Exports of goods and services	44.1	49.8	52.0	51.2	54.3	63.3	63.2	69.6	79.9	86.8
Interest payments	6.4	7.0	6.6	7.1	6.4	6.5	5.7	5.0	5.3	5.1
Oil trade balance	3.2	4.2	4.3	2.6	4.8	8.9	7.0	9.0	10.1	11.2
Middle East and north Africa										
Exports	175.1	203.0	206.2	157.3	199.7	289.6	266.7	275.4	313.7	302.8
Imports	147.3	155.2	161.0	162.3	160.3	174.1	187.1	200.6	217.7	232.8
Trade balance	27.7	47.8	45.2	−5.0	39.4	115.5	79.7	74.7	96.0	70.0
Services, net	−27.9	−31.9	−32.7	−24.5	−24.6	−31.9	−27.5	−30.6	−29.7	−30.4
Balance on goods and services	−0.2	15.9	12.5	−29.4	14.8	83.5	52.2	44.2	66.3	39.6
Income, net	7.5	7.0	10.1	12.7	11.1	12.0	8.6	2.0	−0.5	2.8
Current transfers, net	−12.0	−10.4	−9.8	−10.7	−11.8	−14.1	−13.6	−12.2	−11.8	−12.3
Current account balance	**−4.7**	**12.6**	**12.9**	**−27.4**	**14.1**	**81.4**	**47.2**	**33.9**	**53.9**	**30.1**
Memorandum										
Exports of goods and services	200.5	230.4	236.5	188.5	232.1	323.1	303.9	314.3	356.9	348.2
Interest payments	−11.7	−12.0	−12.3	−12.1	−11.1	−11.5	−10.1	−9.1	−9.4	−10.0
Oil trade balance	110.7	137.0	133.9	90.0	129.1	206.3	175.7	180.4	209.2	192.8

Table 33. Summary of Balance of Payments, Capital Flows, and External Financing

(Billions of U.S. dollars)

	1995	1996	1997	1998	1999	2000	2001	2002	2003	2004
Developing countries										
Balance of payments[1]										
Balance on current account	−97.2	−73.8	−55.6	−82.6	−9.6	67.8	25.9	74.0	65.7	28.0
Balance on goods and services	−59.2	−38.9	−27.0	−46.8	38.3	114.9	72.8	106.1	102.6	67.6
Income, net	−71.0	−72.7	−73.4	−76.4	−92.1	−94.2	−98.7	−97.7	−108.8	−108.3
Current transfers, net	32.9	37.8	44.9	40.6	44.1	47.1	51.8	65.6	71.9	68.8
Balance on capital and financial account	122.5	111.4	109.4	112.9	48.2	−29.4	−1.1	−63.9	−70.3	−17.9
Balance on capital account[2]	5.5	6.7	14.4	6.2	8.5	8.0	8.7	5.8	7.2	7.0
Balance on financial account	117.0	104.7	95.0	106.7	39.7	−37.4	−9.8	−69.7	−77.5	−24.9
Direct investment, net	82.7	104.8	128.2	130.2	142.7	131.9	151.2	116.6	116.0	114.9
Portfolio investment, net	22.3	74.9	36.9	7.7	4.1	−17.5	−49.4	−26.4	−7.9	−2.8
Other investment, net	79.9	16.6	−5.3	−32.3	−75.3	−90.5	−29.3	−27.2	0.7	−38.9
Reserve assets	−68.0	−91.6	−64.8	1.1	−31.8	−61.3	−82.3	−132.7	−186.3	−98.0
Errors and omissions, net	−25.3	−37.5	−53.8	−30.3	−38.5	−38.4	−24.8	−10.1	4.6	−10.1
Capital flows										
Total capital flows, net[3]	185.0	196.3	159.8	105.7	71.5	23.9	72.5	63.0	108.8	73.1
Net official flows	35.0	−6.9	25.1	40.3	26.0	1.0	43.4	24.3	26.0	1.5
Net private flows[4]	149.9	203.1	134.7	65.3	45.5	22.9	29.1	38.7	82.8	71.6
Direct investment, net	82.7	104.8	128.2	130.2	142.7	131.9	151.2	116.6	116.0	114.9
Private portfolio investment, net	19.1	72.5	39.5	5.3	3.4	−14.2	−49.9	−32.8	−9.2	−5.4
Other private flows, net	48.2	25.8	−33.0	−70.2	−100.6	−94.8	−72.3	−45.2	−24.1	−37.8
External financing[5]										
Net external financing[6]	218.8	243.1	246.4	208.5	172.9	158.1	141.2	133.2	147.5	148.6
Nondebt-creating flows	107.0	141.8	169.0	138.5	156.1	154.1	151.8	113.1	122.0	124.9
Capital transfers[7]	5.5	6.7	14.4	6.2	8.5	8.0	8.7	5.8	7.2	7.0
Foreign direct investment and equity security liabilities[8]	101.5	135.1	154.6	132.3	147.6	146.1	143.1	107.3	114.8	117.9
Net external borrowing[9]	111.8	101.3	77.5	70.1	16.7	4.0	−10.6	20.1	25.5	23.7
Borrowing from official creditors[10]	32.8	−1.5	21.6	35.4	26.6	12.8	43.5	15.1	23.1	0.2
of which, credit and loans from IMF[11]	12.6	−2.9	0.8	8.5	1.3	−6.7	23.3	15.0	. . .	. . .
Borrowing from banks[12]	33.2	32.2	18.3	5.8	0.2	−8.4	−8.9	−11.0	5.8	9.1
Borrowing from other private creditors	45.8	70.6	37.6	28.9	−10.0	−0.4	−45.2	16.0	−3.4	14.4
Memorandum										
Balance on goods and services in percent of GDP[13]	−1.3	−0.8	−0.5	−0.9	0.8	2.1	1.3	2.0	1.7	1.1
Scheduled amortization of external debt	150.9	185.1	221.5	214.4	242.6	250.0	249.4	250.8	260.6	234.9
Gross external financing[14]	369.7	428.2	468.0	423.0	415.5	408.1	390.6	384.0	408.1	383.5
Gross external borrowing[15]	262.7	286.4	299.0	284.5	259.4	254.0	238.8	270.9	286.1	258.6
Exceptional external financing, net	22.5	21.4	18.1	20.9	17.9	13.8	14.9	31.6	27.5	17.6
Of which,										
Arrears on debt service	−2.5	−6.8	−7.5	1.1	6.7	−19.1	2.3	1.1	. . .	. . .
Debt forgiveness	2.3	9.6	17.5	1.3	1.9	2.3	3.1	4.8	. . .	. . .
Rescheduling of debt service	20.7	17.9	2.5	5.5	6.1	−2.5	7.2	11.9	. . .	. . .

Table 33 *(concluded)*

	1995	1996	1997	1998	1999	2000	2001	2002	2003	2004
Countries in transition										
Balance of payments[1]										
Balance on current account	−4.6	−11.6	−25.3	−29.5	−2.4	25.1	12.8	9.9	10.0	−2.9
Balance on goods and services	−5.6	−13.8	−21.3	−23.0	2.8	28.4	13.7	11.6	10.6	−2.9
Income, net	−1.5	−3.6	−9.9	−20.1	−13.2	−11.5	−10.1	−13.1	−13.1	−13.2
Current transfers, net	2.5	5.9	5.9	13.6	8.0	8.3	9.1	11.4	12.5	13.2
Balance on capital and financial account	9.8	18.4	31.8	38.0	9.6	−18.1	−6.9	−1.2	−0.4	12.4
Balance on capital account[2]	0.6	1.2	9.5	0.2	—	0.4	0.5	0.5	0.9	1.3
Balance on financial account	9.2	17.1	22.3	37.8	9.6	−18.5	−7.4	−1.6	−1.3	11.1
Direct investment, net	12.9	12.3	14.9	21.2	23.8	23.4	25.9	27.9	25.8	29.2
Portfolio investment, net	−6.4	0.6	20.7	12.1	−0.4	−2.5	−5.4	−6.5	−3.8	−1.1
Other investment, net	39.8	4.4	−3.2	6.2	−6.1	−15.7	−10.1	2.3	6.6	6.4
Reserve assets	−37.2	−0.2	−10.0	−1.7	−7.7	−23.7	−17.8	−25.4	−29.8	−23.5
Errors and omissions, net	−5.2	−6.8	−6.5	−8.5	−7.2	−7.0	−5.8	−8.7	−9.6	−9.5
Capital flows										
Total capital flows, net[3]	46.3	17.4	32.3	39.5	17.3	5.2	10.4	23.7	28.6	34.5
Net official flows	15.6	11.8	6.2	11.7	−0.4	−3.8	−5.6	−1.9	−2.7	−2.1
Net private flows[4]	30.7	5.6	26.1	27.8	17.7	9.0	16.0	25.6	31.2	36.7
Direct investment, net	12.9	12.3	14.9	21.2	23.8	23.4	25.9	27.9	25.8	29.2
Private portfolio investment, net	−6.4	0.5	20.7	12.1	−0.9	−3.4	−5.7	−6.7	−4.2	−1.4
Other private flows, net	24.2	−7.2	−9.4	−5.5	−5.2	−11.0	−4.2	4.4	9.6	8.9
External financing[5]										
Net external financing[6]	46.5	47.5	82.2	57.6	43.4	32.6	23.8	40.2	50.1	55.0
Nondebt-creating flows	15.5	14.7	29.0	22.8	23.8	24.6	26.0	28.4	26.4	30.3
Capital transfers[7]	0.6	1.2	9.5	0.2	—	0.4	0.5	0.5	0.9	1.3
Foreign direct investment and equity security liabilities[8]	14.9	13.5	19.5	22.7	23.8	24.1	25.5	28.0	25.5	29.0
Net external borrowing[9]	31.0	32.8	53.3	34.7	19.6	8.1	−2.2	11.8	23.7	24.7
Borrowing from official creditors[10]	16.3	9.5	4.5	10.6	−1.5	−5.4	−7.6	−2.6	−2.7	−2.1
of which, credit and loans from IMF[11]	4.6	3.6	2.5	5.5	−3.6	−4.1	−4.3	−2.1	...	...
Borrowing from banks[12]	0.1	10.7	16.1	1.7	−1.9	0.1	4.0	14.8	9.9	7.8
Borrowing from other private creditors	14.5	12.5	32.7	22.4	23.0	13.4	1.3	−0.4	16.4	19.1
Memorandum										
Balance on goods and services in percent of GDP[13]	−0.7	−1.6	−2.4	−2.9	0.4	3.8	1.6	1.2	0.9	−0.2
Scheduled amortization of external debt	20.1	23.3	32.0	33.0	35.8	36.5	42.6	47.4	55.0	52.5
Gross external financing[14]	66.6	70.8	114.2	90.6	79.1	69.2	66.4	87.6	105.0	107.5
Gross external borrowing[15]	51.1	56.1	85.2	67.8	55.3	44.6	40.4	59.2	78.7	77.2
Exceptional external financing, net	15.3	13.6	−20.8	7.8	7.6	5.8	1.5	1.6	0.3	0.1
Of which,										
Arrears on debt service	−0.1	1.1	−24.8	5.0	1.8	1.6	0.3	−0.9	...	...
Debt forgiveness	0.9	0.9	—	—	—	—	—	0.2	...	...
Rescheduling of debt service	13.9	9.9	3.3	2.4	4.7	3.9	1.1	2.1	...	...

[1]Standard presentation in accordance with the 5th edition of the International Monetary Fund's *Balance of Payments Manual* (1993).

[2]Comprises capital transfers—including debt forgiveness—and acquisition/disposal of nonproduced, nonfinancial assets.

[3]Comprise net direct investment, net portfolio investment, and other long- and short-term net investment flows, including official and private borrowing. In the standard balance of payments presentation above, total net capital flows are equal to the balance on financial account minus the change in reserve assets.

[4]Because of limitations on the data coverage for net official flows, the residually derived data for net private flows may include some official flows.

[5]As defined in the *World Economic Outlook* (see footnote 6). It should be noted that there is no generally accepted standard definition of external financing.

[6]Defined as the sum of—with opposite sign—the goods and services balance, net income and current transfers, direct investment abroad, the change in reserve assets, the net acquisition of other assets (such as recorded private portfolio assets, export credit, and the collateral for debt-reduction operations), and the net errors and omissions. Thus, net external financing, according to the definition adopted in the *World Economic Outlook*, measures the total amount required to finance the current account, direct investment outflows, net reserve transactions (often at the discretion of the monetary authorities), the net acquisition of nonreserve external assets, and the net transactions underlying the errors and omissions (not infrequently reflecting capital flight).

[7]Including other transactions on capital account.

[8]Debt-creating foreign direct investment liabilities are not included.

[9]Net disbursement of long- and short-term credits, including exceptional financing, by both official and private creditors.

[10]Net disbursement by official creditors, based on directly reported flows and flows derived from information on external debt.

[11]Comprise use of International Monetary Fund resources under the General Resources Account, Trust Fund, and Poverty Reduction and Growth Facility (PRGF). For further detail, see Table 37.

[12]Net disbursement by commercial banks, based on directly reported flows and cross-border claims and liabilities reported in the International Banking section of the International Monetary Fund's *International Financial Statistics*.

[13]This is often referred to as the "resource balance" and, with opposite sign, the "net resource transfer."

[14]Net external financing plus amortization due on external debt.

[15]Net external borrowing plus amortization due on external debt.

Table 34. Developing Countries—by Region: Balance of Payments and External Financing[1]

(Billions of U.S. dollars)

	1995	1996	1997	1998	1999	2000	2001	2002	2003	2004
Africa										
Balance of payments										
Balance on current account	−16.6	−6.2	−6.2	−18.6	−15.9	4.8	−2.2	−5.9	−3.8	−8.1
Balance on capital account	2.2	6.4	11.4	3.3	4.5	3.5	4.7	4.1	4.1	4.3
Balance on financial account	13.8	1.2	−3.1	16.4	13.2	−7.8	−3.9	1.3	−0.9	2.9
Change in reserves (− = increase)	−3.1	−6.6	−11.2	2.7	−3.5	−13.1	−12.6	−7.2	−13.9	−11.0
Other official flows, net	5.6	−2.3	3.9	5.6	4.5	5.1	3.5	3.5	4.8	4.4
Private flows, net	11.3	10.1	4.2	8.1	12.2	0.2	5.2	5.0	8.1	9.5
External financing										
Net external financing	23.9	18.9	27.3	25.0	28.7	12.6	16.2	12.8	17.3	18.7
Nondebt-creating inflows	10.0	13.9	27.4	20.0	24.5	12.9	22.9	15.8	19.2	17.9
Net external borrowing	13.8	5.0	−0.1	4.9	4.2	−0.3	−6.7	−3.0	−1.9	0.8
From official creditors	6.0	−1.9	4.0	6.0	4.8	5.8	3.7	3.8	4.9	4.8
of which, credit and loans from IMF	0.8	0.6	−0.5	−0.4	−0.2	−0.2	−0.4	−0.7	. . .	. . .
From banks	0.9	0.4	0.8	−0.4	1.1	0.3	0.1	1.3	2.0	1.6
From other private creditors	7.0	6.5	−5.0	−0.6	−1.7	−6.5	−10.5	−8.1	−8.9	−5.5
Memorandum										
Exceptional financing	14.5	14.8	17.9	4.9	10.8	8.5	7.7	8.6	8.0	3.9
Sub-Sahara										
Balance of payments										
Balance on current account	−12.4	−7.0	−9.0	−16.9	−15.3	−3.0	−10.0	−10.5	−11.5	−12.7
Balance on capital account	2.2	6.2	11.3	3.2	4.2	3.5	4.6	3.9	4.0	4.2
Balance on financial account	9.8	2.1	−0.3	14.9	11.9	0.1	4.1	5.9	6.8	7.8
Change in reserves (− = increase)	−4.5	−3.9	−6.1	1.6	−3.8	−6.5	−2.5	−2.9	−4.2	−5.5
Other official flows, net	5.9	−2.0	4.9	6.1	5.0	6.0	4.7	4.8	5.9	5.0
Private flows, net	8.3	8.0	0.9	7.2	10.6	0.5	2.0	3.9	5.1	8.3
External financing										
Net external financing	21.3	17.3	25.4	24.5	27.9	14.0	14.8	13.6	15.9	17.9
Nondebt-creating inflows	9.3	12.6	25.5	18.4	22.5	11.3	18.3	13.5	15.2	14.6
Net external borrowing	12.0	4.7	−0.1	6.1	5.4	2.7	−3.5	0.1	0.7	3.3
From official creditors	6.3	−1.6	5.0	6.5	5.4	6.7	4.9	5.2	6.0	5.3
of which, credit and loans from IMF	0.6	0.1	−0.5	−0.3	−0.1	—	−0.2	−0.4	. . .	. . .
From banks	0.4	0.2	0.1	−0.5	−0.3	—	−0.4	0.4	2.1	1.6
From other private creditors	5.2	6.1	−5.2	0.1	0.3	−4.0	−8.0	−5.5	−7.4	−3.6
Memorandum										
Exceptional financing	8.5	10.2	14.3	3.9	10.2	8.4	7.6	8.5	8.0	3.9
Developing Asia										
Balance of payments										
Balance on current account	−43.3	−39.3	8.1	47.8	46.8	43.6	35.6	65.4	42.4	34.9
Balance on capital account	0.5	0.8	0.8	0.5	0.5	0.4	0.5	0.4	0.4	0.5
Balance on financial account	64.4	68.6	26.1	−25.5	−23.2	−20.0	−27.7	−68.2	−52.2	−31.2
Change in reserves (− = increase)	−31.2	−37.5	−28.2	−20.6	−31.0	−17.5	−61.8	−112.9	−120.5	−66.9
Other official flows, net	6.9	−1.6	14.4	21.2	21.9	11.7	5.9	5.7	7.5	9.4
Private flows, net	88.7	107.8	39.9	−26.2	−14.1	−14.2	28.3	39.0	60.9	26.4
External financing										
Net external financing	101.3	108.5	90.6	51.6	50.6	59.0	53.4	68.9	71.8	70.5
Nondebt-creating inflows	58.0	69.1	62.3	52.6	54.2	61.2	52.1	55.5	64.7	62.8
Net external borrowing	43.3	39.5	28.3	−1.0	−3.6	−2.2	1.4	13.4	7.1	7.7
From official creditors	6.9	−1.6	14.4	21.2	21.9	11.7	5.9	5.7	7.5	9.4
of which, credit and loans from IMF	−1.5	−1.7	5.0	6.6	1.7	0.9	−2.2	−2.7	. . .	. . .
From banks	29.6	27.9	13.6	−12.5	−11.8	−22.2	−6.1	−9.2	−0.5	0.4
From other private creditors	6.8	13.2	0.3	−9.8	−13.7	8.4	1.6	16.9	0.1	−2.1
Memorandum										
Exceptional financing	0.6	0.7	0.5	14.6	7.1	6.1	6.6	8.0	6.4	2.9

Table 34 *(concluded)*

	1995	1996	1997	1998	1999	2000	2001	2002	2003	2004
Excluding China and India										
Balance of payments										
Balance on current account	−39.4	−40.5	−25.9	23.2	34.3	28.2	19.0	25.2	19.7	14.5
Balance on capital account	0.5	0.8	0.8	0.6	0.6	0.5	0.6	0.5	0.4	0.5
Balance on financial account	43.4	52.3	36.6	−17.4	−26.1	−16.9	−15.4	−21.0	−16.3	−10.7
Change in reserves (− = increase)	−10.9	−3.1	12.2	−11.5	−16.5	−1.0	−5.8	−18.5	−8.7	−5.1
Other official flows, net	3.0	−3.9	12.8	15.7	14.9	12.1	4.9	3.4	2.2	2.9
Private flows, net	51.3	59.3	11.6	−21.6	−24.4	−28.1	−14.5	−5.9	−9.9	−8.5
External financing										
Net external financing	61.9	55.0	29.6	0.4	2.8	1.5	−2.5	1.9	1.2	−0.5
Nondebt-creating inflows	20.1	24.6	10.6	9.6	13.3	5.5	1.6	2.9	4.3	4.1
Net external borrowing	41.8	30.4	18.9	−9.2	−10.4	−4.0	−4.0	−1.0	−3.1	−4.6
From official creditors	3.0	−3.9	12.8	15.7	14.9	12.1	4.9	3.4	2.2	2.9
of which, credit and loans from IMF	−0.3	−0.4	5.7	7.0	2.1	0.9	−2.2	−2.7	. . .	. . .
From banks	23.9	24.0	6.3	−15.4	−9.8	−15.7	−6.2	−10.8	−5.1	−5.3
From other private creditors	14.9	10.3	−0.1	−9.4	−15.4	−0.5	−2.7	6.4	−0.3	−2.2
Memorandum										
Exceptional financing	0.6	0.7	0.5	14.6	7.1	6.1	6.6	8.0	6.4	2.9
Middle East and Turkey										
Balance of payments										
Balance on current account	0.4	10.8	9.4	−22.1	15.0	65.3	45.0	29.3	40.6	22.2
Balance on capital account	2.3	0.9	0.8	0.7	1.2	2.8	2.7	1.6	1.0	0.7
Balance on financial account	−1.3	−8.6	2.7	23.4	−9.5	−51.8	−32.6	−22.4	−36.4	−16.6
Change in reserves (− = increase)	−10.7	−19.2	−11.1	11.2	−6.0	−27.9	−9.0	−10.9	−22.9	−11.1
Other official flows, net	2.9	1.8	−2.3	3.3	2.4	−5.6	10.6	1.6	1.0	0.6
Private flows, net	6.5	8.8	16.2	9.0	−5.9	−18.3	−34.2	−13.2	−14.5	−6.1
External financing										
Net external financing	5.7	22.0	28.3	30.0	9.6	20.5	−5.6	10.4	7.0	15.0
Nondebt-creating inflows	7.3	7.7	6.3	4.0	5.1	11.4	9.8	6.0	6.9	8.4
Net external borrowing	−1.6	14.3	22.0	26.0	4.5	9.2	−15.5	4.4	0.1	6.6
From official creditors	—	—	−0.1	−0.5	−0.8	2.7	11.6	−3.4	1.3	−1.0
of which, credit and loans from IMF	0.4	0.1	0.2	−0.1	0.6	3.3	10.3	6.5	. . .	. . .
From banks	−2.5	−2.1	0.3	6.6	5.5	4.3	−8.6	−1.3	0.3	1.6
From other private creditors	1.0	16.4	21.8	20.0	−0.2	2.1	−18.4	9.2	−1.5	6.0
Memorandum										
Exceptional financing	3.3	1.0	0.3	0.4	0.2	0.3	0.2	0.7	0.3	—
Western Hemisphere										
Balance of payments										
Balance on current account	−37.6	−39.2	−66.8	−89.7	−55.6	−46.0	−52.5	−14.9	−13.5	−21.0
Balance on capital account	0.6	−1.4	1.4	1.7	2.2	1.3	0.8	−0.3	1.6	1.5
Balance on financial account	40.2	43.4	69.3	92.4	59.2	42.3	54.3	19.6	12.0	19.9
Change in reserves (− = increase)	−22.9	−28.3	−14.4	7.8	8.6	−2.8	1.1	−1.8	−29.0	−8.9
Other official flows, net	19.7	−4.8	9.2	10.2	−2.8	−10.2	23.4	13.6	12.7	−13.0
Private flows, net	43.4	76.4	74.4	74.4	53.4	55.3	29.8	7.8	28.3	41.8
External financing										
Net external financing	88.0	93.7	100.3	102.0	84.0	66.0	77.2	41.1	51.3	44.4
Nondebt-creating inflows	31.7	51.2	73.0	61.8	72.3	68.6	67.0	35.8	31.1	35.8
Net external borrowing	56.2	42.5	27.3	40.1	11.7	−2.6	10.2	5.3	20.3	8.6
From official creditors	19.9	1.9	3.3	8.7	0.6	−7.3	22.3	9.0	9.4	−13.0
of which, credit and loans from IMF	12.9	−2.0	−4.0	2.5	−0.9	−10.7	15.6	11.9	. . .	. . .
From banks	5.2	6.0	3.5	12.1	5.4	9.2	5.8	−1.7	4.0	5.5
From other private creditors	31.1	34.6	20.4	19.3	5.6	−4.5	−17.9	−2.0	6.9	16.0
Memorandum										
Exceptional financing	4.1	4.9	−0.6	0.9	−0.2	−1.1	0.5	14.3	12.8	10.7

[1]For definitions, see footnotes to Table 33.

Table 35. Developing Countries—by Analytical Criteria: Balance of Payments and External Financing[1]
(Billions of U.S. dollars)

	1995	1996	1997	1998	1999	2000	2001	2002	2003	2004
By source of export earnings										
Fuel										
Balance of payments										
Balance on current account	2.3	30.3	24.1	−26.5	18.7	106.2	54.0	40.0	63.7	40.2
Balance on capital account	1.8	4.0	0.9	0.9	1.8	3.2	3.6	2.2	1.2	0.9
Balance on financial account	2.4	−31.5	−11.2	27.2	−9.8	−91.4	−40.8	−30.6	−57.3	−33.5
Change in reserves (− = increase)	−1.2	−21.6	−13.6	17.9	4.4	−42.3	−13.7	−0.8	−27.7	−14.6
Other official flows, net	7.4	—	3.5	9.7	5.9	−9.1	2.0	12.4	6.8	5.0
Private flows, net	−3.8	−9.9	−1.2	−0.3	−20.1	−39.9	−29.1	−42.2	−36.4	−23.9
External financing										
Net external financing	1.4	6.0	18.5	28.4	2.1	2.3	0.2	−6.4	−10.7	1.7
Nondebt-creating inflows	4.2	10.1	6.5	8.0	10.2	13.2	13.4	9.5	9.6	8.9
Net external borrowing	−2.7	−4.1	12.0	20.5	−8.0	−10.9	−13.2	−15.8	−20.3	−7.2
From official creditors	3.8	−0.2	4.5	4.2	4.1	4.3	3.6	4.8	4.2	3.7
of which, credit and loans from IMF	−0.2	0.8	−0.2	−0.5	−0.5	−0.7	−0.3	−0.3	. . .	. . .
From banks	−3.6	−6.2	−3.3	2.6	0.6	1.1	−1.6	−0.1	1.9	2.5
From other private creditors	−3.0	2.3	10.8	13.6	−12.8	−16.2	−15.1	−20.6	−26.4	−13.4
Memorandum										
Exceptional financing	13.2	9.3	8.1	6.1	5.2	2.7	2.1	2.9	1.4	0.9
Nonfuel										
Balance of payments										
Balance on current account	−99.3	−103.6	−78.8	−55.0	−26.8	−36.5	−25.9	36.8	5.5	−8.0
Balance on capital account	3.7	2.7	13.5	5.3	6.7	4.9	5.1	3.6	6.0	6.1
Balance on financial account	114.4	135.7	105.4	78.3	48.0	52.0	28.7	−42.0	−23.7	4.4
Change in reserves (− = increase)	−66.7	−70.0	−51.2	−16.8	−36.3	−19.0	−68.6	−132.5	−159.8	−85.3
Other official flows, net	27.4	−7.1	21.4	30.5	20.0	9.9	41.2	11.7	19.0	−3.7
Private flows, net	153.8	212.7	135.2	64.7	64.3	61.2	56.0	78.8	117.1	93.5
External financing										
Net external financing	217.2	236.6	227.1	178.9	169.2	154.0	138.7	137.3	155.9	144.5
Nondebt-creating inflows	102.9	131.7	162.5	130.5	146.0	141.0	138.5	103.6	112.3	116.0
Net external borrowing	114.3	104.8	64.6	48.4	23.2	13.0	0.3	33.6	43.6	28.6
From official creditors	28.8	−1.5	16.9	31.0	22.2	8.3	39.7	10.1	18.7	−3.7
of which, credit and loans from IMF	12.8	−3.8	1.0	9.0	1.7	−6.1	23.6	15.3	. . .	. . .
From banks	36.7	38.4	21.6	3.1	−0.4	−9.5	−7.2	−11.0	3.9	6.6
From other private creditors	48.8	68.0	26.1	14.3	1.4	14.1	−32.2	34.5	21.0	25.7
Memorandum										
Exceptional financing	9.3	12.1	10.0	14.8	12.7	11.1	12.8	28.7	26.1	16.7
By external financing source										
Net debtor countries										
Balance of payments										
Balance on current account	−104.6	−109.6	−114.9	−92.6	−48.5	−48.0	−42.3	−1.1	−14.7	−28.3
Balance on capital account	4.6	6.8	14.4	6.1	7.8	5.8	5.8	4.2	6.2	6.1
Balance on financial account	97.1	121.0	119.1	96.3	54.1	54.7	42.5	5.6	9.3	24.8
Change in reserves (− = increase)	−45.2	−40.7	−18.2	−9.0	−26.8	−15.2	−22.9	−54.3	−62.1	−37.0
Other official flows, net	23.5	−12.6	22.7	28.1	17.1	14.9	44.4	14.1	18.3	−5.7
Private flows, net	118.7	174.4	114.6	77.2	63.9	55.0	21.0	45.7	53.1	67.5
External financing										
Net external financing	179.4	197.6	181.5	155.0	136.4	112.9	91.2	88.6	95.9	87.3
Nondebt-creating inflows	71.4	101.6	120.7	93.3	116.2	96.4	102.1	62.7	63.3	69.3
Net external borrowing	108.0	96.0	60.8	61.6	20.2	16.5	−10.9	26.0	32.6	18.0
From official creditors	24.7	−7.2	18.0	28.5	19.3	13.3	43.0	12.7	17.8	−5.5
of which, credit and loans from IMF	12.8	−3.6	1.2	9.0	1.8	−6.1	23.6	15.3	. . .	. . .
From banks	31.2	33.8	14.4	0.2	2.1	−2.1	−7.5	−12.0	1.8	3.7
From other private creditors	52.1	69.4	28.3	32.9	−1.2	5.3	−46.5	25.2	13.0	19.7
Memorandum										
Exceptional financing	14.3	17.0	14.7	19.9	17.7	13.8	14.9	31.6	27.5	17.6

Table 35 *(continued)*

	1995	1996	1997	1998	1999	2000	2001	2002	2003	2004
Official financing										
Balance of payments										
Balance on current account	−20.9	−18.5	−13.7	−10.6	−3.5	9.7	3.0	0.4	−1.5	−5.6
Balance on capital account	3.1	3.3	12.1	3.5	4.4	3.3	3.5	3.3	3.2	3.2
Balance on financial account	17.3	21.1	3.0	8.1	−0.4	−11.5	−5.9	−2.8	−1.8	2.4
Change in reserves (− = increase)	−7.6	1.2	−11.8	−2.7	−3.4	−11.6	−4.7	−9.2	−11.6	−5.3
Other official flows, net	7.1	−0.4	9.1	14.0	20.1	18.8	9.8	8.7	11.0	5.9
Private flows, net	17.9	20.2	5.7	−3.1	−17.1	−18.6	−10.9	−2.3	−1.2	1.8
External financing										
Net external financing	28.9	23.1	27.0	14.2	11.8	16.4	7.2	14.0	17.7	11.5
Non-debt-creating inflows	13.2	13.6	16.6	8.5	14.0	11.8	12.7	13.1	13.9	13.5
Net external borrowing	15.8	9.5	10.3	5.7	−2.2	4.6	−5.5	0.9	3.7	−2.0
From official creditors	7.3	—	9.4	14.3	20.5	19.2	9.8	8.5	10.8	5.5
of which, credit and loans from IMF	0.4	0.1	3.0	5.9	1.7	1.1	−0.8	−1.2	. . .	. . .
From banks	7.1	16.2	14.8	0.7	−0.8	−8.5	−2.6	−6.0	−0.8	−0.4
From other private creditors	1.4	−6.7	−13.8	−9.3	−21.9	−6.1	−12.7	−1.6	−6.3	−7.1
Memorandum										
Exceptional financing	8.8	8.9	12.7	22.1	15.1	10.3	11.2	13.2	12.0	5.0
Net debtor countries by debt-servicing experience										
Countries with arrears and/or rescheduling during 1997–2001										
Balance of payments										
Balance on current account	−44.3	−43.7	−47.3	−51.1	−35.2	−17.5	−23.9	−9.5	−8.2	−16.4
Balance on capital account	2.1	3.9	11.9	4.2	5.9	4.2	4.1	2.4	4.1	4.2
Balance on financial account	38.9	46.9	40.9	52.4	32.7	16.0	20.2	9.9	3.7	11.6
Change in reserves (− = increase)	−19.2	−8.8	−4.6	5.2	2.9	−7.6	−11.5	−11.5	−28.7	−6.7
Other official flows, net	6.8	−7.3	7.4	16.0	17.1	8.8	16.5	13.2	20.8	−5.3
Private flows, net	51.3	62.9	38.0	31.2	12.8	14.9	15.2	8.3	11.6	23.6
External financing										
Net external financing	62.4	60.0	54.9	54.3	40.0	42.1	41.8	30.4	41.8	25.3
Non-debt-creating inflows	22.2	34.6	47.4	42.5	52.8	51.8	49.8	34.3	33.4	35.8
Net external borrowing	40.2	25.4	7.5	11.8	−12.8	−9.7	−8.0	−3.9	8.3	−10.5
From official creditors	6.5	−7.4	7.3	15.9	17.0	8.9	16.3	12.8	20.3	−5.6
of which, credit and loans from IMF	0.7	—	2.9	10.5	5.9	−5.6	5.5	9.9	. . .	. . .
From banks	7.2	15.9	15.1	0.6	1.8	−7.5	−1.2	−5.4	1.2	1.1
From other private creditors	26.5	17.0	−14.9	−4.7	−31.6	−11.1	−23.1	−11.3	−13.1	−5.9
Memorandum										
Exceptional financing	10.8	14.5	14.8	19.5	17.0	12.9	13.7	18.1	13.7	6.4
Other groups										
Heavily indebted poor countries										
Balance of payments										
Balance on current account	−12.5	−12.9	−13.9	−14.7	−12.8	−7.8	−11.4	−9.7	−12.7	−13.2
Balance on capital account	2.4	4.8	11.6	3.5	4.8	3.3	4.3	2.2	4.6	4.4
Balance on financial account	9.4	6.1	1.6	10.8	7.9	4.4	6.4	8.3	7.7	8.3
Change in reserves (− = increase)	−1.6	−2.2	−0.4	0.5	−2.2	−2.0	−1.6	−3.0	−3.8	−4.3
Other official flows, net	5.1	−3.0	5.1	5.9	5.1	6.7	5.4	3.7	5.1	5.3
Private flows, net	5.9	11.3	−3.1	4.4	5.0	−0.2	2.6	7.7	6.5	7.2
External financing										
Net external financing	14.4	13.9	12.6	13.8	14.2	8.9	11.5	13.2	15.1	16.2
Non-debt-creating inflows	6.2	8.6	17.1	9.5	12.8	8.9	11.4	10.6	12.8	12.0
Net external borrowing	8.2	5.3	−4.6	4.3	1.4	−0.1	0.1	2.7	2.2	4.2
From official creditors	5.8	−2.4	5.5	6.3	5.6	7.2	5.5	3.5	4.5	4.7
of which, credit and loans from IMF	0.6	0.2	−0.2	0.1	0.1	—	−0.1	−0.5	. . .	. . .
From banks	0.5	0.3	0.1	−0.4	−0.2	0.2	−0.4	0.3	2.1	1.4
From other private creditors	1.9	7.5	−10.2	−1.6	−4.0	−7.4	−5.0	−1.1	−4.4	−1.9
Memorandum										
Exceptional financing	8.1	11.3	12.0	1.6	7.7	6.7	6.3	8.3	6.4	5.7

Table 35 *(concluded)*

	1995	1996	1997	1998	1999	2000	2001	2002	2003	2004
Middle East and north Africa										
Balance of payments										
Balance on current account	−4.7	12.6	12.9	−27.4	14.1	81.4	47.2	33.9	53.9	30.1
Balance on capital account	2.3	1.0	0.9	0.8	1.5	2.9	2.9	1.9	1.4	1.1
Balance on financial account	4.7	−12.4	−3.7	26.8	−6.5	−71.3	−37.9	−28.3	−50.8	−25.7
Change in reserves (− = increase)	−4.3	−17.2	−12.4	12.6	0.2	−34.5	−21.5	−9.1	−32.1	−16.0
Other official flows, net	2.9	2.2	−2.9	3.8	3.3	−9.7	−0.5	6.4	1.3	4.0
Private flows, net	6.2	2.6	11.6	10.3	−10.0	−27.1	−16.0	−25.7	−19.9	−13.6
External financing										
Net external financing	5.6	13.8	21.1	28.1	1.2	2.6	1.2	−0.6	2.1	8.4
Non-debt-creating inflows	6.9	7.8	7.7	6.0	6.4	11.2	12.1	8.8	10.8	10.5
Net external borrowing	−1.3	6.0	13.4	22.0	−5.1	−8.6	−10.9	−9.4	−8.6	−2.1
From official creditors	—	0.4	−0.7	—	—	−1.4	0.6	1.4	1.6	2.4
of which, credit and loans from IMF	0.2	0.6	0.3	−0.1	—	−0.3	−0.2	−0.3	. . .	. . .
From banks	−3.2	−3.7	−1.3	5.7	4.7	0.2	−0.1	0.5	−0.2	0.8
From other private creditors	1.9	9.2	15.3	16.3	−9.9	−7.5	−11.4	−11.3	−10.0	−5.3
Memorandum										
Exceptional financing	9.5	6.8	5.4	2.9	2.4	1.9	1.3	1.6	1.1	0.8

[1]For definitions, see footnotes to Table 33.

Table 36. Developing Countries: Reserves[1]

	1995	1996	1997	1998	1999	2000	2001	2002	2003	2004
					Billions of U.S. dollars					
Developing countries	**470.5**	**564.6**	**620.8**	**615.6**	**641.0**	**711.4**	**792.3**	**933.5**	**1,119.1**	**1,217.0**
Regional groups										
Africa	26.5	31.9	43.8	41.5	42.4	54.5	64.7	72.7	86.7	97.7
Sub-Sahara	18.9	21.6	29.5	28.0	29.6	35.5	35.9	36.8	41.0	46.5
Developing Asia	185.2	230.8	249.0	273.9	306.6	321.0	379.7	495.4	615.2	682.2
Excluding China and India	90.6	102.3	80.4	96.1	115.1	113.7	117.0	135.2	143.1	148.2
Middle East and Turkey	128.4	144.9	157.4	146.9	148.6	179.8	188.7	204.1	227.0	238.1
Western Hemisphere	130.4	157.0	170.6	153.4	143.4	156.1	159.2	161.2	190.2	199.1
Analytical groups										
By source of export earnings										
Fuel	94.1	114.0	131.5	114.8	109.7	156.3	169.4	171.1	198.8	213.4
Nonfuel	376.3	450.4	489.2	500.7	531.3	555.1	622.9	762.8	922.0	1,007.3
of which, primary products	25.7	27.9	30.7	28.6	27.7	27.9	27.4	30.5	32.2	34.9
By external financing source										
Net debtor countries	308.8	354.6	360.4	363.8	385.0	405.4	426.9	488.6	550.0	587.0
of which, official financing	33.9	41.0	44.2	48.8	54.8	63.3	65.7	75.2	86.1	91.4
Net debtor countries by debt-servicing experience										
Countries with arrears and/or rescheduling during 1997–2001	95.0	111.3	108.1	95.9	92.3	107.5	118.0	130.4	158.5	165.2
Other groups										
Heavily indebted poor countries	10.3	12.1	13.0	12.6	14.6	16.5	17.7	21.5	24.6	28.9
Middle East and north Africa	122.0	137.2	151.8	139.3	136.5	175.3	197.3	211.5	243.6	259.7
					Ratio of reserves to imports of goods and services[2]					
Developing countries	**43.1**	**47.2**	**48.2**	**50.6**	**52.6**	**49.5**	**55.3**	**61.7**	**65.8**	**65.8**
Regional groups										
Africa	20.5	24.5	32.5	31.1	31.4	38.9	44.7	46.7	49.1	53.0
Sub-Sahara	19.5	21.7	28.0	27.5	29.0	33.3	32.6	31.2	30.8	33.9
Developing Asia	37.5	42.6	44.4	56.5	59.2	49.6	58.4	68.1	72.4	72.5
Excluding China and India	29.3	30.8	23.8	36.7	43.4	35.3	38.6	42.3	40.9	39.4
Middle East and Turkey	60.0	60.8	61.5	59.4	62.0	65.3	69.9	69.6	70.4	69.7
Western Hemisphere	51.0	54.9	50.7	43.7	43.9	41.8	43.2	47.8	54.0	52.2
Analytical groups										
By source of export earnings										
Fuel	52.3	59.6	63.6	58.4	55.7	71.1	72.0	67.7	74.3	75.6
Nonfuel	41.3	44.9	45.3	49.2	52.1	45.7	52.1	60.6	64.4	64.4
of which, primary products	52.8	53.1	54.2	51.8	54.9	53.3	52.2	56.8	53.8	54.4
By external financing source										
Net debtor countries	38.7	40.5	38.2	41.3	44.4	40.3	43.9	49.6	50.6	50.3
of which, official financing	22.4	25.0	25.6	31.3	37.4	37.4	38.7	41.5	42.9	43.5
Net debtor countries by debt-servicing experience										
Countries with arrears and/or rescheduling during 1997–2001	41.4	44.4	39.6	37.1	38.4	38.9	42.0	45.7	50.5	49.7
Other groups										
Heavily indebted poor countries	18.4	19.6	20.1	18.9	21.6	22.9	23.1	25.8	25.5	28.0
Middle East and north Africa	60.8	64.0	67.7	63.9	62.8	73.2	78.4	78.3	83.9	84.2

[1]In this table, official holdings of gold are valued at SDR 35 an ounce. This convention results in a marked underestimate of reserves for countries that have substantial gold holdings.
[2]Reserves at year-end in percent of imports of goods and services for the year indicated.

Table 37. Net Credit and Loans from IMF[1]

(Billions of U.S. dollars)

	1994	1995	1996	1997	1998	1999	2000	2001	2002
Advanced economies	—	**−0.1**	**−0.1**	**11.3**	**5.2**	**−10.3**	—	**−5.7**	—
Newly industrialized Asian economies	—	—	—	11.3	5.2	−10.3	—	−5.7	—
Developing countries	**−0.8**	**12.6**	**−2.9**	**0.8**	**8.5**	**1.3**	**−6.7**	**23.3**	**15.0**
Regional groups									
Africa	0.9	0.8	0.6	−0.5	−0.4	−0.2	−0.2	−0.4	−0.7
Sub-Sahara	0.5	0.6	0.1	−0.5	−0.3	−0.1	—	−0.2	−0.4
Developing Asia	−0.8	−1.5	−1.7	5.0	6.6	1.7	0.9	−2.2	−2.7
Excluding China and India	0.4	−0.3	−0.4	5.7	7.0	2.1	0.9	−2.2	−2.7
Middle East and Turkey	0.4	0.4	0.1	0.2	−0.1	0.6	3.3	10.3	6.5
Western Hemisphere	−1.3	12.9	−2.0	−4.0	2.5	−0.9	−10.7	15.6	11.9
Analytical groups									
By source of export earnings									
Fuel	0.5	−0.2	0.8	−0.2	−0.5	−0.5	−0.7	−0.3	−0.3
Nonfuel	−1.3	12.8	−3.8	1.0	9.0	1.7	−6.1	23.6	15.3
of which, primary products	0.1	0.4	0.1	−0.1	0.2	−0.1	−0.2	−0.1	−0.4
By external financing source									
Net debtor countries	−1.2	12.8	−3.6	1.2	9.0	1.8	−6.1	23.6	15.3
of which, official financing	0.9	0.3	0.1	3.0	5.9	1.7	1.1	−0.8	−1.2
Net debtor countries by debt-servicing experience									
Countries with arrears and/or rescheduling during 1997–2001	1.0	0.7	—	2.9	10.5	5.9	−5.6	5.5	9.9
Other groups									
Heavily indebted poor countries	0.5	0.6	0.3	—	0.2	0.2	−0.1	−0.1	−0.5
Middle East and north Africa	0.5	0.2	0.6	0.3	−0.1	—	−0.3	−0.2	−0.3
Countries in transition	**2.4**	**4.6**	**3.6**	**2.5**	**5.5**	**−3.6**	**−4.1**	**−4.3**	**−2.1**
Central and eastern Europe	0.1	−2.7	−0.8	0.4	−0.3	—	—	−0.3	−0.3
Commonwealth of Independent States and Mongolia	2.3	7.3	4.4	2.0	5.8	−3.6	−4.1	−3.9	−1.8
Russia	1.5	5.5	3.2	1.5	5.3	−3.6	−2.9	−3.8	−1.5
Excluding Russia	0.7	1.8	1.2	0.5	0.4	—	−1.2	−0.1	−0.3
Memorandum									
Total									
Net credit provided under:									
General Resources Account	0.594	15.472	0.183	14.345	18.801	−12.826	−10.666	13.269	12.863
Trust Fund	−0.014	−0.015	—	−0.007	−0.001	−0.001	—	—	—
PRGF	0.998	1.619	0.325	0.179	0.319	0.185	−0.177	0.087	0.031
Disbursements at year-end under:[2]									
General Resources Account	37.276	53.118	51.565	62.450	84.686	69.675	55.604	66.732	85.697
Trust Fund	0.153	0.141	0.137	0.121	0.126	0.122	0.116	0.111	0.120
PRGF	6.634	8.342	8.392	8.049	8.731	8.697	8.081	7.880	8.557

[1]Includes net disbursements from programs under the General Resources Account, Trust Fund, and Poverty Reduction and Growth Facility (formerly ESAF—Enhanced Structural Adjustment Facility). The data are on a transactions basis, with conversion to U.S. dollar values at annual average exchange rates.
[2]Converted to U.S. dollar values at end-of-period exchange rates.

Table 38. Summary of External Debt and Debt Service

	1995	1996	1997	1998	1999	2000	2001	2002	2003	2004
					Billions of U.S. dollars					
External debt										
Developing countries	**1,864.6**	**1,948.2**	**2,030.4**	**2,201.2**	**2,235.3**	**2,201.9**	**2,170.2**	**2,191.5**	**2,219.2**	**2,211.6**
Regional groups										
Africa	295.3	293.8	283.1	281.0	280.1	272.8	261.6	264.7	267.9	261.8
Developing Asia	577.5	613.4	666.2	703.4	701.1	673.9	681.5	675.5	683.8	699.8
Middle East and Turkey	369.5	391.2	406.1	456.3	472.9	493.9	482.9	507.5	508.9	514.8
Western Hemisphere	622.3	649.8	675.0	760.5	781.2	761.3	744.2	743.8	758.6	735.3
Analytical groups										
By external financing source										
Net debtor countries	1,614.7	1,682.4	1,748.5	1,884.3	1,910.2	1,887.7	1,837.3	1,861.8	1,883.3	1,857.2
of which, official financing	337.3	349.3	362.2	383.3	381.0	367.2	359.5	353.6	351.6	345.1
Net debtor countries by debt-servicing experience										
Countries with arrears and/or rescheduling during 1997–2001	673.3	703.2	742.8	809.3	810.6	794.1	765.0	762.8	767.9	755.7
Countries in transition	**282.9**	**312.6**	**346.0**	**390.2**	**396.1**	**384.0**	**388.4**	**424.2**	**438.5**	**453.5**
Central and eastern Europe	127.2	140.8	146.9	167.4	177.3	184.9	194.4	221.8	237.6	251.9
Commonwealth of Independent States and Mongolia	155.7	171.8	199.1	222.8	218.9	199.1	194.0	202.4	200.9	201.6
Russia	133.2	145.3	167.4	185.7	177.1	158.3	150.4	154.6	150.8	149.7
Excluding Russia	22.5	26.5	31.7	37.1	41.8	40.8	43.6	47.7	50.1	51.9
Debt-service payments[1]										
Developing countries	**230.7**	**264.8**	**301.3**	**309.4**	**335.5**	**342.5**	**341.8**	**324.8**	**327.1**	**314.9**
Regional groups										
Africa	26.8	26.7	26.9	26.9	26.4	26.2	27.0	33.6	27.2	25.4
Developing Asia	74.1	70.5	85.0	98.5	94.6	97.5	99.4	107.4	108.3	95.1
Middle East and Turkey	32.4	43.1	37.7	34.5	35.5	37.0	43.8	40.0	43.0	44.8
Western Hemisphere	97.3	124.4	151.7	149.4	179.0	181.9	171.6	143.9	148.6	149.6
Analytical groups										
By external financing source										
Net debtor countries	185.8	215.5	252.6	261.6	284.7	293.1	288.8	275.0	276.9	263.4
of which, official financing	35.5	37.2	47.3	53.2	43.6	47.6	48.5	57.7	47.0	39.8
Net debtor countries by debt-servicing experience										
Countries with arrears and/or rescheduling during 1997–2001	65.8	70.3	96.0	112.7	124.9	115.6	109.8	116.9	111.9	107.1
Countries in transition	**36.2**	**42.6**	**53.8**	**61.3**	**55.6**	**57.9**	**65.3**	**65.9**	**79.0**	**77.5**
Central and eastern Europe	23.6	27.9	29.9	32.4	29.2	32.1	34.9	36.2	43.3	46.2
Commonwealth of Independent States and Mongolia	12.6	14.7	23.9	28.9	26.4	25.8	30.4	29.7	35.7	31.3
Russia	8.9	11.7	20.4	24.7	21.1	20.2	25.7	25.1	30.4	25.9
Excluding Russia	3.7	3.0	3.5	4.3	5.3	5.5	4.7	4.6	5.3	5.4

Table 38 *(concluded)*

	1995	1996	1997	1998	1999	2000	2001	2002	2003	2004
					Percent of exports of goods and services					
External debt[2]										
Developing countries	**180.5**	**168.3**	**161.1**	**188.3**	**177.7**	**141.9**	**144.1**	**135.3**	**123.0**	**115.4**
Regional groups										
Africa	249.4	224.0	209.3	234.6	219.1	174.2	176.7	173.0	151.1	144.5
Developing Asia	126.9	121.4	117.8	130.5	121.3	96.3	98.1	85.6	76.9	71.6
Middle East and Turkey	172.9	158.3	156.6	209.8	189.6	146.8	152.3	153.1	136.4	138.8
Western Hemisphere	253.2	236.9	224.7	259.8	258.1	212.3	215.1	214.6	208.1	190.3
Analytical groups										
By external financing source										
Net debtor countries	227.6	216.0	207.7	234.2	226.2	191.1	192.9	187.7	174.3	161.8
of which, official financing	262.1	246.8	233.6	277.0	263.8	202.6	212.8	201.6	182.8	173.3
Net debtor countries by debt-servicing experience										
Countries with arrears and/or rescheduling during 1997–2001	337.9	323.7	309.4	361.1	345.9	274.4	272.3	260.6	238.8	225.7
Countries in transition	**110.4**	**111.0**	**117.9**	**136.3**	**142.8**	**115.1**	**110.3**	**109.9**	**96.4**	**94.1**
Central and eastern Europe	102.1	105.0	100.3	105.2	115.2	109.4	104.0	106.6	95.2	93.0
Commonwealth of Independent States and Mongolia	118.2	116.5	135.4	175.2	177.2	120.9	117.5	113.7	97.9	95.7
Russia	143.2	141.1	165.8	213.9	209.3	138.1	133.5	128.5	107.3	104.6
Excluding Russia	58.1	59.6	68.8	91.9	107.3	81.5	83.2	82.8	77.6	76.7
Debt-service payments[1]										
Developing countries	**22.3**	**22.9**	**23.9**	**26.5**	**26.7**	**22.1**	**22.7**	**20.0**	**18.1**	**16.4**
Regional groups										
Africa	22.7	20.4	19.9	22.4	20.7	16.7	18.2	22.0	15.4	14.0
Developing Asia	16.3	13.9	15.0	18.3	16.4	13.9	14.3	13.6	12.2	9.7
Middle East and Turkey	15.2	17.4	14.5	15.9	14.2	11.0	13.8	12.1	11.5	12.1
Western Hemisphere	39.6	45.4	50.5	51.0	59.1	50.7	49.6	41.5	40.7	38.7
Analytical groups										
By external financing source										
Net debtor countries	26.2	27.7	30.0	32.5	33.7	29.7	30.3	27.7	25.6	22.9
of which, official financing	27.6	26.3	30.5	38.5	30.2	26.2	28.7	32.9	24.4	20.0
Net debtor countries by debt-servicing experience										
Countries with arrears and/or rescheduling during 1997–2001	33.0	32.4	40.0	50.3	53.3	39.9	39.1	39.9	34.8	32.0
Countries in transition	**14.1**	**15.1**	**18.4**	**21.4**	**20.0**	**17.4**	**18.6**	**17.1**	**17.4**	**16.1**
Central and eastern Europe	18.9	20.8	20.4	20.4	19.0	19.0	18.7	17.4	17.3	17.1
Commonwealth of Independent States and Mongolia	9.5	10.0	16.3	22.7	21.3	15.6	18.4	16.7	17.4	14.9
Russia	9.6	11.3	20.2	28.4	24.9	17.6	22.8	20.8	21.6	18.1
Excluding Russia	9.4	6.8	7.6	10.6	13.5	11.1	9.0	8.0	8.2	8.0

[1]Debt-service payments refer to actual payments of interest on total debt plus actual amortization payments on long-term debt. The projections incorporate the impact of exceptional financing items.
[2]Total debt at year-end in percent of exports of goods and services in year indicated.

Table 39. Developing Countries—by Region: External Debt, by Maturity and Type of Creditor

(Billions of U.S. dollars)

	1995	1996	1997	1998	1999	2000	2001	2002	2003	2004
Developing countries										
Total debt	**1,864.6**	**1,948.2**	**2,030.4**	**2,201.2**	**2,235.3**	**2,201.9**	**2,170.2**	**2,191.5**	**2,219.2**	**2,211.6**
By maturity										
Short-term	272.3	293.2	296.2	274.6	257.6	236.0	213.0	223.3	230.1	238.8
Long-term	1,592.3	1,655.0	1,734.2	1,926.5	1,977.7	1,965.9	1,957.2	1,968.2	1,989.1	1,972.8
By type of creditor										
Official	820.3	820.5	799.1	845.8	853.1	824.3	845.1	875.4	889.3	881.1
Banks	448.5	534.8	601.2	642.6	641.0	632.6	607.3	596.1	594.5	602.0
Other private	595.7	592.9	630.1	712.8	741.1	745.0	717.9	720.0	735.4	728.5
Regional groups										
Africa										
Total debt	**295.3**	**293.8**	**283.1**	**281.0**	**280.1**	**272.8**	**261.6**	**264.7**	**267.9**	**261.8**
By maturity										
Short-term	27.5	31.9	34.5	36.8	37.8	16.5	14.8	17.8	18.4	17.7
Long-term	267.8	261.9	248.6	244.1	242.2	256.3	246.9	246.9	249.5	244.0
By type of creditor										
Official	210.3	212.6	198.5	202.5	201.0	198.1	194.9	197.8	200.8	197.4
Banks	34.8	32.6	32.9	30.0	29.3	28.6	28.5	27.4	25.9	25.1
Other private	50.2	48.7	51.8	48.5	49.8	46.1	38.2	39.4	41.2	39.2
Sub-Sahara										
Total debt	**228.4**	**227.2**	**221.6**	**218.3**	**220.2**	**218.1**	**211.4**	**211.8**	**214.0**	**210.4**
By maturity										
Short-term	25.6	29.5	32.5	34.4	35.0	13.8	12.1	14.8	15.0	14.2
Long-term	202.8	197.7	189.1	183.9	185.2	204.3	199.3	196.9	198.9	196.2
By type of creditor										
Official	164.1	164.5	153.5	156.0	157.0	157.5	157.4	157.2	158.1	156.6
Banks	24.9	22.5	22.6	18.9	17.2	17.3	17.5	15.9	14.7	14.6
Other private	39.5	40.2	45.6	43.4	46.0	43.3	36.4	38.6	41.2	39.2
Developing Asia										
Total debt	**577.5**	**613.4**	**666.2**	**703.4**	**701.1**	**673.9**	**681.5**	**675.5**	**683.8**	**699.8**
By maturity										
Short-term	106.8	111.5	100.7	90.5	71.9	61.6	57.5	56.5	64.2	70.7
Long-term	470.6	501.9	565.5	613.0	629.2	612.3	624.0	619.0	619.6	629.0
By type of creditor										
Official	245.1	258.6	279.7	301.8	307.7	291.3	287.0	294.5	297.8	303.0
Banks	189.6	201.0	210.6	203.0	197.3	182.6	178.1	168.6	168.3	169.1
Other private	142.8	153.8	175.8	198.6	196.2	200.0	216.4	212.5	217.6	227.7
Middle East and Turkey										
Total debt	**369.5**	**391.2**	**406.1**	**456.3**	**472.9**	**493.9**	**482.9**	**507.5**	**508.9**	**514.8**
By maturity										
Short-term	43.0	44.5	50.2	57.3	60.5	63.7	50.0	48.6	50.5	52.9
Long-term	326.5	346.7	355.9	398.9	412.5	430.2	432.9	459.0	458.4	461.8
By type of creditor										
Official	172.1	171.7	164.7	164.9	165.6	169.5	180.7	182.6	185.4	183.8
Banks	91.7	110.9	148.9	176.8	188.6	201.9	185.7	207.3	206.6	213.3
Other private	105.8	108.7	92.6	114.6	118.8	122.5	116.5	117.6	116.9	117.7
Western Hemisphere										
Total debt	**622.3**	**649.8**	**675.0**	**760.5**	**781.2**	**761.3**	**744.2**	**743.8**	**758.6**	**735.3**
By maturity										
Short-term	94.9	105.3	110.9	90.0	87.4	94.2	90.8	100.5	96.9	97.3
Long-term	527.4	544.5	564.1	670.5	693.8	667.1	653.4	643.3	661.7	637.9
By type of creditor										
Official	192.9	177.7	156.2	176.6	178.9	165.5	182.5	200.5	205.3	196.8
Banks	132.4	190.4	208.9	232.8	225.9	219.5	214.9	192.8	193.6	194.6
Other private	297.0	281.7	309.9	351.1	376.4	376.3	346.8	350.6	359.7	343.8

Table 40. Developing Countries—by Analytical Criteria: External Debt, by Maturity and Type of Creditor
(Billions of U.S. dollars)

	1995	1996	1997	1998	1999	2000	2001	2002	2003	2004
By source of export earnings										
Fuel										
Total debt	**373.2**	**382.5**	**387.4**	**428.0**	**437.0**	**440.2**	**432.3**	**435.2**	**424.8**	**423.2**
By maturity										
Short-term	33.0	35.7	43.7	50.3	54.0	32.1	29.8	30.8	29.4	30.1
Long-term	340.2	346.7	343.7	377.7	383.0	408.1	402.5	404.4	395.4	393.1
By type of creditor										
Official	168.3	166.1	158.9	162.2	165.1	165.9	166.7	175.8	176.8	176.3
Banks	73.2	90.5	102.5	115.8	117.5	118.5	115.5	111.4	102.6	100.2
Other private	131.7	125.8	125.9	150.0	154.3	155.9	150.1	148.0	145.4	146.7
Nonfuel										
Total debt	**1,486.6**	**1,560.6**	**1,637.2**	**1,766.0**	**1,789.6**	**1,751.1**	**1,725.0**	**1,741.0**	**1,776.6**	**1,768.3**
By maturity										
Short-term	239.2	257.1	251.9	223.0	201.9	201.8	180.8	189.8	197.5	205.2
Long-term	1,247.4	1,303.5	1,385.3	1,543.0	1,587.7	1,549.3	1,544.2	1,551.2	1,579.1	1,563.0
By type of creditor										
Official	647.2	649.4	635.3	678.4	682.6	652.8	672.5	693.6	706.1	698.2
Banks	375.3	444.3	498.7	526.8	523.5	514.1	491.8	484.7	491.8	501.8
Other private	464.1	466.9	503.3	560.8	583.6	584.1	560.7	562.8	578.7	568.3
Nonfuel primary products										
Total debt	**113.0**	**114.6**	**111.5**	**114.4**	**116.9**	**119.0**	**121.5**	**121.3**	**122.0**	**122.5**
By maturity										
Short-term	11.5	10.5	10.0	7.4	6.9	8.9	9.1	10.9	9.9	7.9
Long-term	101.4	104.1	101.5	107.0	110.0	110.0	112.4	110.4	112.0	114.6
By type of creditor										
Official	82.7	84.2	77.1	78.9	78.9	78.2	79.2	76.7	75.3	73.8
Banks	20.3	18.8	20.7	19.3	20.1	19.7	20.1	20.3	21.5	23.2
Other private	9.9	11.6	13.7	16.1	17.9	21.1	22.2	24.3	25.2	25.5
By external financing source										
Net debtor countries										
Total debt	**1,614.7**	**1,682.4**	**1,748.5**	**1,884.3**	**1,910.2**	**1,887.7**	**1,837.3**	**1,861.8**	**1,883.3**	**1,857.2**
By maturity										
Short-term	236.4	254.7	248.4	223.2	206.7	188.3	170.0	177.7	180.2	184.5
Long-term	1,378.4	1,427.7	1,500.1	1,661.1	1,703.6	1,699.4	1,667.4	1,684.1	1,703.1	1,672.7
By type of creditor										
Official	726.4	724.9	700.6	744.7	757.6	739.5	761.7	787.1	795.3	781.7
Banks	384.7	452.8	508.1	533.3	524.4	517.8	497.7	490.9	491.5	496.1
Other private	503.6	504.7	539.8	606.3	628.3	630.4	577.9	583.8	596.5	579.4
Official financing										
Total debt	**337.3**	**349.3**	**362.2**	**383.3**	**381.0**	**367.2**	**359.5**	**353.6**	**351.6**	**345.1**
By maturity										
Short-term	36.1	36.7	33.2	39.8	39.4	17.1	15.4	11.2	11.1	11.4
Long-term	301.2	312.6	329.0	343.5	341.6	350.1	344.0	342.4	340.6	333.7
By type of creditor										
Official	222.6	242.9	235.4	245.8	254.9	248.4	246.7	253.5	254.6	250.5
Banks	53.8	47.8	58.4	60.6	56.7	48.7	47.4	39.6	38.4	37.3
Other private	60.8	58.5	68.4	76.9	69.4	70.1	65.3	60.4	58.6	57.3

Table 40 *(concluded)*

	1995	1996	1997	1998	1999	2000	2001	2002	2003	2004
Net debtor countries by debt-servicing experience										
Countries with arrears and/or rescheduling during 1997–2001										
Total debt	**673.3**	**703.2**	**742.8**	**809.3**	**810.6**	**794.1**	**765.0**	**762.8**	**767.9**	**755.7**
By maturity										
Short-term	67.6	79.0	74.5	68.0	68.2	45.9	44.1	35.6	35.6	35.2
Long-term	605.8	624.2	668.4	741.3	742.4	748.2	720.8	727.2	732.4	720.6
By type of creditor										
Official	385.2	396.2	392.4	422.4	438.2	427.1	432.1	455.0	468.2	457.8
Banks	141.9	193.8	222.6	234.8	229.8	223.8	216.5	194.1	186.4	183.3
Other private	146.2	113.2	127.8	152.1	142.6	143.2	116.4	113.6	113.3	114.7
Other groups										
Heavily indebted poor countries										
Total debt	**189.4**	**185.4**	**178.1**	**178.7**	**178.1**	**174.3**	**174.3**	**171.6**	**173.2**	**176.4**
By maturity										
Short-term	7.3	7.0	6.6	5.5	4.2	3.7	3.5	3.5	3.4	3.5
Long-term	182.0	178.4	171.5	173.2	174.0	170.6	170.9	168.1	169.8	172.9
By type of creditor										
Official	162.7	158.3	150.2	154.4	154.4	151.5	151.9	149.8	151.5	154.4
Banks	20.8	18.8	18.6	14.8	13.4	13.7	14.0	13.2	11.9	11.9
Other private	5.9	8.4	9.3	9.5	10.3	9.1	8.4	8.5	9.9	10.1
Middle East and north Africa										
Total debt	**382.8**	**398.5**	**404.2**	**444.3**	**452.5**	**453.7**	**443.6**	**453.6**	**451.7**	**451.2**
By maturity										
Short-term	28.8	29.0	33.6	37.9	39.0	36.7	34.9	34.7	34.1	34.5
Long-term	354.0	369.5	370.6	406.4	413.5	416.9	408.7	418.9	417.6	416.6
By type of creditor										
Official	203.8	205.2	196.6	200.4	200.9	199.2	198.0	209.6	216.1	216.8
Banks	77.9	96.5	109.5	125.0	129.8	129.9	128.1	126.5	119.6	117.6
Other private	101.1	96.8	98.1	118.9	121.8	124.6	117.6	117.5	116.0	116.8

Table 41. Developing Countries: Ratio of External Debt to GDP[1]

	1995	1996	1997	1998	1999	2000	2001	2002	2003	2004
Developing countries	**41.5**	**39.4**	**38.7**	**43.5**	**44.7**	**40.6**	**40.1**	**40.9**	**37.7**	**35.0**
Regional groups										
Africa	72.1	67.7	63.5	65.9	65.5	63.0	61.0	59.3	49.2	46.5
Sub-Sahara	72.1	68.7	64.2	67.6	68.2	67.0	66.1	63.5	52.3	50.0
Developing Asia	32.6	31.1	32.5	37.0	34.1	30.7	29.9	27.4	25.3	23.8
Excluding China and India	52.5	51.4	59.1	84.7	72.2	65.4	65.4	57.7	51.7	47.4
Middle East and Turkey	58.5	55.5	54.8	63.0	62.5	59.2	61.2	62.7	54.8	52.2
Western Hemisphere	36.9	35.5	33.7	37.9	44.3	38.7	38.9	45.3	44.1	40.0
Analytical groups										
By source of export earnings										
Fuel	71.8	65.2	62.3	73.5	69.4	60.8	58.4	61.4	55.1	53.0
Nonfuel	37.6	36.0	35.6	39.7	41.2	37.5	37.2	37.7	35.0	32.3
of which, primary products	71.3	67.6	62.0	66.7	71.5	74.1	77.0	71.1	68.4	66.4
By external financing source										
Net debtor countries	48.9	47.1	46.6	53.0	56.0	51.5	51.8	54.1	49.4	45.5
of which, official financing	67.5	64.4	67.0	93.0	82.3	75.9	74.9	64.7	57.6	53.5
Net debtor countries by debt-servicing experience										
Countries with arrears and/or rescheduling during 1997–2001	55.0	52.0	53.7	65.2	79.1	70.4	73.0	72.4	64.1	59.3
Other groups										
Heavily indebted poor countries	125.8	111.6	100.5	99.2	97.2	94.4	92.1	83.5	74.8	70.7
Middle East and north Africa	68.6	62.4	61.0	70.0	66.9	60.2	57.9	59.6	53.5	52.0

[1]Debt at year-end in percent of GDP in year indicated.

Table 42. Developing Countries: Debt-Service Ratios[1]
(Percent of exports of goods and services)

	1995	1996	1997	1998	1999	2000	2001	2002	2003	2004
Interest payments[2]										
Developing countries	**8.8**	**8.4**	**7.7**	**9.0**	**8.7**	**7.2**	**7.1**	**5.9**	**5.0**	**4.9**
Regional groups										
Africa	9.7	9.8	8.9	9.7	8.8	6.8	6.9	9.0	5.5	4.9
Sub-Sahara	7.9	8.6	7.9	8.9	8.2	6.4	6.7	10.0	5.7	4.9
Developing Asia	6.1	6.0	5.0	5.9	5.5	4.4	3.9	3.2	2.9	3.1
Excluding China and India	6.2	6.3	6.5	7.4	6.0	5.2	4.5	3.4	3.4	3.9
Middle East and Turkey	4.7	4.1	4.2	5.1	4.7	3.9	4.1	3.5	3.5	3.8
Western Hemisphere	17.0	16.1	15.5	17.3	17.9	15.9	16.2	13.0	11.3	10.5
Analytical groups										
By source of export earnings										
Fuel	5.0	4.9	4.6	5.8	4.7	3.3	3.3	2.7	2.7	2.6
Nonfuel	9.7	9.3	8.5	9.6	9.6	8.3	8.1	6.7	5.6	5.4
of which, primary products	9.6	7.8	7.7	8.4	8.4	8.9	8.4	17.1	4.9	5.1
By external financing source										
Net debtor countries	10.6	10.4	10.1	11.2	10.8	9.5	9.3	7.9	6.7	6.5
of which, official financing	9.7	10.1	9.8	11.9	9.8	8.0	7.0	7.9	5.2	6.7
Net debtor countries by debt-servicing experience										
Countries with arrears and/or rescheduling during 1997–2001	13.2	13.9	13.1	15.4	14.4	11.8	11.4	10.6	8.7	9.2
Other groups										
Heavily indebted poor countries	10.6	9.9	8.3	9.1	7.6	6.9	6.6	12.1	4.5	3.6
Middle East and north Africa	5.0	4.4	4.3	5.2	4.2	3.1	2.8	2.5	2.1	2.3
Amortization[2]										
Developing countries	**13.5**	**14.4**	**16.2**	**17.5**	**18.0**	**14.9**	**15.6**	**14.2**	**13.1**	**11.5**
Regional groups										
Africa	12.9	10.6	11.0	12.7	11.9	9.9	11.4	13.0	9.8	9.1
Sub-Sahara	10.9	9.3	9.5	10.6	9.5	8.5	10.5	12.4	8.9	7.9
Developing Asia	10.2	7.9	10.0	12.3	10.9	9.5	10.4	10.5	9.3	6.6
Excluding China and India	10.9	10.1	12.8	17.2	14.4	12.9	16.6	17.1	15.3	10.6
Middle East and Turkey	10.5	13.4	10.3	10.8	9.5	7.1	9.7	8.6	8.0	8.3
Western Hemisphere	22.6	29.2	35.1	33.8	41.2	34.8	33.4	28.5	29.4	28.2
Analytical groups										
By source of export earnings										
Fuel	11.7	13.8	12.1	13.4	10.4	6.7	8.8	6.8	6.9	6.9
Nonfuel	13.9	14.6	17.1	18.2	19.7	17.3	17.4	16.0	14.7	12.6
of which, primary products	15.5	16.0	11.5	11.5	13.1	13.6	15.5	26.7	14.4	10.2
By external financing source										
Net debtor countries	15.6	17.3	19.9	21.3	22.9	20.2	21.0	19.8	18.9	16.4
of which, official financing	17.9	16.2	20.7	26.5	20.4	18.2	21.7	25.0	19.3	13.3
Net debtor countries by debt-servicing experience										
Countries with arrears and/or rescheduling during 1997–2001	19.8	18.5	26.9	34.9	38.9	28.1	27.7	29.3	26.1	22.8
Other groups										
Heavily indebted poor countries	16.8	12.7	12.6	13.8	12.3	12.0	13.5	16.6	9.0	7.4
Middle East and north Africa	11.2	13.9	11.1	12.5	10.2	6.7	8.6	6.6	6.1	6.9

[1]Excludes service payments to the International Monetary Fund.
[2]Interest payments on total debt and amortization on long-term debt. Estimates through 2002 reflect debt-service payments actually made. The estimates for 2003 and 2004 take into account projected exceptional financing items, including accumulation of arrears and rescheduling agreements. In some cases, amortization on account of debt-reduction operations is included.

Table 43. IMF Charges and Repurchases to the IMF[1]
(Percent of exports of goods and services)

	1995	1996	1997	1998	1999	2000	2001	2002
Developing countries	**0.9**	**0.6**	**0.6**	**0.5**	**1.0**	**1.1**	**0.5**	**1.2**
Regional groups								
Africa	2.5	0.4	0.9	1.1	0.5	0.2	0.3	0.4
Sub-Sahara	2.8	0.3	0.7	0.8	0.2	0.1	0.1	0.2
Developing Asia	0.4	0.4	0.2	0.2	0.2	0.2	0.6	0.6
Excluding China and India	0.2	0.2	0.2	0.2	0.3	0.4	1.2	1.4
Middle East and Turkey	0.1	0.1	0.1	0.1	0.2	0.1	0.5	2.2
Western Hemisphere	1.6	1.6	1.9	1.1	3.2	4.2	0.6	2.0
Analytical groups								
By source of export earnings								
Fuel	0.5	0.3	0.4	0.6	0.4	0.2	0.2	0.1
Nonfuel	1.0	0.7	0.7	0.5	1.1	1.3	0.6	1.5
By external financing source								
Net debtor countries	1.2	0.8	0.9	0.6	1.3	1.6	0.8	1.9
of which, official financing	0.3	0.4	0.3	0.5	0.7	0.6	1.5	1.9
Net debtor countries by debt-servicing experience								
Countries with arrears and/or rescheduling during 1997–2001	1.5	0.4	0.3	0.3	1.4	2.8	1.0	2.9
Other groups								
Heavily indebted poor countries	5.7	0.5	0.6	0.6	0.4	0.3	0.3	0.4
Middle East and north Africa	0.3	0.2	0.3	0.4	0.3	0.1	0.1	0.2
Countries in transition	**1.4**	**0.8**	**0.6**	**1.0**	**2.4**	**1.7**	**1.6**	**0.7**
Central and eastern Europe	2.7	0.8	0.3	0.5	0.3	0.3	0.3	0.3
Commonwealth of Independent States and Mongolia	0.3	0.8	0.9	1.7	4.9	3.2	3.0	1.2
Russia	0.3	1.0	1.1	1.9	5.9	3.1	3.8	1.4
Excluding Russia	0.3	0.4	0.5	1.2	2.8	3.3	1.3	0.6
Memorandum								
Total, billions of U.S. dollars								
General Resources Account	12.721	9.497	9.986	8.810	18.503	22.788	13.793	22.322
Charges	2.762	2.266	2.200	2.510	2.832	2.846	2.639	2.807
Repurchases	9.960	7.231	7.786	6.300	15.672	19.942	11.154	19.515
Trust Fund	0.015	—	0.007	0.001	0.001	—	—	—
Interest	—	—	—	—	—	—	—	—
Repayments	0.015	—	0.007	0.001	0.001	—	—	—
PRGF[2]	0.585	0.750	0.866	0.881	0.855	0.812	1.046	1.197
Interest	0.033	0.046	0.039	0.040	0.042	0.038	0.038	0.040
Repayments	0.552	0.703	0.827	0.842	0.813	0.776	1.009	1.158

[1]Excludes advanced economies. Charges on, and repurchases (or repayments of principal) for, use of International Monetary Fund credit.
[2]Poverty Reduction and Growth Facility (formerly ESAF—Enhanced Structural Adjustment Facility).

Table 44. Summary of Sources and Uses of World Saving
(Percent of GDP)

	Averages		1997	1998	1999	2000	2001	2002	2003	2004	Average 2005–08
	1981–88	1989–96									
World											
Saving	22.8	23.1	23.8	23.2	23.0	23.6	23.1	23.4	23.3	23.0	23.6
Investment	24.0	24.2	24.3	23.5	23.2	23.5	23.1	22.9	23.2	23.3	23.8
Advanced economies											
Saving	21.9	21.5	21.8	21.8	21.4	21.6	20.4	19.6	19.1	19.0	20.1
Private	21.4	20.7	19.7	19.1	18.3	17.9	17.4	18.2	18.6	18.5	18.5
Public	0.5	0.8	2.1	2.7	3.2	3.7	2.9	1.4	0.5	0.5	1.7
Investment	22.6	22.0	21.9	21.7	21.9	22.2	20.7	20.0	19.8	19.8	20.2
Private	18.3	17.7	17.9	17.9	17.9	18.4	16.9	16.3	16.2	16.2	16.7
Public	4.3	4.3	3.9	3.9	3.9	3.7	3.8	3.6	3.6	3.6	3.5
Net lending	−0.7	−0.5	−0.1	0.1	−0.4	−0.6	−0.3	−0.4	−0.7	−0.8	—
Private	3.2	3.0	1.8	1.3	0.4	−0.5	0.5	1.9	2.4	2.2	1.8
Public	−3.8	−3.5	−1.8	−1.2	−0.8	—	−0.8	−2.3	−3.1	−3.1	−1.8
Current transfers	−0.2	−0.3	−0.3	−0.3	−0.4	−0.4	—	—	—	—	—
Factor income	−0.2	−0.4	−0.3	−0.2	—	0.4	—	−0.2	−0.3	−0.5	—
Resource balance	−0.3	0.2	0.6	0.6	—	−0.6	−0.3	−0.2	−0.4	−0.3	—
United States											
Saving	18.4	16.7	18.1	18.8	18.4	18.4	16.5	15.0	13.6	13.2	15.4
Private	19.5	17.5	16.2	15.7	14.6	14.0	13.9	15.2	15.5	15.5	15.5
Public	−1.1	−0.8	1.9	3.1	3.8	4.4	2.6	−0.2	−1.9	−2.3	−0.2
Investment	20.6	18.3	19.9	20.7	20.9	21.1	19.1	18.6	18.3	18.2	18.5
Private	16.9	14.9	16.7	17.5	17.6	17.9	15.7	15.3	15.0	15.0	15.3
Public	3.6	3.4	3.2	3.2	3.3	3.3	3.3	3.4	3.3	3.3	3.1
Net lending	−2.2	−1.6	−1.8	−1.9	−2.6	−2.7	−2.6	−3.6	−4.7	−5.0	−3.1
Private	2.5	2.6	−0.6	−1.9	−3.0	−3.9	−1.9	—	0.5	0.5	0.2
Public	−4.7	−4.2	−1.3	−0.1	0.5	1.2	−0.7	−3.6	−5.2	−5.6	−3.3
Current transfers	−0.5	−0.4	−0.5	−0.5	−0.5	−0.5	0.5	0.6	0.6	0.5	0.5
Factor income	0.5	—	−0.1	0.5	0.8	1.7	0.5	−0.2	−0.8	−1.4	—
Resource balance	−2.1	−1.1	−1.3	−1.9	−2.8	−3.9	−3.5	−4.0	−4.5	−4.2	−3.6
Euro area											
Saving	...	21.0	21.3	21.2	21.2	21.1	20.6	20.7	20.9	21.2	22.1
Private	...	22.3	21.2	20.3	19.3	18.8	18.9	18.8	19.3	19.5	19.9
Public	...	−1.4	0.1	0.8	1.9	2.3	1.7	1.8	1.6	1.7	2.2
Investment	...	21.3	20.3	21.0	21.3	22.0	21.0	20.0	19.8	20.1	20.8
Private	...	18.0	17.7	18.3	18.5	19.2	18.1	17.2	17.0	17.2	18.0
Public	...	3.3	2.7	2.7	2.8	2.8	2.9	2.8	2.9	2.9	2.9
Net lending	...	−0.4	0.9	0.1	−0.1	−0.9	−0.4	0.6	1.0	1.1	1.3
Private	...	4.3	3.6	2.1	0.9	−0.4	0.8	1.7	2.3	2.3	2.0
Public	...	−4.7	−2.6	−1.9	−1.0	−0.5	−1.2	−1.0	−1.3	−1.2	−0.7
Current transfers[1]	−0.2	−0.5	−0.5	−0.6	−0.6	−0.7	−0.7	−0.6	−0.6	−0.7	−0.7
Factor income[1]	−0.9	−0.8	−0.9	−1.3	−0.9	−0.8	−1.1	−1.1	−0.5	−0.4	−0.4
Resource balance[1]	0.6	1.0	2.3	2.0	1.3	0.5	1.3	2.2	1.9	1.9	2.1
Japan[2]											
Saving	31.8	32.4	30.8	29.7	28.4	28.7	27.7	26.5	26.3	26.3	27.0
Private	26.3	24.5	25.7	25.9	26.0	26.9	24.1	25.5	25.8	25.0	25.5
Public	5.5	7.9	5.1	3.8	2.4	1.8	3.5	1.0	0.5	1.3	1.4
Investment	29.4	30.3	28.6	26.8	25.9	26.2	25.6	23.7	23.5	23.5	24.0
Private	21.9	22.7	21.0	19.3	18.1	19.3	19.0	17.4	17.9	17.9	18.7
Public	7.5	7.5	7.6	7.4	7.8	6.9	6.6	6.3	5.7	5.5	5.2
Net lending	2.4	2.2	2.2	2.9	2.5	2.5	2.1	2.8	2.8	2.9	3.0
Private	4.4	1.8	4.7	6.5	7.9	7.6	5.2	8.1	7.9	7.1	6.8
Public	−2.0	0.4	−2.5	−3.6	−5.4	−5.1	−3.1	−5.3	−5.1	−4.2	−3.8
Current transfers	−0.1	−0.2	−0.2	−0.2	−0.3	−0.2	−0.2	−0.1	−0.2	−0.2	−0.3
Factor income	0.4	0.8	1.3	1.3	1.3	1.2	1.6	1.6	1.5	1.7	1.8
Resource balance	2.2	1.5	1.1	1.9	1.5	1.4	0.6	1.3	1.4	1.4	1.4

Table 44 *(continued)*

	Averages		1997	1998	1999	2000	2001	2002	2003	2004	Average 2005–08
	1981–88	1989–96									
Newly industrialized Asian economies											
Saving	...	34.5	32.3	32.6	31.8	30.7	28.8	28.7	29.4	29.8	29.5
Private	...	27.5	24.9	26.0	25.5	22.7	20.9	21.7	22.9	23.0	20.3
Public	...	6.9	7.3	6.6	6.3	8.0	7.9	7.0	6.5	6.8	9.2
Investment	...	32.1	31.6	24.2	25.9	26.9	23.8	22.8	22.9	23.2	23.6
Private	...	22.6	22.1	14.9	17.6	19.3	16.2	16.5	16.2	16.5	17.2
Public	...	9.4	9.6	9.3	8.3	7.6	7.7	6.2	6.8	6.7	6.4
Net lending	...	2.4	0.6	8.4	5.9	3.9	5.0	5.9	6.5	6.6	6.0
Private	...	4.9	2.9	11.1	7.9	3.4	4.7	5.2	6.8	6.5	3.1
Public	...	−2.5	−2.2	−2.7	−2.0	0.4	0.2	0.7	−0.3	0.1	2.8
Current transfers	...	−0.1	−0.4	0.1	−0.2	−0.4	−0.5	−0.6	−0.6	−0.6	−0.6
Factor income	...	1.1	0.5	−0.3	−0.1	0.3	0.7	0.8	0.6	0.5	0.5
Resource balance	...	1.4	0.5	8.5	6.2	4.0	4.8	5.7	6.5	6.7	6.0
Developing countries											
Saving	21.5	25.3	27.6	26.1	26.4	27.0	27.1	29.0	29.2	28.9	28.5
Investment	24.2	27.2	28.3	26.7	25.8	25.9	26.6	27.3	28.1	28.3	28.6
Net lending	−2.7	−2.0	−0.6	−0.7	0.6	1.1	0.5	1.7	1.1	0.6	−0.1
Current transfers	0.8	1.1	1.1	0.8	0.8	1.1	1.3	1.6	1.6	1.5	1.3
Factor income	−2.2	−1.9	−1.7	−1.9	−1.8	−2.2	−2.1	−1.7	−1.6	−1.5	−1.3
Resource balance	−1.2	−1.1	—	0.4	1.6	2.2	1.2	1.7	1.0	0.6	−0.1
Memorandum											
Acquisition of foreign assets	0.1	1.9	4.1	3.2	3.5	4.2	3.2	4.3	3.6	2.8	2.2
Change in reserves	−0.4	1.4	1.6	0.3	0.8	1.2	2.1	3.2	3.7	1.9	1.2
Regional groups											
Africa											
Saving	18.2	16.5	17.5	15.4	16.0	18.9	18.3	18.6	19.7	19.5	20.5
Investment	22.7	20.2	19.6	20.5	20.1	18.5	19.8	20.4	21.6	22.0	22.7
Net lending	−4.5	−3.8	−2.2	−5.1	−4.1	0.3	−1.5	−1.8	−1.9	−2.6	−2.2
Current transfers	1.8	3.2	2.9	3.1	2.8	3.4	3.8	4.0	4.2	4.0	3.7
Factor income	−5.0	−5.2	−4.3	−4.3	−4.3	−4.8	−4.4	−3.7	−4.2	−4.3	−3.3
Resource balance	−1.3	−1.8	−0.8	−3.9	−2.6	1.7	−0.9	−2.1	−1.8	−2.2	−2.6
Memorandum											
Acquisition of foreign assets	0.1	1.1	3.5	0.7	1.9	3.3	3.7	1.5	2.2	1.4	1.3
Change in reserves	−0.3	0.7	2.5	−0.6	0.6	2.6	2.7	1.8	2.5	1.9	1.5
Developing Asia											
Saving	25.4	31.1	33.4	32.1	32.2	31.8	32.9	34.9	35.1	34.7	33.9
Investment	27.5	32.3	32.8	30.0	29.5	29.6	31.0	31.8	33.2	33.2	33.0
Net lending	−2.1	−1.2	0.6	2.2	2.7	2.2	1.9	3.1	1.9	1.6	0.9
Current transfers	1.0	1.0	1.5	1.2	1.3	1.3	1.4	1.7	1.6	1.4	1.1
Factor income	−0.5	−0.8	−1.4	−1.5	−1.1	−1.2	−1.2	−0.8	−0.8	−0.8	−0.8
Resource balance	−2.6	−1.4	0.5	2.5	2.5	2.1	1.8	2.2	1.1	1.0	0.5
Memorandum											
Acquisition of foreign assets	0.3	2.6	5.2	5.0	4.5	4.7	3.5	5.4	4.2	3.5	2.7
Change in reserves	—	1.7	1.9	1.1	1.4	0.9	2.8	4.7	4.7	2.4	1.4
Middle East and Turkey											
Saving	18.8	21.7	24.8	21.7	23.6	25.8	22.7	24.1	23.2	21.9	20.2
Investment	22.8	24.9	25.0	25.1	22.9	23.2	21.5	23.5	21.6	21.7	21.5
Net lending	−4.1	−3.2	−0.2	−3.5	0.7	2.6	1.1	0.7	1.6	0.2	−1.4
Current transfers	−0.2	−0.7	−2.4	−3.6	−4.4	−2.5	−1.1	−0.6	−0.4	−0.3	−0.4
Factor income	−0.6	−0.8	0.3	−0.9	−1.4	−4.5	−2.9	−1.6	−0.7	−0.3	0.1
Resource balance	−3.3	−1.7	2.0	1.1	6.5	9.6	5.1	2.9	2.7	0.8	−1.1
Memorandum											
Acquisition of foreign assets	−1.0	−1.1	3.9	2.3	3.6	9.7	4.2	5.1	4.1	3.0	2.2
Change in reserves	−1.6	1.4	0.8	−1.2	1.1	3.5	1.3	2.2	2.5	1.1	0.9

Table 44 *(continued)*

	Averages		1997	1998	1999	2000	2001	2002	2003	2004	Average 2005–08
	1981–88	1989–96									
Western Hemisphere											
Saving	18.9	18.9	19.2	17.7	17.2	18.3	16.8	18.5	18.6	18.7	18.6
Investment	20.9	21.0	22.5	22.2	20.2	20.6	19.8	18.8	18.9	19.5	20.2
Net lending	−1.9	−2.1	−3.2	−4.5	−2.9	−2.3	−3.0	−0.4	−0.3	−0.8	−1.6
Current transfers	0.6	1.1	1.0	1.1	1.3	1.3	1.5	1.8	1.8	1.7	1.7
Factor income	−4.3	−3.2	−2.4	−2.4	−2.9	−2.9	−3.1	−3.4	−3.2	−3.1	−2.9
Resource balance	1.8	−0.1	−1.8	−3.2	−1.3	−0.7	−1.4	1.3	1.1	0.6	−0.3
Memorandum											
Acquisition of foreign assets	0.3	2.1	1.7	0.4	1.4	0.9	1.5	1.6	2.2	1.3	0.9
Change in reserves	−0.3	1.2	1.0	−0.5	−0.6	0.2	0.1	−0.1	1.8	0.5	0.3
Analytical groups											
By source of export earnings											
Fuel											
Saving	20.3	22.4	27.7	21.5	25.7	32.9	28.1	28.9	29.7	27.3	24.9
Investment	23.0	24.1	24.5	26.2	23.5	22.4	24.0	25.5	24.3	24.7	25.0
Net lending	−2.7	−1.7	3.1	−4.6	2.2	10.6	4.1	3.5	5.3	2.6	−0.1
Current transfers	−2.2	−2.9	−4.3	−5.7	−6.8	−4.5	−2.6	−2.0	−1.6	−1.4	−1.3
Factor income	−0.4	−1.7	−0.8	−2.4	−2.3	−6.0	−3.4	−2.4	−2.4	−1.9	−1.1
Resource balance	−0.2	2.9	8.2	3.5	11.3	21.1	10.1	7.9	9.3	5.9	2.4
Memorandum											
Acquisition of foreign assets	−1.2	−0.7	5.6	1.5	3.1	14.5	6.7	4.5	5.3	3.7	2.0
Change in reserves	−2.3	1.0	1.7	−2.6	−0.5	6.5	2.6	1.1	3.8	1.8	1.0
Nonfuel											
Saving	21.7	25.6	27.6	26.5	26.5	26.4	27.0	29.0	29.2	29.1	28.8
Investment	24.3	27.6	28.7	26.8	26.0	26.3	26.8	27.5	28.5	28.7	28.9
Net lending	−2.7	−2.0	−1.0	−0.3	0.4	0.1	0.1	1.5	0.7	0.4	−0.1
Current transfers	1.2	1.5	1.6	1.5	1.6	1.7	1.8	2.0	2.0	1.8	1.5
Factor income	−2.6	−1.9	−1.8	−1.9	−1.8	−1.9	−2.0	−1.6	−1.5	−1.5	−1.3
Resource balance	−1.3	−1.6	−0.9	0.1	0.6	0.3	0.3	1.1	0.2	0.1	−0.3
Memorandum											
Acquisition of foreign assets	0.3	2.2	3.9	3.4	3.5	3.2	2.8	4.2	3.5	2.7	2.2
Change in reserves	—	1.5	1.6	0.6	1.0	0.6	2.0	3.4	3.7	1.9	1.2
By external financing source											
Net debtor countries											
Saving	18.2	20.5	20.9	19.3	19.9	20.2	19.7	20.6	20.5	20.7	21.2
Investment	21.7	23.5	24.2	21.5	20.3	20.9	20.4	20.0	20.4	20.9	21.9
Net lending	−3.5	−3.1	−3.3	−2.2	−0.3	−0.6	−0.7	0.6	0.1	−0.2	−0.8
Current transfers	1.4	2.0	1.7	1.4	1.3	1.7	2.1	2.5	2.5	2.3	2.2
Factor income	−3.1	−2.8	−2.2	−2.4	−2.1	−2.7	−2.5	−2.2	−1.9	−1.8	−1.7
Resource balance	−1.8	−2.2	−2.8	−1.2	0.5	0.4	−0.4	0.3	−0.4	−0.7	−1.3
Memorandum											
Acquisition of foreign assets	—	1.2	1.4	1.8	2.7	2.3	1.8	2.8	2.1	1.4	1.3
Change in reserves	−0.3	1.2	0.6	0.5	1.0	0.6	0.9	1.8	1.6	1.0	1.0
Official financing											
Saving	15.3	19.8	20.9	16.2	19.1	20.5	21.2	21.0	20.8	20.7	22.1
Investment	21.2	23.7	25.0	19.3	16.5	17.9	18.9	18.3	19.4	20.1	22.3
Net lending	−5.9	−3.9	−4.1	−3.1	2.6	2.6	2.3	2.7	1.4	0.7	−0.2
Current transfers	2.4	2.8	3.4	3.6	3.7	4.0	4.3	4.7	4.8	4.4	4.0
Factor income	−3.5	−2.9	−3.5	−3.7	−1.5	−3.6	−2.3	−1.0	−1.5	−1.6	−1.7
Resource balance	−4.8	−3.8	−4.0	−3.0	0.3	2.2	0.3	−1.0	−1.9	−2.1	−2.5
Memorandum											
Acquisition of foreign assets	0.3	1.0	1.9	1.1	1.6	4.9	1.8	3.1	3.0	1.0	0.7
Change in reserves	−0.3	0.7	1.8	1.1	0.8	1.9	0.9	2.0	1.9	0.8	0.8

Table 44 *(concluded)*

	Averages										Average
	1981–88	1989–96	1997	1998	1999	2000	2001	2002	2003	2004	2005–08
Net debtor countries by debt-servicing experience											
Countries with arrears and/or rescheduling during 1997–2001											
Saving	15.7	19.2	19.1	15.7	17.0	18.6	18.7	19.2	19.3	19.5	20.2
Investment	20.7	22.5	23.4	20.0	17.9	19.1	19.7	18.7	19.4	20.1	21.7
Net lending	−5.0	−3.2	−4.2	−4.2	−0.9	−0.5	−1.0	0.5	−0.1	−0.7	−1.5
Current transfers	0.9	1.8	0.8	0.2	−0.2	0.9	2.1	2.6	2.7	2.5	2.2
Factor income	−4.0	−4.0	−3.2	−4.3	−3.3	−5.0	−3.8	−2.7	−2.7	−2.8	−2.8
Resource balance	−2.0	−0.9	−1.8	−0.1	2.5	3.6	0.7	0.6	—	−0.4	−0.9
Memorandum											
Acquisition of foreign assets	−0.8	0.4	0.7	1.2	1.3	3.6	1.7	2.3	2.8	0.6	0.5
Change in reserves	−0.6	0.9	0.8	0.3	0.1	0.9	1.1	1.4	2.3	0.5	0.6
Countries in transition											
Saving	...	...	20.1	18.4	17.4	21.3	23.8	23.8	23.9	21.4	22.2
Investment	...	...	23.2	20.3	19.6	21.6	23.1	22.3	22.4	22.9	24.4
Net lending	...	...	−3.2	−1.9	−2.2	−0.3	0.7	1.5	1.5	−1.5	−2.2
Current transfers	...	...	0.7	1.7	1.1	1.1	1.1	1.2	1.2	1.1	1.0
Factor income	...	...	−1.3	−1.3	−7.0	−7.9	−3.4	−2.3	−1.8	−3.0	−2.2
Resource balance	...	...	−2.6	−2.3	3.7	6.6	3.1	2.6	2.0	0.4	−1.1
Memorandum											
Acquisition of foreign assets	...	...	5.8	3.4	6.9	8.3	4.3	5.5	5.6	4.1	2.2
Change in reserves	...	...	1.2	−0.4	1.0	3.6	2.3	2.7	3.0	2.0	0.8

Note: The estimates in this table are based on individual countries' national accounts and balance of payments statistics. For many countries, the estimates of national saving are built up from national accounts data on gross domestic investment and from balance-of-payments-based data on net foreign investment. The latter, which is equivalent to the current account balance, comprises three components: current transfers, net factor income, and the resource balance. The mixing of data sources, which is dictated by availability, implies that the estimates for national saving that are derived incorporate the statistical discrepancies. Furthermore, errors, omissions, and asymmetries in balance of payments statistics affect the estimates for net lending; at the global level, net lending, which in theory would be zero, equals the world current account discrepancy.

Notwithstanding these statistical shortcomings, flow of funds estimates, such as those presented in this table, provide a useful framework for analyzing development in saving and investment, both over time and across regions and countries. Country group composites are weighted by GDP valued at purchasing power parities (PPPs) as a share of total world GDP.

[1]Calculated from the data of individual euro area countries.
[2]Annual data are calculated from seasonally adjusted quarterly data.

Table 45. Summary of World Medium-Term Baseline Scenario

	Eight-Year Averages		Four-Year Average 2001–04	2001	2002	2003	2004	Four-Year Average 2005–08
	1985–92	1993–2000						
	Annual percent change unless otherwise noted							
World real GDP	**3.3**	**3.6**	**3.2**	**2.4**	**3.0**	**3.2**	**4.1**	**4.3**
Advanced economies	3.2	3.0	1.9	1.0	1.8	1.8	2.9	3.0
Developing countries	4.8	5.6	4.8	4.1	4.6	5.0	5.6	5.9
Countries in transition	−0.7	−0.8	4.7	5.1	4.2	4.9	4.7	4.5
Memorandum								
Potential output								
Major advanced economies	2.9	2.5	2.4	2.5	2.4	2.4	2.4	2.4
World trade, volume[1]	5.3	7.7	2.9	0.1	3.2	2.9	5.5	6.6
Imports								
Advanced economies	6.1	7.7	2.2	−1.0	2.2	2.8	4.8	6.3
Developing countries	4.0	7.9	5.1	1.6	6.0	5.1	7.8	8.0
Countries in transition	−4.2	7.4	8.2	11.9	6.3	6.6	8.1	6.8
Exports								
Advanced economies	5.7	7.4	2.0	−0.8	2.2	1.6	5.2	6.4
Developing countries	7.0	9.6	5.1	2.7	6.5	4.3	6.9	7.4
Countries in transition	−3.0	6.7	6.0	6.0	6.3	5.8	5.6	5.8
Terms of trade								
Advanced economies	1.1	−0.2	0.5	0.2	0.6	0.9	0.2	0.2
Developing countries	−3.9	0.7	−1.1	−3.9	1.1	—	−1.4	−0.6
Countries in transition	−2.6	1.7	−0.7	0.3	−1.2	−0.6	−1.1	−0.2
World prices in U.S. dollars								
Manufactures	6.7	−1.6	3.5	−2.4	2.6	12.8	1.7	1.0
Oil	−4.9	5.1	−2.5	−14.0	2.8	14.2	−10.5	−4.2
Nonfuel primary commodities	0.1	−0.6	0.9	−4.0	0.6	5.0	2.4	1.3
Consumer prices								
Advanced economies	4.1	2.2	1.7	2.2	1.5	1.8	1.3	2.0
Developing countries	49.3	20.7	5.5	5.8	5.3	5.9	4.9	4.0
Countries in transition	54.3	99.1	11.5	16.2	11.1	9.7	9.1	4.9
Interest rates (in percent)								
Real six-month LIBOR[2]	4.1	3.6	0.7	1.4	0.7	−0.2	0.8	3.3
World real long-term interest rate[3]	4.8	3.6	2.5	2.4	2.8	1.8	2.9	3.2
	Percent of GDP							
Balances on current account								
Advanced economies	−0.3	—	−0.8	−0.8	−0.7	−0.9	−0.8	−0.6
Developing countries	−1.9	−1.3	0.9	0.5	1.4	1.1	0.4	−0.5
Countries in transition	−0.1	−0.9	0.8	1.5	1.0	0.9	−0.2	−1.7
Total external debt								
Developing countries	40.1	41.6	38.4	40.1	40.9	37.7	35.0	30.7
Countries in transition	15.8	45.0	41.2	45.4	44.5	38.9	35.9	32.0
Debt service								
Developing countries	5.1	5.7	5.7	6.3	6.1	5.6	5.0	4.5
Countries in transition	2.9	5.9	6.9	7.6	6.9	7.0	6.1	5.7

[1]Data refer to trade in goods and services.
[2]London interbank offered rate on U.S. dollar deposits less percent change in U.S. GDP deflator.
[3]GDP-weighted average of 10-year (or nearest maturity) government bond rates for the United States, Japan, Germany, France, Italy, the United Kingdom, and Canada.

Table 46. Developing Countries—Medium-Term Baseline Scenario: Selected Economic Indicators

	Eight-Year Averages		Four-Year Average					Four-Year Average
	1985–92	1993–2000	2001–04	2001	2002	2003	2004	2005–08
	Annual percent change							
Developing countries								
Real GDP	4.8	5.6	4.8	4.1	4.6	5.0	5.6	5.9
Export volume[1]	7.0	9.6	5.1	2.7	6.5	4.3	6.9	7.4
Terms of trade[1]	–3.9	0.7	–1.1	–3.9	1.1	—	–1.4	–0.6
Import volume[1]	4.0	7.9	5.1	1.6	6.0	5.1	7.8	8.0
Regional groups								
Africa								
Real GDP	2.0	2.9	3.8	3.7	3.1	3.7	4.8	4.9
Export volume[1]	4.9	5.3	3.3	1.7	1.8	4.3	5.5	6.6
Terms of trade[1]	–3.7	1.2	–1.7	–7.5	–1.2	3.9	–1.8	–1.7
Import volume[1]	2.0	4.8	5.7	4.7	4.6	6.4	7.4	5.1
Developing Asia								
Real GDP	7.2	7.5	6.3	5.8	6.4	6.4	6.5	6.8
Export volume[1]	9.3	13.4	7.1	2.1	11.9	6.0	8.6	9.0
Terms of trade[1]	–1.0	–0.7	–0.2	–0.6	1.3	–1.8	0.3	0.1
Import volume[1]	7.3	10.9	7.9	2.6	11.8	7.9	9.7	10.1
Middle East and Turkey								
Real GDP	3.3	3.7	4.1	2.0	4.8	5.1	4.6	5.0
Export volume[1]	8.2	5.2	4.4	4.3	4.2	5.3	3.9	5.0
Terms of trade[1]	–8.0	3.3	–2.7	–7.7	2.2	—	–4.9	–2.1
Import volume[1]	–0.5	3.9	4.7	–0.3	12.0	2.8	4.6	5.4
Western Hemisphere								
Real GDP	2.7	3.3	1.3	0.7	–0.1	1.1	3.6	3.8
Export volume[1]	4.2	8.7	2.3	3.0	—	–0.1	6.6	6.0
Terms of trade[1]	–2.2	0.9	–1.0	–5.2	1.0	2.0	–1.7	–0.6
Import volume[1]	7.8	8.5	–0.1	0.2	–7.9	1.0	6.9	6.6
Analytical groups								
Net debtor countries by debt-servicing experience								
Countries with arrears and/or rescheduling during 1997–2001								
Real GDP	3.5	3.7	3.5	3.4	3.1	3.2	4.4	4.9
Export volume[1]	4.5	7.8	4.1	3.3	4.8	3.9	4.6	6.1
Terms of trade[1]	–3.2	0.2	–1.7	–5.1	–1.2	—	–0.2	–0.6
Import volume[1]	1.2	7.6	3.7	3.6	0.2	4.3	6.9	6.1

Table 46 (*concluded*)

	1992	1996	2000	2001	2002	2003	2004	2008
				Percent of exports of good and services				
Developing countries								
Current account balance	−11.0	−6.4	4.4	1.7	4.6	3.6	1.5	−3.0
Total external debt	202.4	168.3	141.9	144.1	135.3	123.0	115.4	93.4
Debt-service payments[2]	24.0	22.9	22.1	22.7	20.0	18.1	16.4	13.4
Interest payments	9.6	8.4	7.2	7.1	5.9	5.0	4.9	4.8
Amortization	14.4	14.4	14.9	15.6	14.2	13.1	11.5	8.6
Regional groups								
Africa								
Current account balance	−9.8	−4.7	3.1	−1.5	−3.8	−2.1	−4.5	−4.9
Total external debt	246.6	224.0	174.2	176.7	173.0	151.1	144.5	114.2
Debt-service payments[2]	29.8	20.4	16.7	18.2	22.0	15.4	14.0	10.8
Interest payments	11.5	9.8	6.8	6.9	9.0	5.5	4.9	4.1
Amortization	18.3	10.6	9.9	11.4	13.0	9.8	9.1	6.8
Developing Asia								
Current account balance	−5.2	−7.8	6.2	5.1	8.3	4.8	3.6	−0.1
Total external debt	151.0	121.4	96.3	98.1	85.6	76.9	71.6	56.0
Debt-service payments[2]	19.6	13.9	13.9	14.3	13.6	12.2	9.7	7.1
Interest payments	7.9	6.0	4.4	3.9	3.2	2.9	3.1	2.7
Amortization	11.7	7.9	9.5	10.4	10.5	9.3	6.6	4.5
Middle East and Turkey								
Current account balance	−11.8	4.4	19.4	14.2	8.9	10.9	6.0	−2.8
Total external debt	181.6	158.3	146.8	152.3	153.1	136.4	138.8	127.3
Debt-service payments[2]	10.0	17.4	11.0	13.8	12.1	11.5	12.1	11.1
Interest payments	4.0	4.1	3.9	4.1	3.5	3.5	3.8	4.0
Amortization	6.0	13.4	7.1	9.7	8.6	8.0	8.3	7.1
Western Hemisphere								
Current account balance	−19.6	−14.3	−12.8	−15.2	−4.3	−3.7	−5.4	−10.8
Total external debt	275.7	236.9	212.3	215.1	214.6	208.1	190.3	164.1
Debt-service payments[2]	41.5	45.4	50.7	49.6	41.5	40.7	38.7	34.6
Interest payments	16.6	16.1	15.9	16.2	13.0	11.3	10.5	11.8
Amortization	24.8	29.2	34.8	33.4	28.5	29.4	28.2	22.8
Analytical groups								
Net debtor countries by debt-servicing experience								
Countries with arrears and/or rescheduling during 1997–2001								
Current account balance	−8.5	−20.1	−6.1	−8.5	−3.3	−2.6	−4.9	−7.9
Total external debt	372.7	323.7	274.4	272.3	260.6	238.8	225.7	172.4
Debt-service payments[2]	34.6	32.4	39.9	39.1	39.9	34.8	32.0	20.7
Interest payments	14.4	13.9	11.8	11.4	10.6	8.7	9.2	7.1
Amortization	20.2	18.5	28.1	27.7	29.3	26.1	22.8	13.6

[1]Data refer to trade in goods and services.
[2]Interest payments on total debt plus amortization payments on long-term debt only. Projections incorporate the impact of exceptional financing items. Excludes service payments to the International Monetary Fund.

WORLD ECONOMIC OUTLOOK AND STAFF STUDIES FOR THE WORLD ECONOMIC OUTLOOK, SELECTED TOPICS, 1993–2003

III. Economic Growth—Sources and Patterns

IV. Inflation and Deflation; Commodity Markets

V. Fiscal Policy

VI. Monetary Policy; Financial Markets; Flow of Funds

VII. Labor Market Issues

VIII. Exchange Rate Issues

IX. External Payments, Trade, Capital Movements, and Foreign Debt

X. Regional Issues

Staff Studies for the
World Economic Outlook

December 1997

May 2000

XI. Country-Specific Analyses

World Economic Outlook

Staff Studies for the World Economic Outlook

World Economic and Financial Surveys

This series (ISSN 0258-7440) contains biannual, annual, and periodic studies covering monetary and financial issues of importance to the global economy. The core elements of the series are the *World Economic Outlook* report, usually published in May and October, and the quarterly *Global Financial Stability Report*. Other studies assess international trade policy, private market and official financing for developing countries, exchange and payments systems, export credit policies, and issues discussed in the *World Economic Outlook*. Please consult the IMF *Publications Catalog* for a complete listing of currently available World Economic and Financial Surveys.

World Economic Outlook: A Survey by the Staff of the International Monetary Fund

The *World Economic Outlook,* published twice a year in English, French, Spanish, and Arabic, presents IMF staff economists' analyses of global economic developments during the near and medium term. Chapters give an overview of the world economy; consider issues affecting industrial countries, developing countries, and economies in transition to the market; and address topics of pressing current interest.

ISSN 0256-6877.
$49.00 (academic rate: $46.00); paper.
2003. (April). ISBN 1-58906-212-4. **Stock #WEO EA 0012003.**
2002. (Sep.). ISBN 1-58906-179-9. **Stock #WEO EA 0022002.**
2002. (April). ISBN 1-58906-107-1. **Stock #WEO EA 0012002.**

Exchange Arrangements and Foreign Exchange Markets: Developments and Issues
By a staff team led by Shogo Ishii

This study updates developments in exchange arrangements during 1998–2001. It also discusses the evolution of exchange rate regimes based on de facto policies since 1990, reviews foreign exchange market organization and regulations in a number of countries, and examines factors affecting exchange rate volatility.

ISSN 0258-7440
$42.00 (academic rate $35.00)
2003 (March) ISBN 1-58906-177-2. **Stock #WEO EA 0192003.**

Official Financing for Developing Countries
by a staff team in the IMF's Policy Development and Review Department led by Martin Gilman and Jian-Je Wang

This study provides information on official financing for developing countries, with the focus on low-income countries. It updates the 2001 edition and reviews developments in direct financing by official and multilateral sources.

$42.00 (academic rate: $35.00); paper.
2003. ISBN 1-58906-228-0. **Stock #WEO EA 0132003.**
2001. ISBN 1-58906-038-5. **Stock #WEO EA 0132001.**

Exchange Rate Arrangements and Currency Convertibility: Developments and Issues
by a staff team led by R. Barry Johnston

A principal force driving the growth in international trade and investment has been the liberalization of financial transactions, including the liberalization of trade and exchange controls. This study reviews the developments and issues in the exchange arrangements and currency convertibility of IMF members.

$20.00 (academic rate: $12.00); paper.
1999. ISBN 1-55775-795-X. **Stock #WEO EA 0191999.**

World Economic Outlook Supporting Studies
by the IMF's Research Department

These studies, supporting analyses and scenarios of the *World Economic Outlook*, provide a detailed examination of theory and evidence on major issues currently affecting the global economy.

$25.00 (academic rate: $20.00); paper.
2000. ISBN 1-55775-893-X. **Stock #WEO EA 0032000.**

Global Financial Stability Report: Market Developments and Issues

The *Global Financial Stability Report,* published twice a year, examines trends and issues that influence world financial markets. It replaces two IMF publications—the annual *International Capital Markets* report and the electronic quarterly *Emerging Market Financing* report. The report is designed to deepen understanding of international capital flows and explores developments that could pose a risk to international financial market stability.

$49.00 (academic rate: $46.00); paper.
September 2003 ISBN 1-58906-236-1. **Stock #GFSR EA0022003.**
March 2003 ISBN 1-58906-210-8. **Stock #GFSR EA0012003.**
December 2002 ISBN-1-58906-192-6. **Stock #GFSR EA0042002.**
September 2002 ISBN 1-58906-157-8. **Stock #GFSR EA0032002.**
June 2002 ISBN 1-58906-131-4. **Stock #GFSR EA0022002.**

International Capital Markets: Developments, Prospects, and Key Policy Issues (back issues)
$42.00 (academic rate: $35.00); paper.
2001. ISBN 1-58906-056-3. **Stock #WEO EA 0062001.**

Toward a Framework for Financial Stability
by a staff team led by David Folkerts-Landau and Carl-Johan Lindgren

This study outlines the broad principles and characteristics of stable and sound financial systems, to facilitate IMF surveillance over banking sector issues of macroeconomic significance and to contribute to the general international effort to reduce the likelihood and diminish the intensity of future financial sector crises.

$25.00 (academic rate: $20.00); paper.
1998. ISBN 1-55775-706-2. **Stock #WEO-016.**

Trade Liberalization in IMF-Supported Programs
by a staff team led by Robert Sharer

This study assesses trade liberalization in programs supported by the IMF by reviewing multiyear arrangements in the 1990s and six detailed case studies. It also discusses the main economic factors affecting trade policy targets.

$25.00 (academic rate: $20.00); paper.
1998. ISBN 1-55775-707-0. **Stock #WEO-1897.**

Available by series subscription or single title (including back issues); academic rate available only to full-time university faculty and students. For earlier editions please inquire about prices.

The IMF *Catalog of Publications* is available on-line at the Internet address listed below.

Please send orders and inquiries to:
International Monetary Fund, Publication Services, 700 19th Street, N.W.
Washington, D.C. 20431, U.S.A.
Tel.: (202) 623-7430   Telefax: (202) 623-7201
E-mail: publications@imf.org
Internet: http://www.imf.org